[redacted]

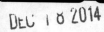

DEC 1 8 2014

KICK-ASS 3

KICK-ASS 3. Contains material originally published in magazine form as KICK-ASS 3 #1-8. First printing 2014. ISBN# 978-0-7851-8488-1. Published by MARVEL WORLDWIDE, INC., a subsidiary of MARVEL ENTERTAINMENT, LLC. OFFICE OF PUBLICATION: 135 West 50th Street, New York, NY 10020. Copyright © 2013 and 2014 Millarworld Limited and John S. Romita. All rights reserved. KICK-ASS, KICK-ASS 3, the Kick-Ass and Kick-Ass 3 logos, and all characters and content herein and the likenesses thereof are trademarks of Millarworld Limited and John S. Romita, unless otherwise expressly noted. The events and characters presented are intended as fiction. Any similarity to real events or to persons living or dead is purely coincidental. This work may not be reproduced, except in small amounts for journalistic or review purposes, without permission of the authors. ICON and the Icon logo are trademarks of Marvel Characters, Inc. MILLARWORLD and the Millarworld logos are trademarks of Millarworld Limited. **Printed in the U.S.A.** ALAN FINE, EVP - Office of the President, Marvel Worldwide, Inc. and EVP & CMO Marvel Characters B.V.; DAN BUCKLEY, Publisher & President - Print, Animation & Digital Divisions; JOE QUESADA, Chief Creative Officer; TOM BREVOORT, SVP of Publishing; DAVID BOGART, SVP of Operations & Procurement, Publishing; C.B. CEBULSKI, SVP of Creator & Content Development; DAVID GABRIEL, SVP Print, Sales & Marketing; JIM O'KEEFE, VP of Operations & Logistics; DAN CARR, Executive Director of Publishing Technology; SUSAN CRESPI, Editorial Operations Manager; ALEX MORALES, Publishing Operations Manag[er]. [...] regarding advertising in Marvel Comics or on Marvel.com, please contact Niza Disla, Director of Marvel Partnerships, at ndisla@marvel.com. For [...] 158. **Manufactured between 7/7/2014 and 8/18/2014 by R.R. DONNELLEY, INC., SALEM, VA, USA.**

10 9 8 7 6 5 4 3 2 1

KICK-ASS 3

Writer & Co-Creator
MARK MILLAR

Pencils & Co-Creator
JOHN ROMITA JR.

Inks & Washes
TOM PALMER

Colorist
DEAN WHITE
with MICHAEL KELLEHER

Letterer
CHRIS ELIOPOULOS

Editor
JENNIFER LEE

Collection Editor: **JENNIFER LEE**

Book Designer: **SPRING HOTELING**

Production: **IDETTE WINECOOR**

Special Thanks: **JENNIFER GRÜNWALD**

SVP Print, Sales & Marketing: **DAVID GABRIEL**

SVP of Operations & Procurement, Publishing: **DAVID BOGART**

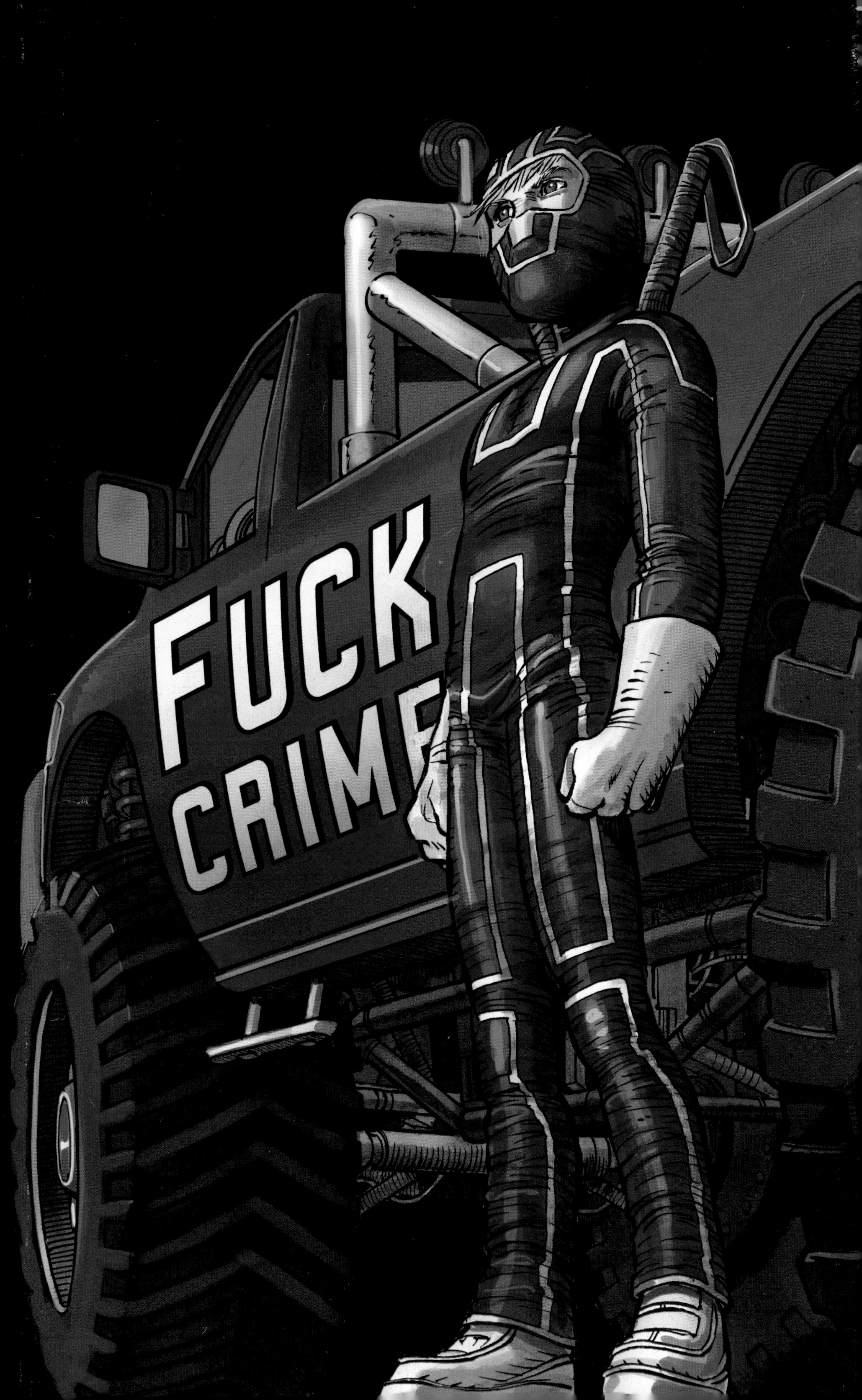
FUCK
CRIME

INTRODUCTION
by Jeff Wadlow

I fucking hate Mark Millar and John Romita Jr.

The end of KICK-ASS?!?! What kind of demon-semen are those two ass clowns mainlining? Why would they end KICK-ASS?

I love KICK-ASS. From the moment I read the first issue, I was gobsmacked by their utterly unique vision. KICK-ASS was so singular in conception and execution that for the longest time, I couldn't adequately describe it. I mean, it is obviously *not* a superhero parody. It can't be. I feel too much for Dave and his insane quest to become a real-life superhero. I thrill too much when cute little, katana-wielding Mindy goes into battle. I worry too much about Chris trying to find himself in his father's pitch-black shadow. But if it's not a satire, why am I laughing my ass off as Mark and John twist, turn, and eviscerate every single superhero cliché imaginable? *What the hell is this thing?*

The answer to that question lies in Matthew Vaughn's brilliant big-screen adaption: In a world gagging on remakes and reboots, KICK-ASS is a genuine original. It stands alone in its ability to do it all.

The only meaningful comparison I can make is to Wes Craven and Kevin Williamson's *Scream* (bear with me), a movie that both mocked horror tropes while simultaneously executing them better than anyone else. When I saw *Scream*, 1996-me wet his pants laughing and then turned them brown in terror (I had a couple of beers in me at the time). KICK-ASS is similar in that it both sends up the superhero genre while still being a really good superhero story — arguably one of the best ever.

Now that I've proclaimed my undying love and affection for all things KICK-ASS, I have a confession to make: *I haven't read a single page of the book you're holding.*

Don't get me wrong, I had every intention of reading KICK-ASS 3. I bought the issues. I put them on the top of my "read" pile. I even picked up issue #1 a few times and stared at the cover. But inevitably I always put it down. I couldn't bring myself to even glance at John, Tom, and Dean's glorious art because I knew what was going to happen.

It was going to end. Badly.

Mark told us all. It had to end. Imagine a charismatic madman with a barely intelligible Scottish brogue uttering the following phrase to our collective anguish and his genuine glee: "KICK-ASS 3 is going to be the last one."

Knowing this, how could I even consider reading KICK-ASS 3? From August 2011 when I started writing the *Kick-Ass 2* screenplay on spec (that's how they say "for free" in Hollywood) until August 2013 when *Kick-Ass 2* ripped into theaters like a German Shepherd's canines into Mr. Kim's man-sack, Dave, Mindy, and Chris were my life.

I ate, drank, and dreamed KICK-ASS. I had the pages of the comics wallpapering my office. I moved to London for a year to direct the movie. And let me tell you about ol' blighty: great place to visit — the people are lovely and I made some life-long friends — but it is the last city you want to live in if you're partial to sunlight, cold beer, or salads that aren't mayonnaise-based.

Point is I suffered for these characters. I talked to them. I spent hour after hour with them. And not just in my head while I was writing; they became very real during production. I hung out with them on set, laughing with Chloë while she called me "Wide Load" and I called her "Slow-ie," marveling at ATJ's emotional depth and physical prowess as he took Dave from zero to hero, and witnessing Chris's jaw-dropping transformation from the laughable Red Mist to the menacing Motherfucker.

I honestly care as much about Dave, Mindy, and Chris as I do about my closest friends — and now Mark and John are going to end it all in what will surely be a grizzly blood bath of depravity, more graphic and visceral than anything I've ever seen in my three decades of reading comics. I guess on some subconscious level, I felt that as long as I didn't read KICK-ASS 3, it couldn't end… Dave, Mindy, and Chris could live forever in my mind.

But damn, Mark and John are good at telling stories. And I want to know what comes next. Matthew, Mark, and I had agreed that teenage Mindy in the movie needed to ride off into the sunset… but Mindy in the comics? The pre-adolescent assassin who could stay eleven years old forever? She was incarcerated. Dave was on the run with Justice Forever. And a mutilated Chris was on death's door. What's going to happen to them?

No, I don't want to know. But I *need* to know. So I guess it's time to bite the bullet and read these eight final issues. It's one thing to start writing an intro when you haven't looked at the material, it's another to finish said preface without even peeking at the pages. So okay, here goes… deep breath… flip that first cover… and… (one hour and fifty-seven minutes later — *no joke, I timed it*).

I fucking worship Mark Millar and John Romita Jr.

They are insane geniuses who have left an indelible mark on not just comics, but all of pop culture with KICK-ASS. They are giants. Legends. And I can sincerely say that working with them to bring the second chapter of their opus to the big screen has been one of the highlights of my life. I'm going to miss Dave, Mindy, and Chris… but goddamn, what a ride. So sit down, strap in, and get ready for an epic conclusion that's as surprising as it is satisfying. It doesn't get better than this.

JUSTICE FOREVER!!!!!!!!!

Jeff Wadlow
June 5th, 2014

Jeff Wadlow is the screenwriter and director of *Kick-Ass 2*. When he's not working on film and TV projects, he's buying comic books and writing them off as a business expense.

ONE

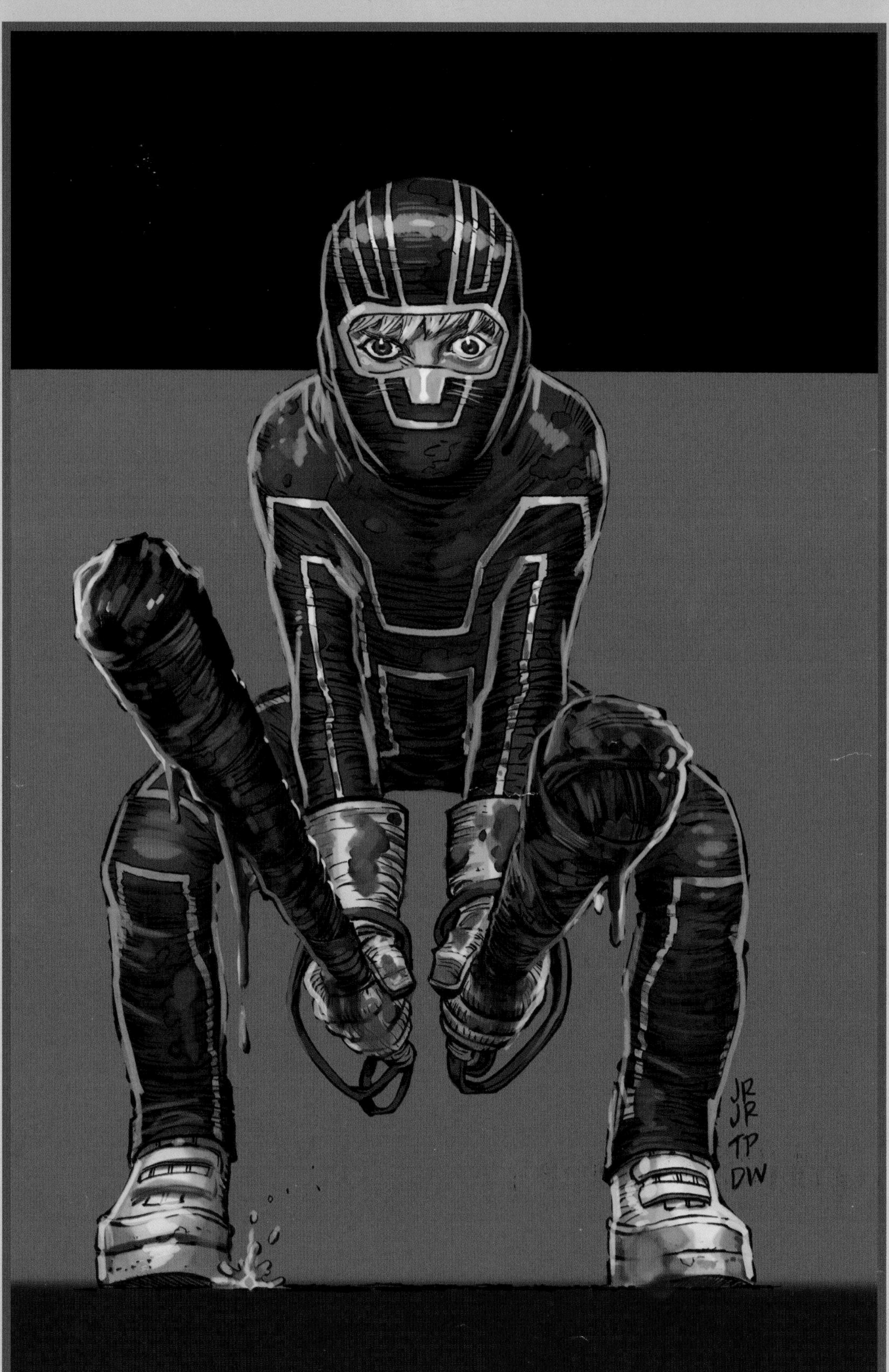

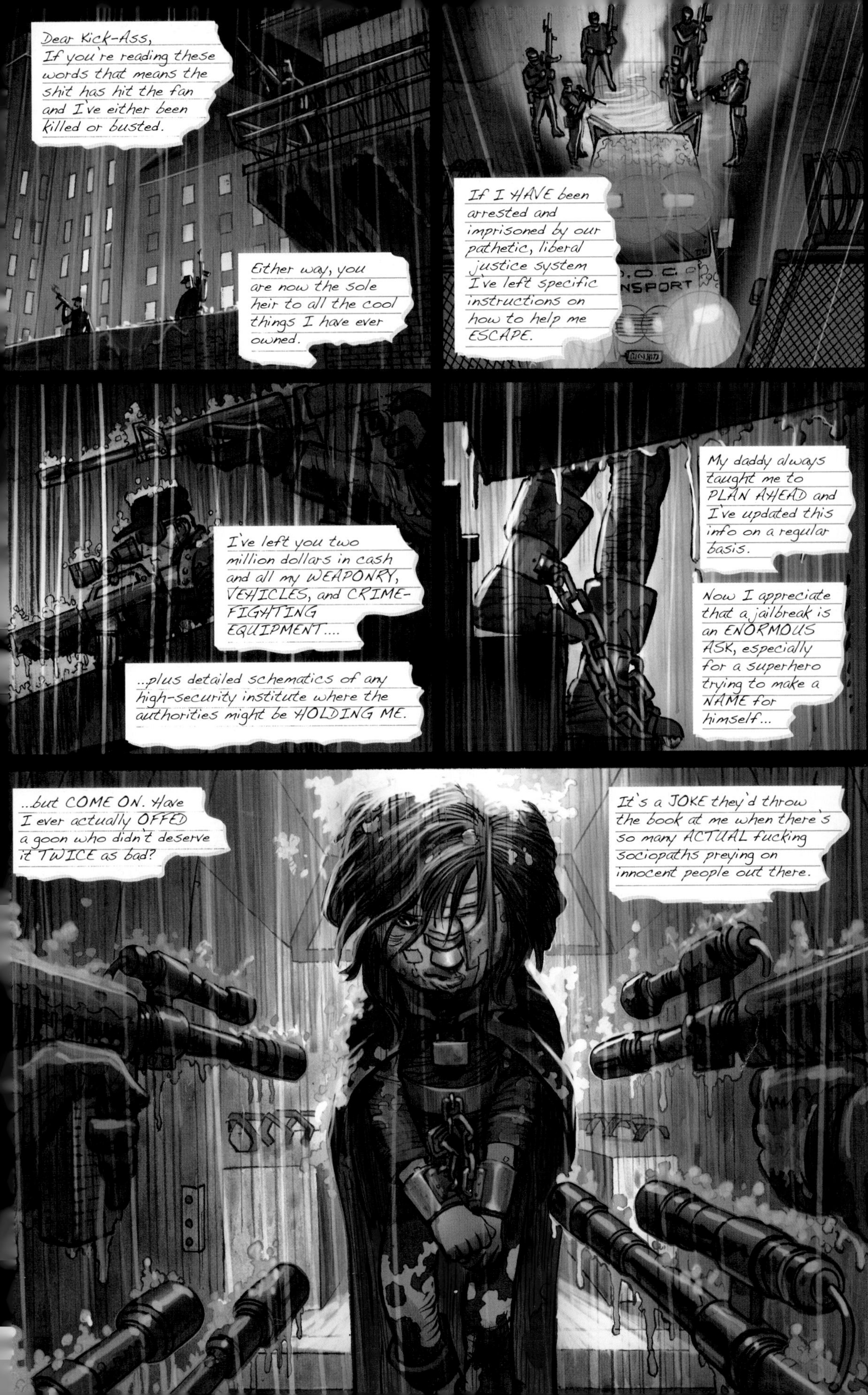

Dear Kick-Ass,
If you're reading these words that means the shit has hit the fan and I've either been killed or busted.
Either way, you are now the sole heir to all the cool things I have ever owned.
If I HAVE been arrested and imprisoned by our pathetic, liberal justice system I've left specific instructions on how to help me ESCAPE.
I've left you two million dollars in cash and all my WEAPONRY, VEHICLES, and CRIME-FIGHTING EQUIPMENT....
...plus detailed schematics of any high-security institute where the authorities might be HOLDING ME.
My daddy always taught me to PLAN AHEAD and I've updated this info on a regular basis.
Now I appreciate that a jailbreak is an ENORMOUS ASK, especially for a superhero trying to make a NAME for himself...
...but COME ON. Have I ever actually OFFED a goon who didn't deserve it TWICE as bad?
It's a JOKE they'd throw the book at me when there's so many ACTUAL fucking sociopaths preying on innocent people out there.

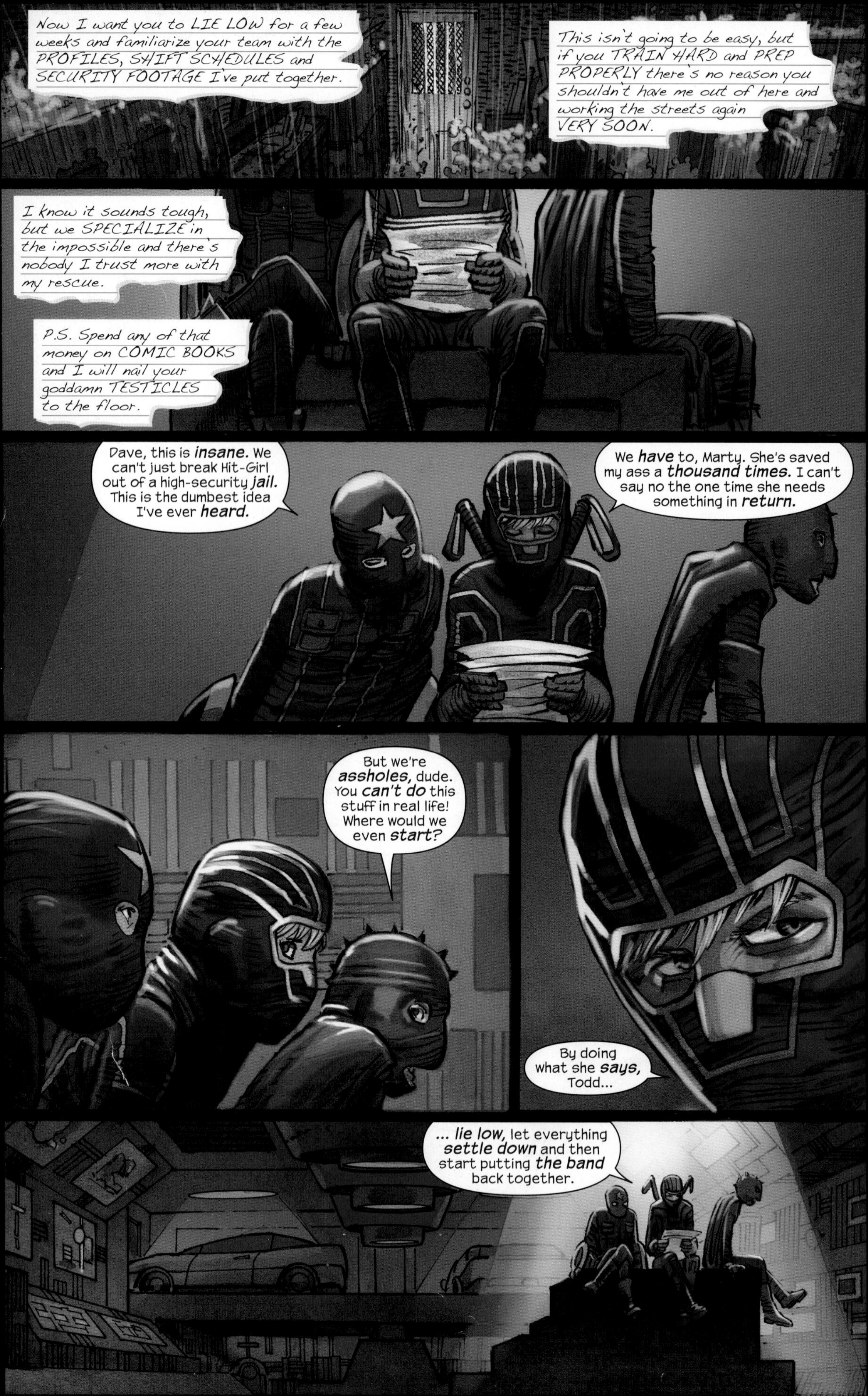
Now I want you to LIE LOW for a few weeks and familiarize your team with the PROFILES, SHIFT SCHEDULES and SECURITY FOOTAGE I've put together.
This isn't going to be easy, but if you TRAIN HARD and PREP PROPERLY there's no reason you shouldn't have me out of here and working the streets again VERY SOON.
I know it sounds tough, but we SPECIALIZE in the impossible and there's nobody I trust more with my rescue.
P.S. Spend any of that money on COMIC BOOKS and I will nail your goddamn TESTICLES to the floor.
Dave, this is insane. We can't just break Hit-Girl out of a high-security jail. This is the dumbest idea I've ever heard.
We have to, Marty. She's saved my ass a thousand times. I can't say no the one time she needs something in return.
But we're assholes, dude. You can't do this stuff in real life! Where would we even start?
By doing what she says, Todd...
... lie low, let everything settle down and then start putting the band back together.

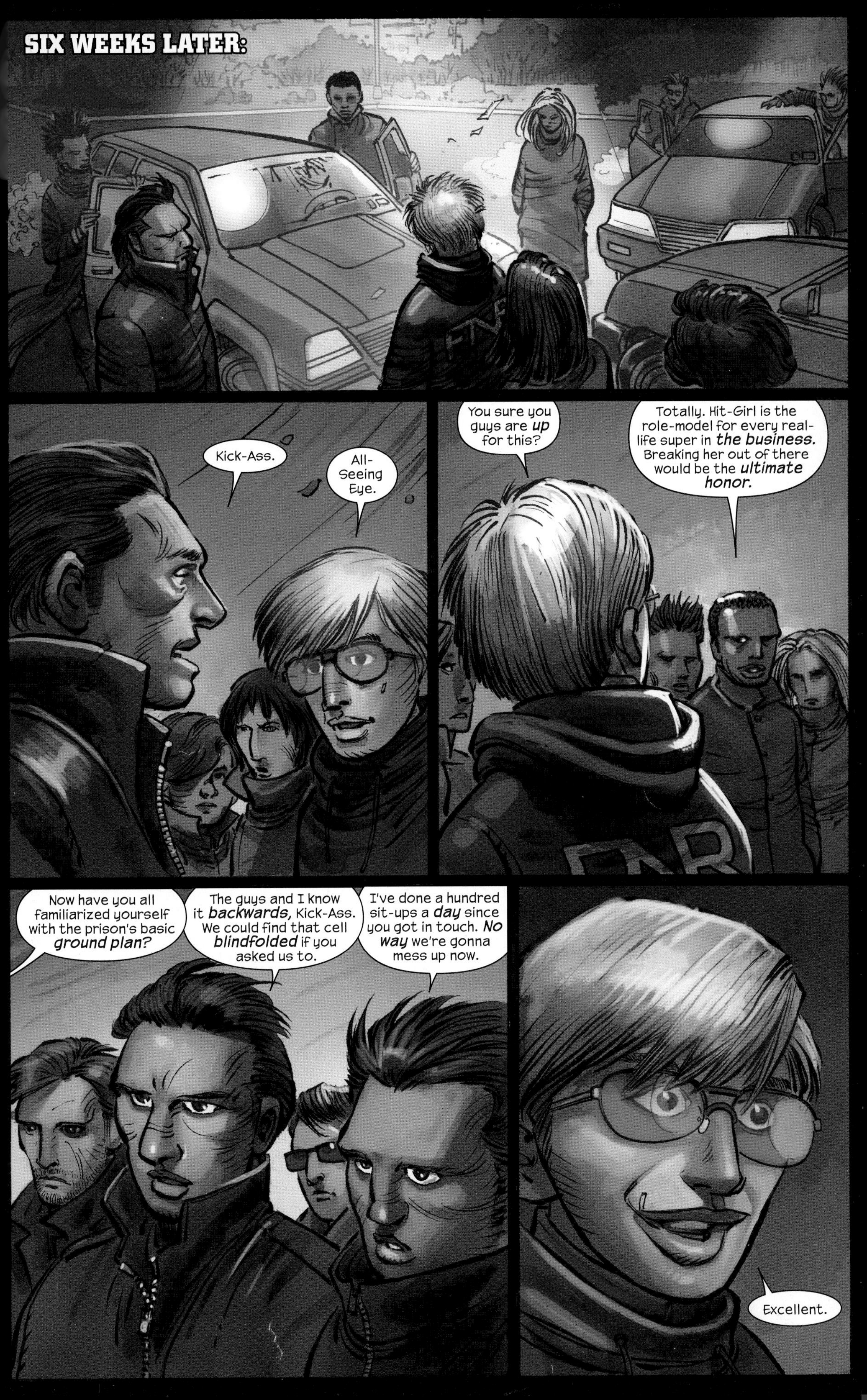

SIX WEEKS LATER:
Kick-Ass.
All-Seeing Eye.
You sure you guys are up for this?
Totally. Hit-Girl is the role-model for every real-life super in the business. Breaking her out of there would be the ultimate honor.
Now have you all familiarized yourself with the prison's basic ground plan?
The guys and I know it backwards, Kick-Ass. We could find that cell blindfolded if you asked us to.
I've done a hundred sit-ups a day since you got in touch. No way we're gonna mess up now.
Excellent.

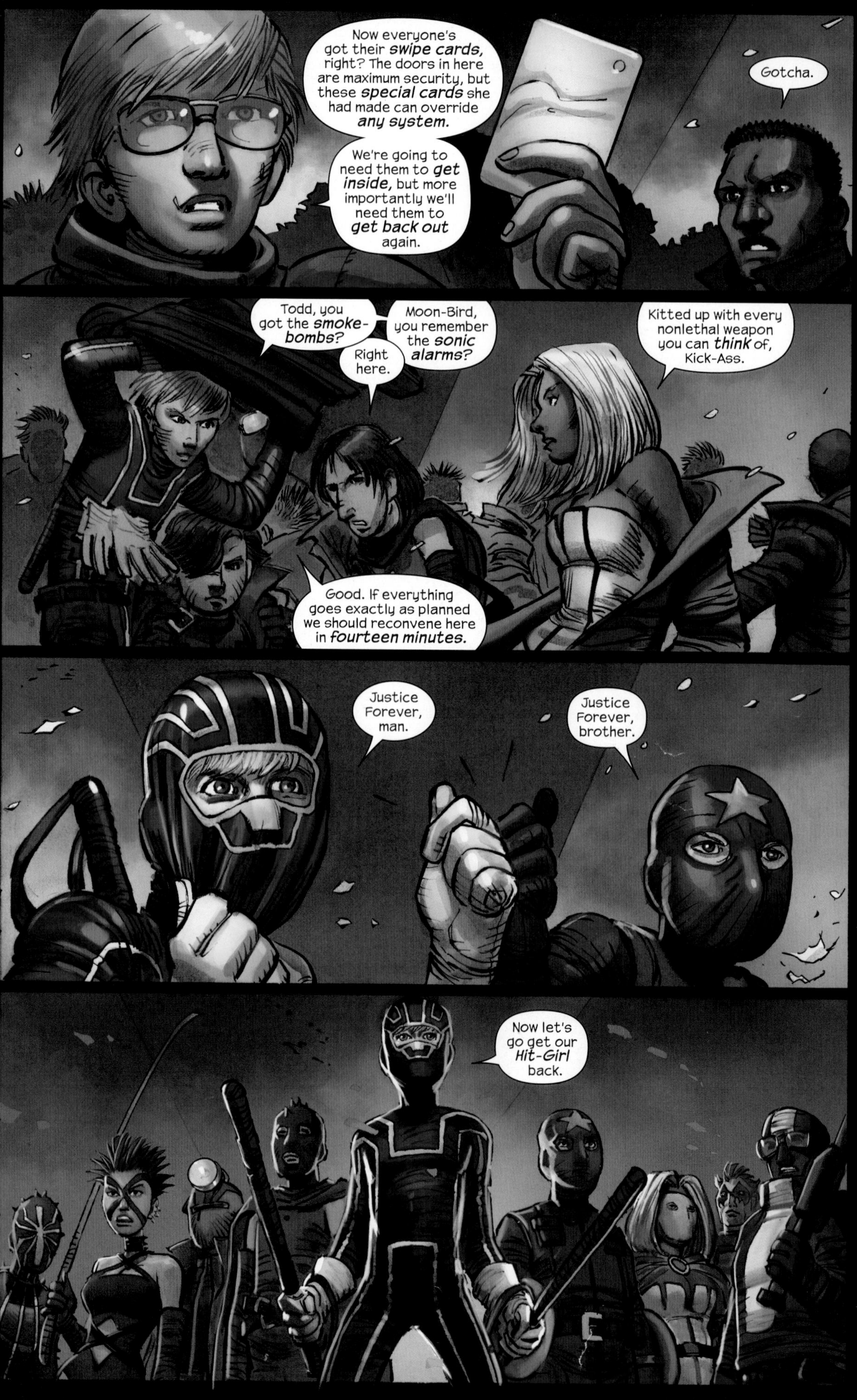
Now everyone's got their swipe cards, right? The doors in here are maximum security, but these special cards she had made can override any system.
We're going to need them to get inside, but more importantly we'll need them to get back out again.
Gotcha.
Todd, you got the smoke-bombs?
Right here.
Moon-Bird, you remember the sonic alarms?
Kitted up with every nonlethal weapon you can think of, Kick-Ass.
Good. If everything goes exactly as planned we should reconvene here in fourteen minutes.
Justice Forever, man.
Justice Forever, brother.
Now let's go get our Hit-Girl back.

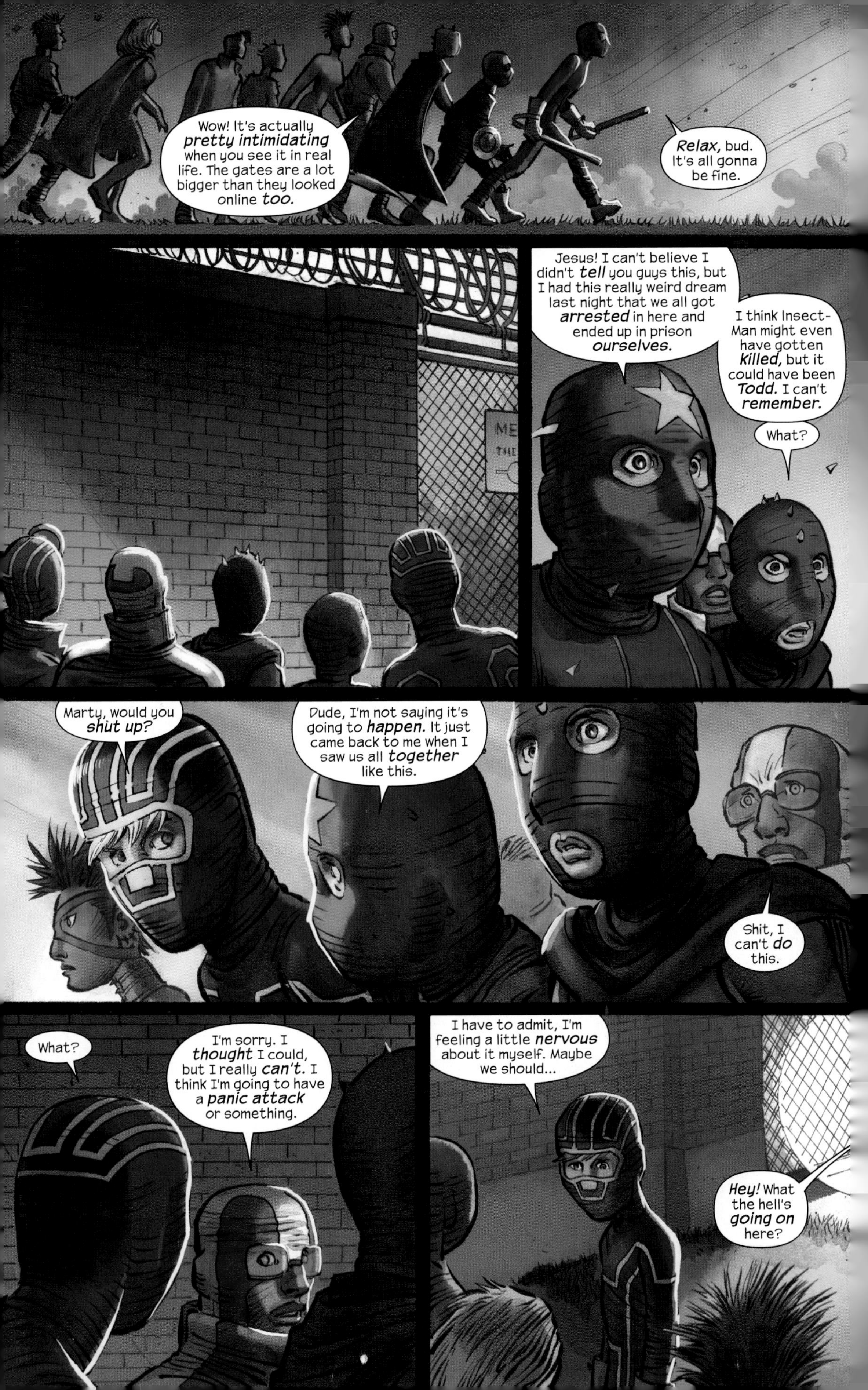

Wow! It's actually pretty intimidating when you see it in real life. The gates are a lot bigger than they looked online too.
Relax, bud. It's all gonna be fine.
Jesus! I can't believe I didn't tell you guys this, but I had this really weird dream last night that we all got arrested in here and ended up in prison ourselves.
I think Insect-Man might even have gotten killed, but it could have been Todd. I can't remember.
What?
Marty, would you shut up?
Dude, I'm not saying it's going to happen. It just came back to me when I saw us all together like this.
Shit, I can't do this.
What?
I'm sorry. I thought I could, but I really can't. I think I'm going to have a panic attack or something.
I have to admit, I'm feeling a little nervous about it myself. Maybe we should...
Hey! What the hell's going on here?

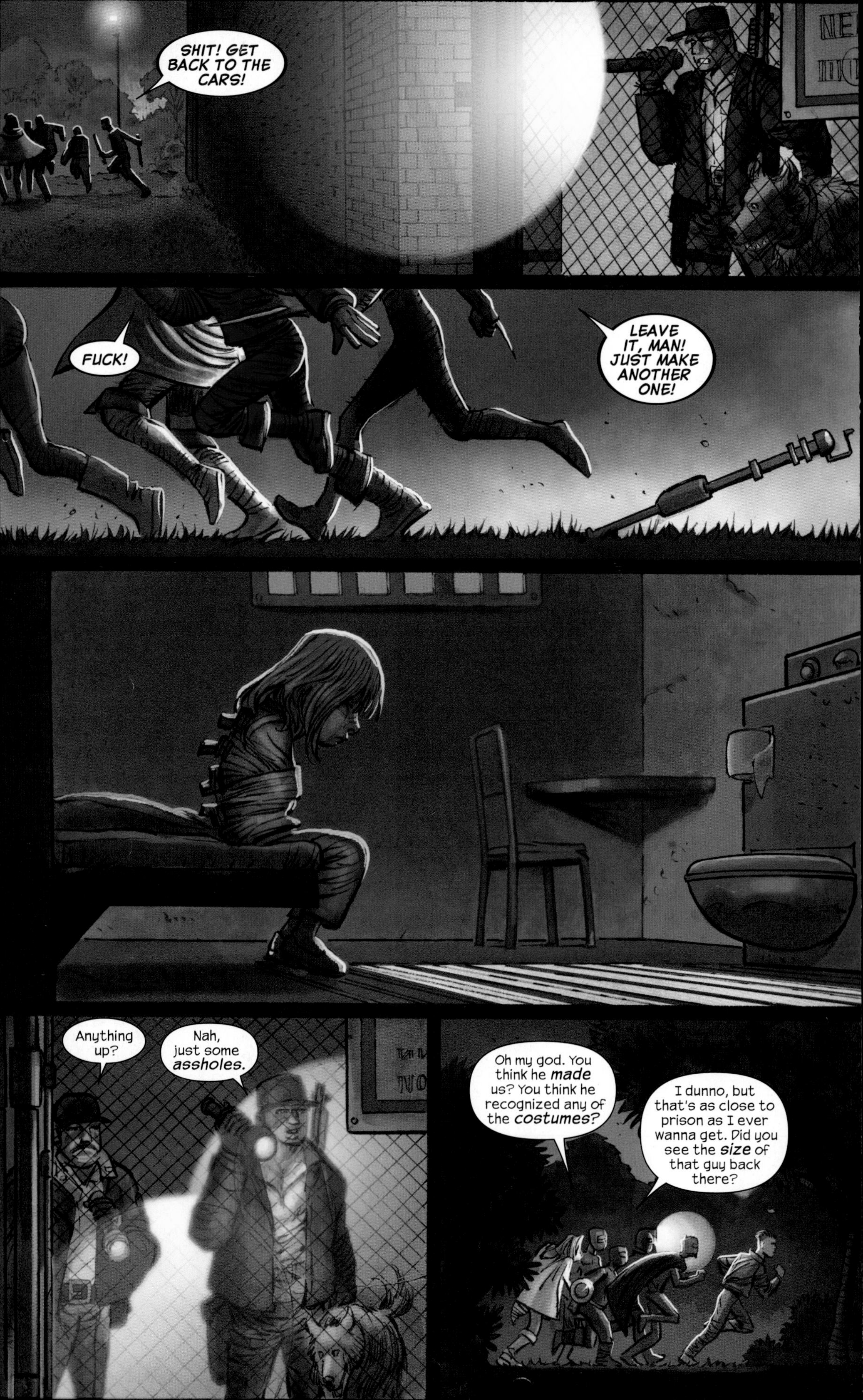
SHIT! GET BACK TO THE CARS!
FUCK!
LEAVE IT, MAN! JUST MAKE ANOTHER ONE!
Anything up?
Nah, just some *assholes.*
Oh my god. You think he *made* us? You think he recognized any of the *costumes?*
I dunno, but that's as close to prison as I ever wanna get. Did you see the *size* of that guy back there?

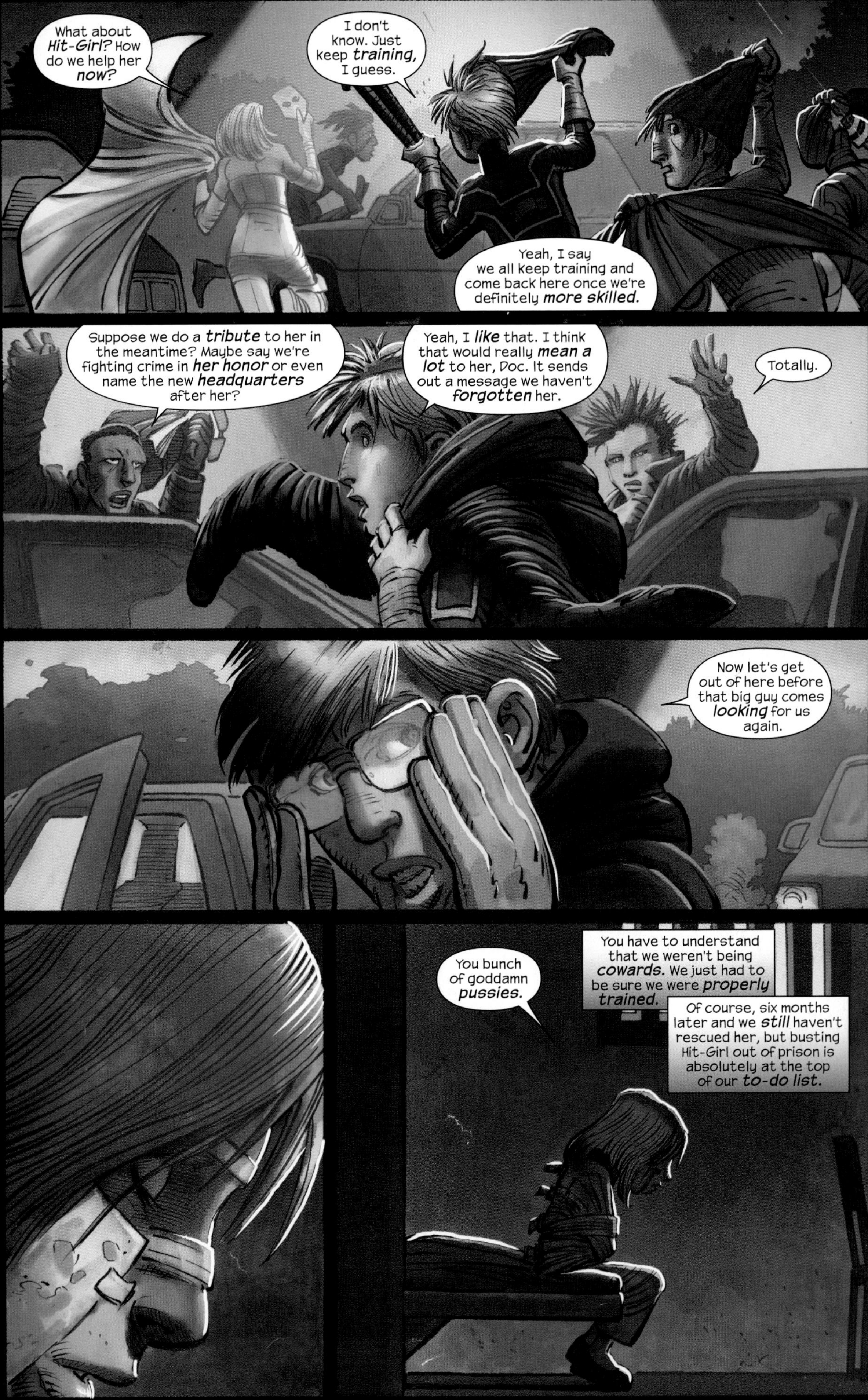
What about Hit-Girl? How do we help her now?
I don't know. Just keep training, I guess.
Yeah, I say we all keep training and come back here once we're definitely more skilled.
Suppose we do a tribute to her in the meantime? Maybe say we're fighting crime in her honor or even name the new headquarters after her?
Yeah, I like that. I think that would really mean a lot to her, Doc. It sends out a message we haven't forgotten her.
Totally.
Now let's get out of here before that big guy comes looking for us again.
You bunch of goddamn pussies.
You have to understand that we weren't being cowards. We just had to be sure we were properly trained.
Of course, six months later and we still haven't rescued her, but busting Hit-Girl out of prison is absolutely at the top of our to-do list.

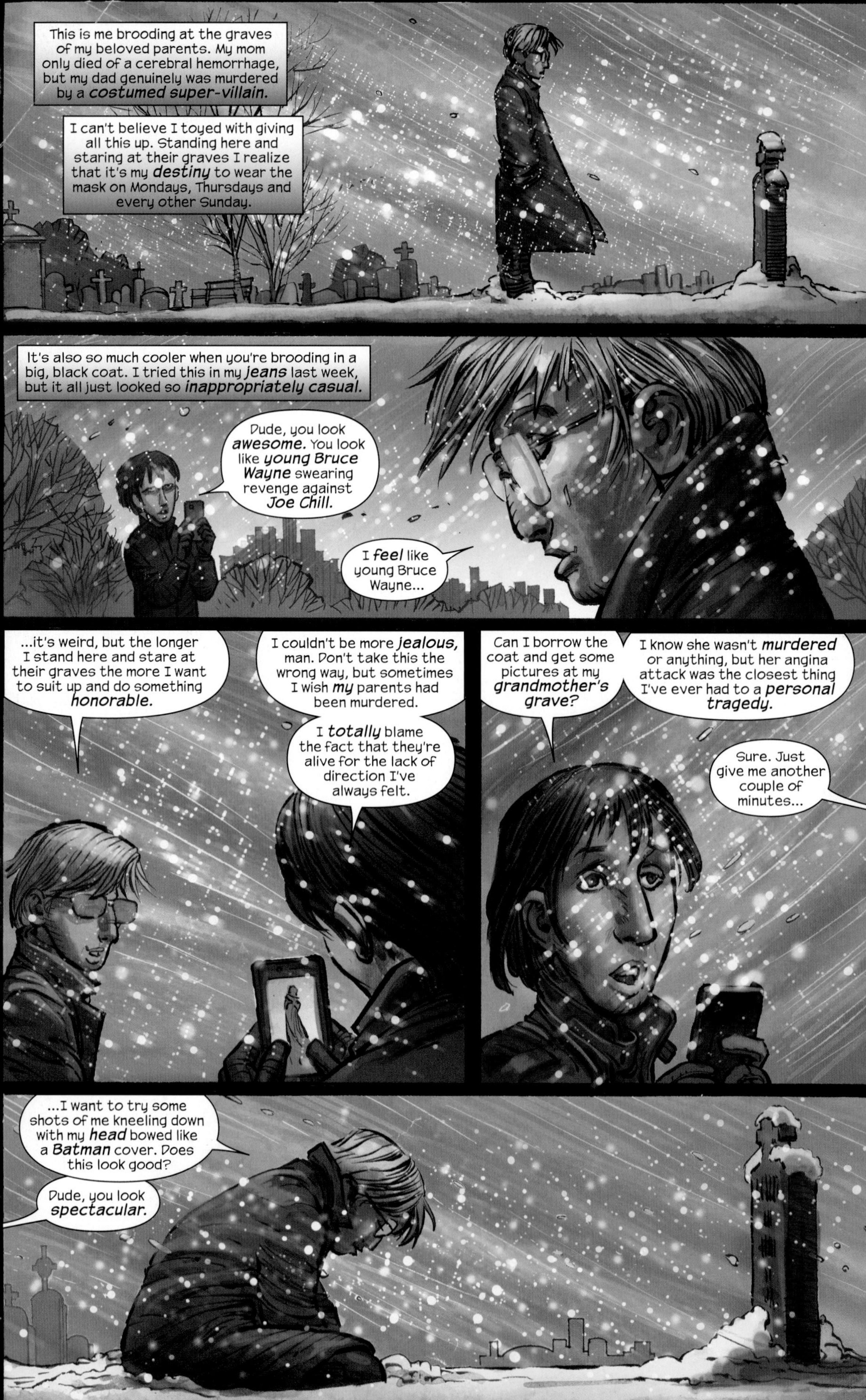
This is me brooding at the graves of my beloved parents. My mom only died of a cerebral hemorrhage, but my dad genuinely was murdered by a costumed super-villain.
I can't believe I toyed with giving all this up. Standing here and staring at their graves I realize that it's my destiny to wear the mask on Mondays, Thursdays and every other Sunday.
It's also so much cooler when you're brooding in a big, black coat. I tried this in my jeans last week, but it all just looked so inappropriately casual.
Dude, you look awesome. You look like young Bruce Wayne swearing revenge against Joe Chill.
I feel like young Bruce Wayne...
...it's weird, but the longer I stand here and stare at their graves the more I want to suit up and do something honorable.
I couldn't be more jealous, man. Don't take this the wrong way, but sometimes I wish my parents had been murdered.
I totally blame the fact that they're alive for the lack of direction I've always felt.
Can I borrow the coat and get some pictures at my grandmother's grave?
I know she wasn't murdered or anything, but her angina attack was the closest thing I've ever had to a personal tragedy.
Sure. Just give me another couple of minutes...
...I want to try some shots of me kneeling down with my head bowed like a Batman cover. Does this look good?
Dude, you look spectacular.

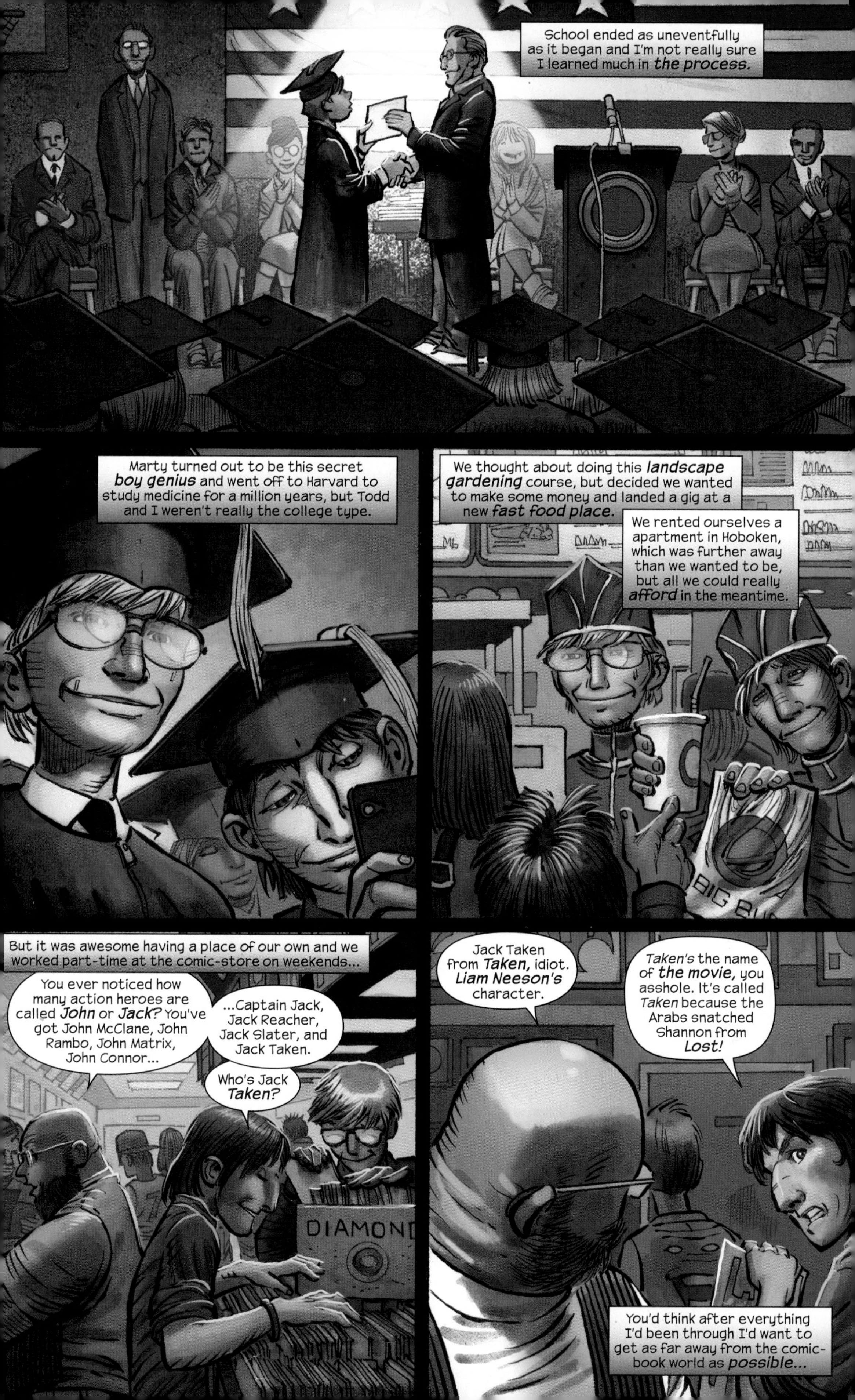

School ended as uneventfully as it began and I'm not really sure I learned much in *the process.*
Marty turned out to be this secret *boy genius* and went off to Harvard to study medicine for a million years, but Todd and I weren't really the college type.
We thought about doing this *landscape gardening* course, but decided we wanted to make some money and landed a gig at a new *fast food place.*
We rented ourselves a apartment in Hoboken, which was further away than we wanted to be, but all we could really *afford* in the meantime.
BIG BU
But it was awesome having a place of our own and we worked part-time at the comic-store on weekends...
You ever noticed how many action heroes are called *John* or *Jack?* You've got John McClane, John Rambo, John Matrix, John Connor...
...Captain Jack, Jack Reacher, Jack Slater, and Jack Taken.
Who's Jack *Taken?*
DIAMOND
Jack Taken from *Taken,* idiot. *Liam Neeson's* character.
Taken's the name of *the movie,* you asshole. It's called *Taken* because the Arabs snatched Shannon from *Lost!*
You'd think after everything I'd been through I'd want to get as far away from the comic-book world as *possible...*

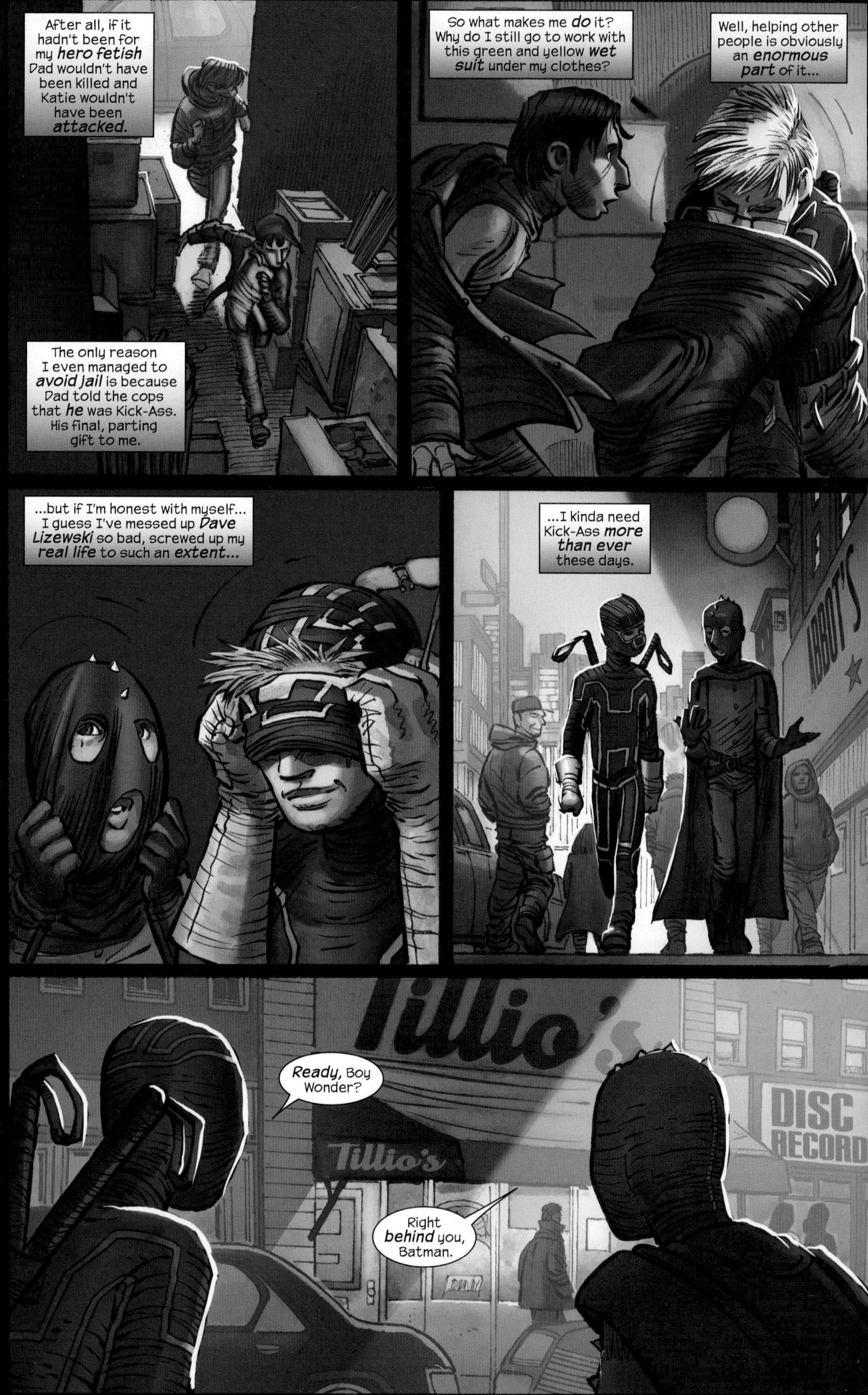
After all, if it hadn't been for my hero fetish Dad wouldn't have been killed and Katie wouldn't have been attacked.
The only reason I even managed to avoid jail is because Dad told the cops that he was Kick-Ass. His final, parting gift to me.
So what makes me do it? Why do I still go to work with this green and yellow wet suit under my clothes?
Well, helping other people is obviously an enormous part of it...
...but if I'm honest with myself... I guess I've messed up Dave Lizewski so bad, screwed up my real life to such an extent...
...I kinda need Kick-Ass more than ever these days.
ABBOT'S
Tillio's
Ready, Boy Wonder?
DISC RECORD
Tillio's
Right behind you, Batman.

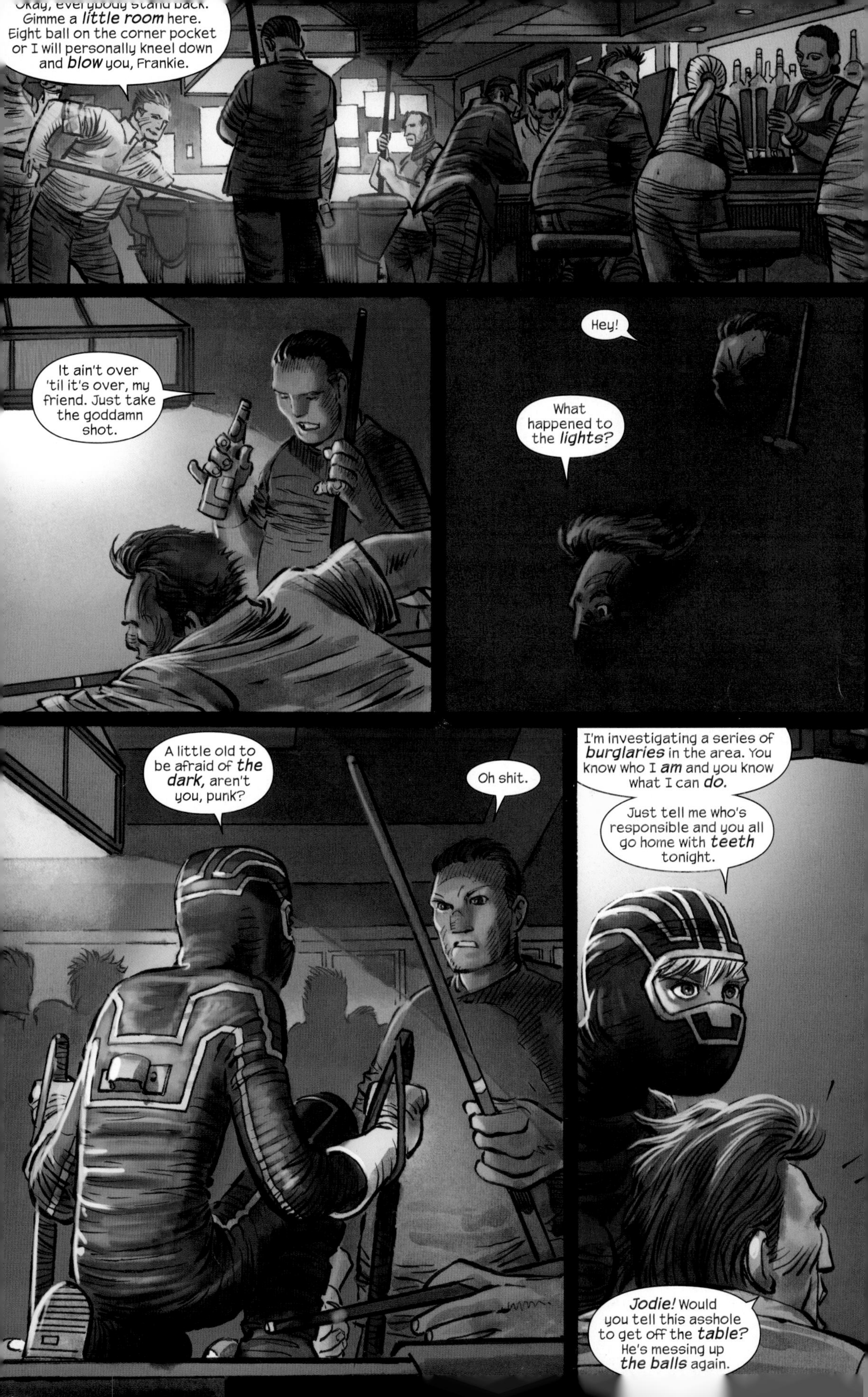
Okay, everybody stand back. Gimme a little room here. Eight ball on the corner pocket or I will personally kneel down and blow you, Frankie.
It ain't over 'til it's over, my friend. Just take the goddamn shot.
Hey!
What happened to the lights?
A little old to be afraid of the dark, aren't you, punk?
Oh shit.
I'm investigating a series of burglaries in the area. You know who I am and you know what I can do.
Just tell me who's responsible and you all go home with teeth tonight.
Jodie! Would you tell this asshole to get off the table? He's messing up the balls again.

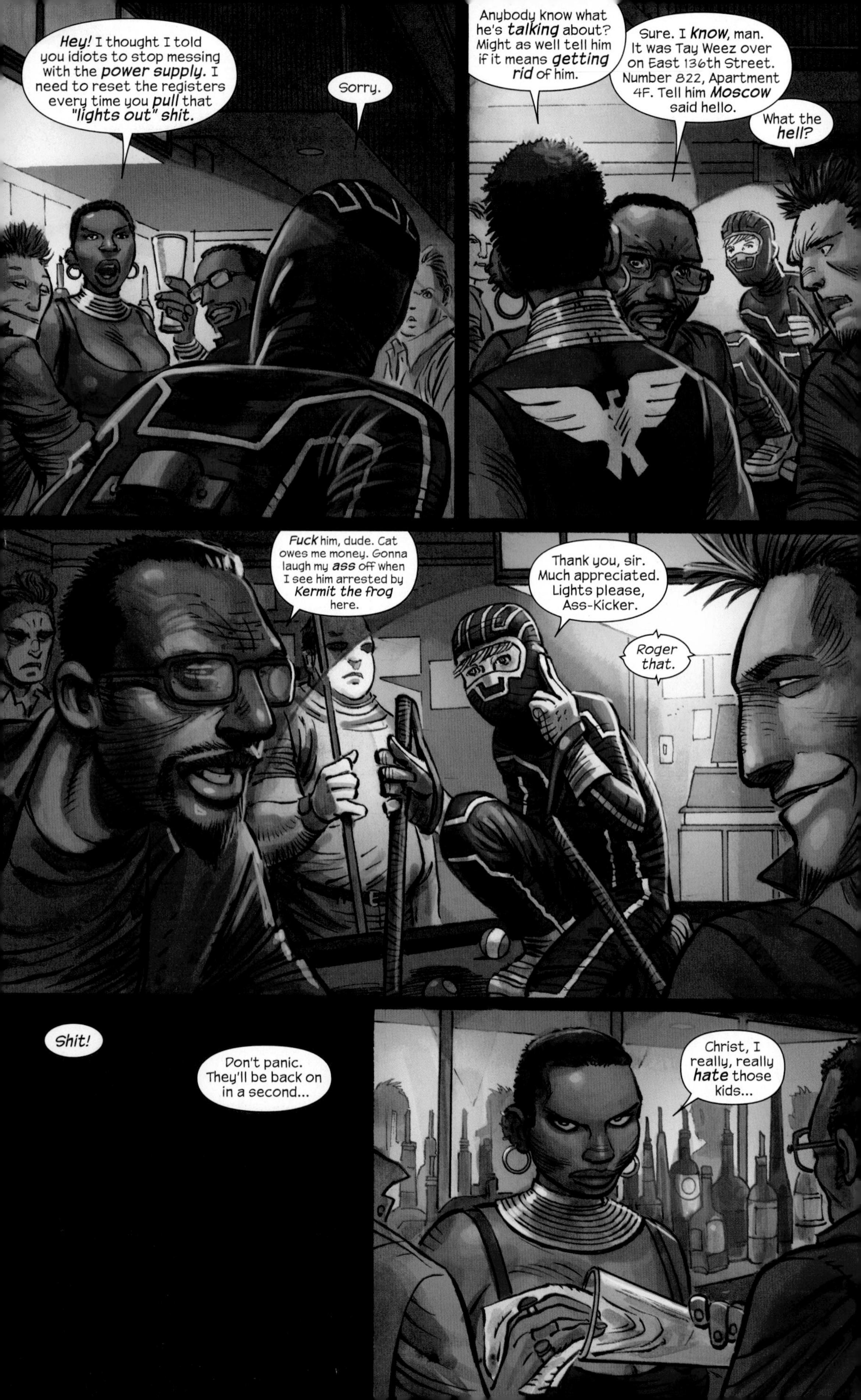

Hey! I thought I told you idiots to stop messing with the power supply. I need to reset the registers every time you pull that "lights out" shit.
Sorry.
Anybody know what he's talking about? Might as well tell him if it means getting rid of him.
Sure. I know, man. It was Tay Weez over on East 136th Street. Number 822, Apartment 4F. Tell him Moscow said hello.
What the hell?
Fuck him, dude. Cat owes me money. Gonna laugh my ass off when I see him arrested by Kermit the frog here.
Thank you, sir. Much appreciated. Lights please, Ass-Kicker.
Roger that.
Shit!
Don't panic. They'll be back on in a second...
Christ, I really, really hate those kids...

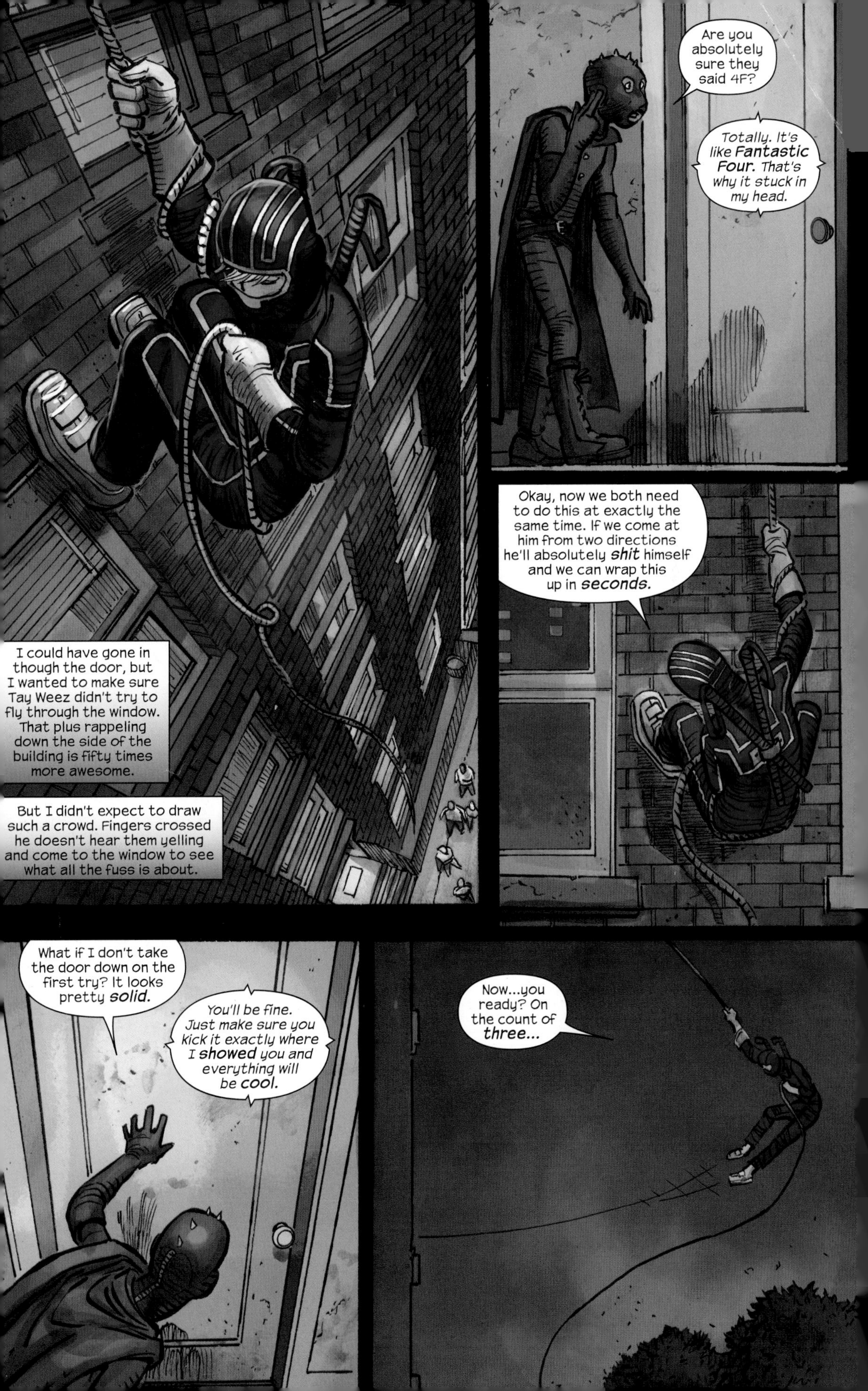
I could have gone in though the door, but I wanted to make sure Tay Weez didn't try to fly through the window. That plus rappeling down the side of the building is fifty times more awesome.
But I didn't expect to draw such a crowd. Fingers crossed he doesn't hear them yelling and come to the window to see what all the fuss is about.
Are you absolutely sure they said 4F?
Totally. It's like Fantastic Four. That's why it stuck in my head.
Okay, now we both need to do this at exactly the same time. If we come at him from two directions he'll absolutely shit himself and we can wrap this up in seconds.
What if I don't take the door down on the first try? It looks pretty solid.
You'll be fine. Just make sure you kick it exactly where I showed you and everything will be cool.
Now...you ready? On the count of three...

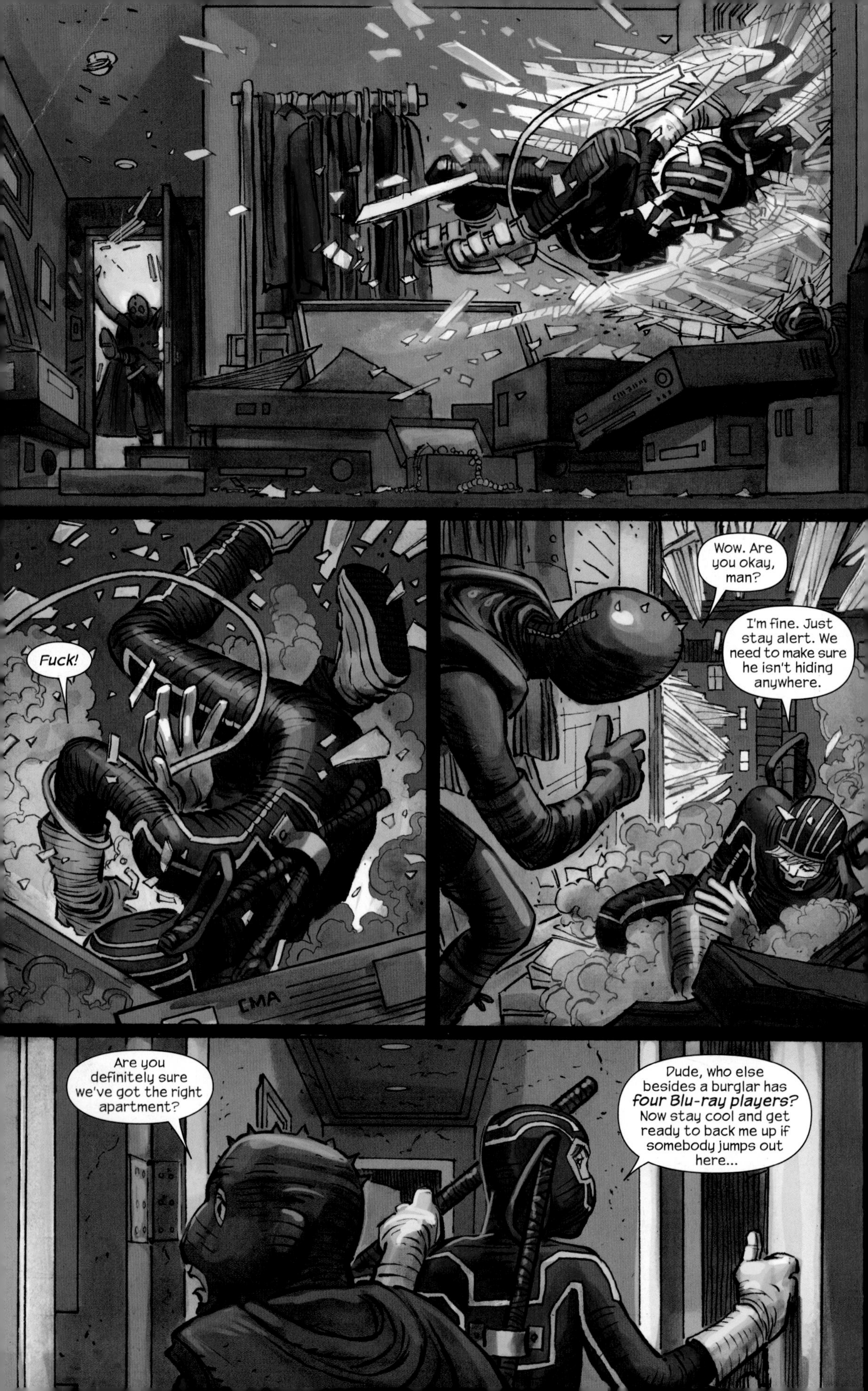
Fuck!
Wow. Are you okay, man?
I'm fine. Just stay alert. We need to make sure he isn't hiding anywhere.
Are you definitely sure we've got the right apartment?
Dude, who else besides a burglar has *four Blu-ray players?* Now stay cool and get ready to back me up if somebody jumps out here...

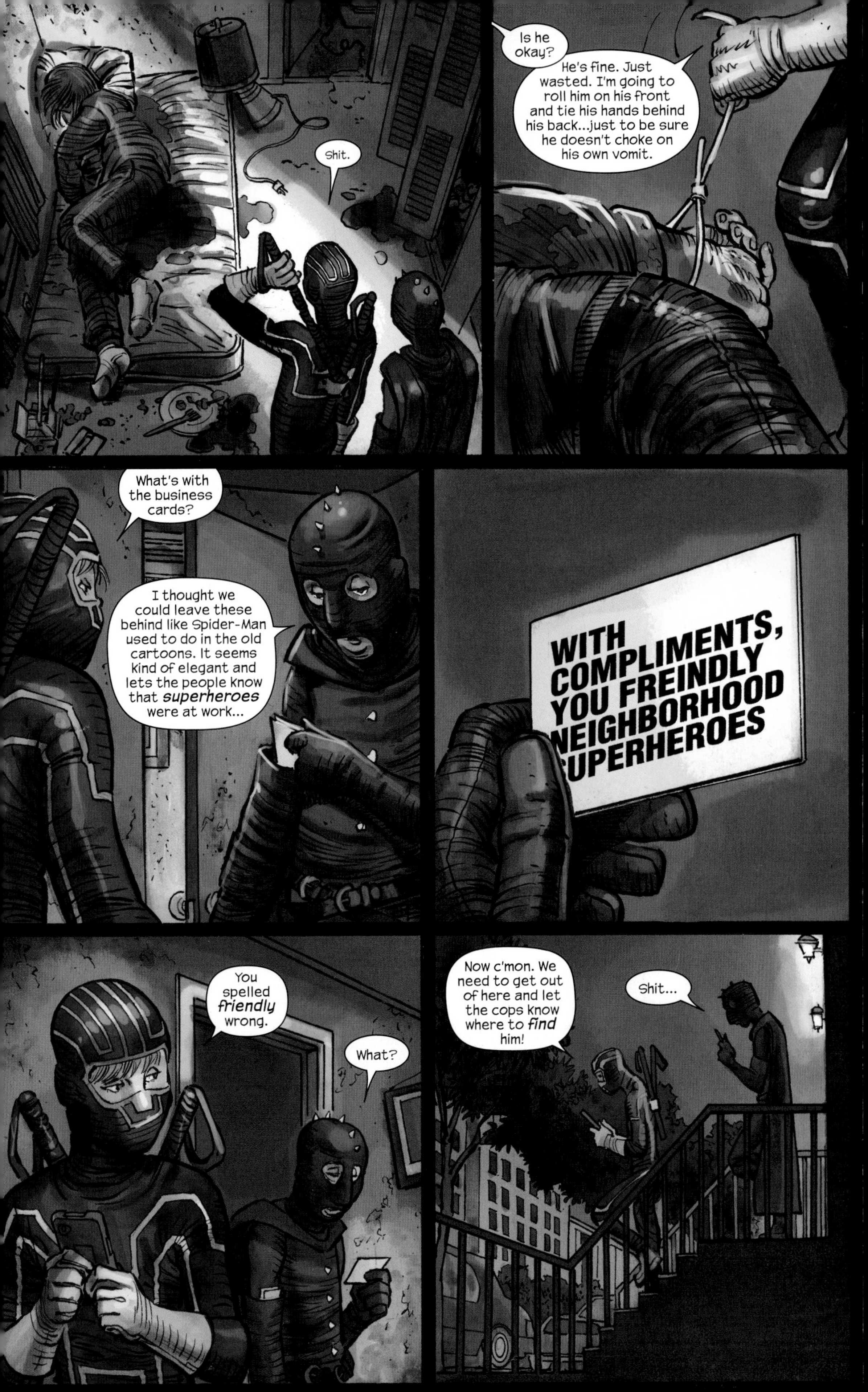

Shit.
Is he okay?
He's fine. Just wasted. I'm going to roll him on his front and tie his hands behind his back...just to be sure he doesn't choke on his own vomit.
What's with the business cards?
I thought we could leave these behind like Spider-Man used to do in the old cartoons. It seems kind of elegant and lets the people know that *superheroes* were at work...
WITH COMPLIMENTS, YOU FREINDLY NEIGHBORHOOD SUPERHEROES
You spelled *friendly* wrong.
What?
Now c'mon. We need to get out of here and let the cops know where to *find* him!
Shit...

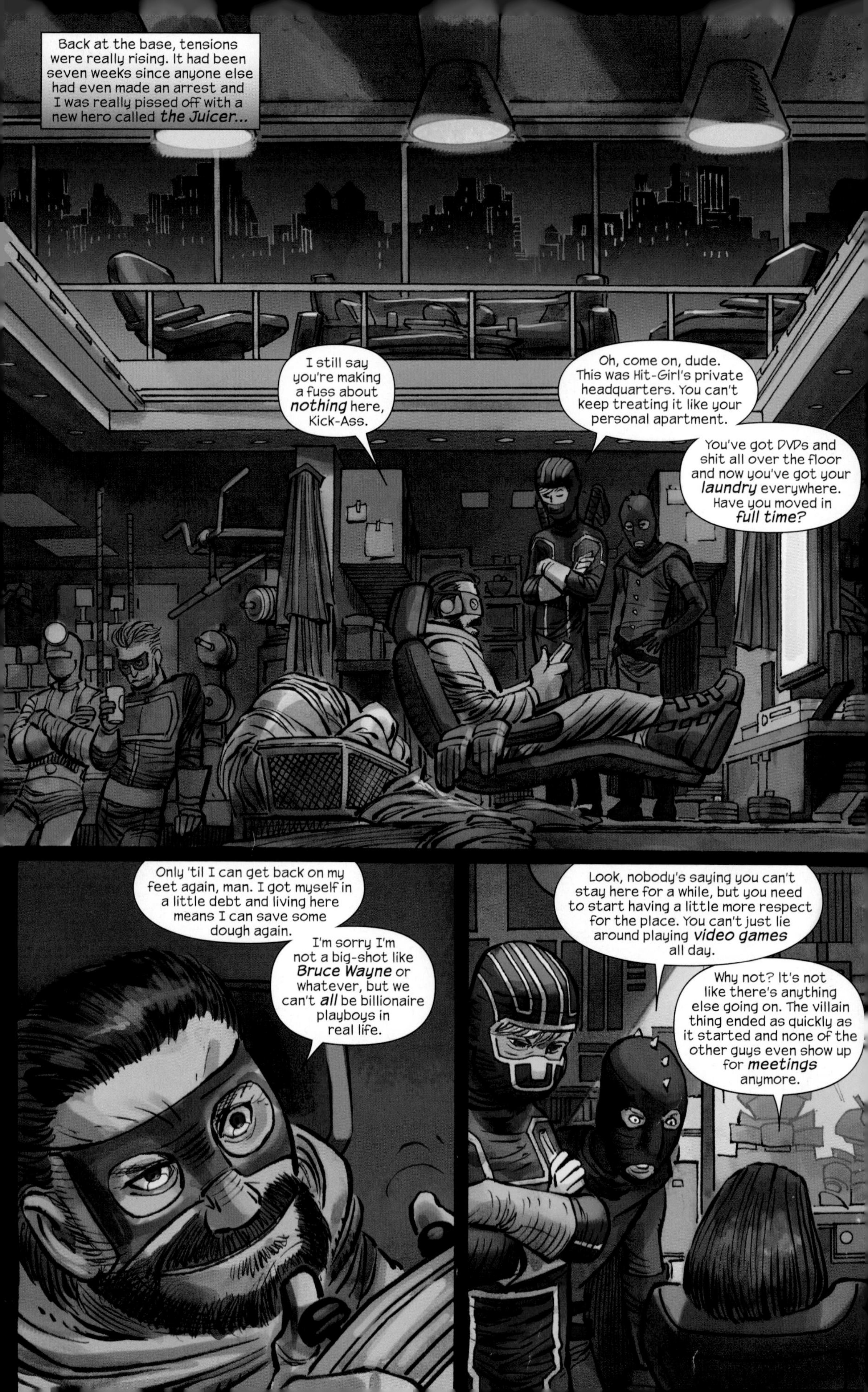
Back at the base, tensions were really rising. It had been seven weeks since anyone else had even made an arrest and I was really pissed off with a new hero called the Juicer...
I still say you're making a fuss about nothing here, Kick-Ass.
Oh, come on, dude. This was Hit-Girl's private headquarters. You can't keep treating it like your personal apartment.
You've got DVDs and shit all over the floor and now you've got your laundry everywhere. Have you moved in full time?
Only 'til I can get back on my feet again, man. I got myself in a little debt and living here means I can save some dough again.
I'm sorry I'm not a big-shot like Bruce Wayne or whatever, but we can't all be billionaire playboys in real life.
Look, nobody's saying you can't stay here for a while, but you need to start having a little more respect for the place. You can't just lie around playing video games all day.
Why not? It's not like there's anything else going on. The villain thing ended as quickly as it started and none of the other guys even show up for meetings anymore.

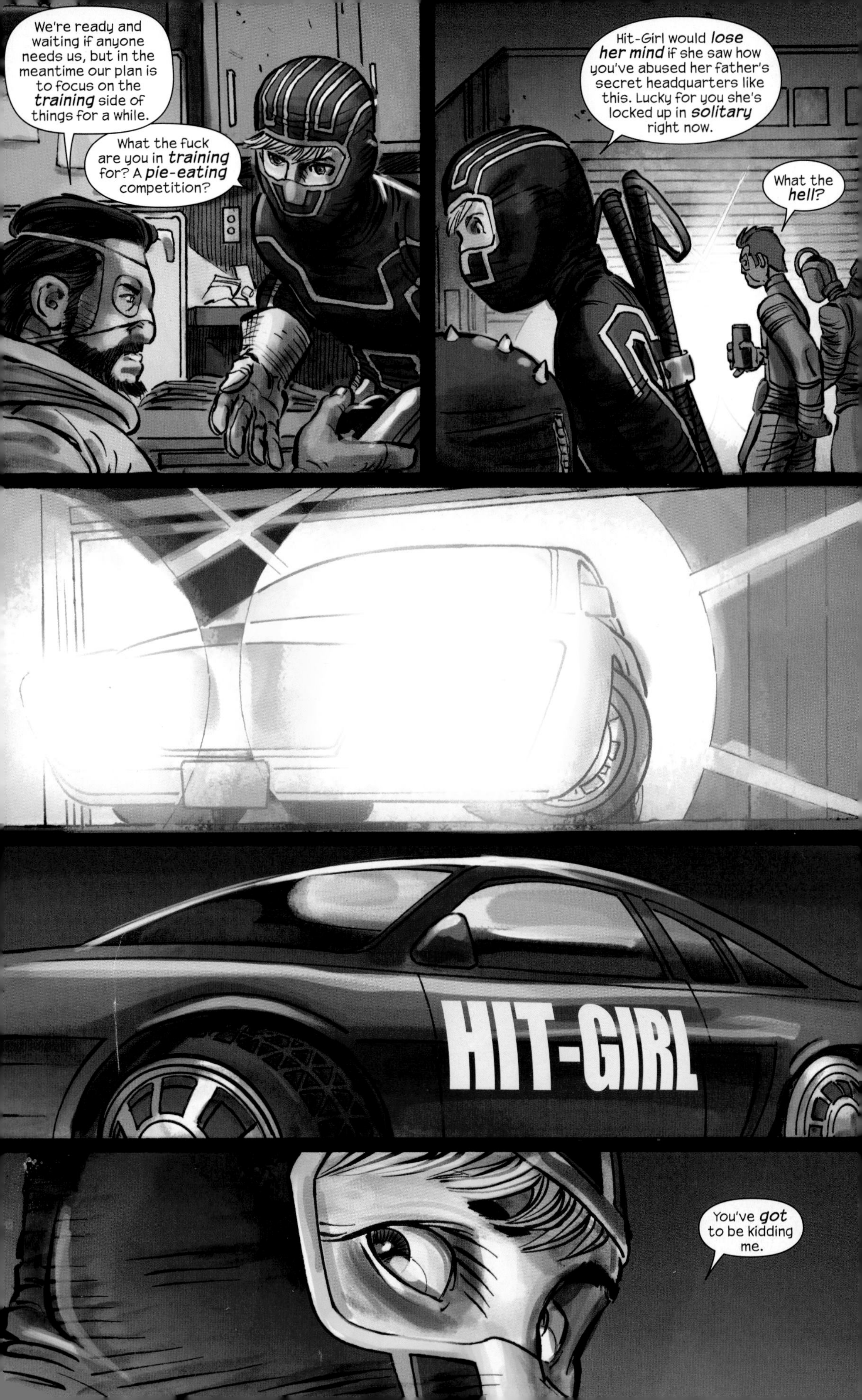
We're ready and waiting if anyone needs us, but in the meantime our plan is to focus on the training side of things for a while.
What the fuck are you in training for? A pie-eating competition?
Hit-Girl would lose her mind if she saw how you've abused her father's secret headquarters like this. Lucky for you she's locked up in solitary right now.
What the hell?
HIT-GIRL
You've got to be kidding me.

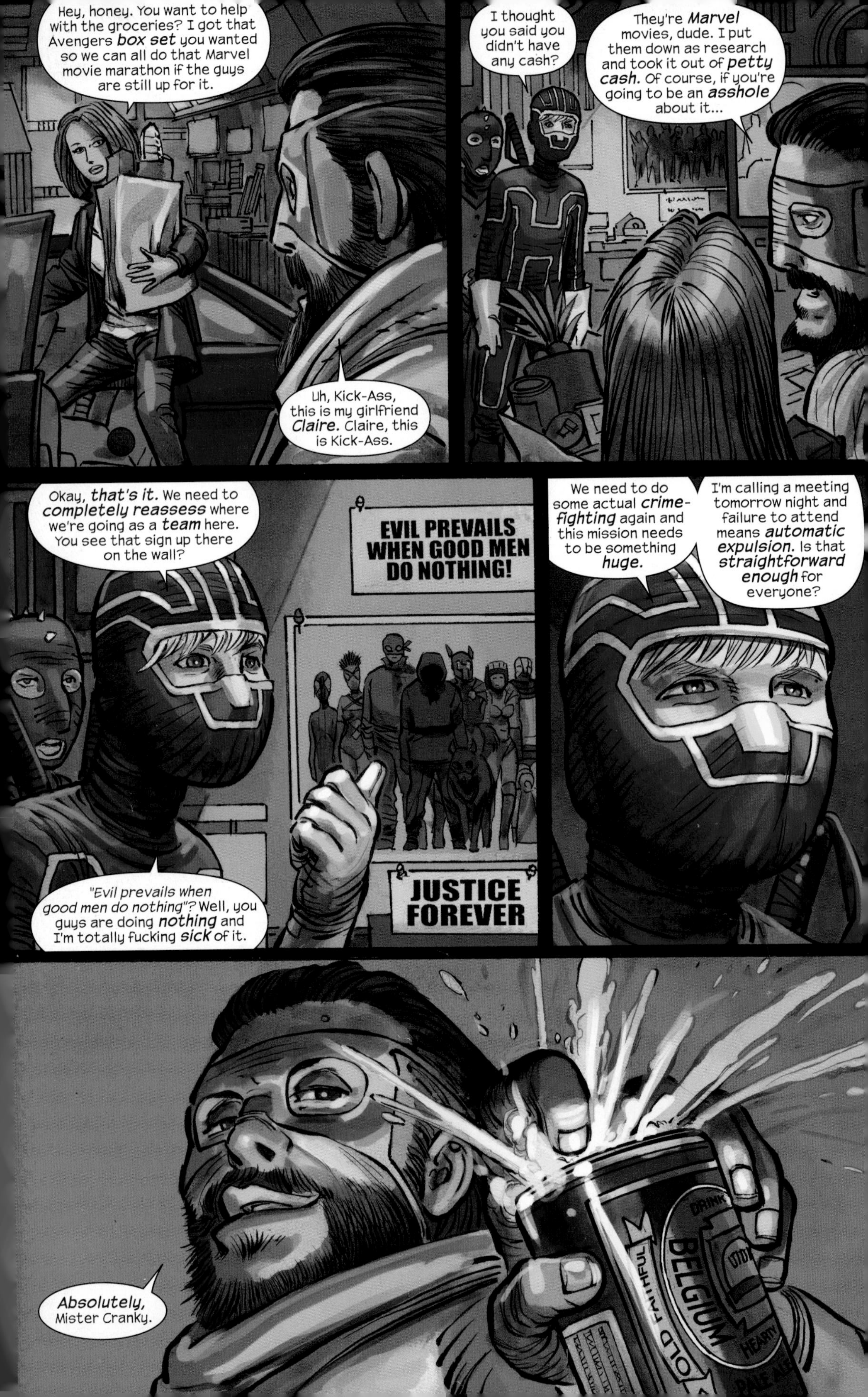
Hey, honey. You want to help with the groceries? I got that Avengers box set you wanted so we can all do that Marvel movie marathon if the guys are still up for it.
Uh, Kick-Ass, this is my girlfriend Claire. Claire, this is Kick-Ass.
I thought you said you didn't have any cash?
They're Marvel movies, dude. I put them down as research and took it out of petty cash. Of course, if you're going to be an asshole about it...
Okay, that's it. We need to completely reassess where we're going as a team here. You see that sign up there on the wall?
EVIL PREVAILS WHEN GOOD MEN DO NOTHING!
JUSTICE FOREVER
"Evil prevails when good men do nothing"? Well, you guys are doing nothing and I'm totally fucking sick of it.
We need to do some actual crime-fighting again and this mission needs to be something huge.
I'm calling a meeting tomorrow night and failure to attend means automatic expulsion. Is that straightforward enough for everyone?
Absolutely, Mister Cranky.
BELGIUM
OLD FAITHFUL
DRINK
HEARTY

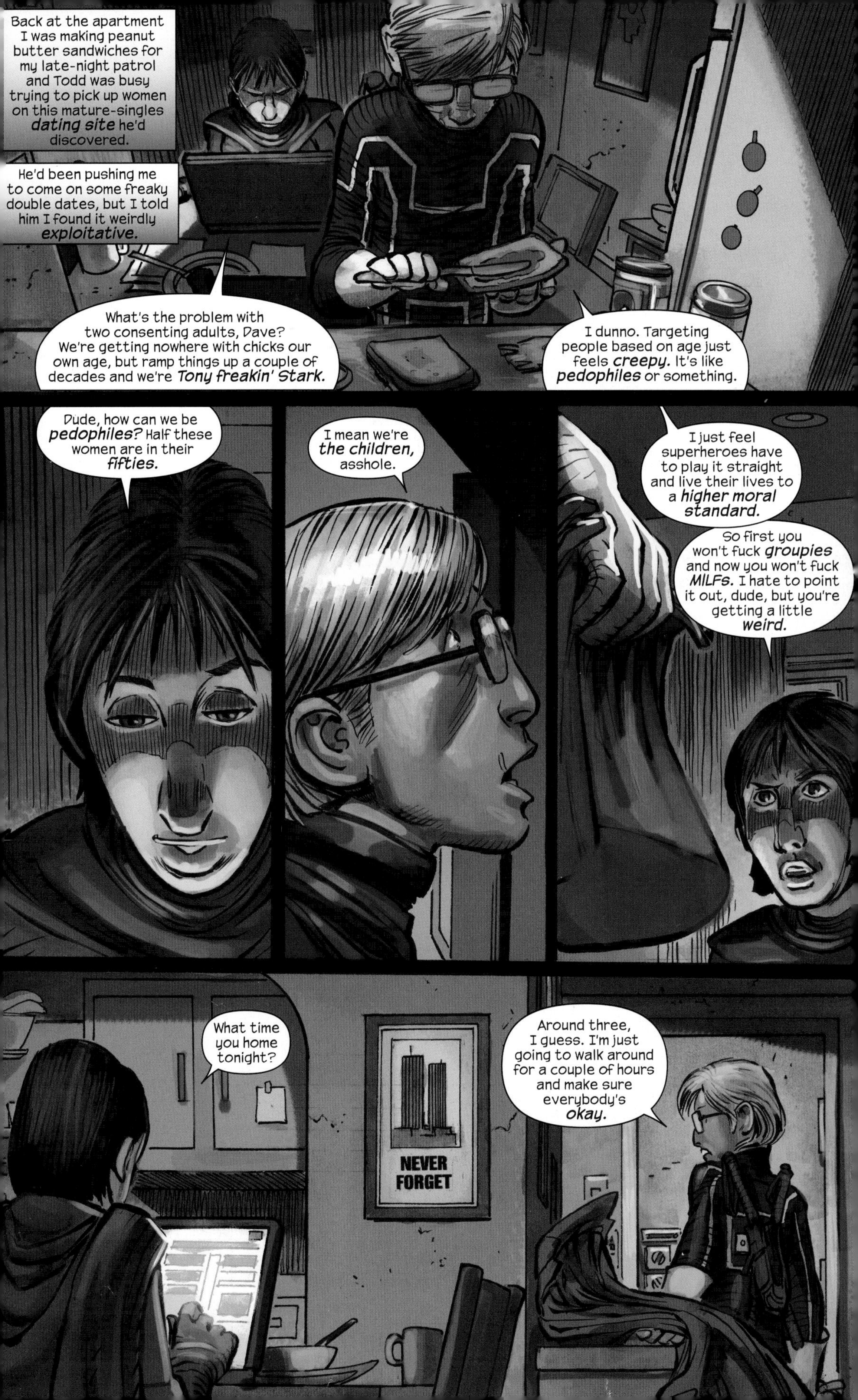
Back at the apartment I was making peanut butter sandwiches for my late-night patrol and Todd was busy trying to pick up women on this mature-singles *dating site* he'd discovered.
He'd been pushing me to come on some freaky double dates, but I told him I found it weirdly *exploitative.*
What's the problem with two consenting adults, Dave? We're getting nowhere with chicks our own age, but ramp things up a couple of decades and we're *Tony freakin' Stark.*
I dunno. Targeting people based on age just feels *creepy.* It's like *pedophiles* or something.
Dude, how can we be *pedophiles?* Half these women are in their *fifties.*
I mean we're *the children,* asshole.
I just feel superheroes have to play it straight and live their lives to a *higher moral standard.*
So first you won't fuck *groupies* and now you won't fuck *MILFs.* I hate to point it out, dude, but you're getting a little *weird.*
What time you home tonight?
NEVER FORGET
Around three, I guess. I'm just going to walk around for a couple of hours and make sure everybody's *okay.*

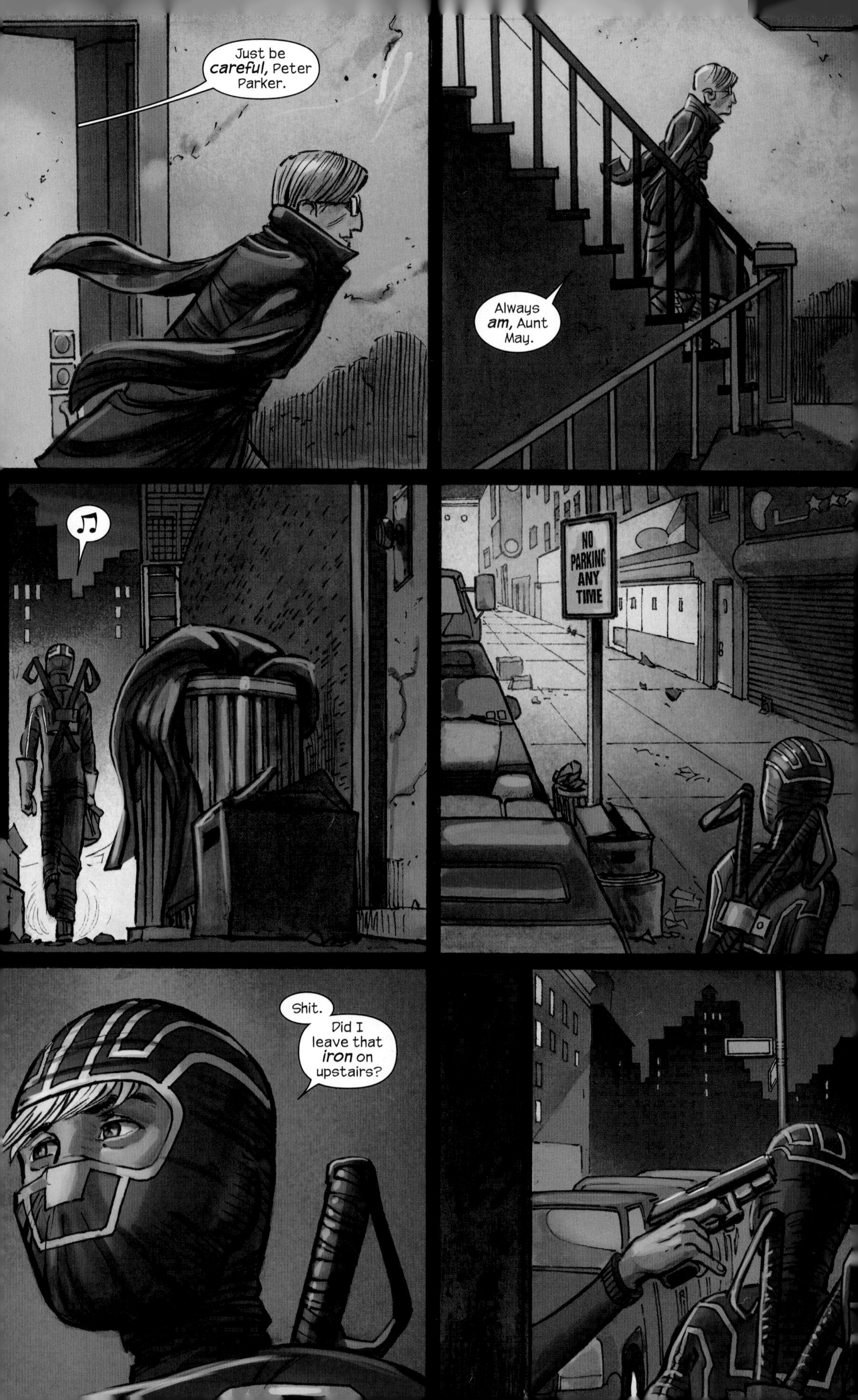
Just be *careful,* Peter Parker.
Always *am,* Aunt May.
♫
NO PARKING ANY TIME
Shit.
Did I leave that *iron* on upstairs?

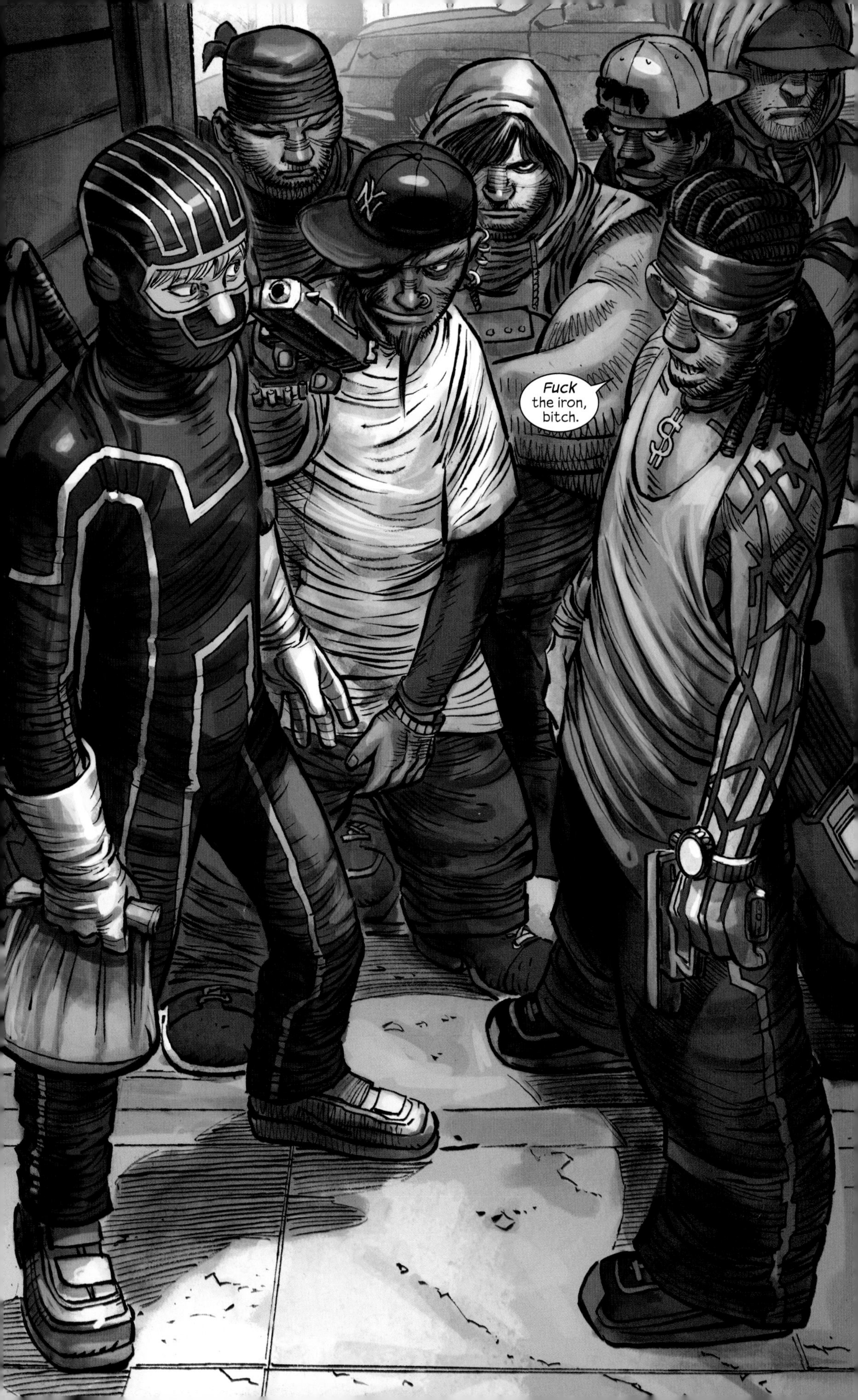
Fuck the iron, bitch.

TWO

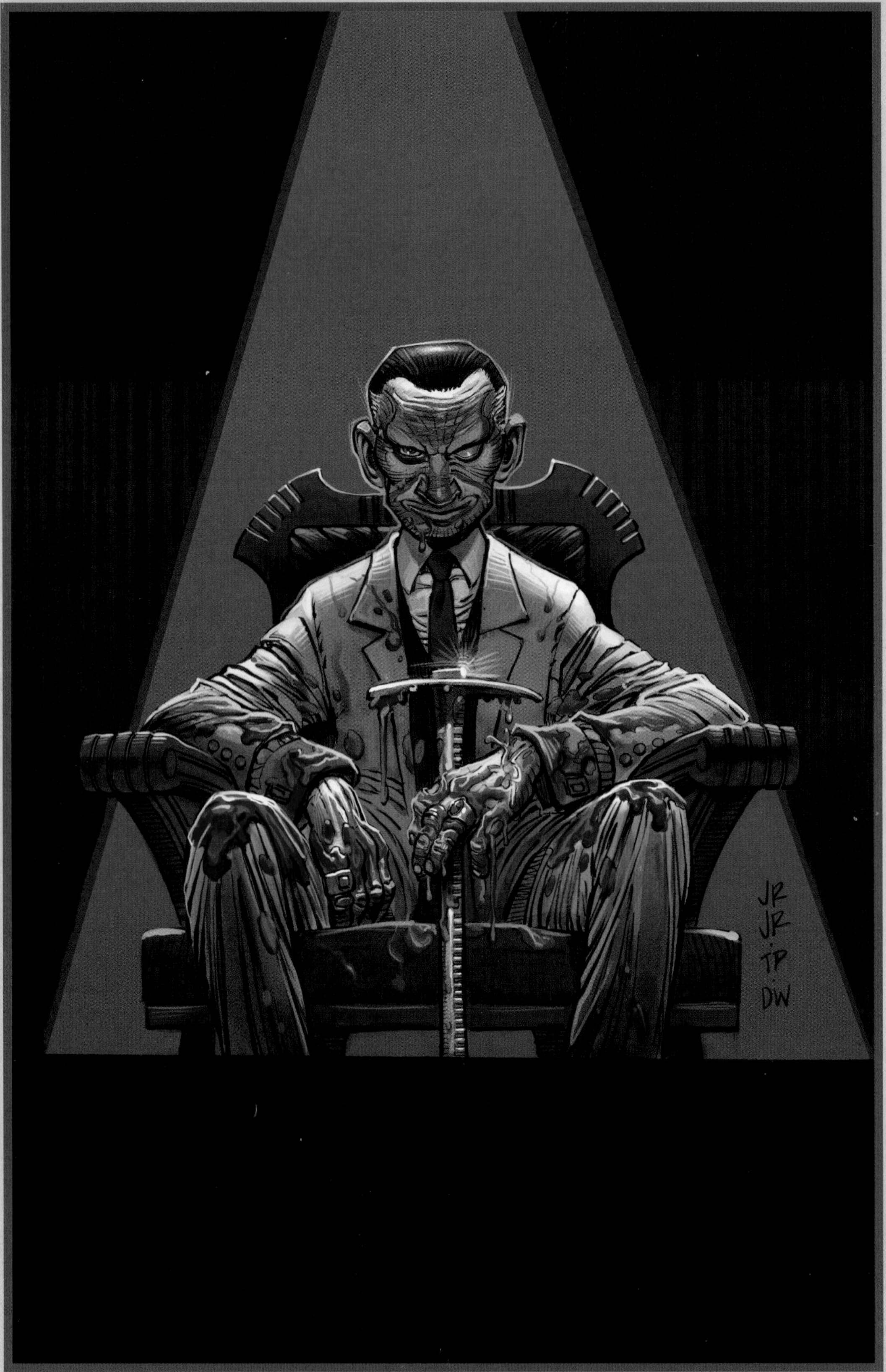
JR
JR
TP
DW

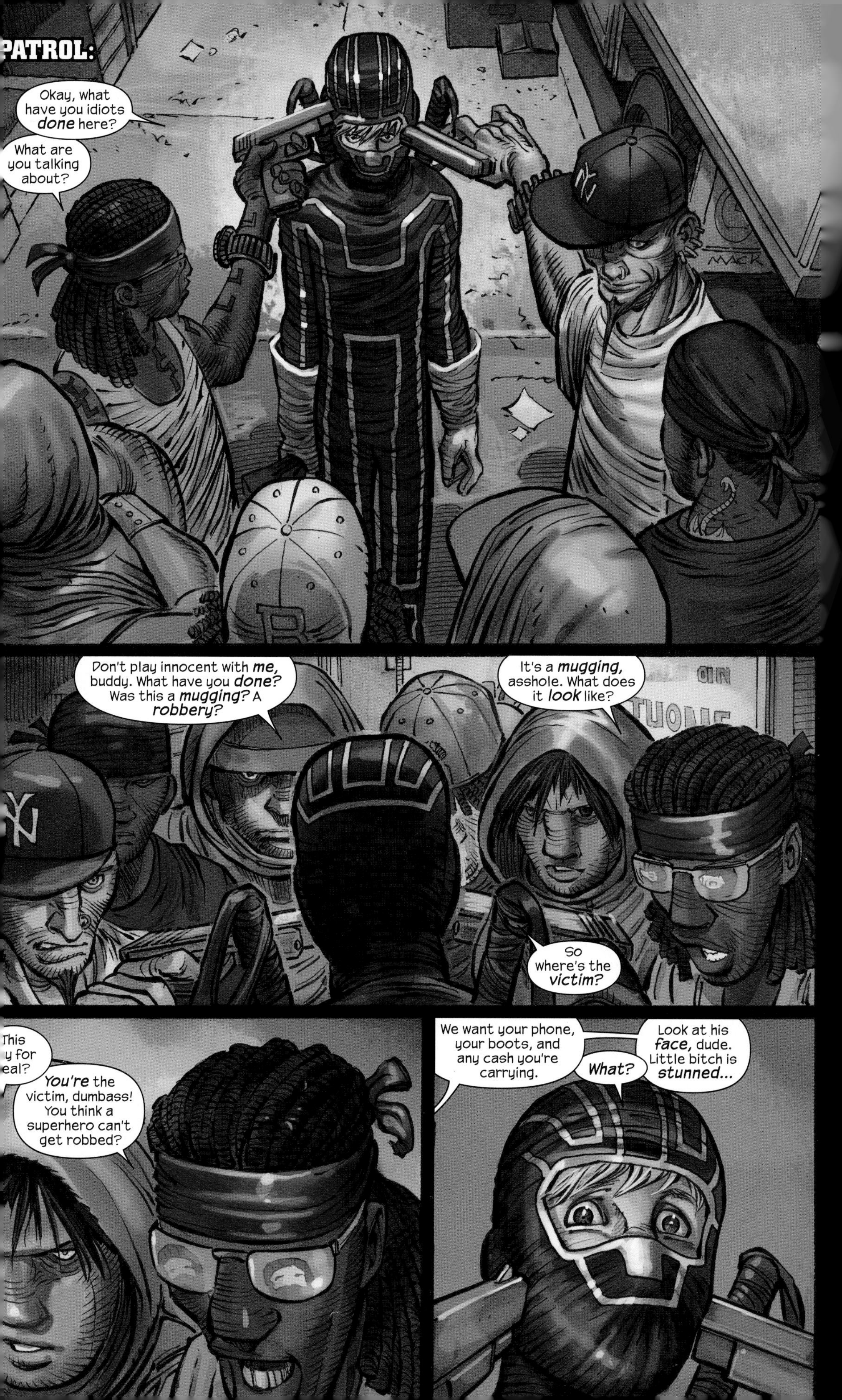
PATROL:
Okay, what have you idiots done here?
What are you talking about?
Don't play innocent with me, buddy. What have you done? Was this a mugging? A robbery?
It's a mugging, asshole. What does it look like?
So where's the victim?
This y for eal?
You're the victim, dumbass! You think a superhero can't get robbed?
We want your phone, your boots, and any cash you're carrying.
What?
Look at his face, dude. Little bitch is stunned...

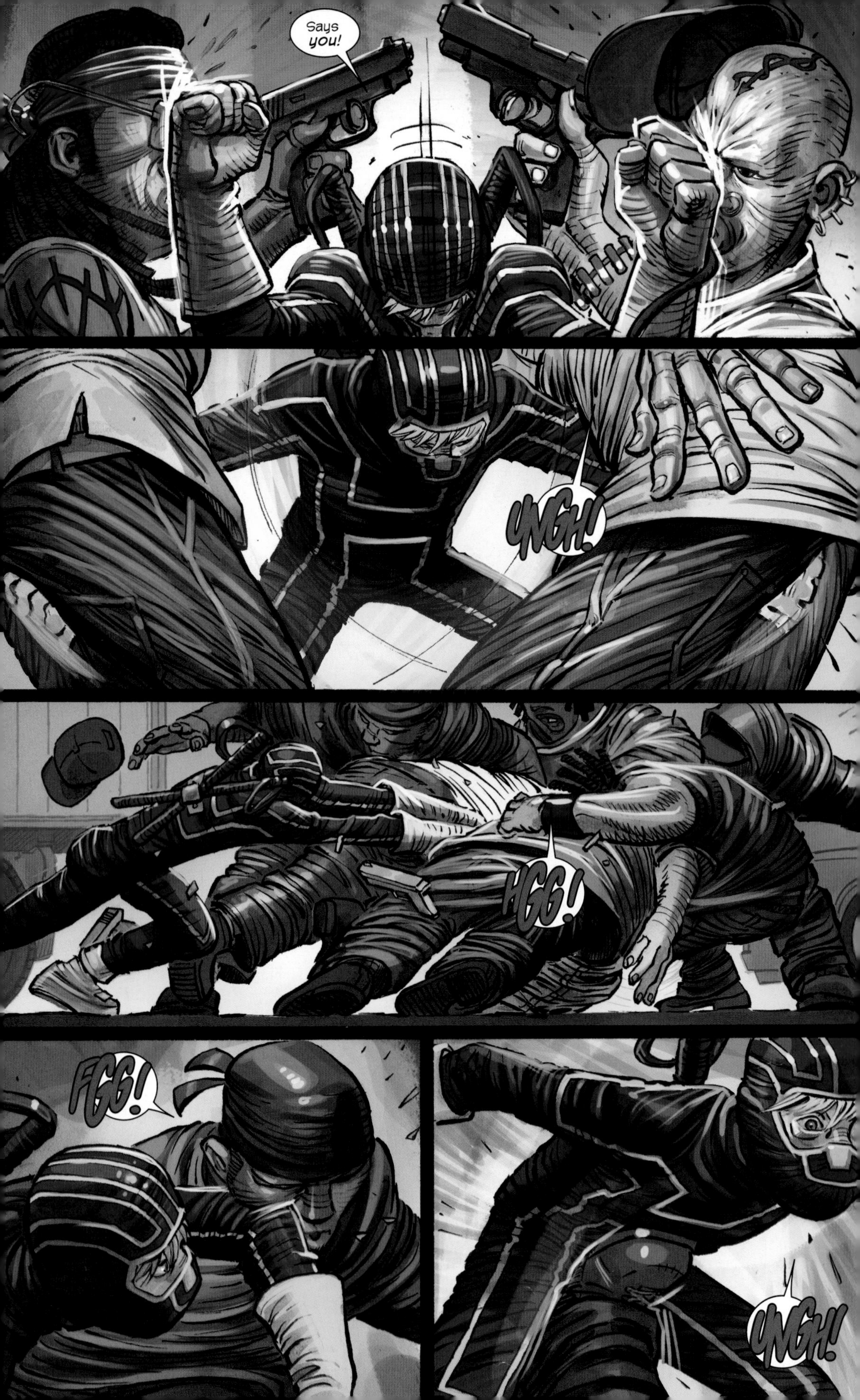
Says you!
UNGH!
HGG!
FGG!
UNGH!

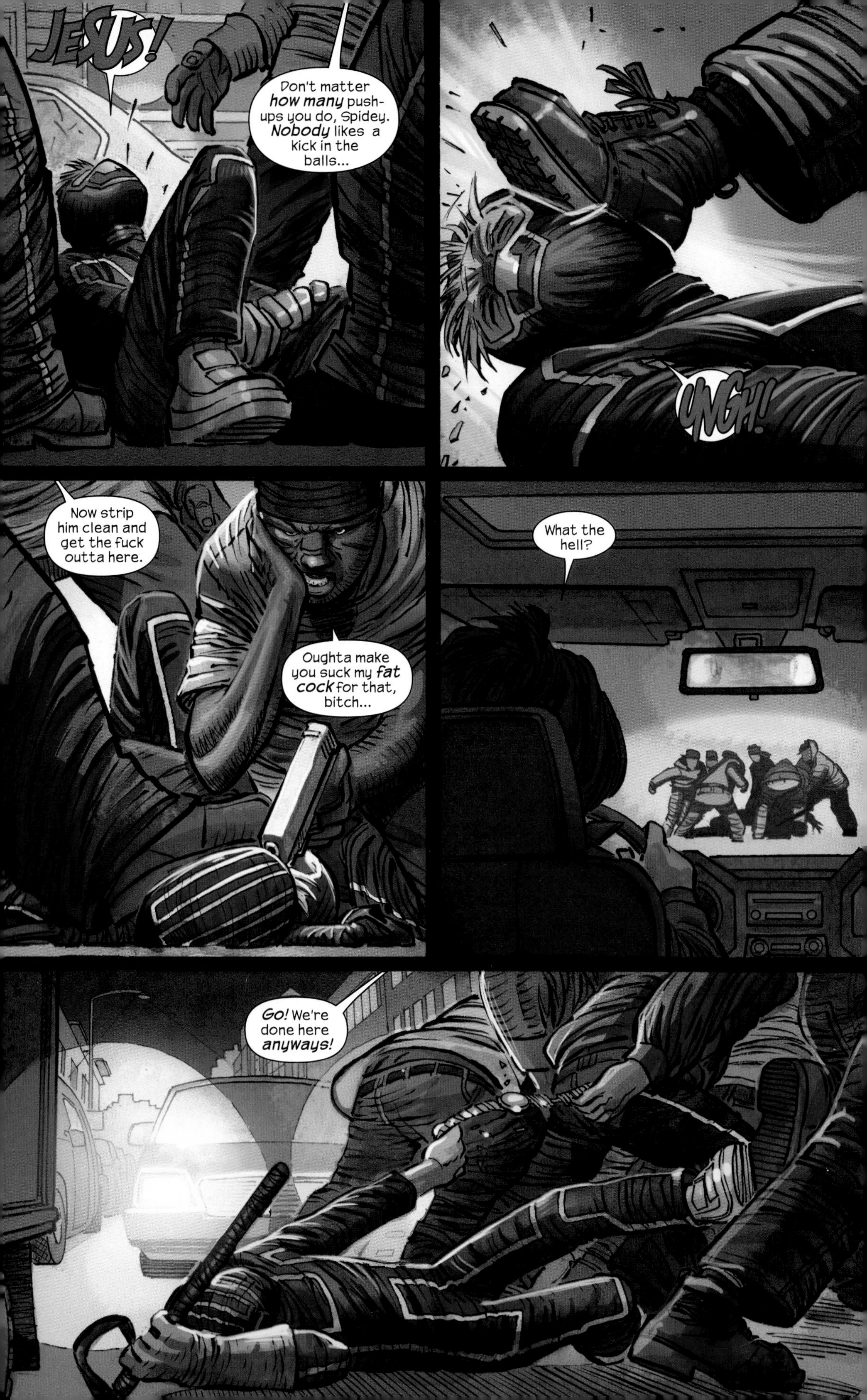
JESUS!
Don't matter *how many* push-ups you do, Spidey. *Nobody* likes a kick in the balls...
UNGH!
Now strip him clean and get the fuck outta here.
Oughta make you suck my *fat cock* for that, bitch...
What the hell?
Go! We're done here *anyways!*

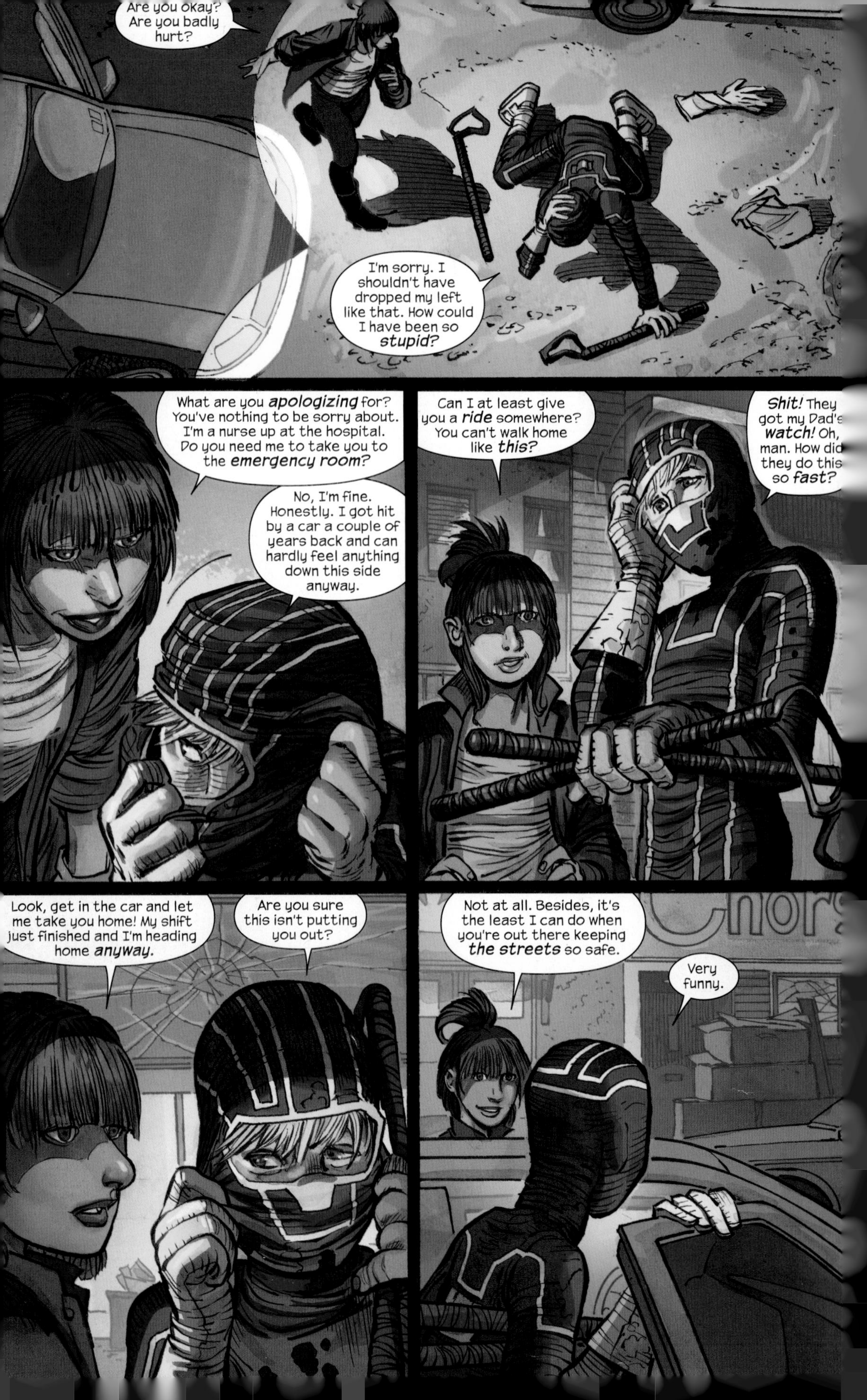
Are you okay? Are you badly hurt?
I'm sorry. I shouldn't have dropped my left like that. How could I have been so stupid?
What are you apologizing for? You've nothing to be sorry about. I'm a nurse up at the hospital. Do you need me to take you to the emergency room?
No, I'm fine. Honestly. I got hit by a car a couple of years back and can hardly feel anything down this side anyway.
Can I at least give you a ride somewhere? You can't walk home like this?
Shit! They got my Dad's watch! Oh, man. How did they do this so fast?
Look, get in the car and let me take you home! My shift just finished and I'm heading home anyway.
Are you sure this isn't putting you out?
Not at all. Besides, it's the least I can do when you're out there keeping the streets so safe.
Very funny.

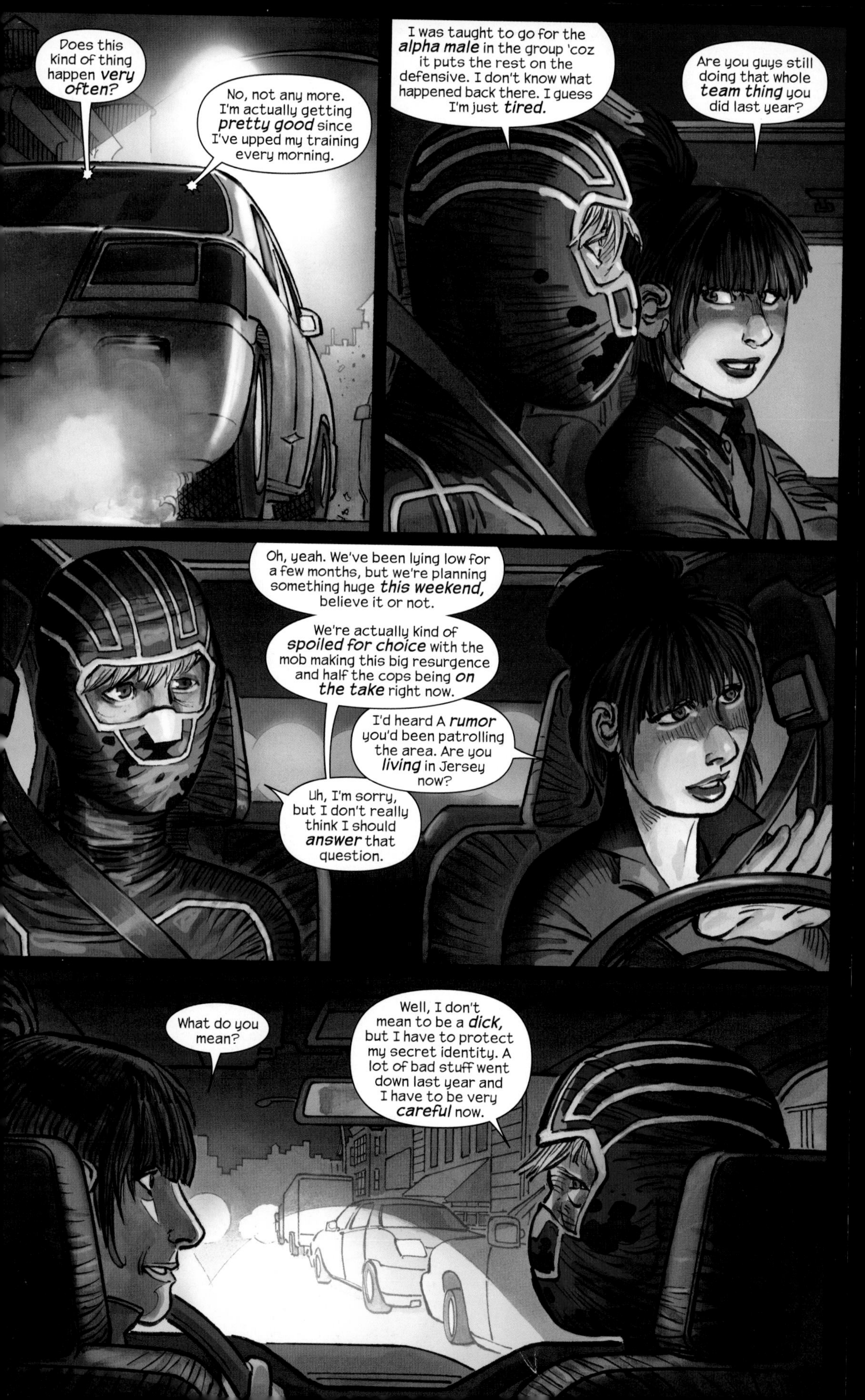

Does this kind of thing happen very often?
No, not any more. I'm actually getting pretty good since I've upped my training every morning.
I was taught to go for the alpha male in the group 'coz it puts the rest on the defensive. I don't know what happened back there. I guess I'm just tired.
Are you guys still doing that whole team thing you did last year?
Oh, yeah. We've been lying low for a few months, but we're planning something huge this weekend, believe it or not.
We're actually kind of spoiled for choice with the mob making this big resurgence and half the cops being on the take right now.
I'd heard A rumor you'd been patrolling the area. Are you living in Jersey now?
Uh, I'm sorry, but I don't really think I should answer that question.
What do you mean?
Well, I don't mean to be a dick, but I have to protect my secret identity. A lot of bad stuff went down last year and I have to be very careful now.

In fact, if you could just drop me over here on the corner that would be perfect.

What are you talking about? I thought you said you were another mile up the road.

Yeah, but it's a nice night and I don't mind *walking* the rest of the way. It's only another ten minutes.

Okay, Captain Paranoia. Whatever you feel *comfortable* with.

Listen, I know the circumstances were hardly ideal, but I have to say it was a pleasure to meet my first real-life superhero. My name's *Valerie*, by the way.

Kick-Ass.

I know.

Look after yourself, Kick-Ass.

You too, Valerie.

From the diary of Angie Genovese...

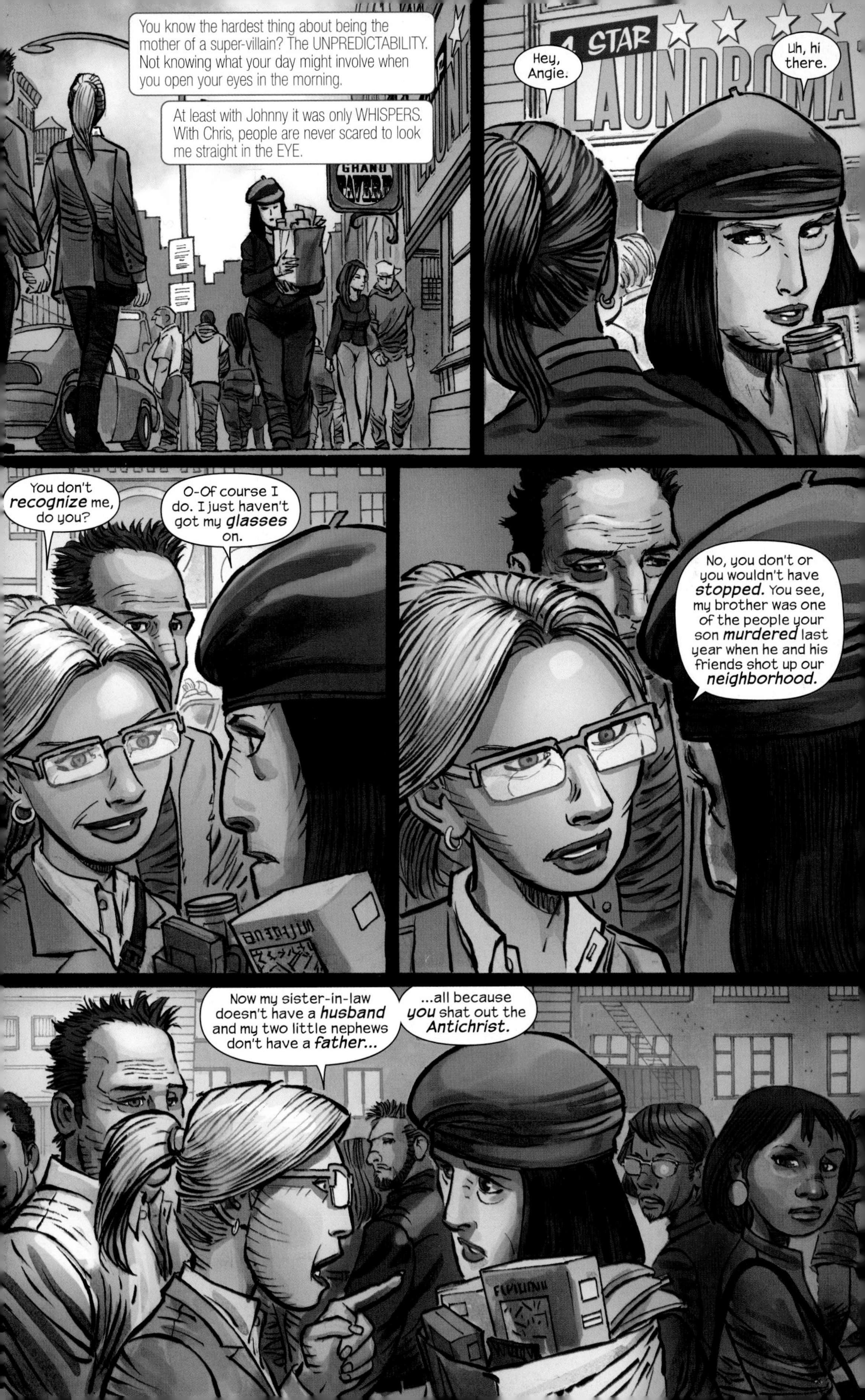
You know the hardest thing about being the mother of a super-villain? The UNPREDICTABILITY. Not knowing what your day might involve when you open your eyes in the morning.
At least with Johnny it was only WHISPERS. With Chris, people are never scared to look me straight in the EYE.
GRAND TAVERN
4 STAR LAUNDROMAT
Hey, Angie.
Uh, hi there.
You don't *recognize* me, do you?
O-Of course I do. I just haven't got my *glasses* on.
No, you don't or you wouldn't have *stopped.* You see, my brother was one of the people your son *murdered* last year when he and his friends shot up our *neighborhood.*
Now my sister-in-law doesn't have a *husband* and my two little nephews don't have a *father...*
...all because *you* shat out the *Antichrist.*

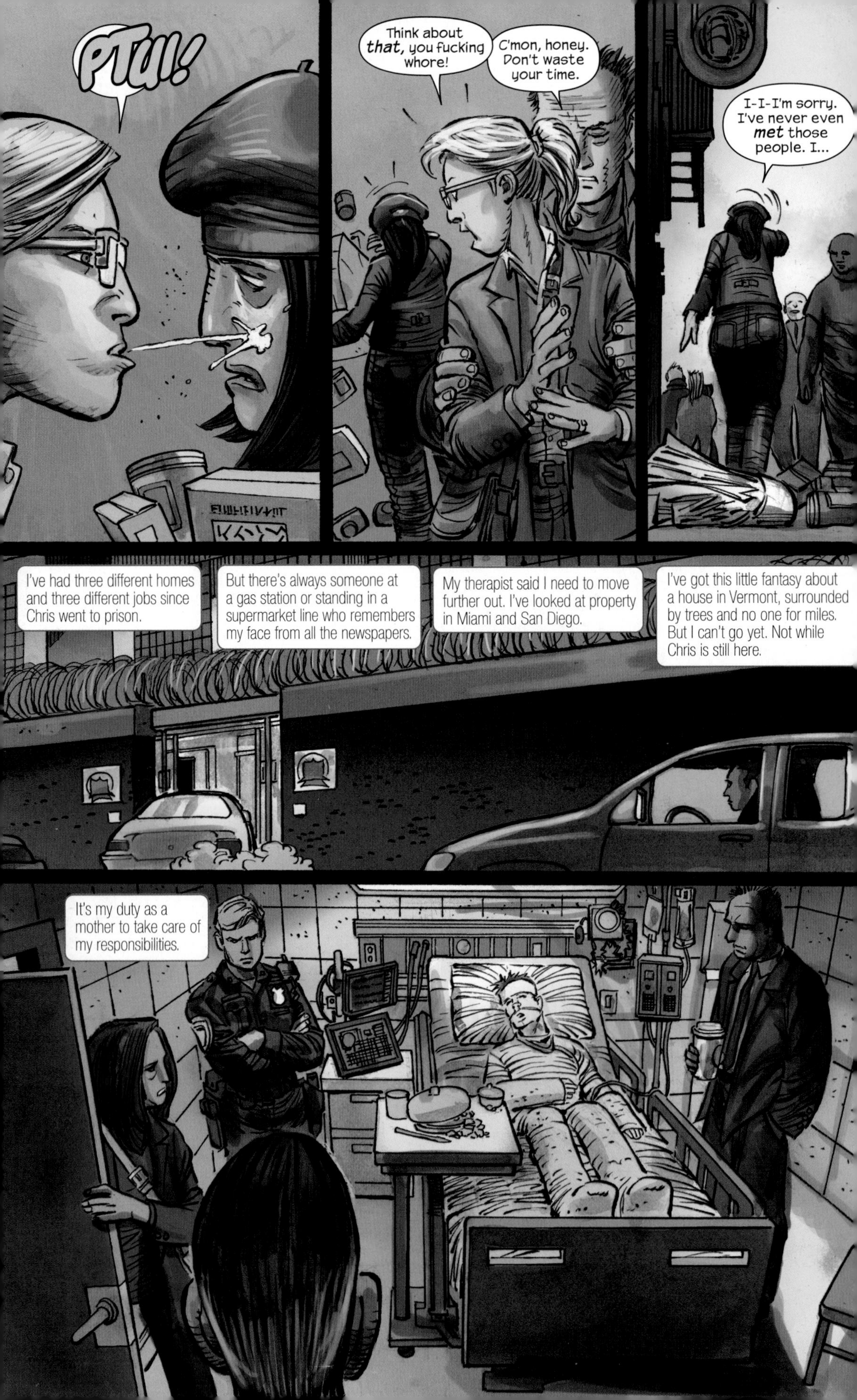
PTUI!
Think about that, you fucking whore!
C'mon, honey. Don't waste your time.
I-I-I'm sorry. I've never even met those people. I...
I've had three different homes and three different jobs since Chris went to prison.
But there's always someone at a gas station or standing in a supermarket line who remembers my face from all the newspapers.
My therapist said I need to move further out. I've looked at property in Miami and San Diego.
I've got this little fantasy about a house in Vermont, surrounded by trees and no one for miles. But I can't go yet. Not while Chris is still here.
It's my duty as a mother to take care of my responsibilities.

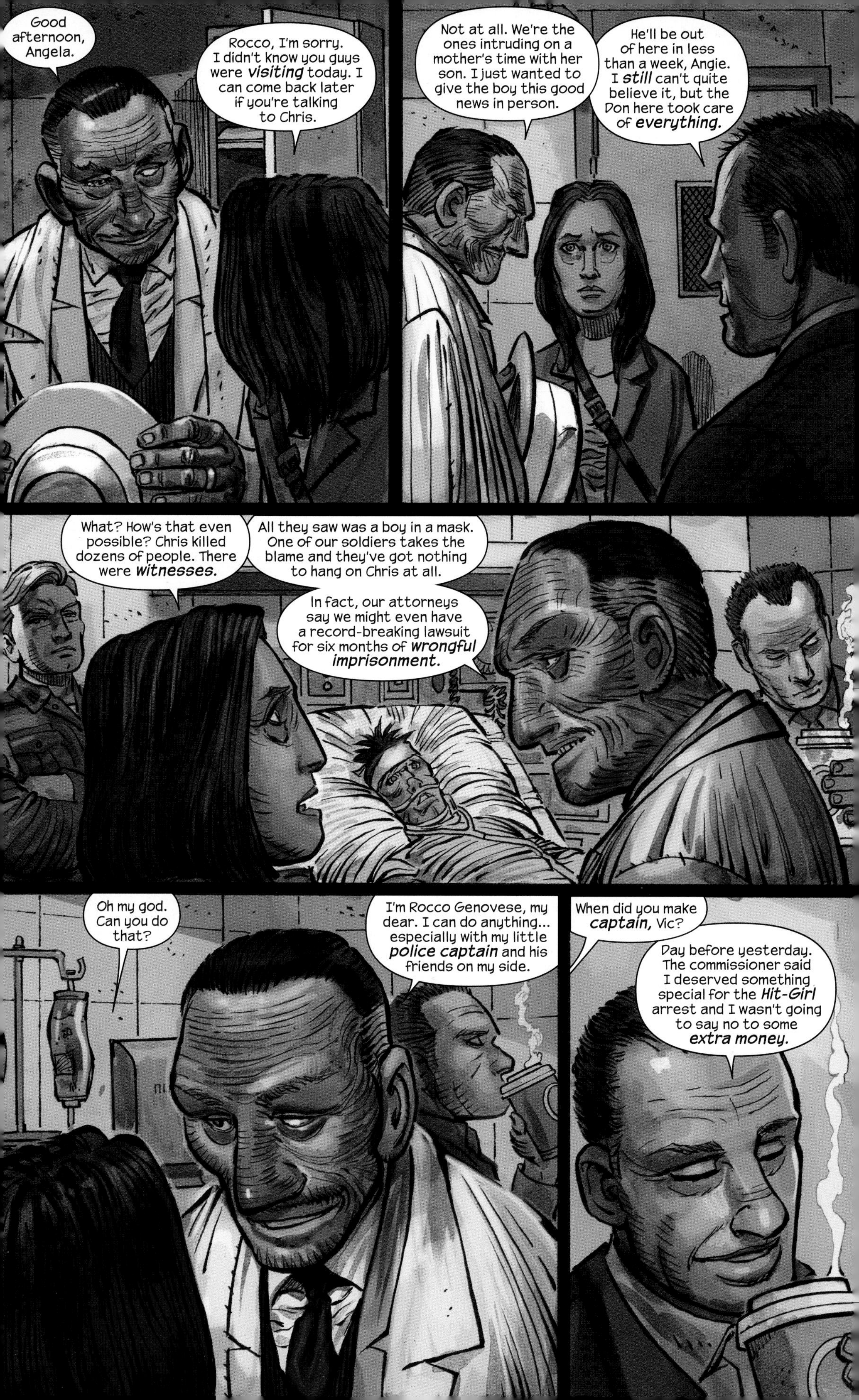
Good afternoon, Angela.
Rocco, I'm sorry. I didn't know you guys were *visiting* today. I can come back later if you're talking to Chris.
Not at all. We're the ones intruding on a mother's time with her son. I just wanted to give the boy this good news in person.
He'll be out of here in less than a week, Angie. I *still* can't quite believe it, but the Don here took care of *everything.*
What? How's that even possible? Chris killed dozens of people. There were *witnesses.*
All they saw was a boy in a mask. One of our soldiers takes the blame and they've got nothing to hang on Chris at all.
In fact, our attorneys say we might even have a record-breaking lawsuit for six months of *wrongful imprisonment.*
Oh my god. Can you do that?
I'm Rocco Genovese, my dear. I can do anything... especially with my little *police captain* and his friends on my side.
When did you make *captain,* Vic?
Day before yesterday. The commissioner said I deserved something special for the *Hit-Girl* arrest and I wasn't going to say no to some *extra money.*

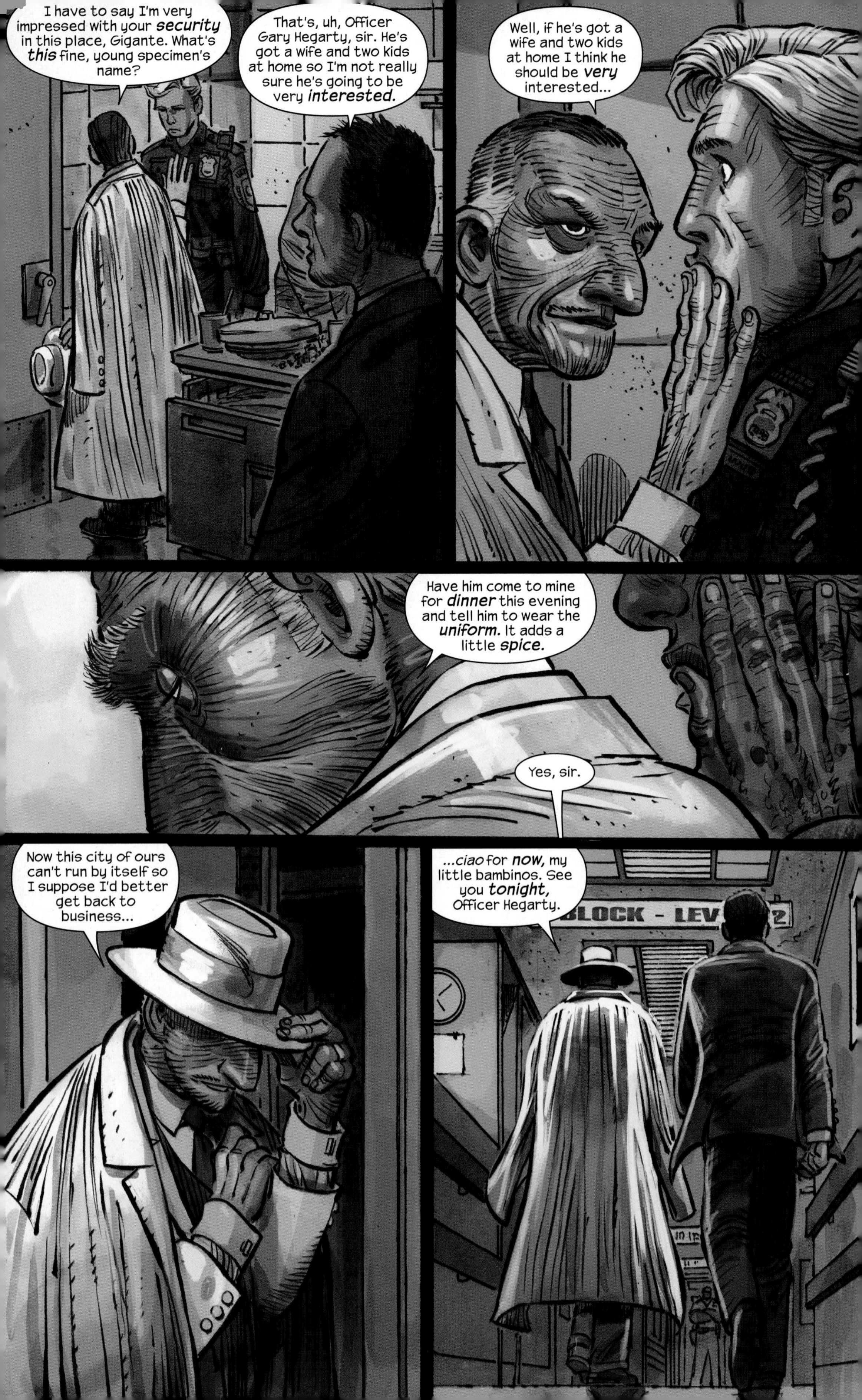
I have to say I'm very impressed with your *security* in this place, Gigante. What's *this* fine, young specimen's name?
That's, uh, Officer Gary Hegarty, sir. He's got a wife and two kids at home so I'm not really sure he's going to be very *interested.*
Well, if he's got a wife and two kids at home I think he should be *very* interested...
Have him come to mine for *dinner* this evening and tell him to wear the *uniform.* It adds a little *spice.*
Yes, sir.
Now this city of ours can't run by itself so I suppose I'd better get back to business...
...*ciao* for *now,* my little bambinos. See you *tonight,* Officer Hegarty.

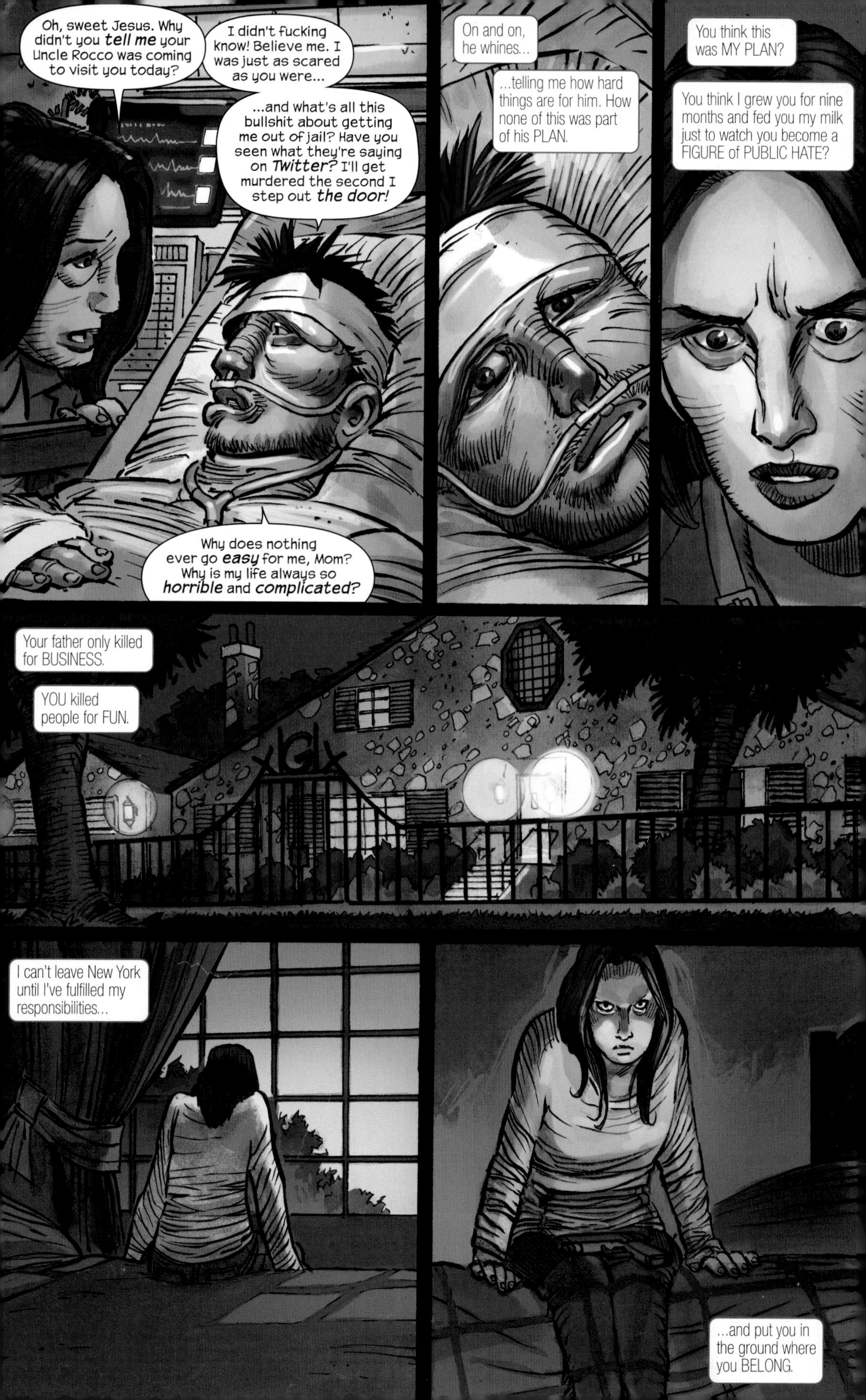
Oh, sweet Jesus. Why didn't you *tell me* your Uncle Rocco was coming to visit you today?
I didn't fucking know! Believe me. I was just as scared as you were...
...and what's all this bullshit about getting me out of jail? Have you seen what they're saying on *Twitter?* I'll get murdered the second I step out *the door!*
Why does nothing ever go *easy* for me, Mom? Why is my life always so *horrible* and *complicated?*
On and on, he whines...
...telling me how hard things are for him. How none of this was part of his PLAN.
You think this was MY PLAN?
You think I grew you for nine months and fed you my milk just to watch you become a FIGURE of PUBLIC HATE?
Your father only killed for BUSINESS.
YOU killed people for FUN.
I can't leave New York until I've fulfilled my responsibilities...
...and put you in the ground where you BELONG.

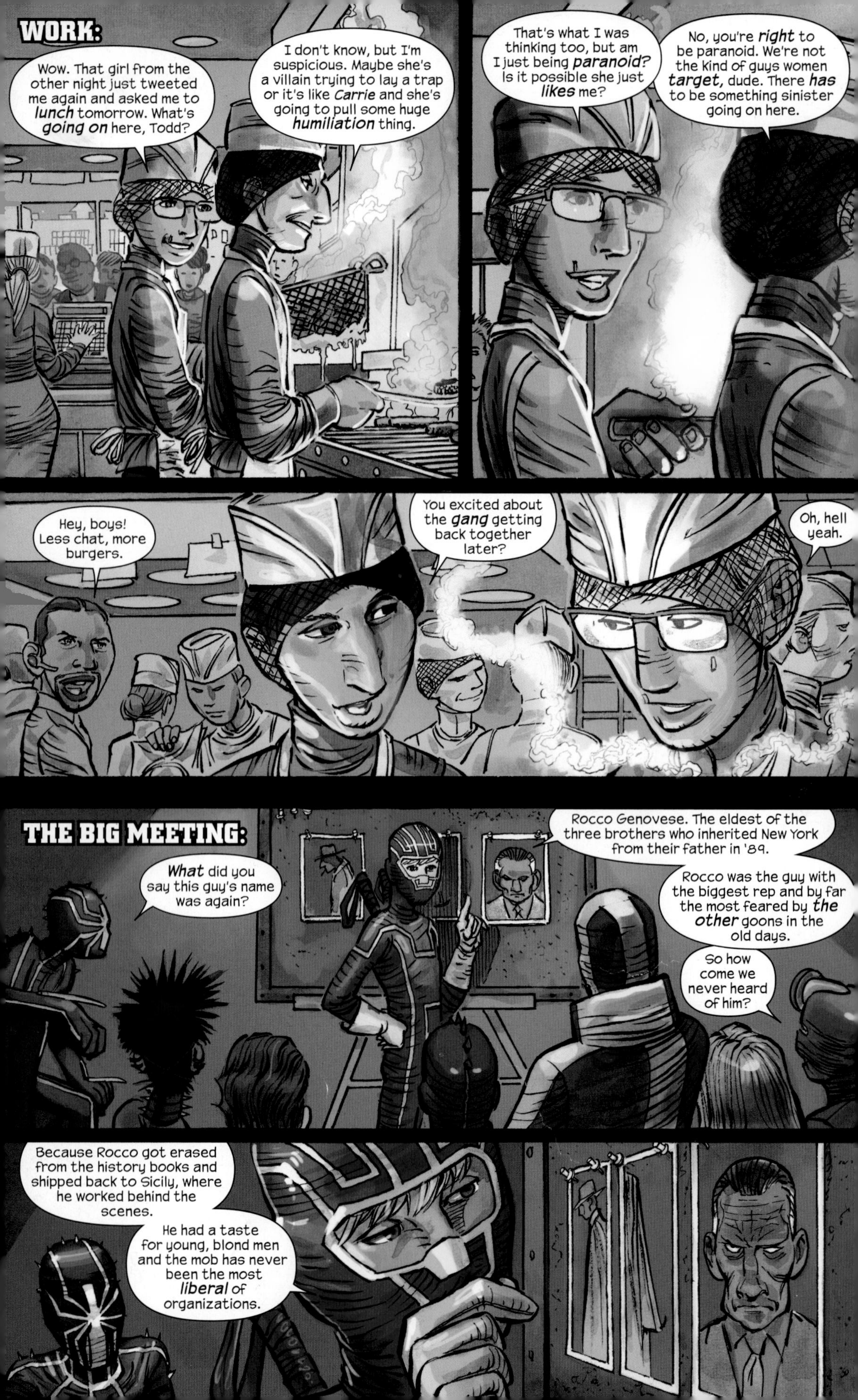
WORK:
Wow. That girl from the other night just tweeted me again and asked me to lunch tomorrow. What's going on here, Todd?
I don't know, but I'm suspicious. Maybe she's a villain trying to lay a trap or it's like Carrie and she's going to pull some huge humiliation thing.
That's what I was thinking too, but am I just being paranoid? Is it possible she just likes me?
No, you're right to be paranoid. We're not the kind of guys women target, dude. There has to be something sinister going on here.
Hey, boys! Less chat, more burgers.
You excited about the gang getting back together later?
Oh, hell yeah.
THE BIG MEETING:
What did you say this guy's name was again?
Rocco Genovese. The eldest of the three brothers who inherited New York from their father in '89.
Rocco was the guy with the biggest rep and by far the most feared by the other goons in the old days.
So how come we never heard of him?
Because Rocco got erased from the history books and shipped back to Sicily, where he worked behind the scenes.
He had a taste for young, blond men and the mob has never been the most liberal of organizations.

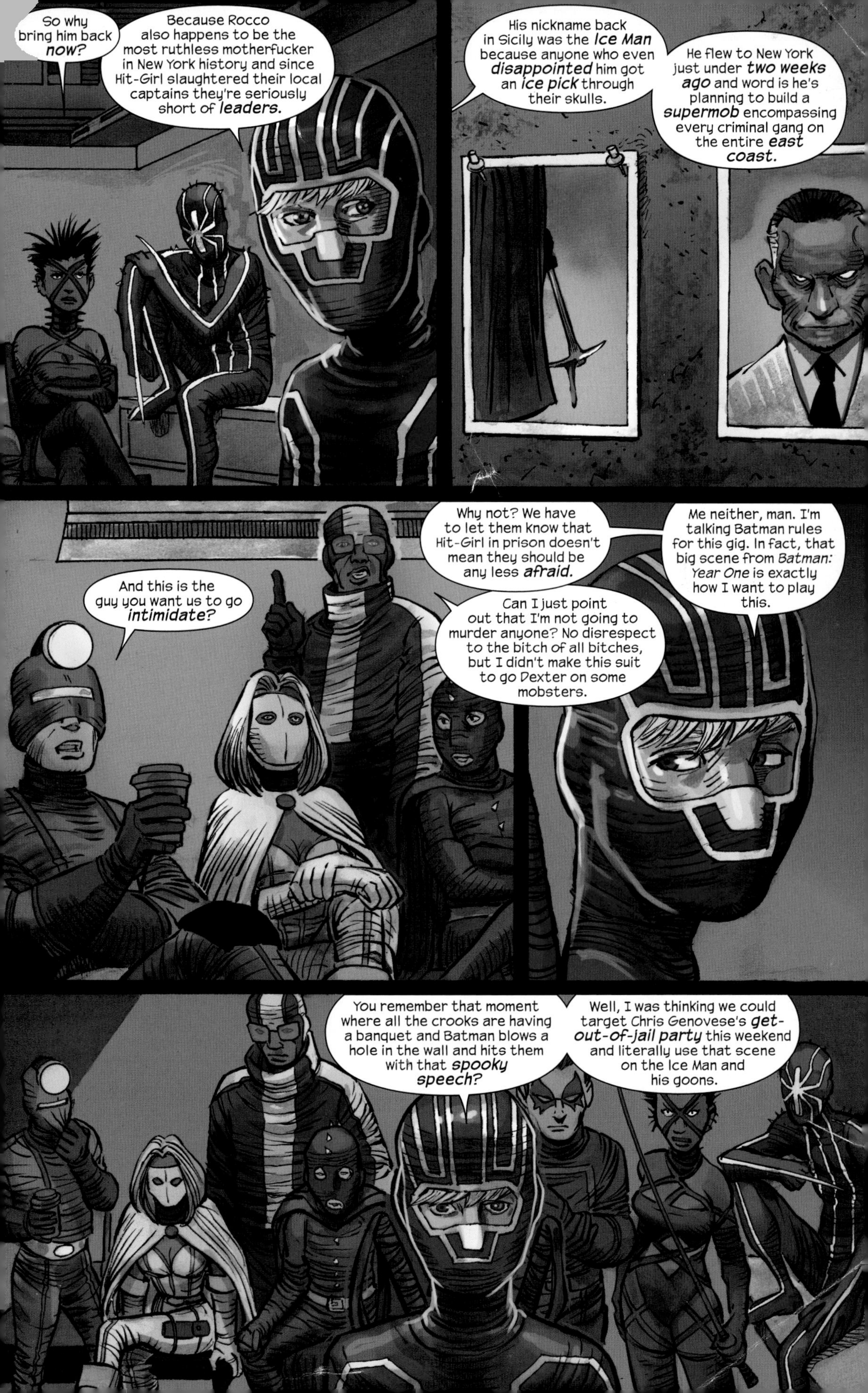
So why bring him back *now?*
Because Rocco also happens to be the most ruthless motherfucker in New York history and since Hit-Girl slaughtered their local captains they're seriously short of *leaders.*
His nickname back in Sicily was the *Ice Man* because anyone who even *disappointed* him got an *ice pick* through their skulls.
He flew to New York just under *two weeks ago* and word is he's planning to build a *supermob* encompassing every criminal gang on the entire *east coast.*
And this is the guy you want us to go *intimidate?*
Why not? We have to let them know that Hit-Girl in prison doesn't mean they should be any less *afraid.*
Can I just point out that I'm not going to murder anyone? No disrespect to the bitch of all bitches, but I didn't make this suit to go Dexter on some mobsters.
Me neither, man. I'm talking Batman rules for this gig. In fact, that big scene from *Batman: Year One* is exactly how I want to play this.
You remember that moment where all the crooks are having a banquet and Batman blows a hole in the wall and hits them with that *spooky speech?*
Well, I was thinking we could target Chris Genovese's *get-out-of-jail party* this weekend and literally use that scene on the Ice Man and his goons.

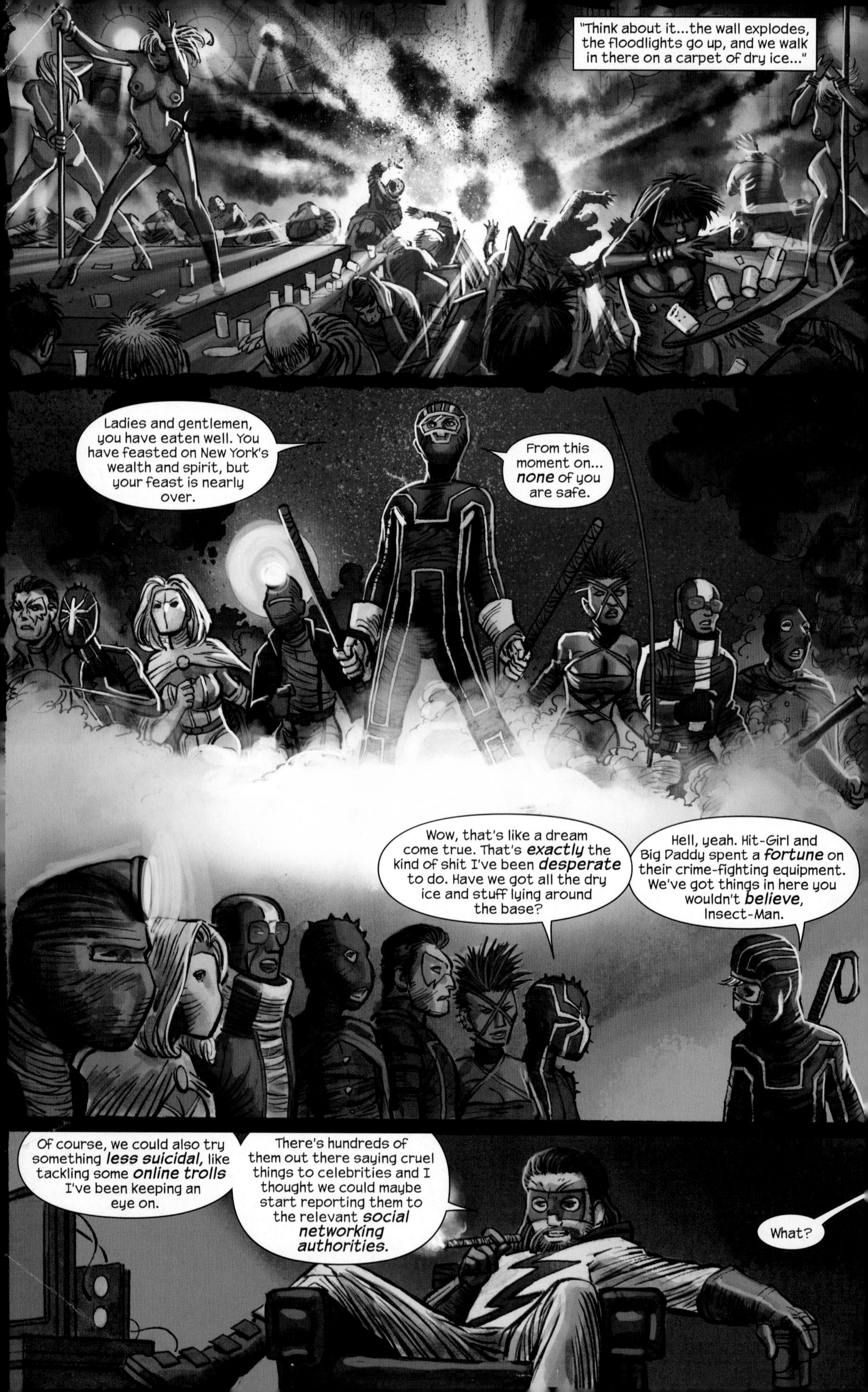

"Think about it...the wall explodes, the floodlights go up, and we walk in there on a carpet of dry ice..."
Ladies and gentlemen, you have eaten well. You have feasted on New York's wealth and spirit, but your feast is nearly over.
From this moment on... none of you are safe.
Wow, that's like a dream come true. That's exactly the kind of shit I've been desperate to do. Have we got all the dry ice and stuff lying around the base?
Hell, yeah. Hit-Girl and Big Daddy spent a fortune on their crime-fighting equipment. We've got things in here you wouldn't believe, Insect-Man.
Of course, we could also try something less suicidal, like tackling some online trolls I've been keeping an eye on.
There's hundreds of them out there saying cruel things to celebrities and I thought we could maybe start reporting them to the relevant social networking authorities.
What?

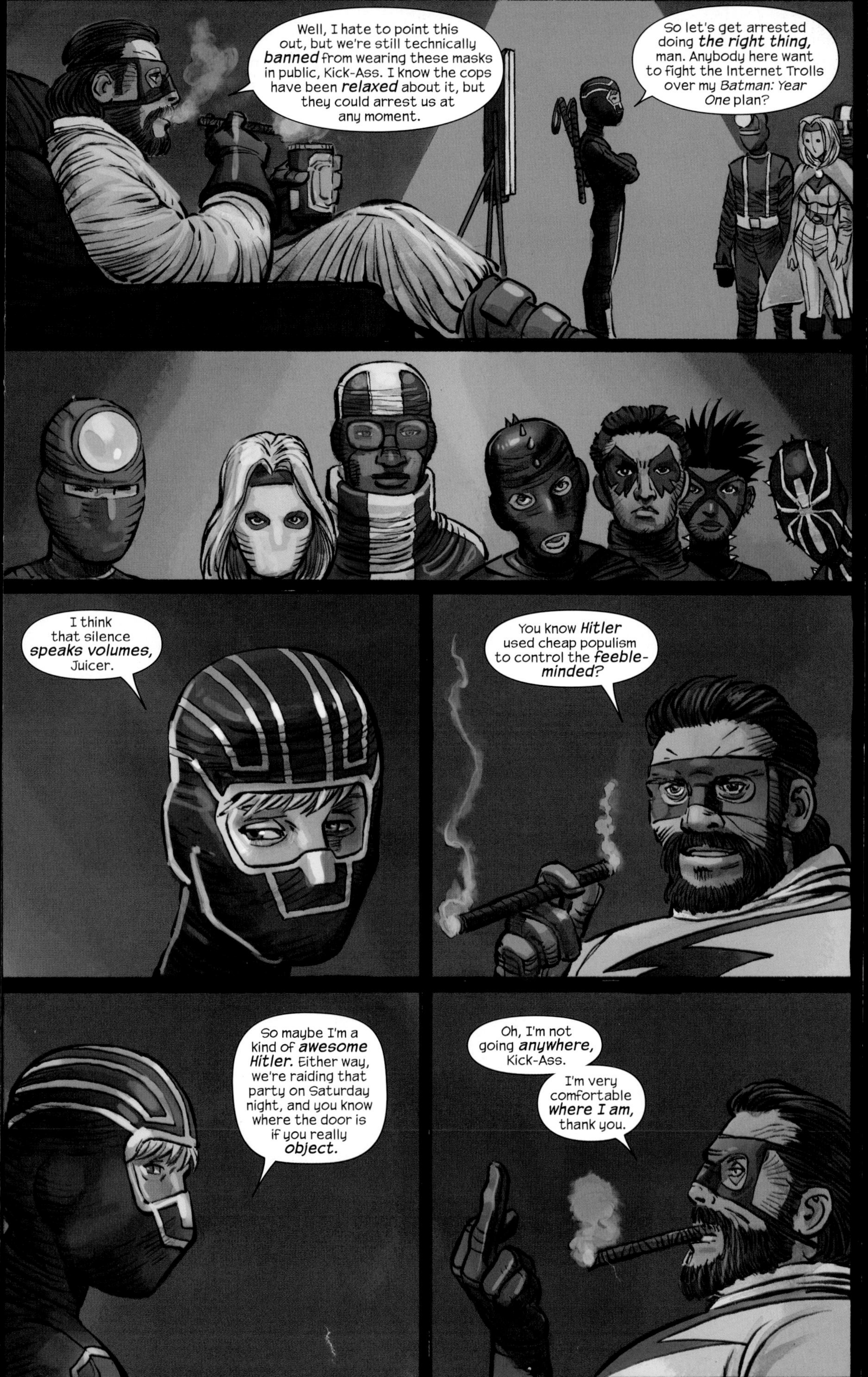
Well, I hate to point this out, but we're still technically banned from wearing these masks in public, Kick-Ass. I know the cops have been relaxed about it, but they could arrest us at any moment.
So let's get arrested doing the right thing, man. Anybody here want to fight the Internet Trolls over my Batman: Year One plan?
I think that silence speaks volumes, Juicer.
You know Hitler used cheap populism to control the feeble-minded?
So maybe I'm a kind of awesome Hitler. Either way, we're raiding that party on Saturday night, and you know where the door is if you really object.
Oh, I'm not going anywhere, Kick-Ass.
I'm very comfortable where I am, thank you.

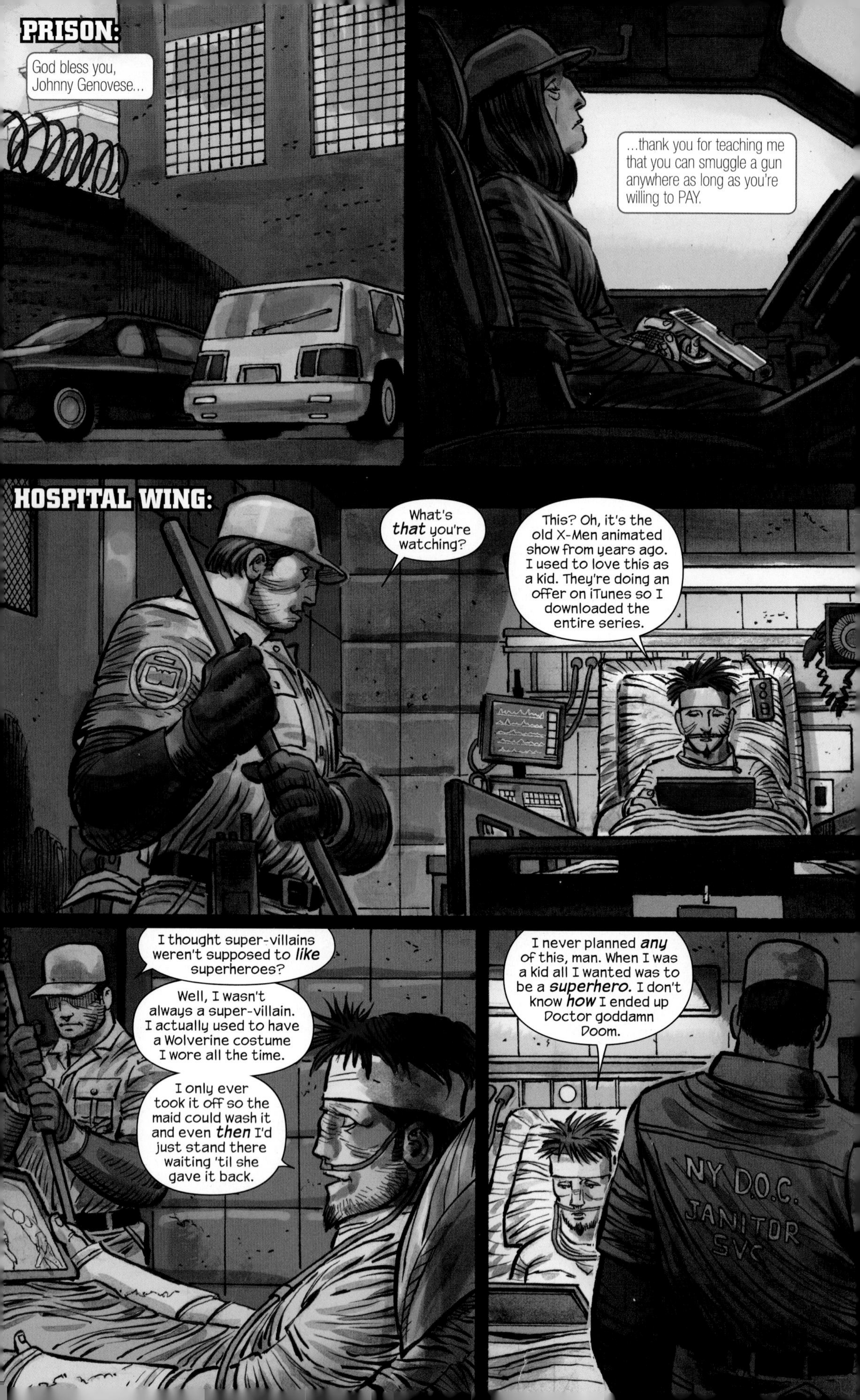
PRISON:
God bless you, Johnny Genovese...
...thank you for teaching me that you can smuggle a gun anywhere as long as you're willing to PAY.
HOSPITAL WING:
What's *that* you're watching?
This? Oh, it's the old X-Men animated show from years ago. I used to love this as a kid. They're doing an offer on iTunes so I downloaded the entire series.
I thought super-villains weren't supposed to *like* superheroes?
Well, I wasn't always a super-villain. I actually used to have a Wolverine costume I wore all the time.
I only ever took it off so the maid could wash it and even *then* I'd just stand there waiting 'til she gave it back.
I never planned *any* of this, man. When I was a kid all I wanted was to be a *superhero.* I don't know *how* I ended up Doctor goddamn Doom.
NY D.O.C. JANITOR SVC

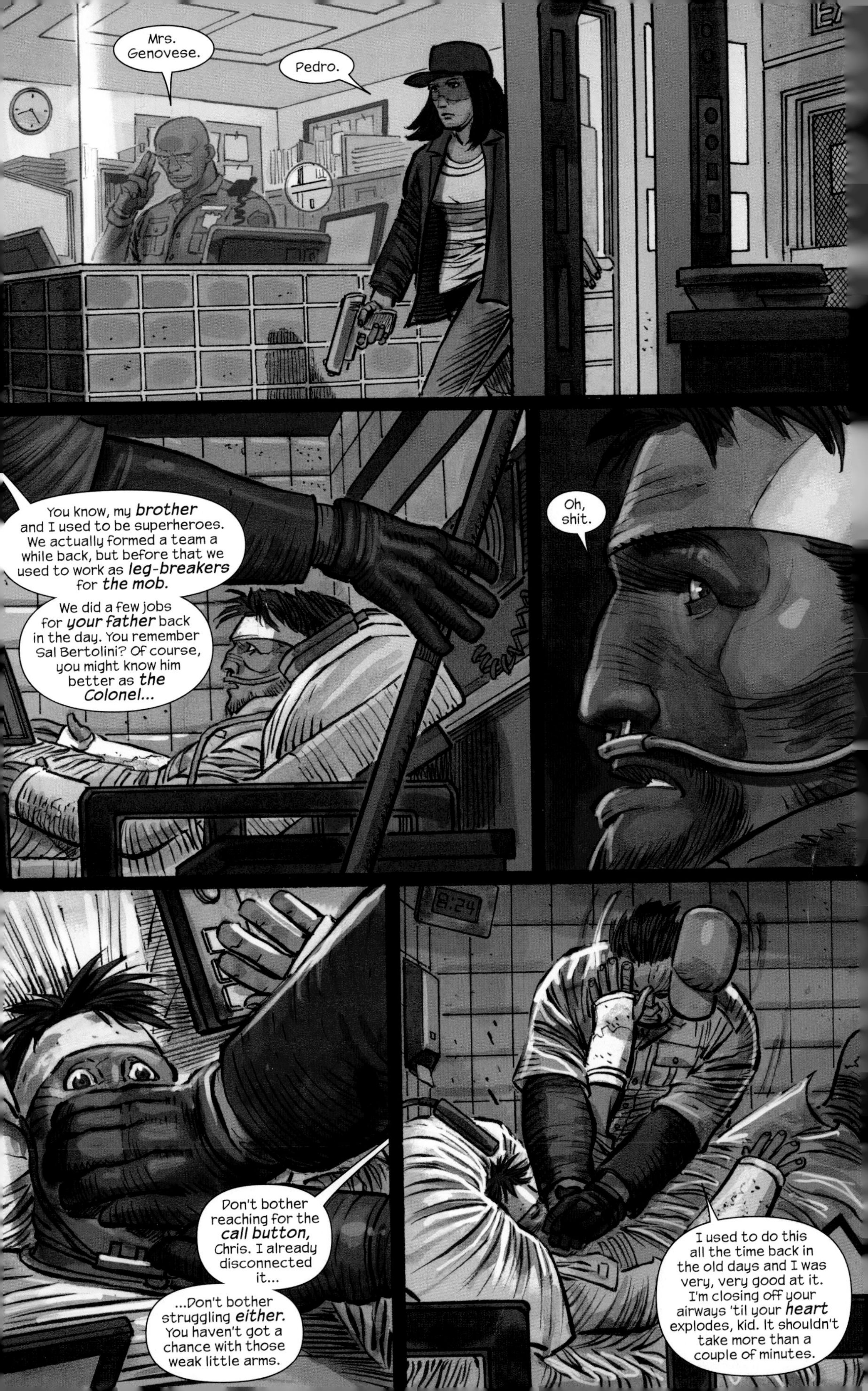
Mrs. Genovese.
Pedro.
You know, my brother and I used to be superheroes. We actually formed a team a while back, but before that we used to work as leg-breakers for the mob.
We did a few jobs for your father back in the day. You remember Sal Bertolini? Of course, you might know him better as the Colonel...
Oh, shit.
Don't bother reaching for the call button, Chris. I already disconnected it...
...Don't bother struggling either. You haven't got a chance with those weak little arms.
I used to do this all the time back in the old days and I was very, very good at it. I'm closing off your airways 'til your heart explodes, kid. It shouldn't take more than a couple of minutes.

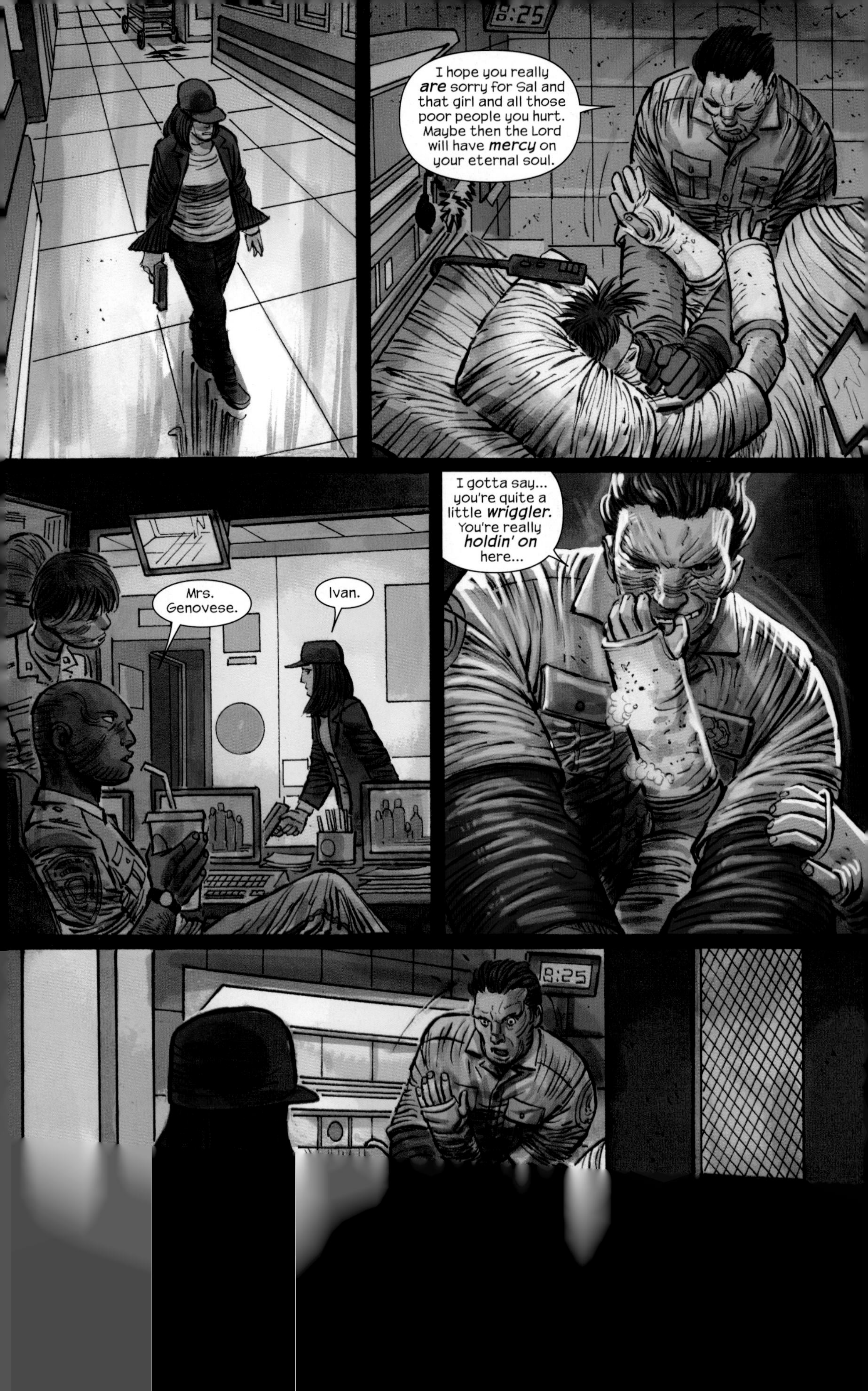
I hope you really are sorry for Sal and that girl and all those poor people you hurt. Maybe then the Lord will have mercy on your eternal soul.
8:25
Mrs. Genovese.
Ivan.
I gotta say... you're quite a little wriggler. You're really holdin' on here...
8:25

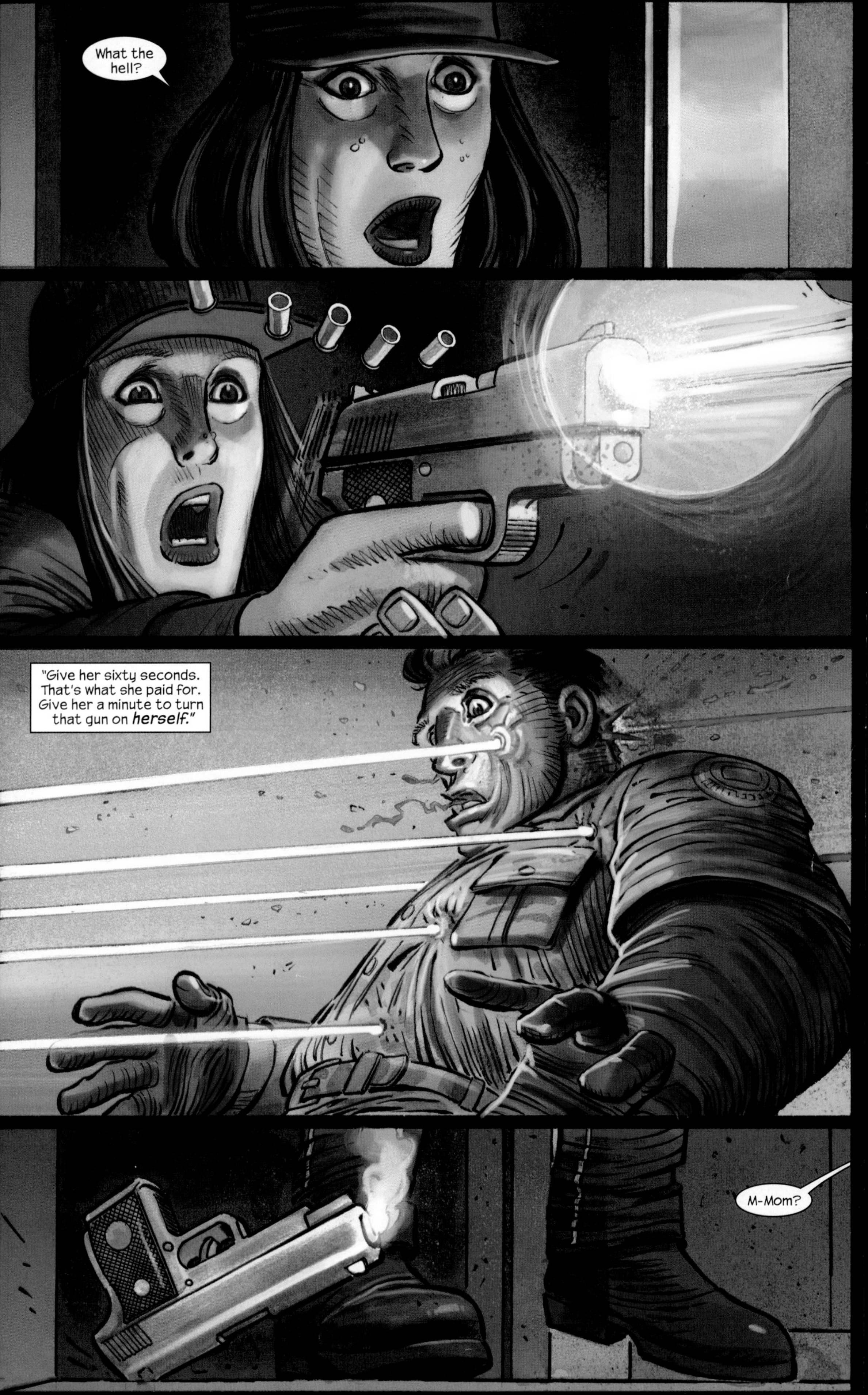
What the hell?
"Give her sixty seconds. That's what she paid for. Give her a minute to turn that gun on *herself*."
M-Mom?

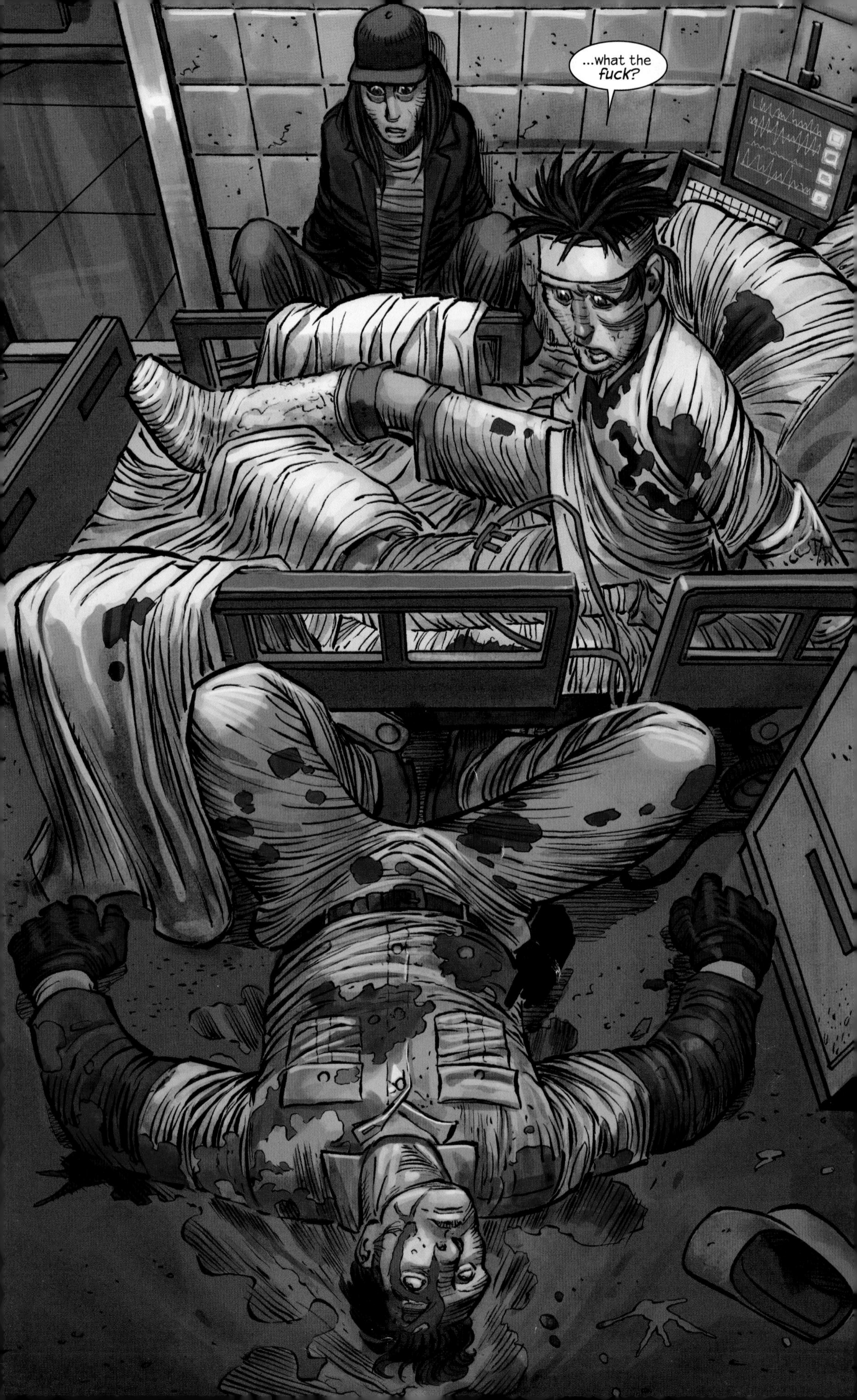
...what the *fuck?*

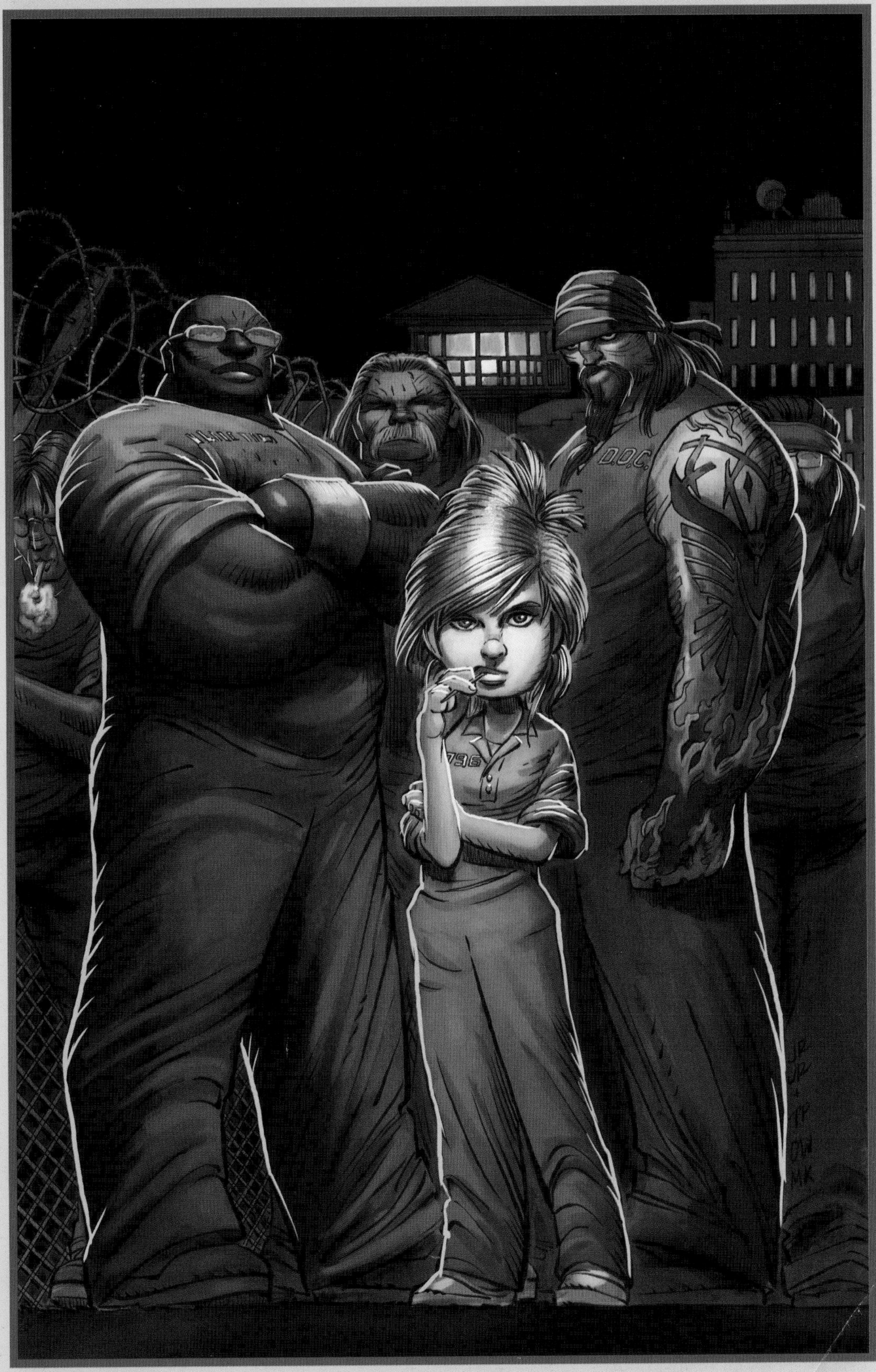
D.O.C.

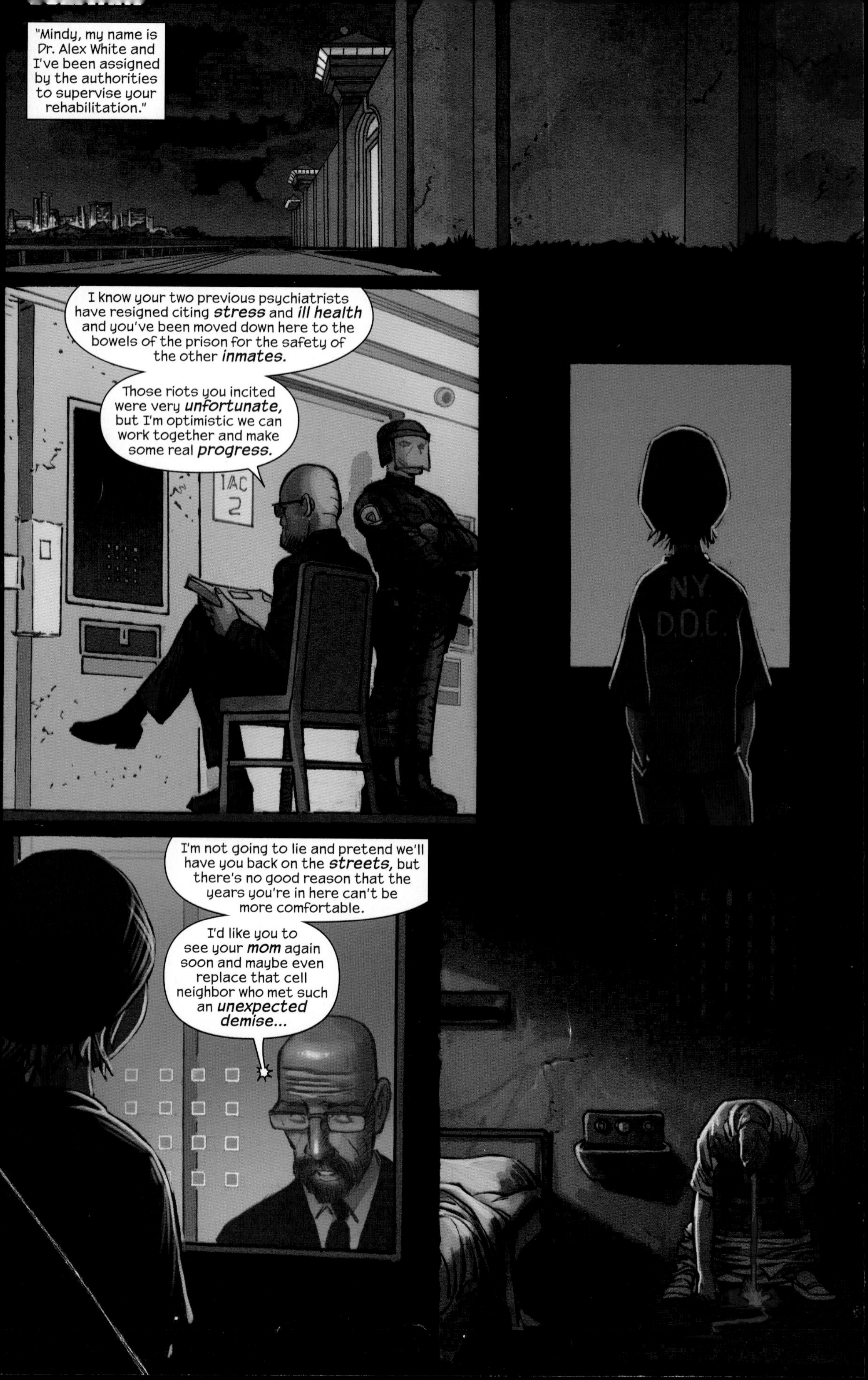
"Mindy, my name is Dr. Alex White and I've been assigned by the authorities to supervise your rehabilitation."
I know your two previous psychiatrists have resigned citing stress and ill health and you've been moved down here to the bowels of the prison for the safety of the other inmates.
Those riots you incited were very unfortunate, but I'm optimistic we can work together and make some real progress.
1/AC 2
N.Y. D.O.C.
I'm not going to lie and pretend we'll have you back on the streets, but there's no good reason that the years you're in here can't be more comfortable.
I'd like you to see your mom again soon and maybe even replace that cell neighbor who met such an unexpected demise...

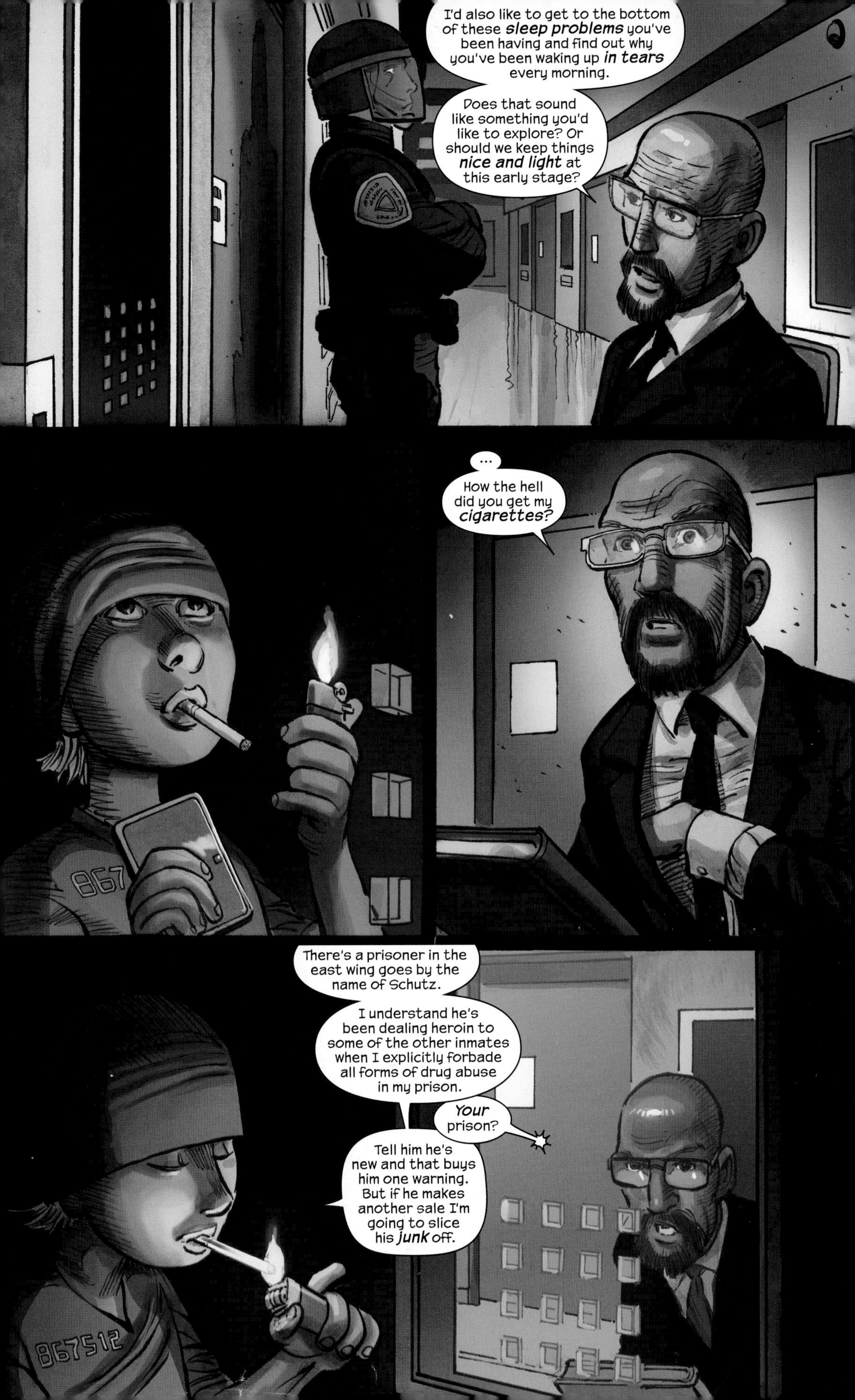
I'd also like to get to the bottom of these sleep problems you've been having and find out why you've been waking up in tears every morning.
Does that sound like something you'd like to explore? Or should we keep things nice and light at this early stage?
...
How the hell did you get my cigarettes?
867
There's a prisoner in the east wing goes by the name of Schutz.
I understand he's been dealing heroin to some of the other inmates when I explicitly forbade all forms of drug abuse in my prison.
Your prison?
Tell him he's new and that buys him one warning. But if he makes another sale I'm going to slice his junk off.
867512

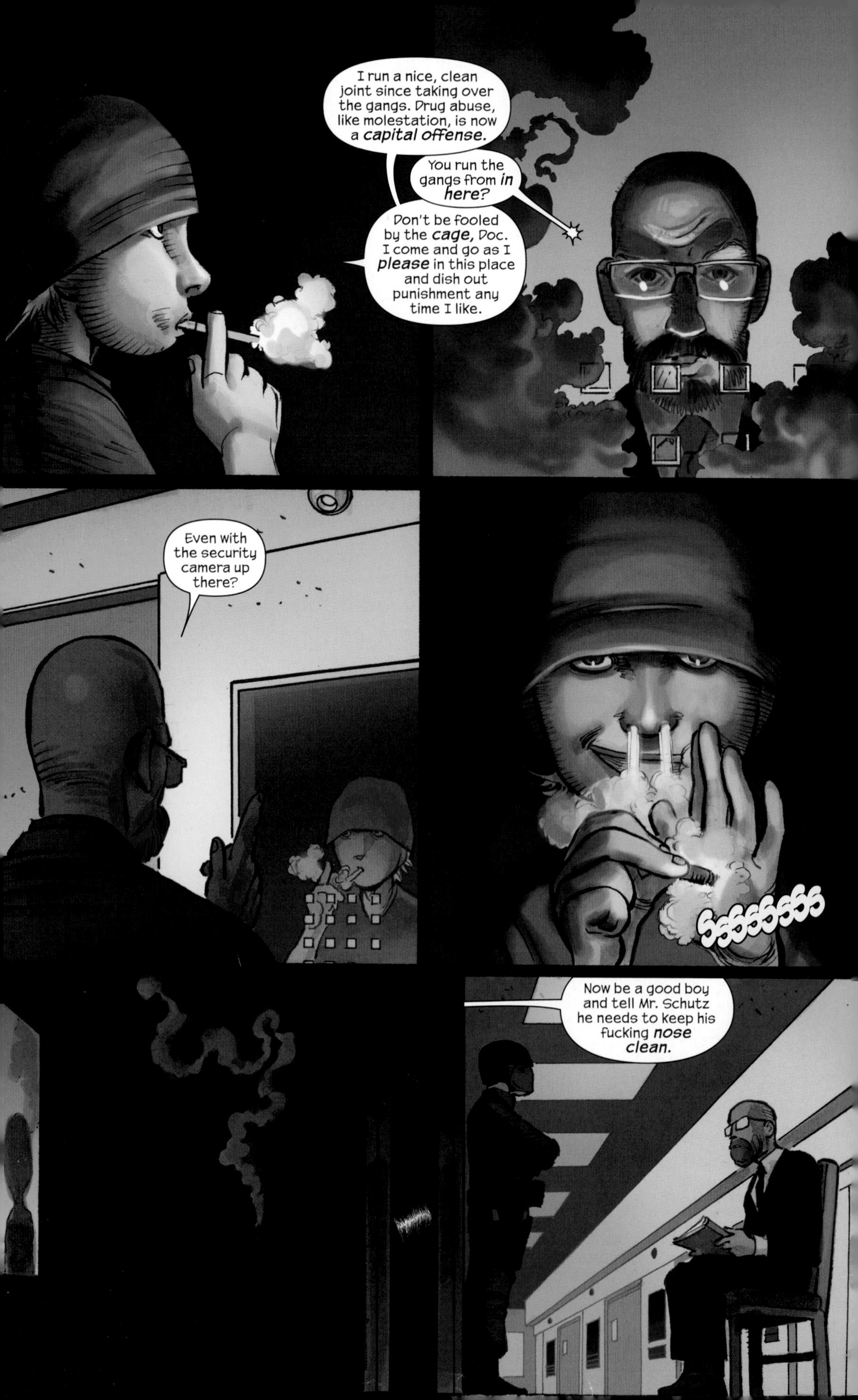
I run a nice, clean joint since taking over the gangs. Drug abuse, like molestation, is now a *capital offense.*
You run the gangs from *in here?*
Don't be fooled by the *cage,* Doc. I come and go as I *please* in this place and dish out punishment any time I like.
Even with the security camera up there?
SSSSSSSS
Now be a good boy and tell Mr. Schutz he needs to keep his fucking *nose clean.*

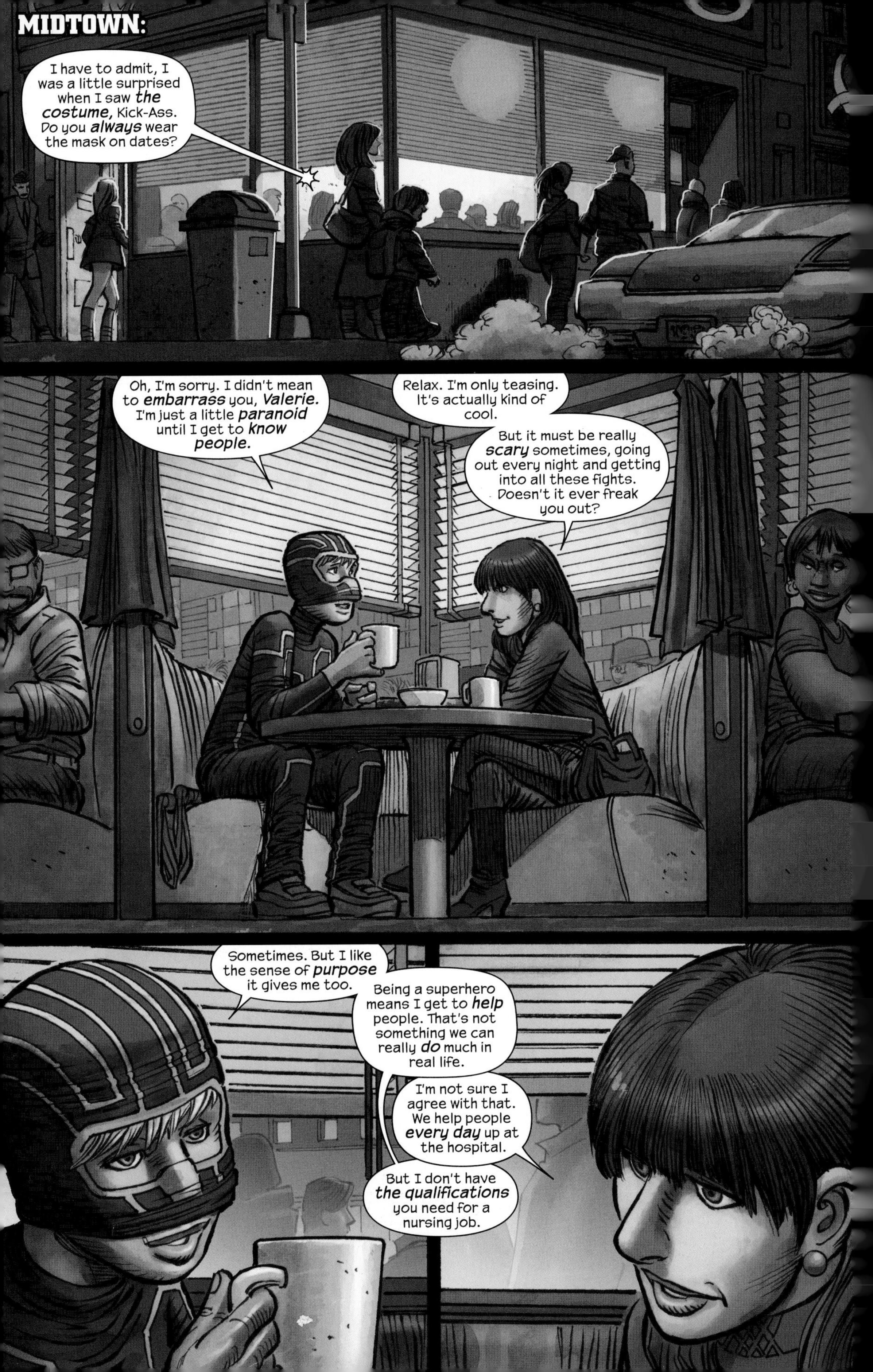
MIDTOWN:
I have to admit, I was a little surprised when I saw the costume, Kick-Ass. Do you always wear the mask on dates?
Oh, I'm sorry. I didn't mean to embarrass you, Valerie. I'm just a little paranoid until I get to know people.
Relax. I'm only teasing. It's actually kind of cool.
But it must be really scary sometimes, going out every night and getting into all these fights. Doesn't it ever freak you out?
Sometimes. But I like the sense of purpose it gives me too.
Being a superhero means I get to help people. That's not something we can really do much in real life.
I'm not sure I agree with that. We help people every day up at the hospital.
But I don't have the qualifications you need for a nursing job.

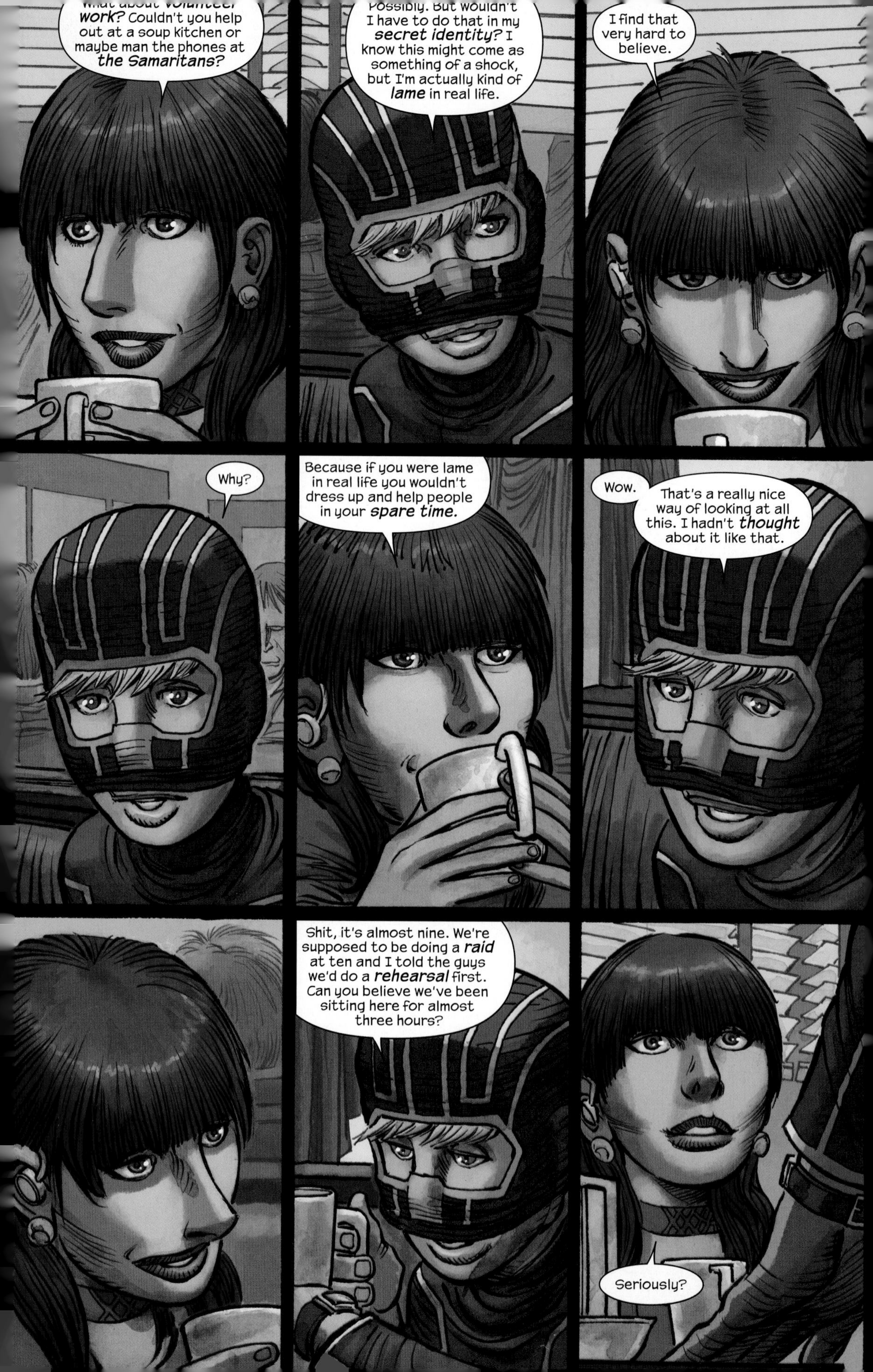
What about *volunteer* *work?* Couldn't you help out at a soup kitchen or maybe man the phones at *the Samaritans?*
Possibly. But wouldn't I have to do that in my *secret identity?* I know this might come as something of a shock, but I'm actually kind of *lame* in real life.
I find that very hard to believe.
Why?
Because if you were lame in real life you wouldn't dress up and help people in your *spare time.*
Wow.
That's a really nice way of looking at all this. I hadn't *thought* about it like that.
Shit, it's almost nine. We're supposed to be doing a *raid* at ten and I told the guys we'd do a *rehearsal* first. Can you believe we've been sitting here for almost three hours?
Seriously?

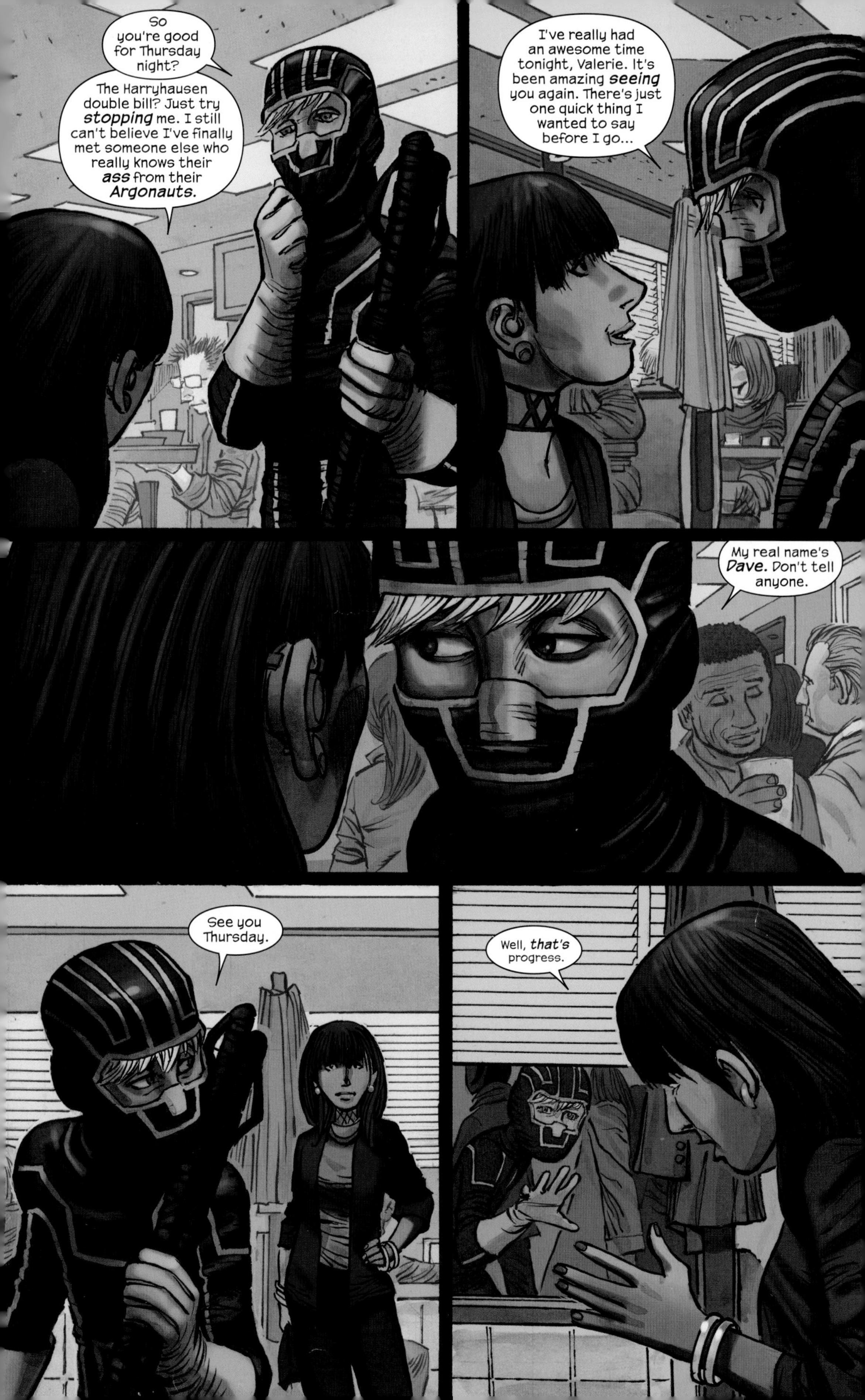
So you're good for Thursday night?
The Harryhausen double bill? Just try stopping me. I still can't believe I've finally met someone else who really knows their ass from their Argonauts.
I've really had an awesome time tonight, Valerie. It's been amazing seeing you again. There's just one quick thing I wanted to say before I go...
My real name's Dave. Don't tell anyone.
See you Thursday.
Well, that's progress.

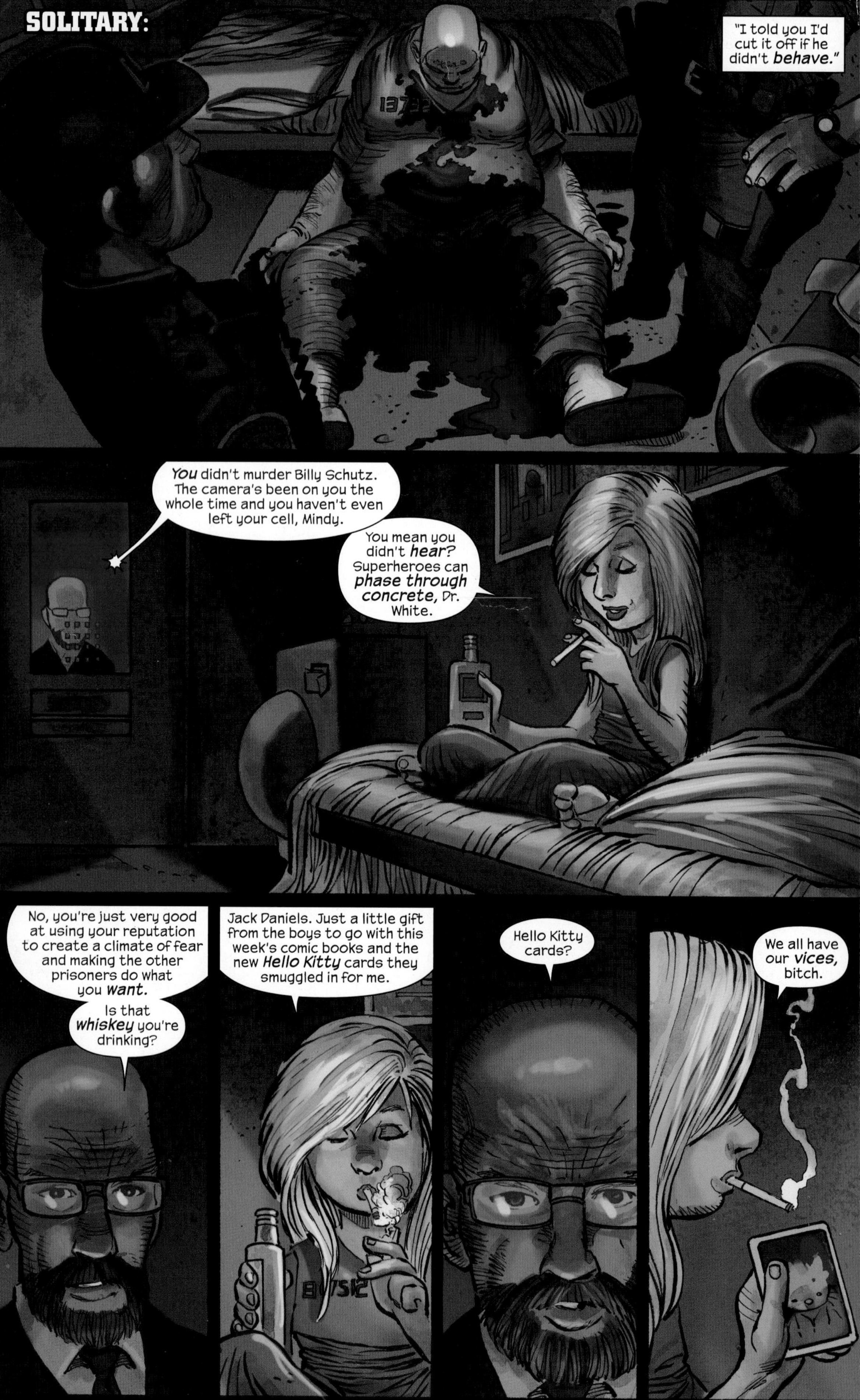
SOLITARY:
"I told you I'd cut it off if he didn't behave."
You didn't murder Billy Schutz. The camera's been on you the whole time and you haven't even left your cell, Mindy.
You mean you didn't hear? Superheroes can phase through concrete, Dr. White.
No, you're just very good at using your reputation to create a climate of fear and making the other prisoners do what you want.
Is that whiskey you're drinking?
Jack Daniels. Just a little gift from the boys to go with this week's comic books and the new Hello Kitty cards they smuggled in for me.
Hello Kitty cards?
We all have our vices, bitch.

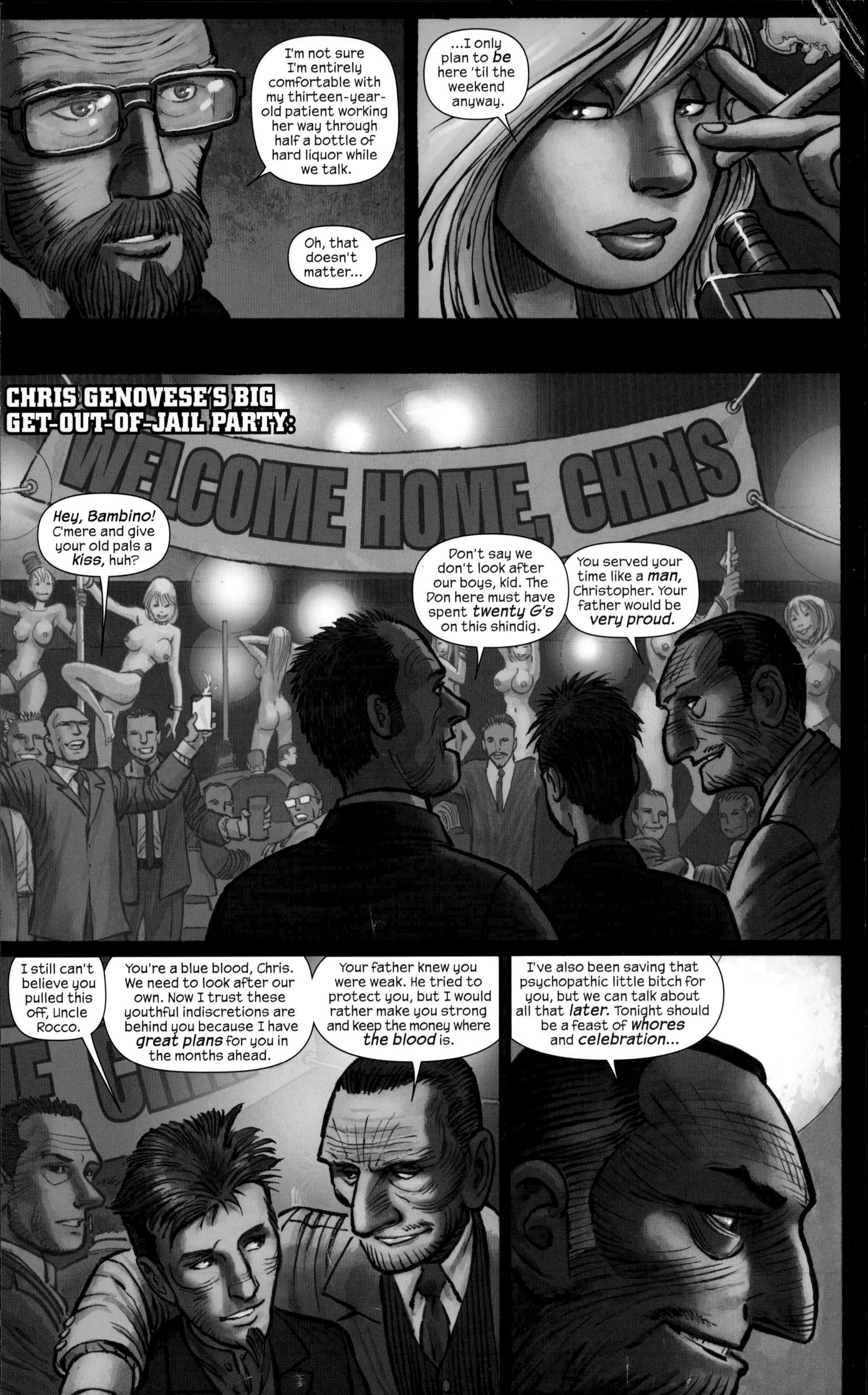
I'm not sure I'm entirely comfortable with my thirteen-year-old patient working her way through half a bottle of hard liquor while we talk.
Oh, that doesn't matter...
...I only plan to be here 'til the weekend anyway.
CHRIS GENOVESE'S BIG GET-OUT-OF-JAIL PARTY:
WELCOME HOME, CHRIS
Hey, Bambino! C'mere and give your old pals a kiss, huh?
Don't say we don't look after our boys, kid. The Don here must have spent twenty G's on this shindig.
You served your time like a man, Christopher. Your father would be very proud.
I still can't believe you pulled this off, Uncle Rocco.
You're a blue blood, Chris. We need to look after our own. Now I trust these youthful indiscretions are behind you because I have great plans for you in the months ahead.
Your father knew you were weak. He tried to protect you, but I would rather make you strong and keep the money where the blood is.
I've also been saving that psychopathic little bitch for you, but we can talk about all that later. Tonight should be a feast of whores and celebration...

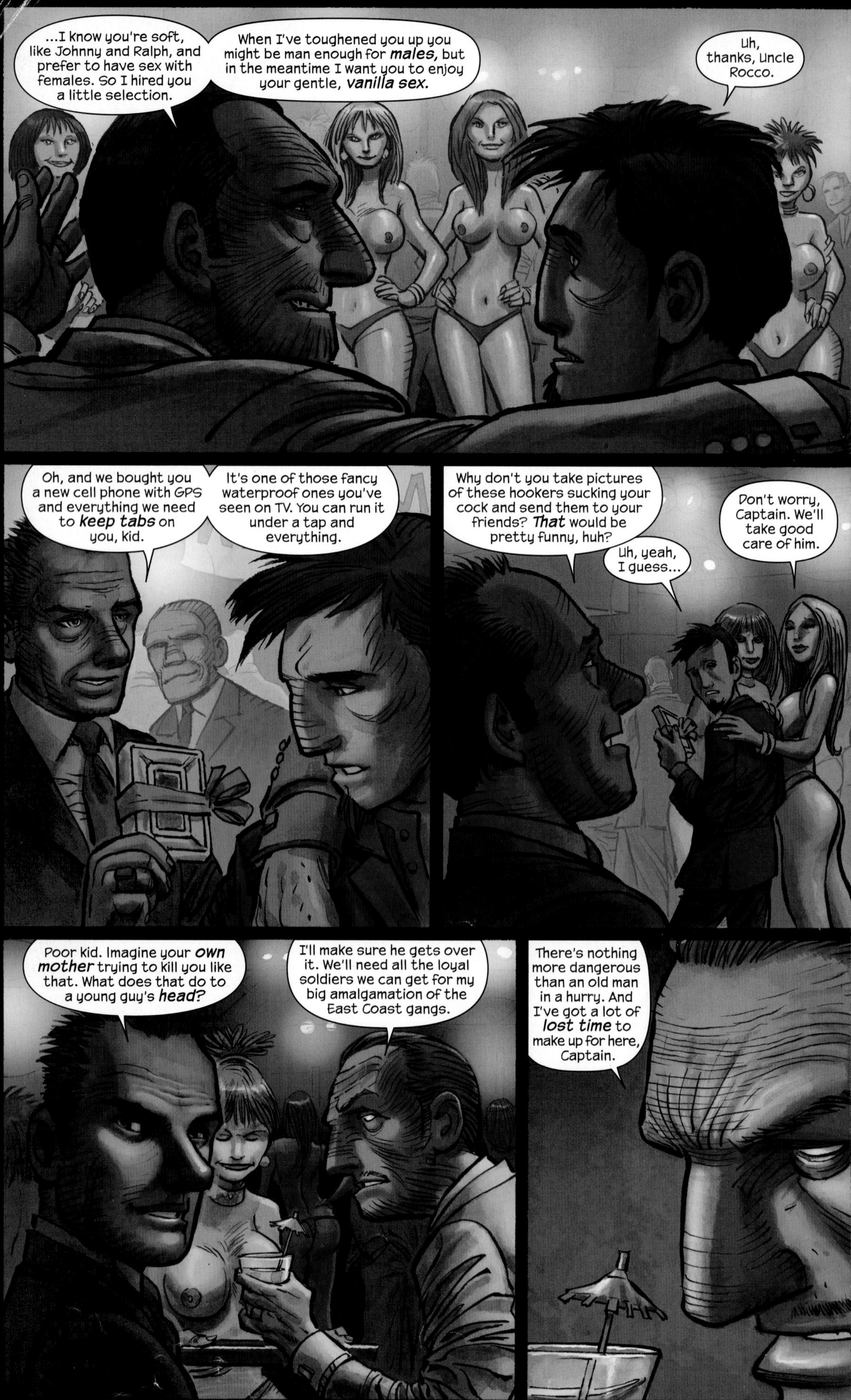
...I know you're soft, like Johnny and Ralph, and prefer to have sex with females. So I hired you a little selection.
When I've toughened you up you might be man enough for *males,* but in the meantime I want you to enjoy your gentle, *vanilla sex.*
Uh, thanks, Uncle Rocco.
Oh, and we bought you a new cell phone with GPS and everything we need to *keep tabs* on you, kid.
It's one of those fancy waterproof ones you've seen on TV. You can run it under a tap and everything.
Why don't you take pictures of these hookers sucking your cock and send them to your friends? *That* would be pretty funny, huh?
Uh, yeah, I guess...
Don't worry, Captain. We'll take good care of him.
Poor kid. Imagine your *own mother* trying to kill you like that. What does that do to a young guy's *head?*
I'll make sure he gets over it. We'll need all the loyal soldiers we can get for my big amalgamation of the East Coast gangs.
There's nothing more dangerous than an old man in a hurry. And I've got a lot of *lost time* to make up for here, Captain.

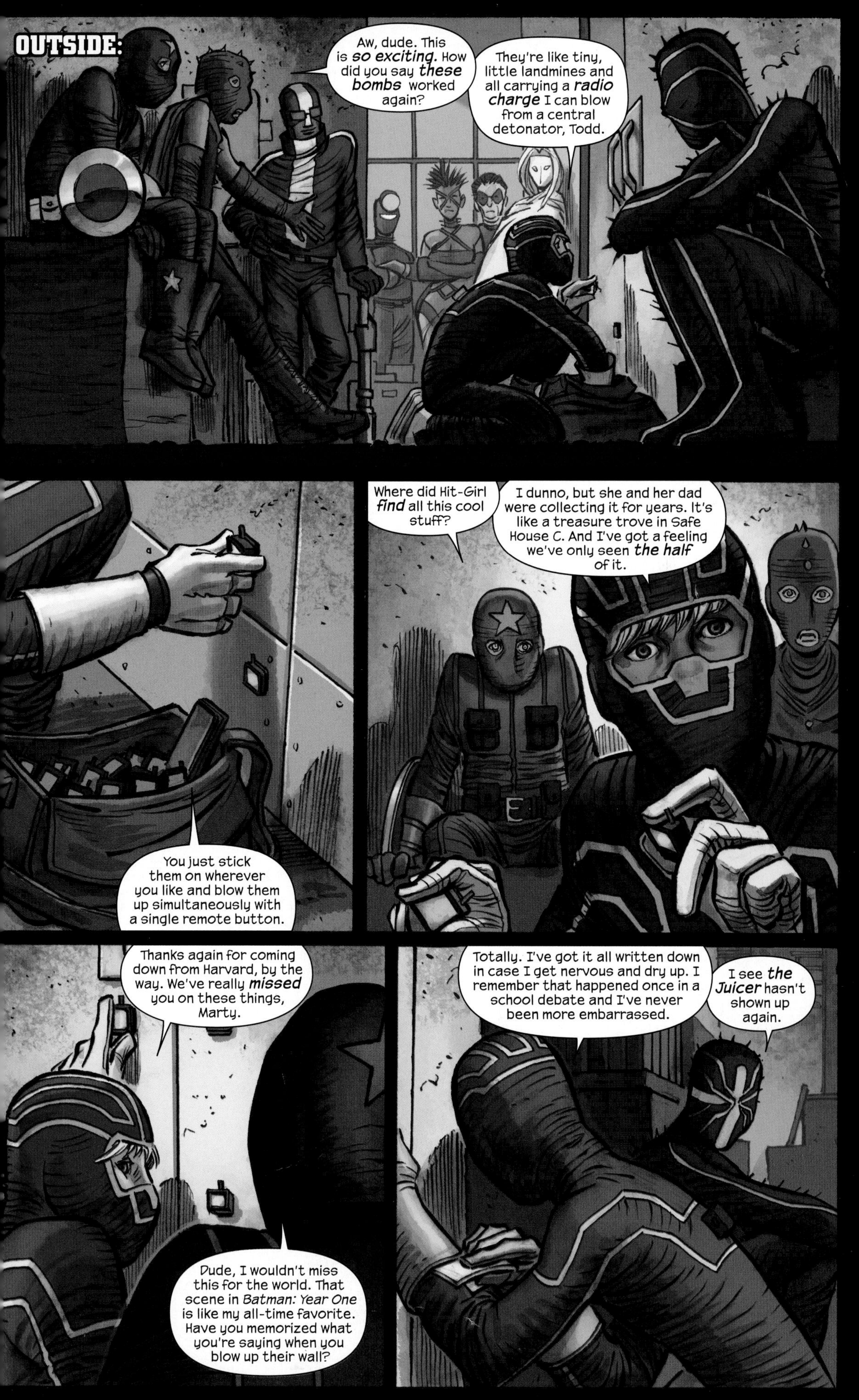
OUTSIDE:
Aw, dude. This is so exciting. How did you say these bombs worked again?
They're like tiny, little landmines and all carrying a radio charge I can blow from a central detonator, Todd.
You just stick them on wherever you like and blow them up simultaneously with a single remote button.
Where did Hit-Girl find all this cool stuff?
I dunno, but she and her dad were collecting it for years. It's like a treasure trove in Safe House C. And I've got a feeling we've only seen the half of it.
Thanks again for coming down from Harvard, by the way. We've really missed you on these things, Marty.
Dude, I wouldn't miss this for the world. That scene in Batman: Year One is like my all-time favorite. Have you memorized what you're saying when you blow up their wall?
Totally. I've got it all written down in case I get nervous and dry up. I remember that happened once in a school debate and I've never been more embarrassed.
I see the Juicer hasn't shown up again.

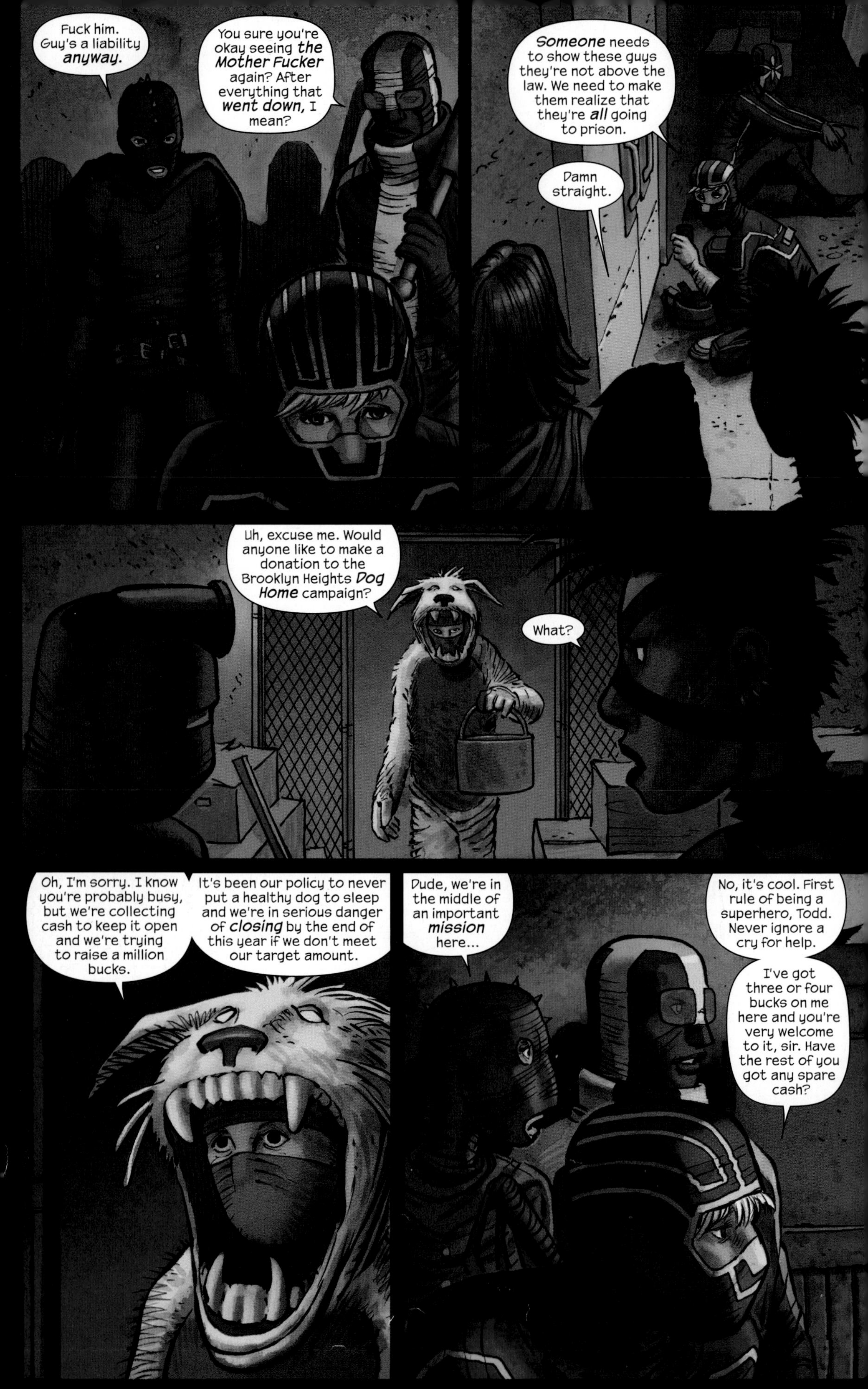
Fuck him. Guy's a liability anyway.
You sure you're okay seeing the Mother Fucker again? After everything that went down, I mean?
Someone needs to show these guys they're not above the law. We need to make them realize that they're all going to prison.
Damn straight.
Uh, excuse me. Would anyone like to make a donation to the Brooklyn Heights Dog Home campaign?
What?
Oh, I'm sorry. I know you're probably busy, but we're collecting cash to keep it open and we're trying to raise a million bucks.
It's been our policy to never put a healthy dog to sleep and we're in serious danger of closing by the end of this year if we don't meet our target amount.
Dude, we're in the middle of an important mission here...
No, it's cool. First rule of being a superhero, Todd. Never ignore a cry for help.
I've got three or four bucks on me here and you're very welcome to it, sir. Have the rest of you got any spare cash?

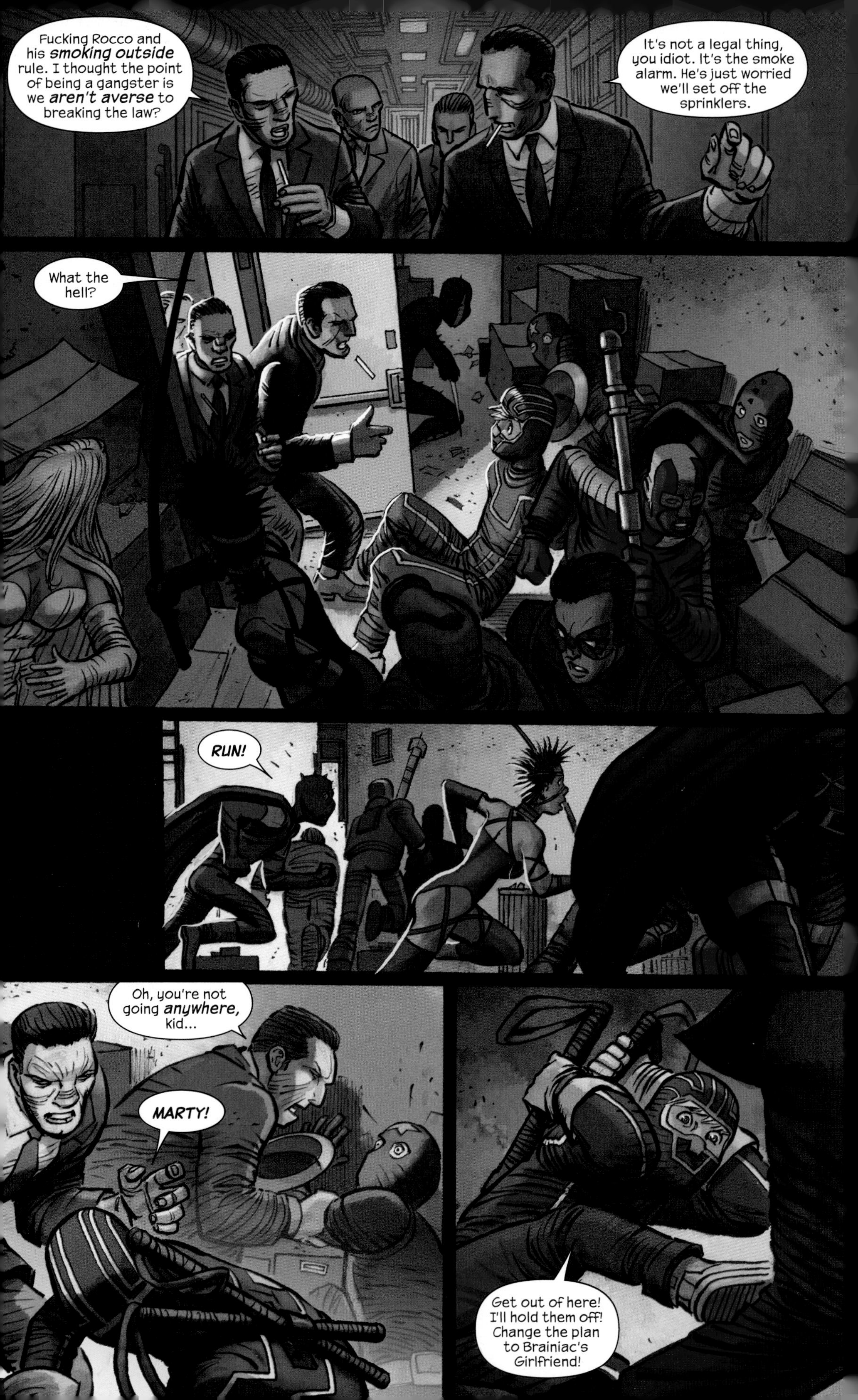
Fucking Rocco and his smoking outside rule. I thought the point of being a gangster is we aren't averse to breaking the law?
It's not a legal thing, you idiot. It's the smoke alarm. He's just worried we'll set off the sprinklers.
What the hell?
RUN!
Oh, you're not going anywhere, kid...
MARTY!
Get out of here! I'll hold them off! Change the plan to Brainiac's Girlfriend!

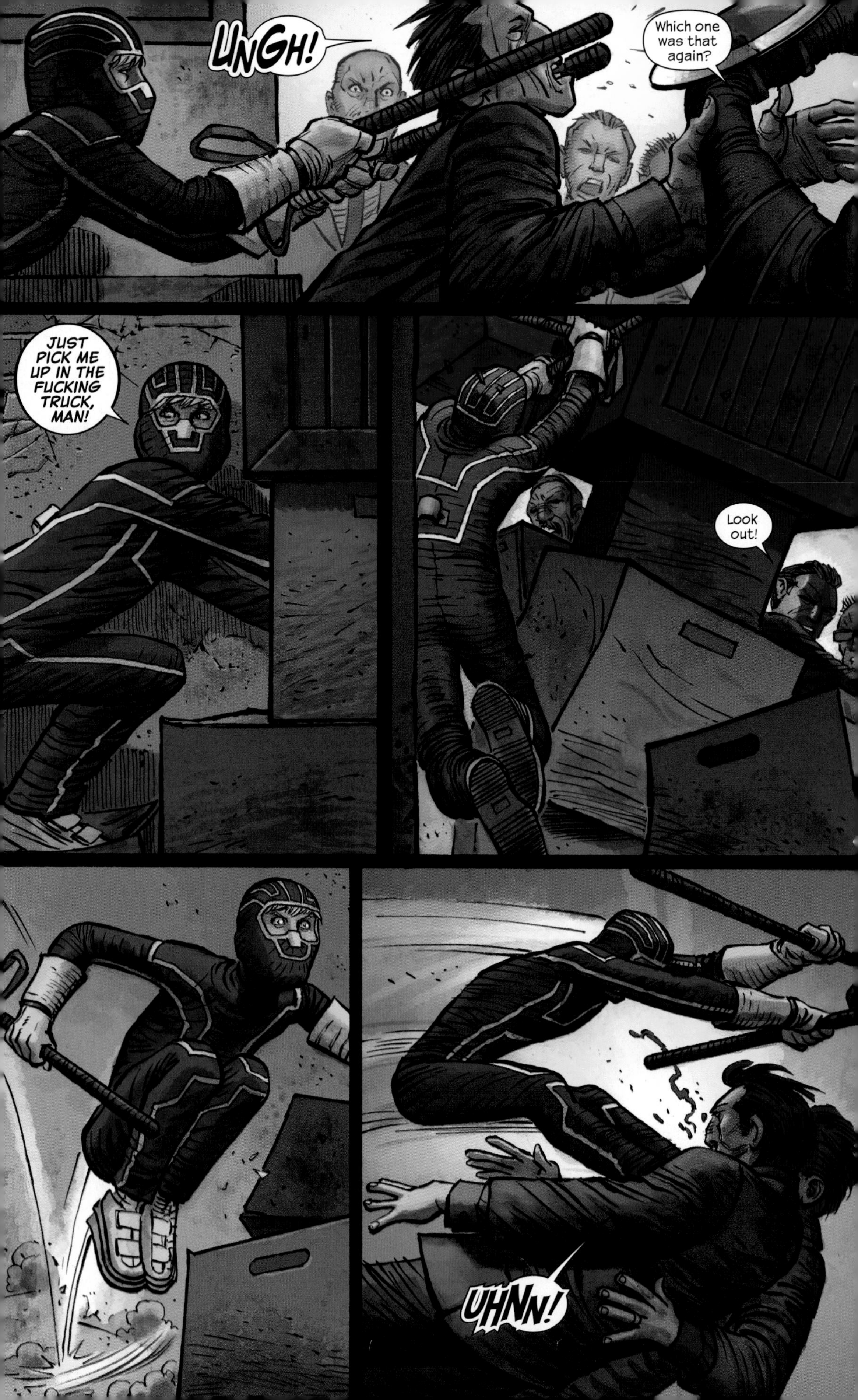
UNGH!
Which one was that again?
JUST PICK ME UP IN THE FUCKING TRUCK, MAN!
Look out!
UHNN!

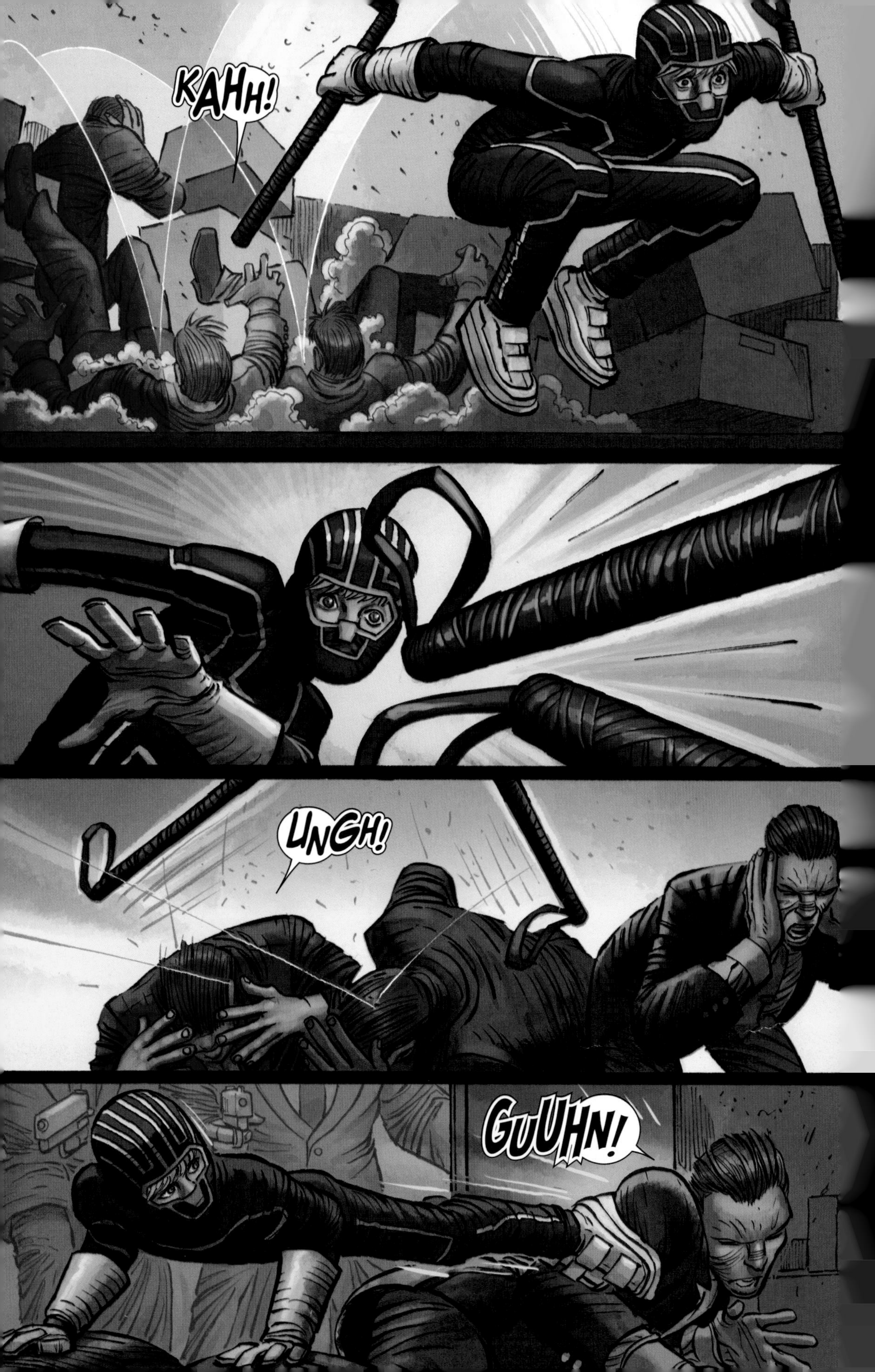
KAHH!
UNGH!
GUUHN!

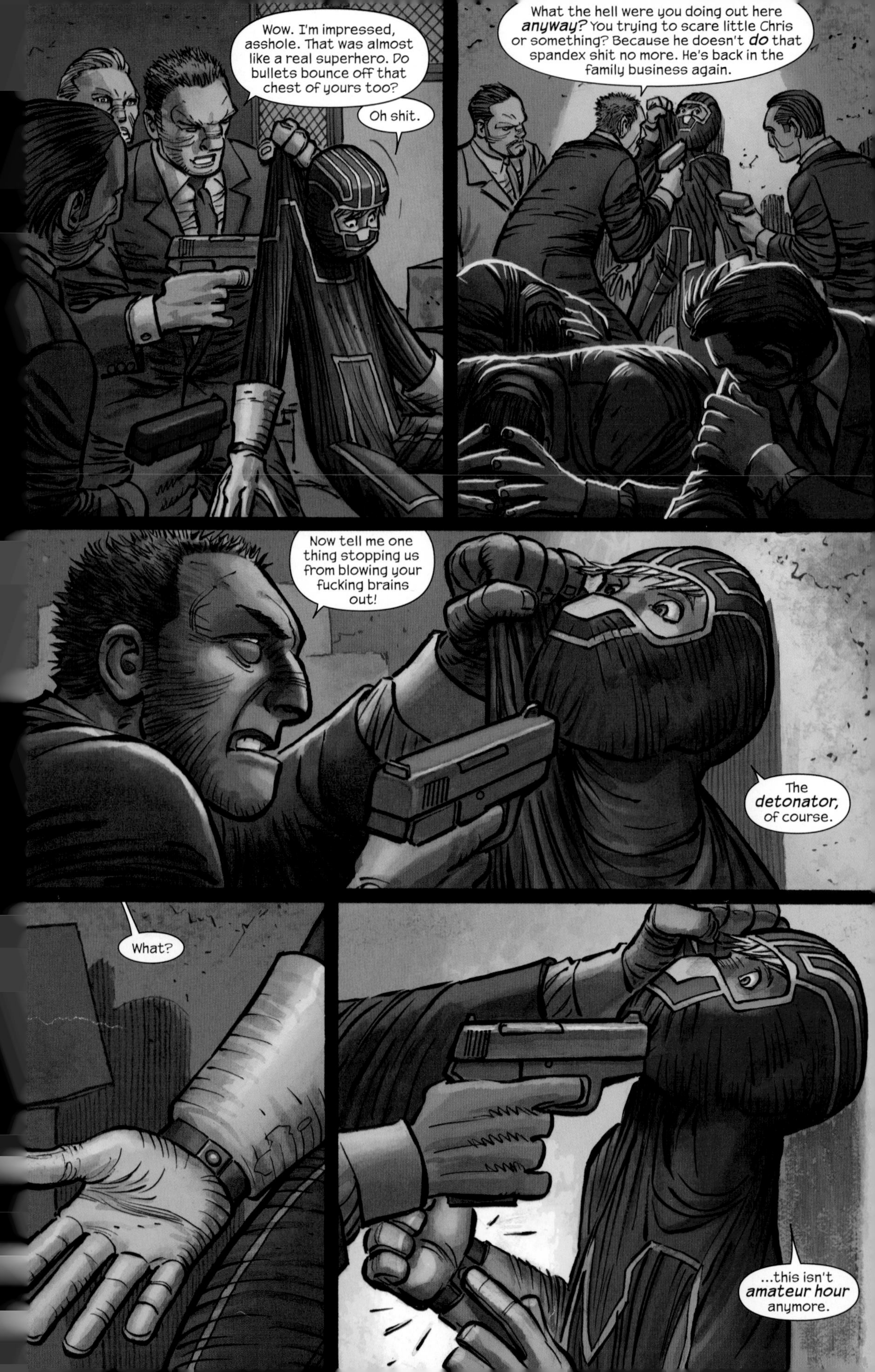
Wow. I'm impressed, asshole. That was almost like a real superhero. Do bullets bounce off that chest of yours too?
Oh shit.
What the hell were you doing out here *anyway?* You trying to scare little Chris or something? Because he doesn't *do* that spandex shit no more. He's back in the family business again.
Now tell me one thing stopping us from blowing your fucking brains out!
The *detonator,* of course.
What?
...this isn't *amateur hour* anymore.

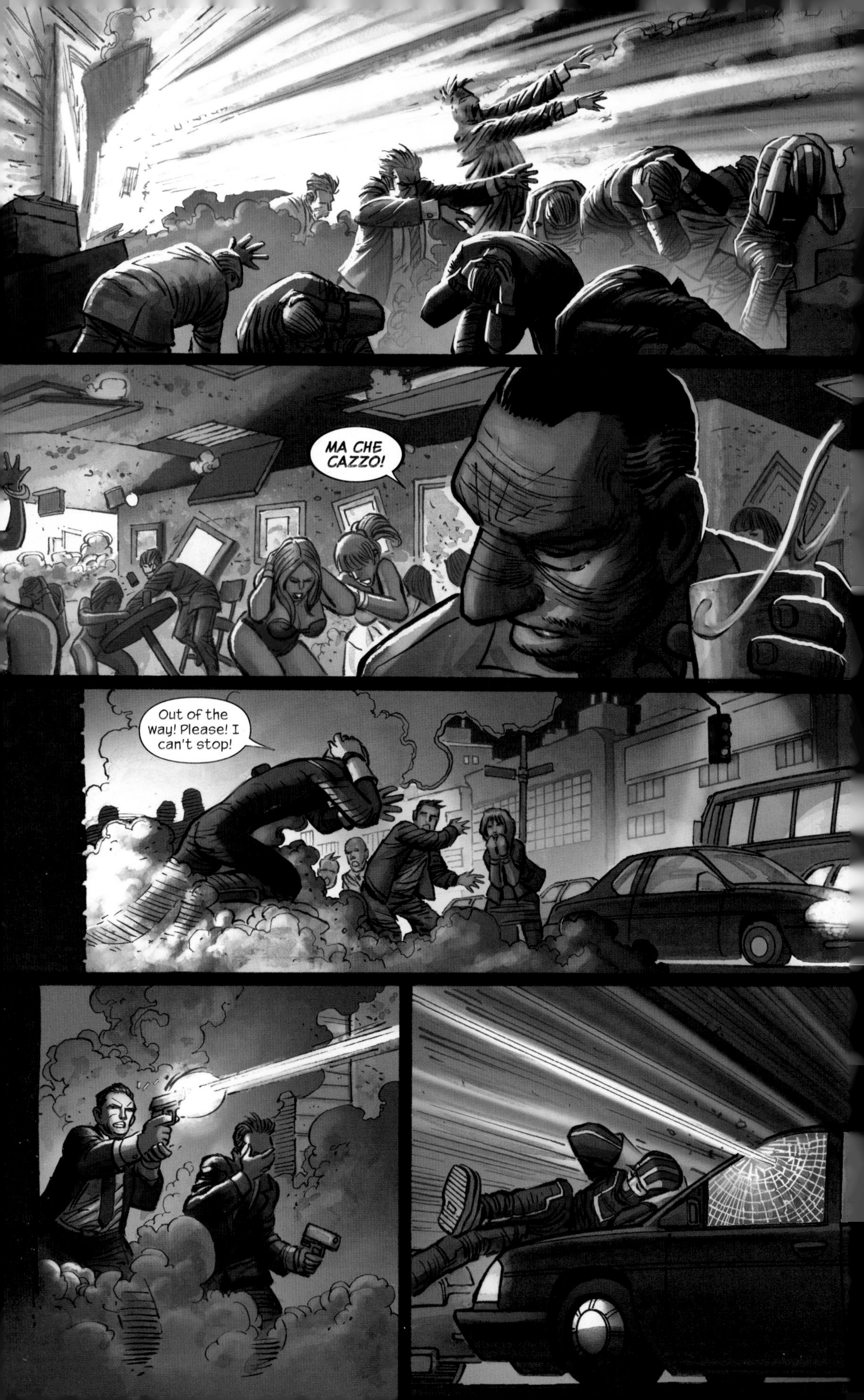
MA CHE CAZZO!
Out of the way! Please! I can't stop!

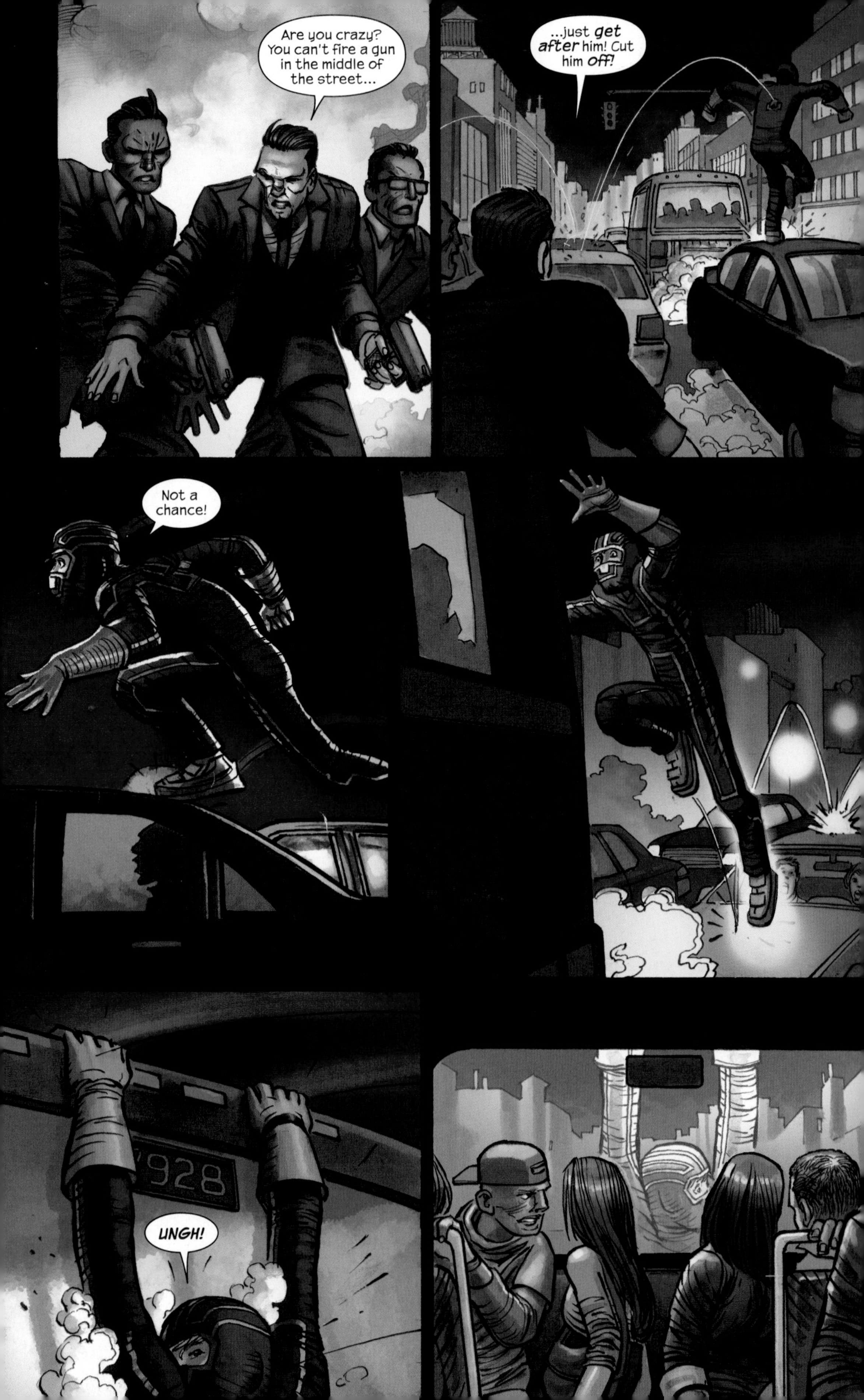
Are you crazy? You can't fire a gun in the middle of the street...
...just get after him! Cut him off!
Not a chance!
UNGH!
7928

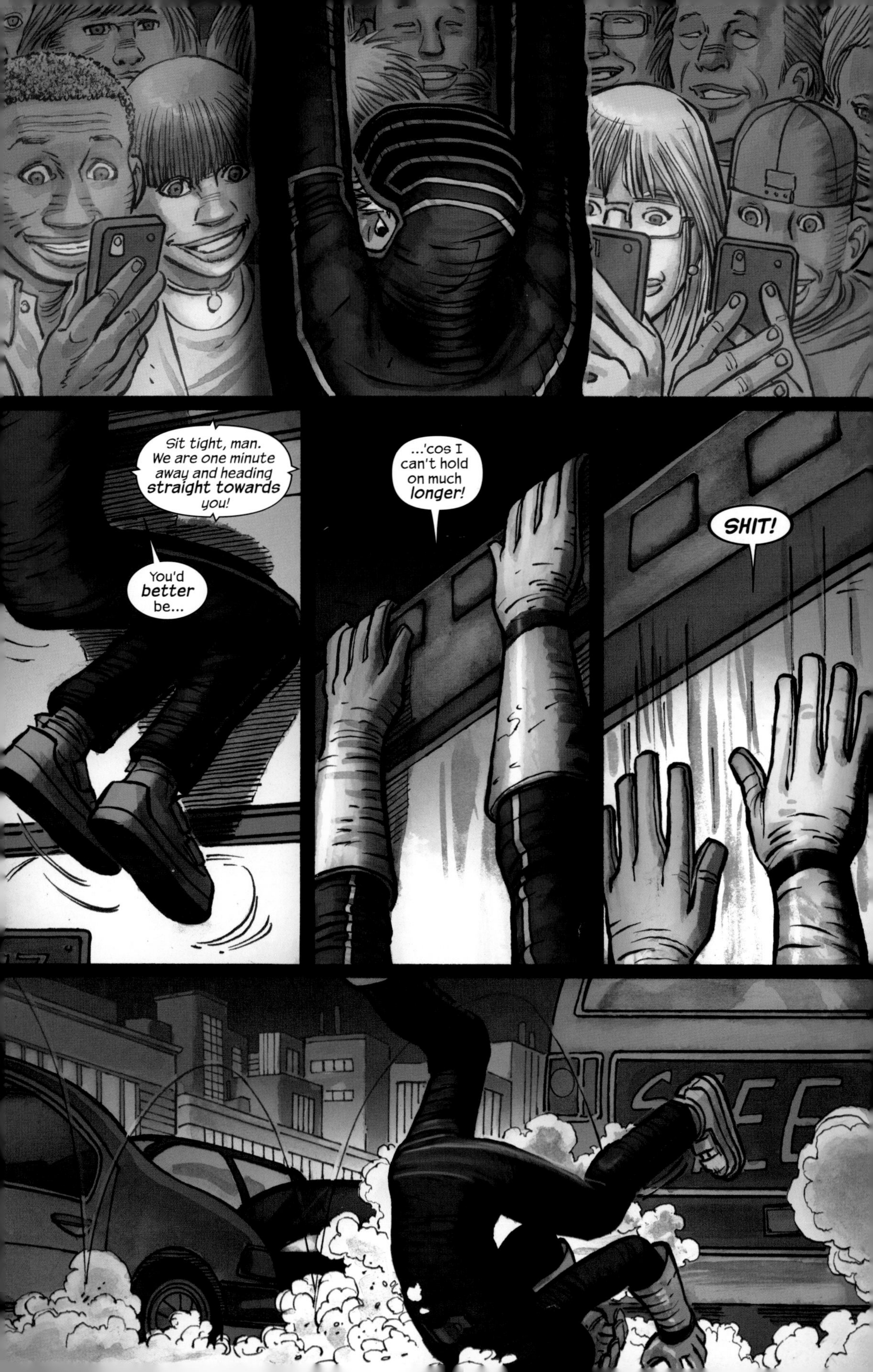
Sit tight, man. We are one minute away and heading straight towards you!
You'd better be...
...'cos I can't hold on much longer!
SHIT!

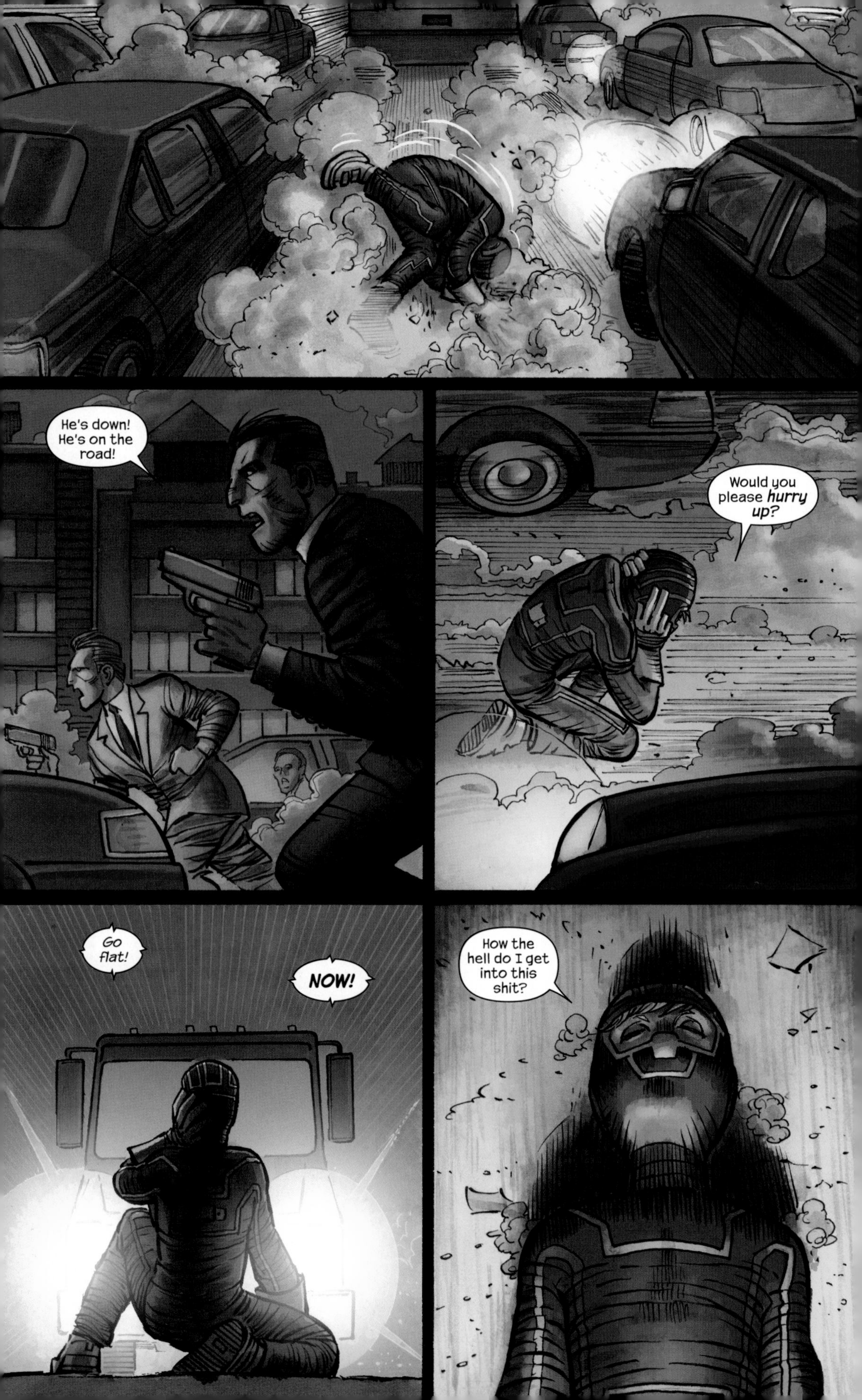
He's down! He's on the road!
Would you please *hurry up?*
Go flat!
NOW!
How the hell do I get into this shit?

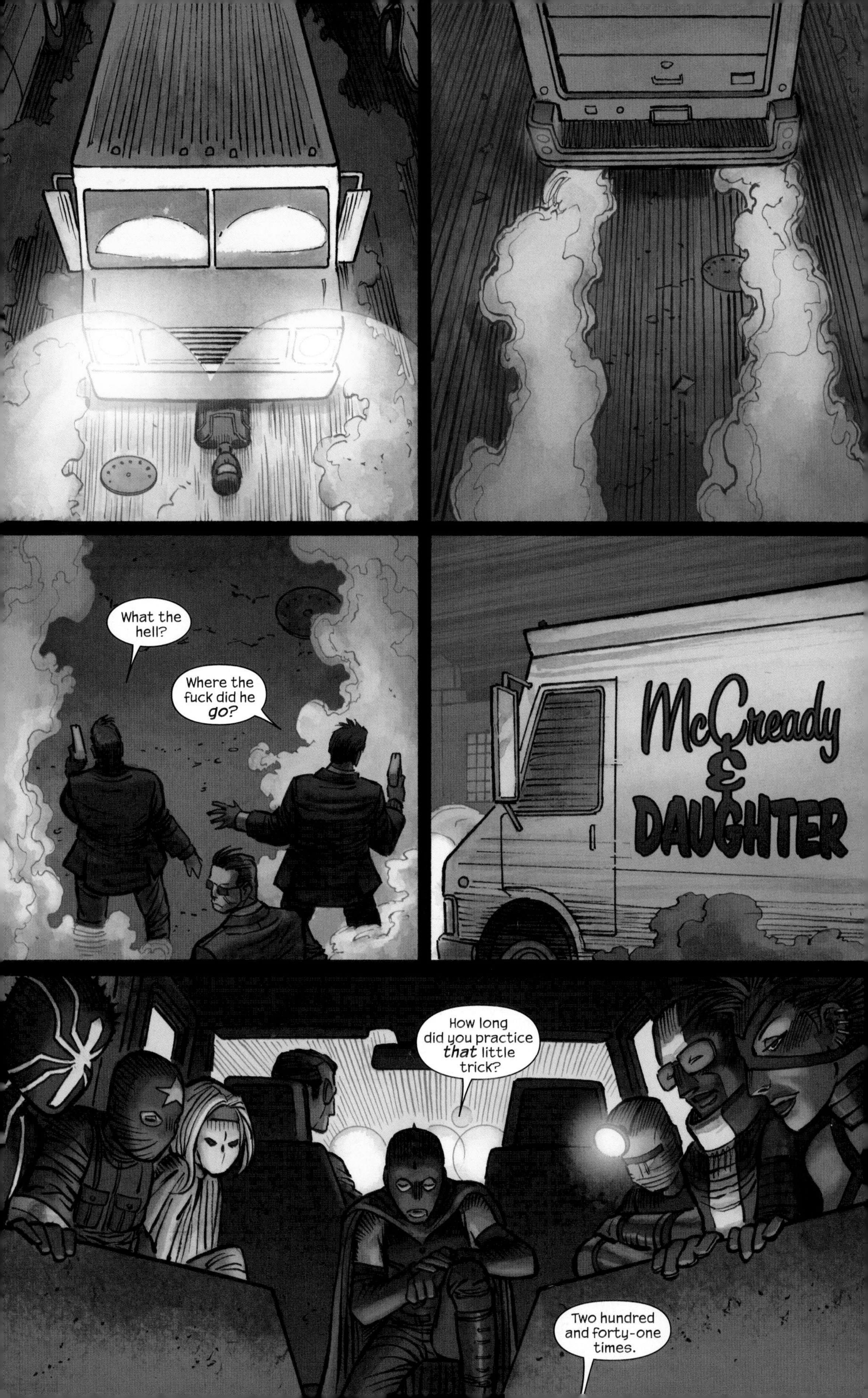
What the hell?
Where the fuck did he *go?*
McCready & DAUGHTER
How long did you practice *that* little trick?
Two hundred and forty-one times.

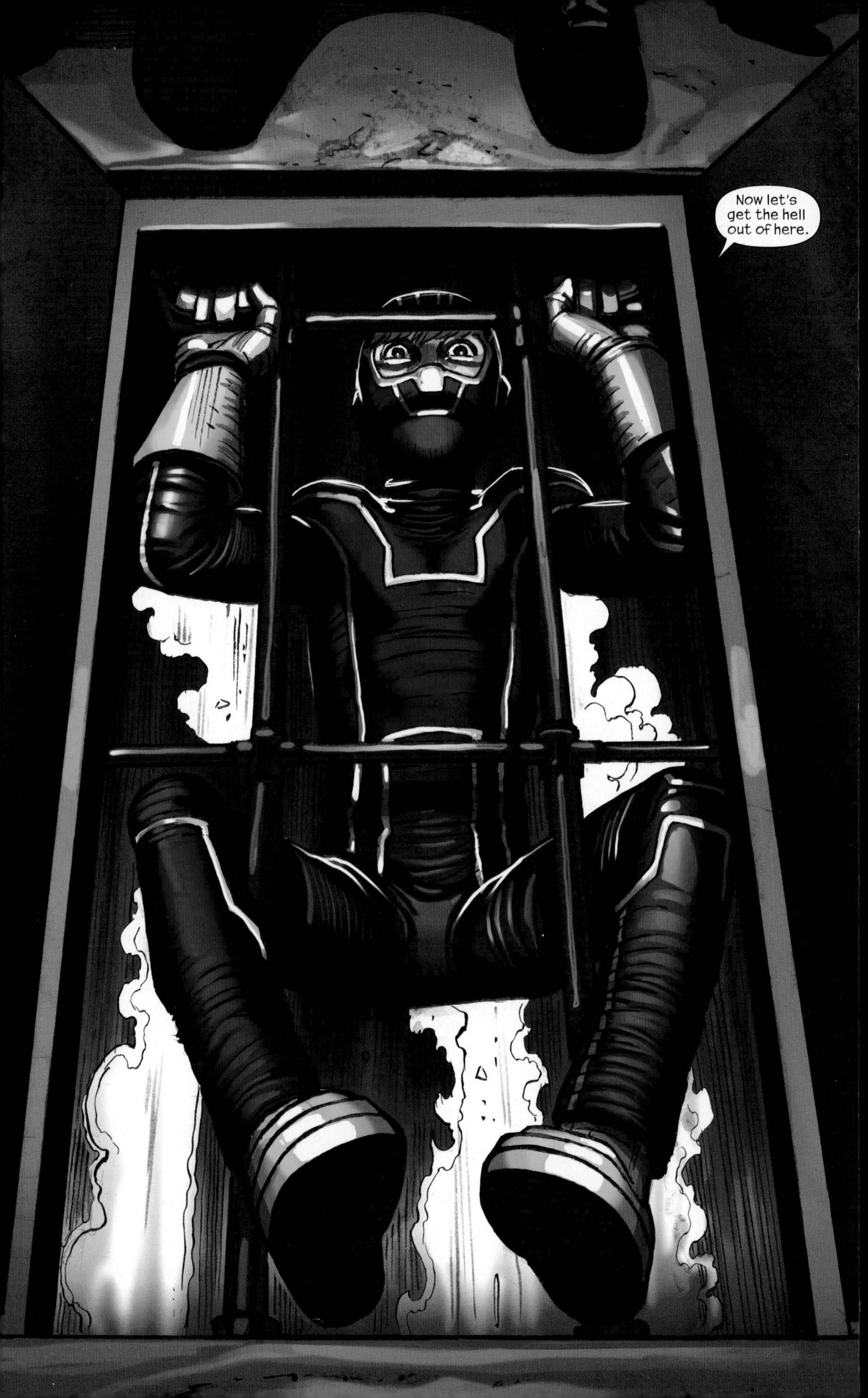
Now let's get the hell out of here.

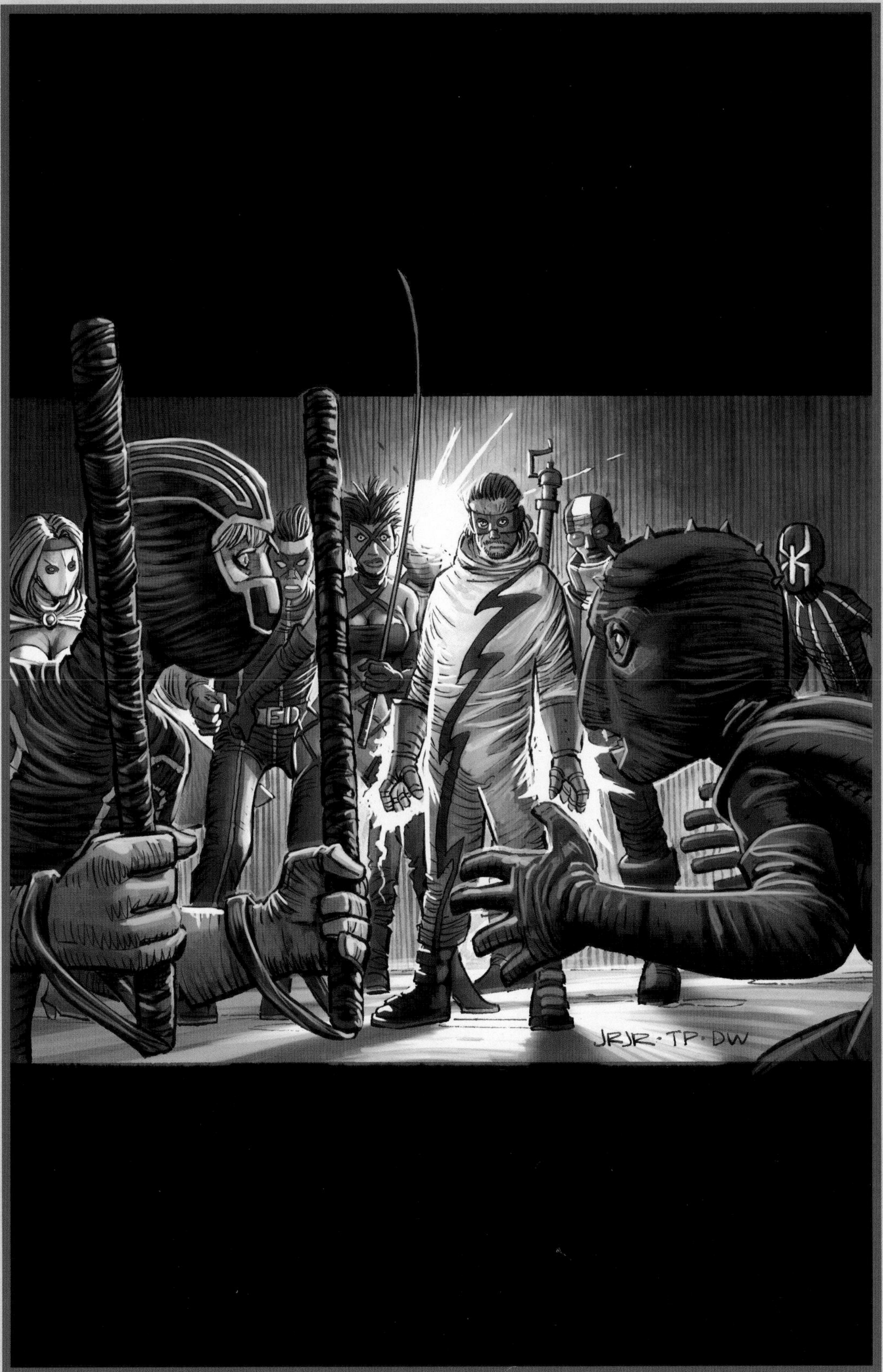
JRJR · TP · DW

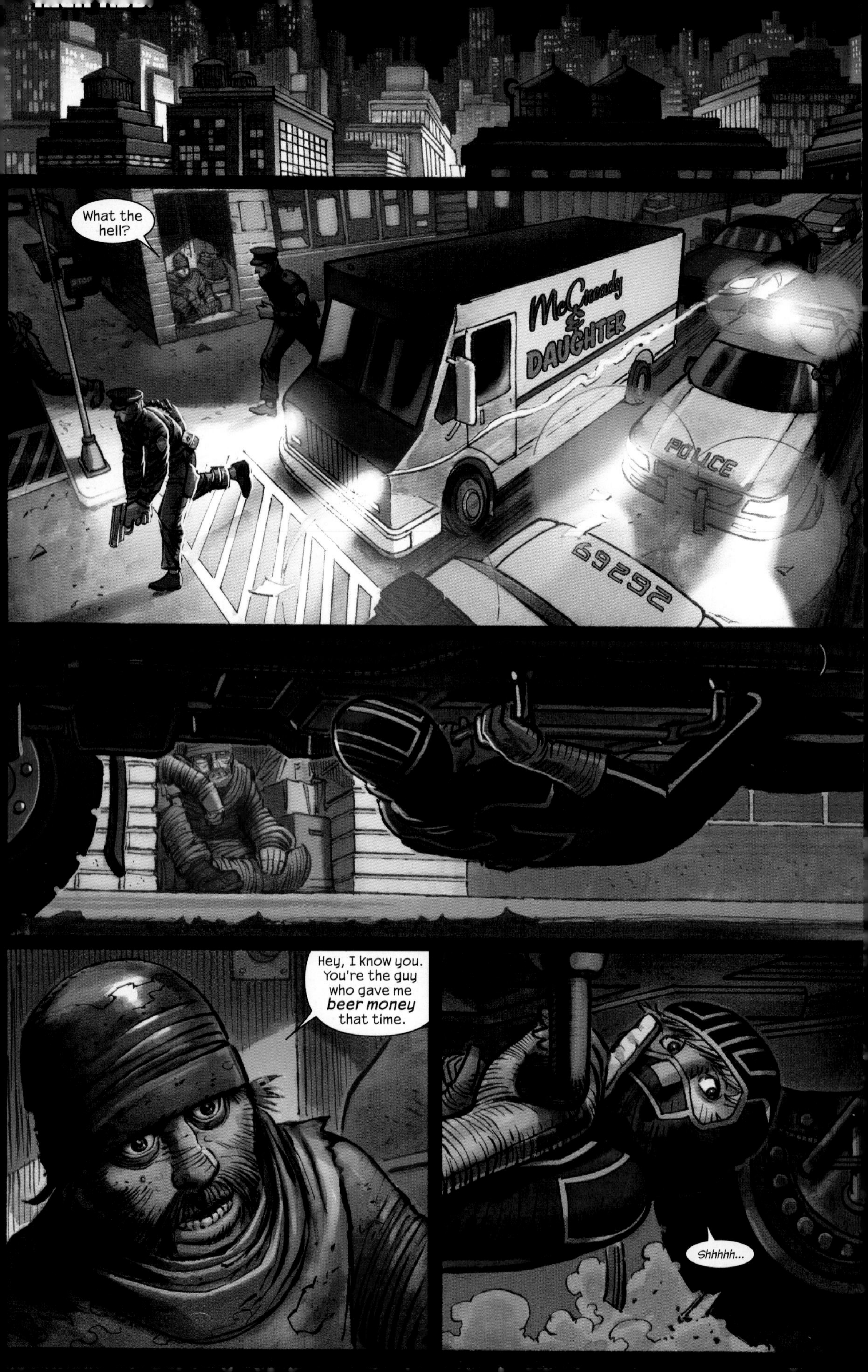
What the hell?
McCreedy & Daughter
POLICE
69292
Hey, I know you. You're the guy who gave me *beer money* that time.
Shhhhh...

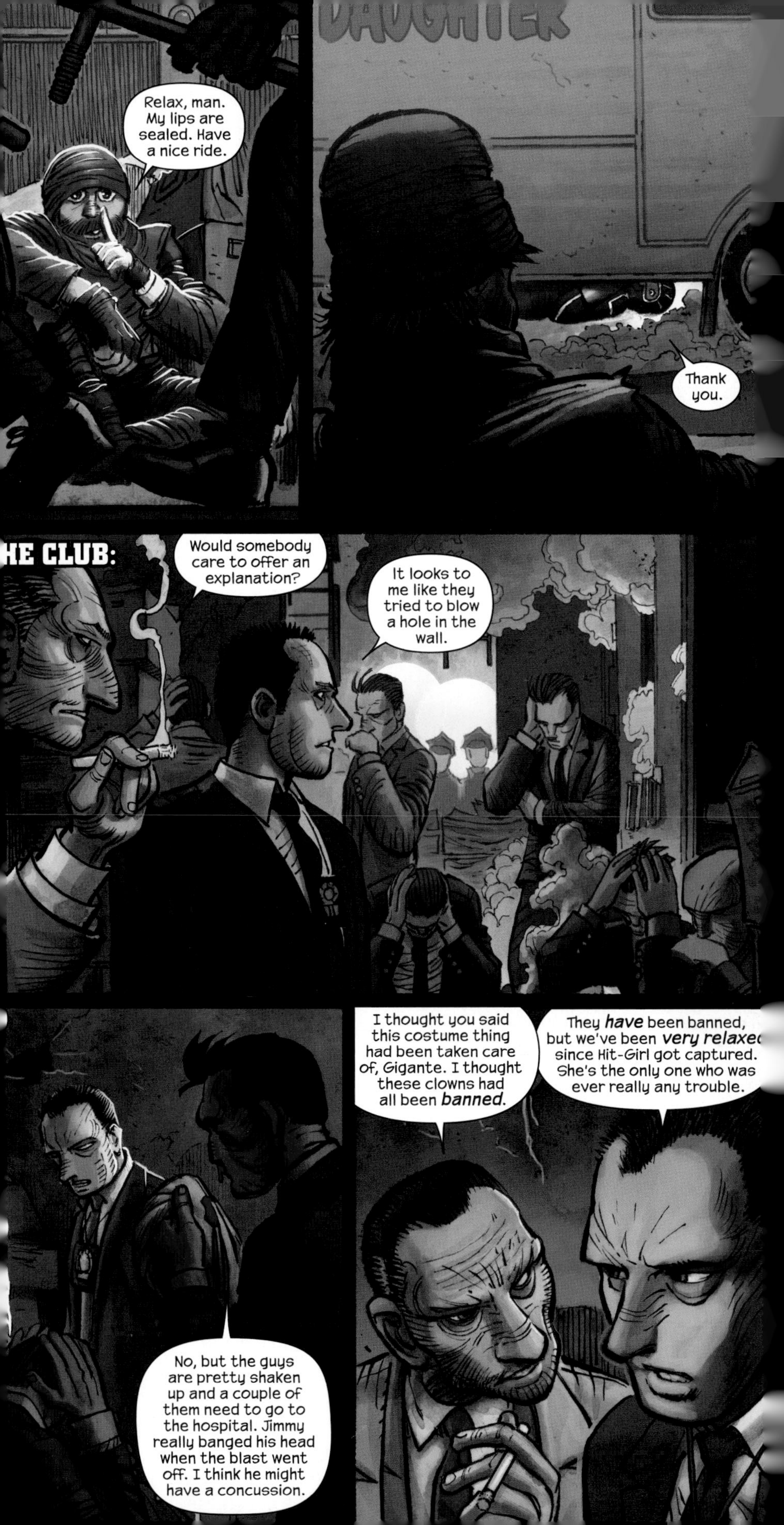
Relax, man. My lips are sealed. Have a nice ride.
Thank you.
HE CLUB:
Would somebody care to offer an explanation?
It looks to me like they tried to blow a hole in the wall.
No, but the guys are pretty shaken up and a couple of them need to go to the hospital. Jimmy really banged his head when the blast went off. I think he might have a concussion.
I thought you said this costume thing had been taken care of, Gigante. I thought these clowns had all been *banned*.
They *have* been banned, but we've been *very relaxe* since Hit-Girl got captured. She's the only one who was ever really any trouble.

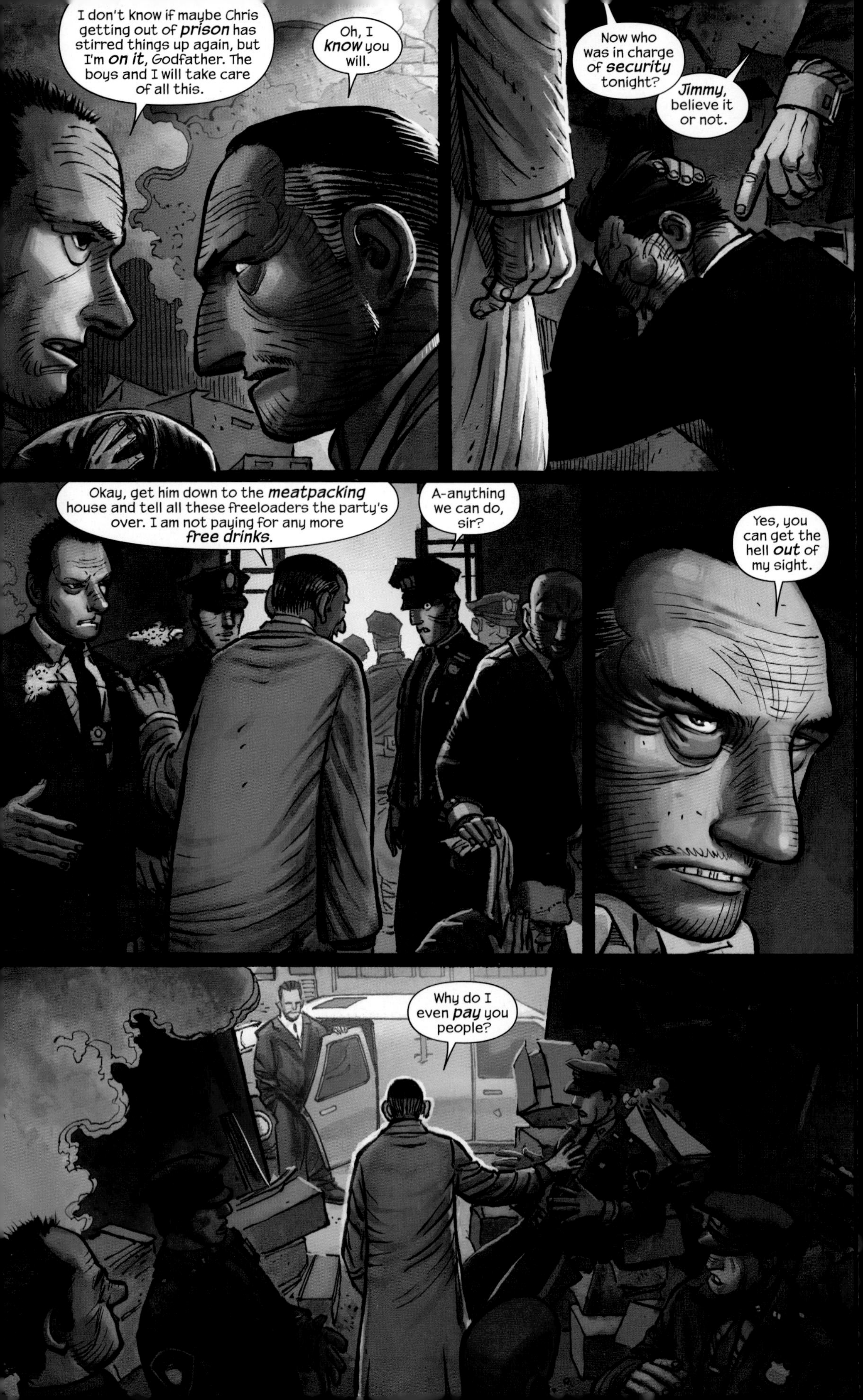
I don't know if maybe Chris getting out of *prison* has stirred things up again, but I'm *on it*, Godfather. The boys and I will take care of all this.
Oh, I *know* you will.
Now who was in charge of *security* tonight?
Jimmy, believe it or not.
Okay, get him down to the *meatpacking* house and tell all these freeloaders the party's over. I am not paying for any more *free drinks*.
A-anything we can do, sir?
Yes, you can get the hell *out* of my sight.
Why do I even *pay* you people?

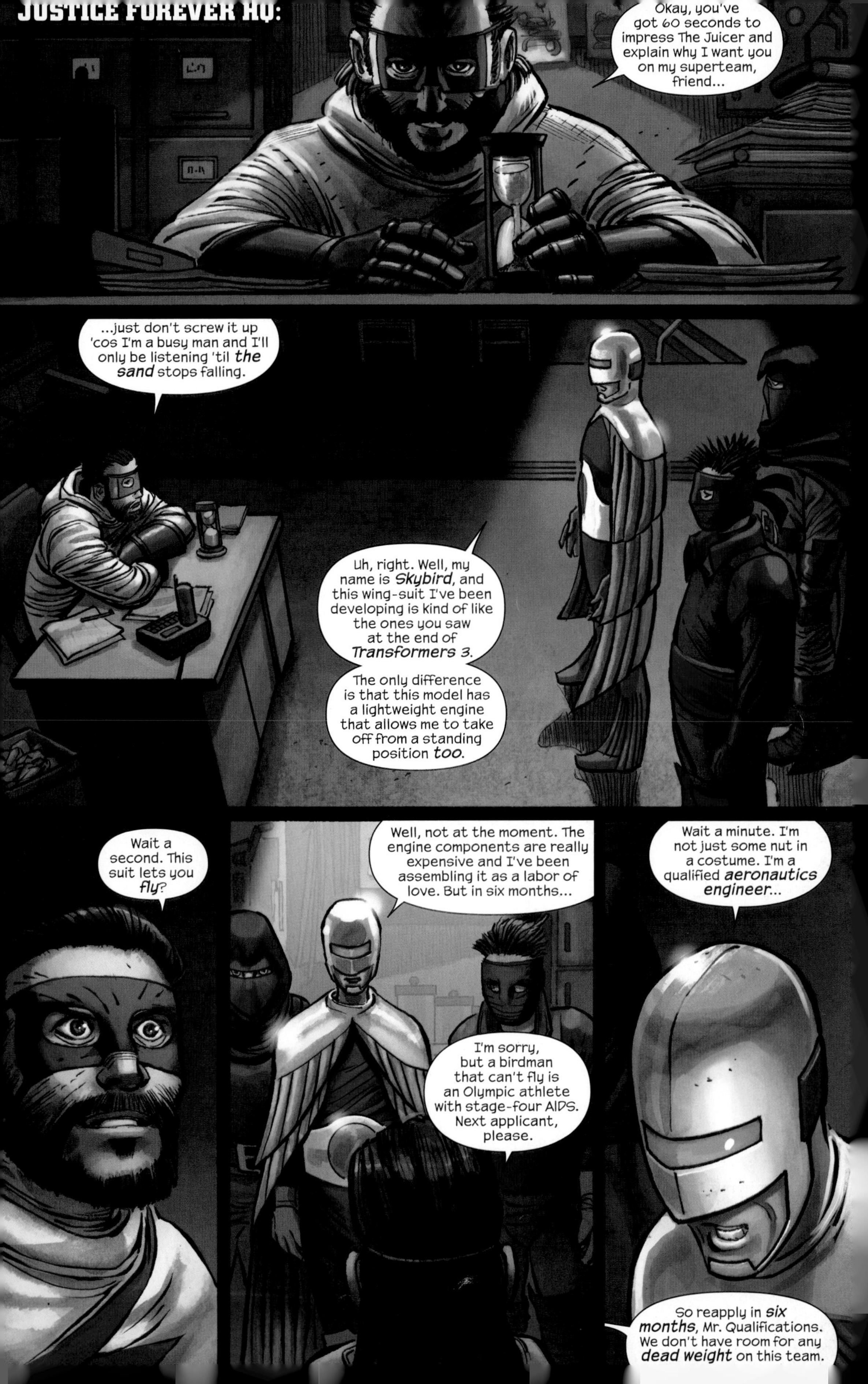
JUSTICE FOREVER HQ:
Okay, you've got 60 seconds to impress The Juicer and explain why I want you on my superteam, friend...
...just don't screw it up 'cos I'm a busy man and I'll only be listening 'til *the sand* stops falling.
Uh, right. Well, my name is *Skybird*, and this wing-suit I've been developing is kind of like the ones you saw at the end of *Transformers 3*.
The only difference is that this model has a lightweight engine that allows me to take off from a standing position *too*.
Wait a second. This suit lets you *fly*?
Well, not at the moment. The engine components are really expensive and I've been assembling it as a labor of love. But in six months...
I'm sorry, but a birdman that can't fly is an Olympic athlete with stage-four AIDS. Next applicant, please.
Wait a minute. I'm not just some nut in a costume. I'm a qualified *aeronautics engineer*...
So reapply in *six months*, Mr. Qualifications. We don't have room for any *dead weight* on this team.

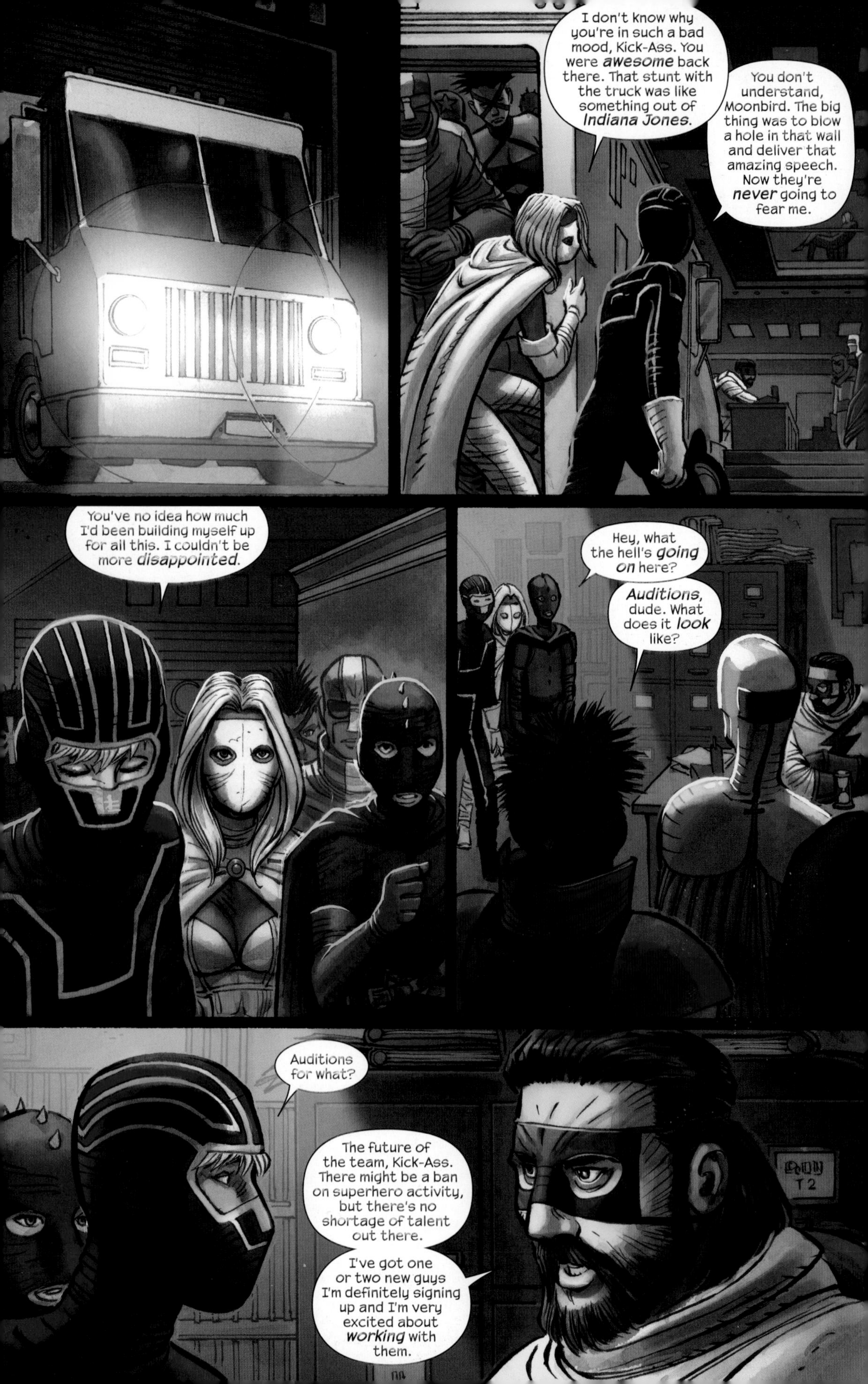
I don't know why you're in such a bad mood, Kick-Ass. You were *awesome* back there. That stunt with the truck was like something out of *Indiana Jones*.
You don't understand, Moonbird. The big thing was to blow a hole in that wall and deliver that amazing speech. Now they're *never* going to fear me.
You've no idea how much I'd been building myself up for all this. I couldn't be more *disappointed*.
Hey, what the hell's *going on* here?
Auditions, dude. What does it *look* like?
Auditions for what?
The future of the team, Kick-Ass. There might be a ban on superhero activity, but there's no shortage of talent out there.
I've got one or two new guys I'm definitely signing up and I'm very excited about *working* with them.

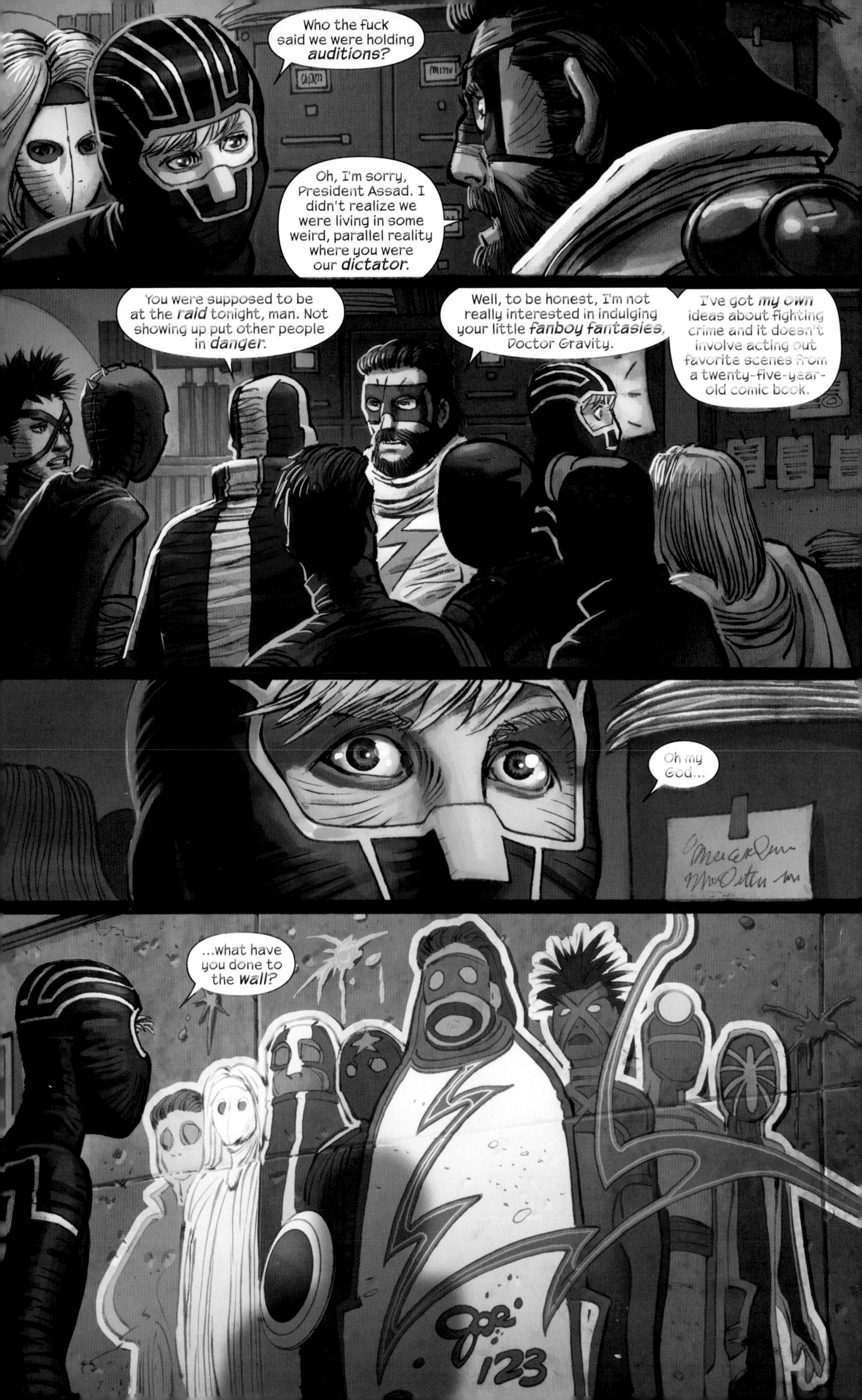
Who the fuck said we were holding *auditions*?
Oh, I'm sorry, President Assad. I didn't realize we were living in some weird, parallel reality where you were our *dictator*.
You were supposed to be at the *raid* tonight, man. Not showing up put other people in *danger*.
Well, to be honest, I'm not really interested in indulging your little *fanboy fantasies*, Doctor Gravity.
I've got *my own* ideas about fighting crime and it doesn't involve acting out favorite scenes from a twenty-five-year-old comic book.
Oh my God...
...what have you done to the *wall*?
123

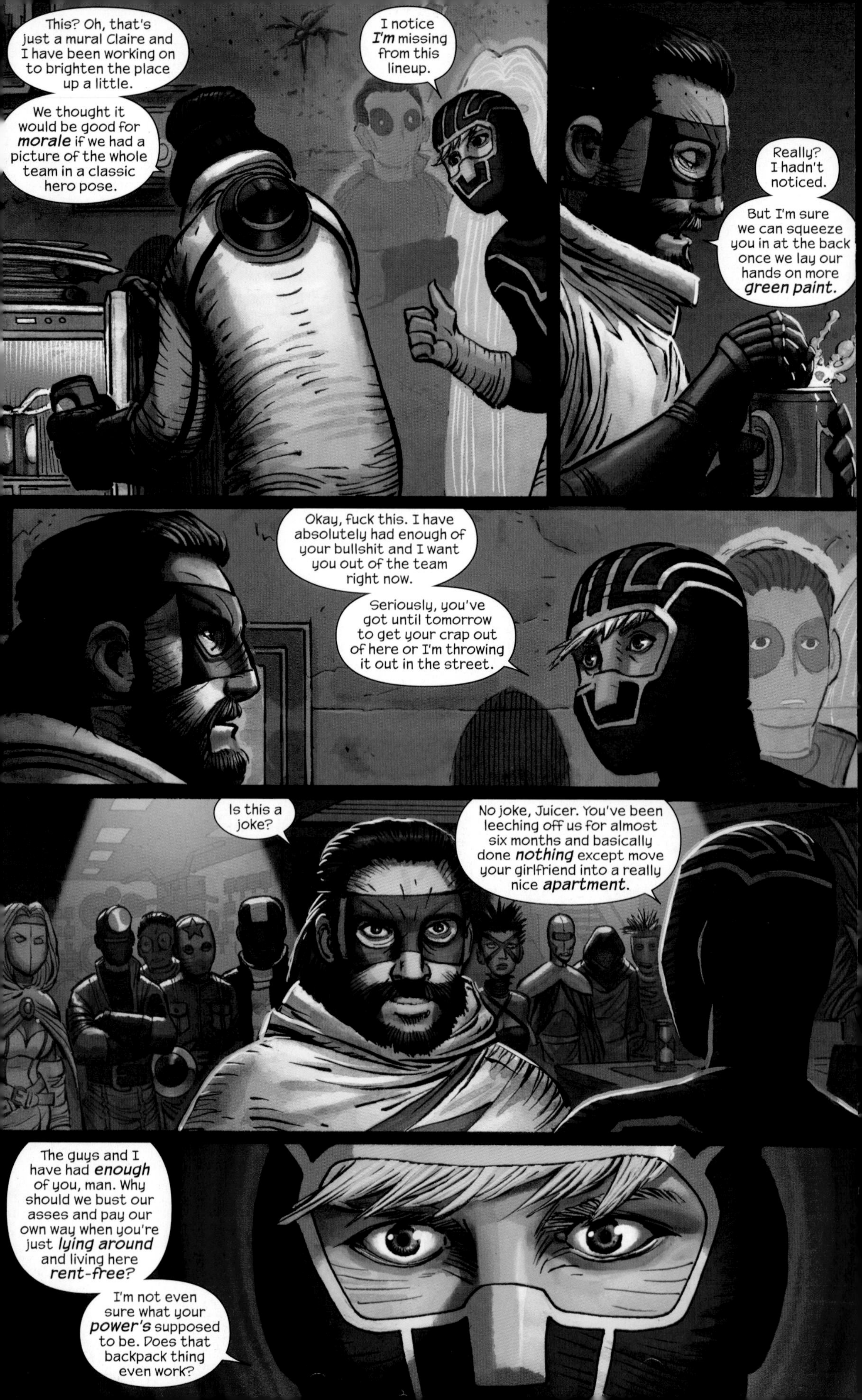

This? Oh, that's just a mural Claire and I have been working on to brighten the place up a little.
We thought it would be good for *morale* if we had a picture of the whole team in a classic hero pose.
I notice *I'm* missing from this lineup.
Really? I hadn't noticed.
But I'm sure we can squeeze you in at the back once we lay our hands on more *green paint.*
Okay, fuck this. I have absolutely had enough of your bullshit and I want you out of the team right now.
Seriously, you've got until tomorrow to get your crap out of here or I'm throwing it out in the street.
Is this a joke?
No joke, Juicer. You've been leeching off us for almost six months and basically done *nothing* except move your girlfriend into a really nice *apartment*.
The guys and I have had *enough* of you, man. Why should we bust our asses and pay our own way when you're just *lying around* and living here *rent-free?*
I'm not even sure what your *power's* supposed to be. Does that backpack thing even work?

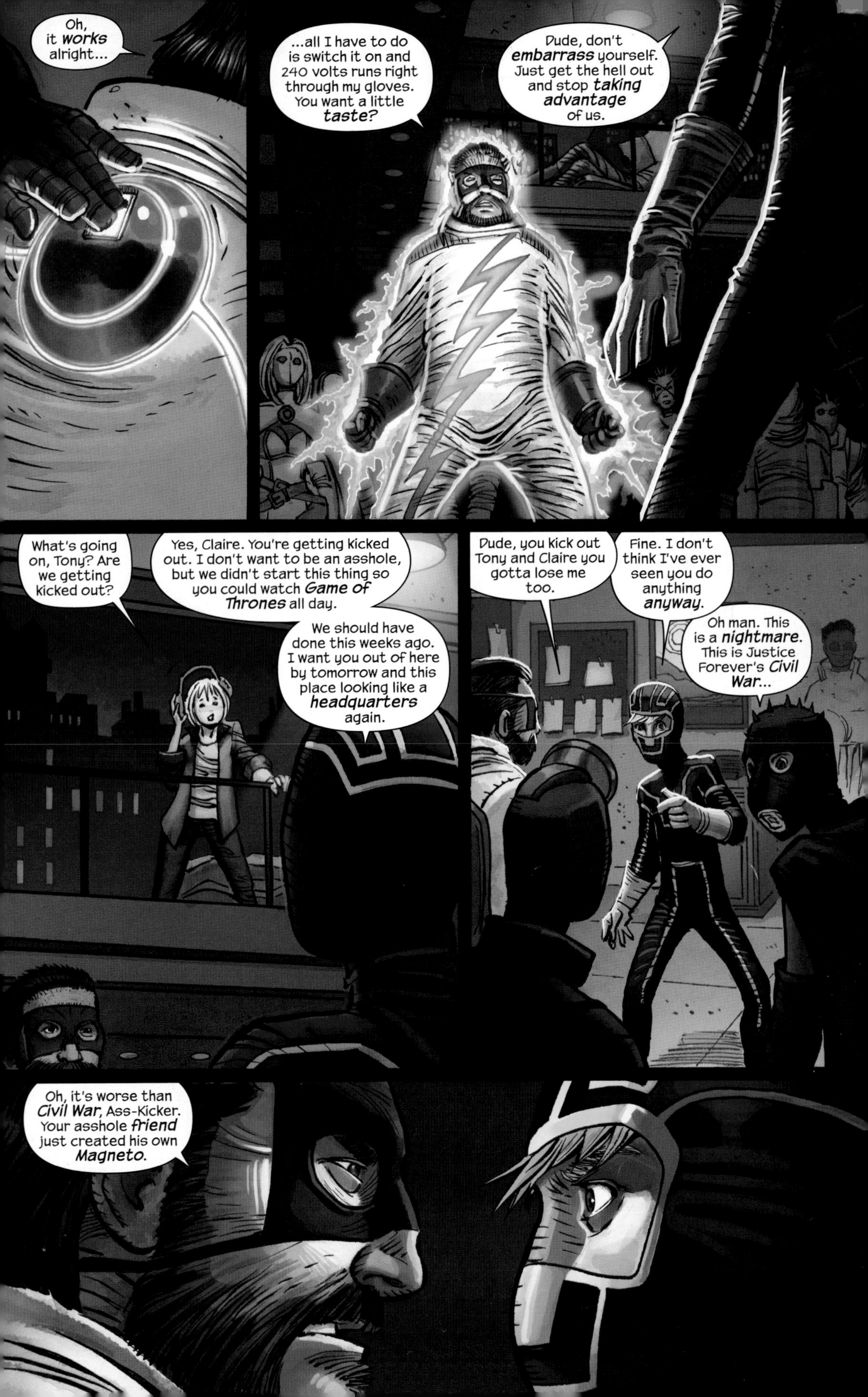
Oh, it works alright...
...all I have to do is switch it on and 240 volts runs right through my gloves. You want a little taste?
Dude, don't embarrass yourself. Just get the hell out and stop taking advantage of us.
What's going on, Tony? Are we getting kicked out?
Yes, Claire. You're getting kicked out. I don't want to be an asshole, but we didn't start this thing so you could watch Game of Thrones all day.
We should have done this weeks ago. I want you out of here by tomorrow and this place looking like a headquarters again.
Dude, you kick out Tony and Claire you gotta lose me too.
Fine. I don't think I've ever seen you do anything anyway.
Oh man. This is a nightmare. This is Justice Forever's Civil War...
Oh, it's worse than Civil War, Ass-Kicker. Your asshole friend just created his own Magneto.

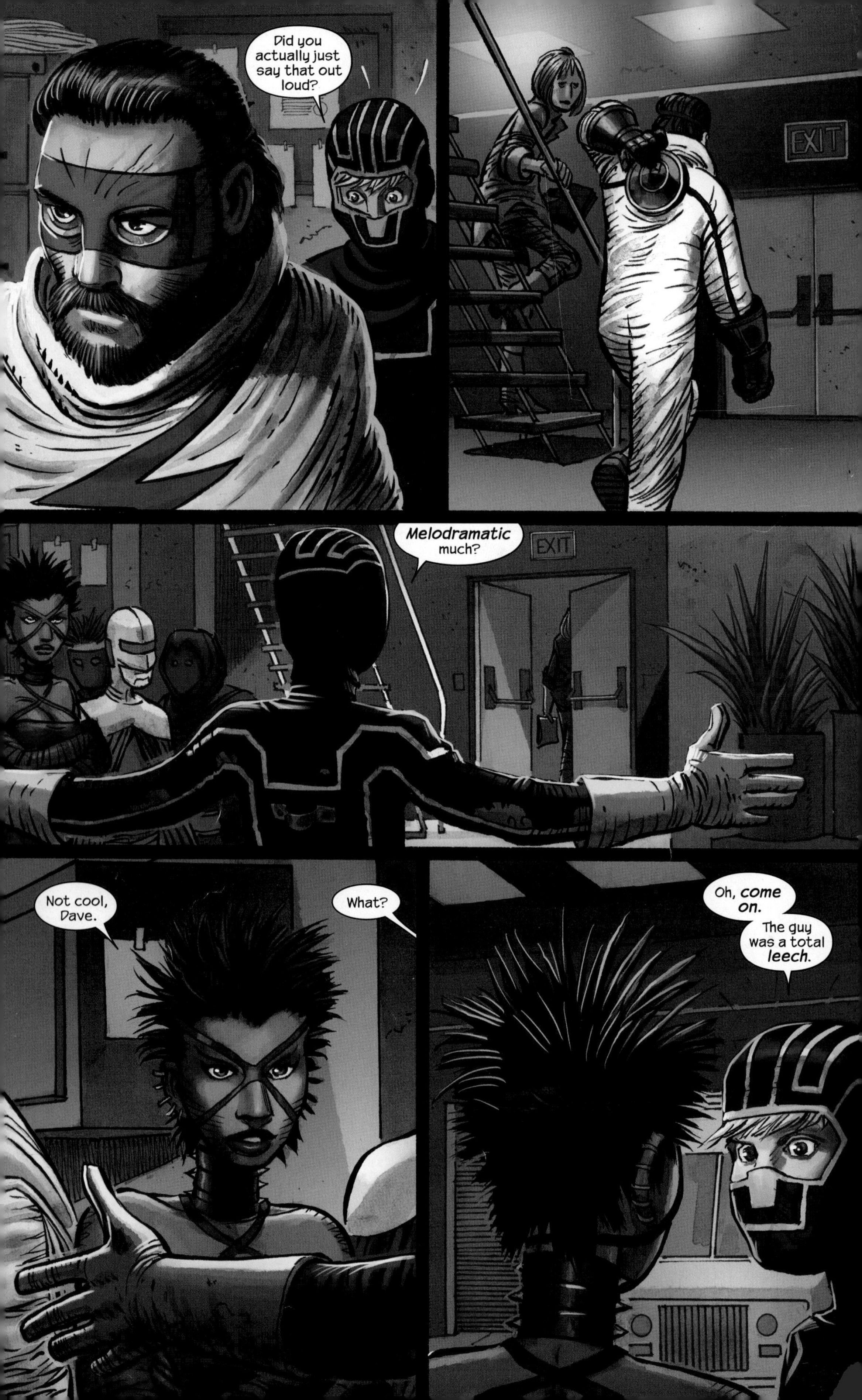
Did you actually just say that out loud?
Melodramatic much?
Not cool, Dave.
What?
Oh, come on.
The guy was a total leech.

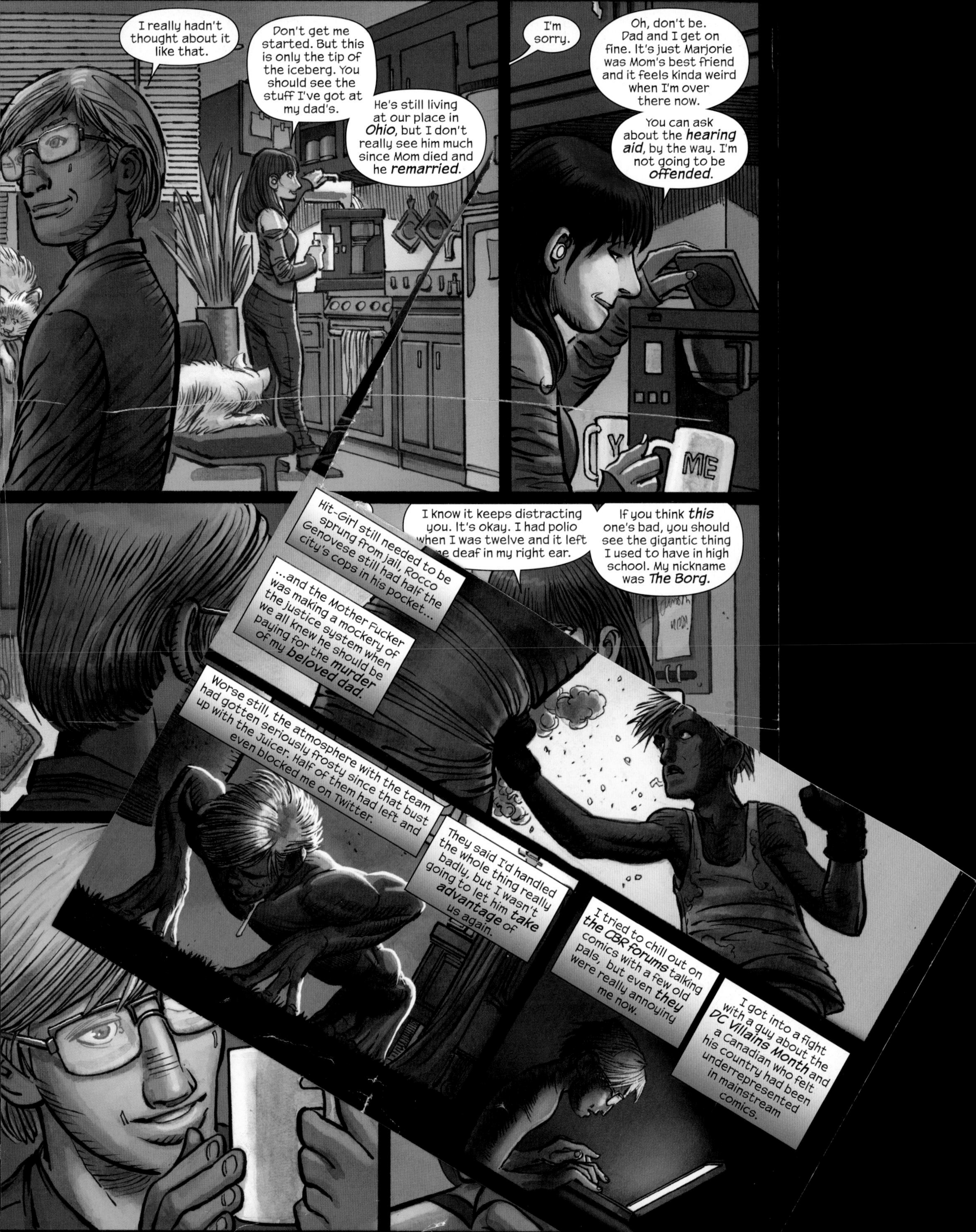

I really hadn't thought about it like that.
Don't get me started. But this is only the tip of the iceberg. You should see the stuff I've got at my dad's.
He's still living at our place in *Ohio*, but I don't really see him much since Mom died and he *remarried*.
I'm sorry.
Oh, don't be. Dad and I get on fine. It's just Marjorie was Mom's best friend and it feels kinda weird when I'm over there now.
You can ask about the *hearing aid*, by the way. I'm not going to be *offended*.
I know it keeps distracting you. It's okay. I had polio when I was twelve and it left me deaf in my right ear.
If you think *this* one's bad, you should see the gigantic thing I used to have in high school. My nickname was *The Borg*.
Hit-Girl still needed to be sprung from jail, Rocco Genovese still had half the city's cops in his pocket...
...and the Mother Fucker was making a mockery of the justice system when we all knew he should be paying for the *murder* of my *beloved dad*.
Worse still, the atmosphere with the team had gotten seriously frosty since that bust up with the Juicer. Half of them had left and even blocked me on Twitter.
They said I'd handled the whole thing really badly, but I wasn't going to let him *take advantage* of us again.
I tried to chill out on *the CBR forums* talking comics with a few old pals, but even *they* were really annoying me now.
I got into a fight with a guy about the *DC Villains Month* and a Canadian who felt his country had been underrepresented in mainstream comics.

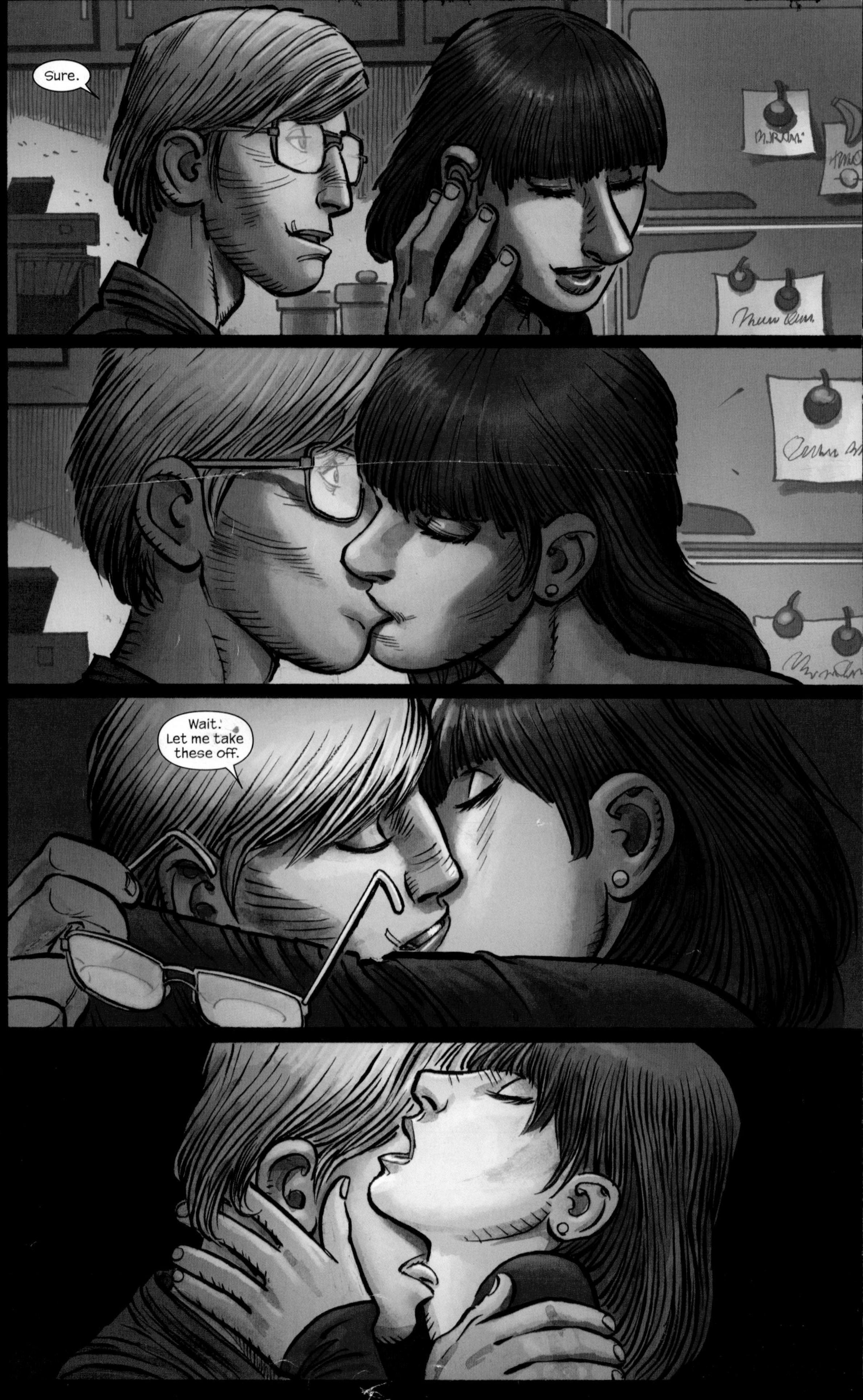
Sure.
Wait. Let me take these off.

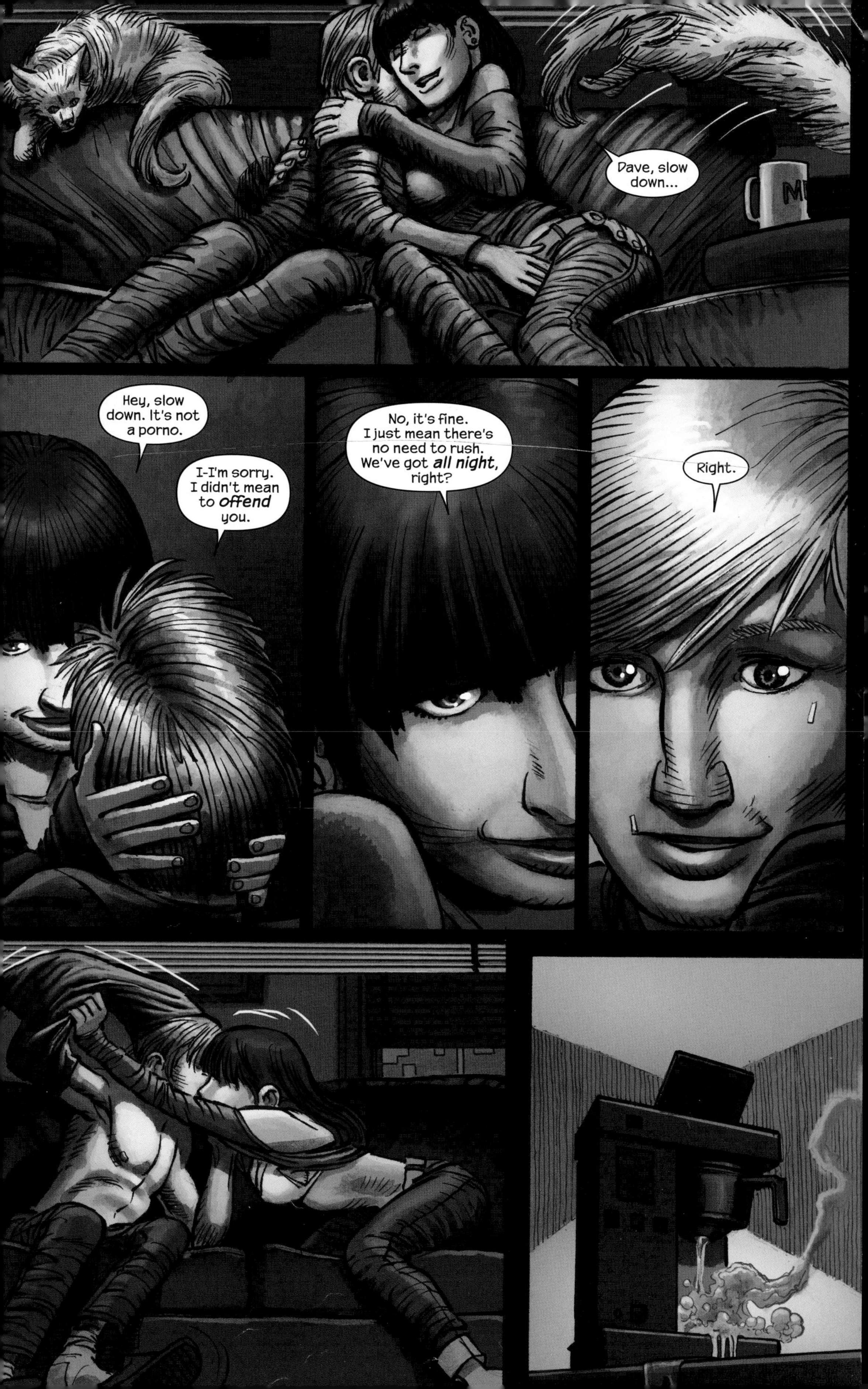
Dave, slow down...
Hey, slow down. It's not a porno.
I-I'm sorry. I didn't mean to *offend* you.
No, it's fine. I just mean there's no need to rush. We've got *all night*, right?
Right.

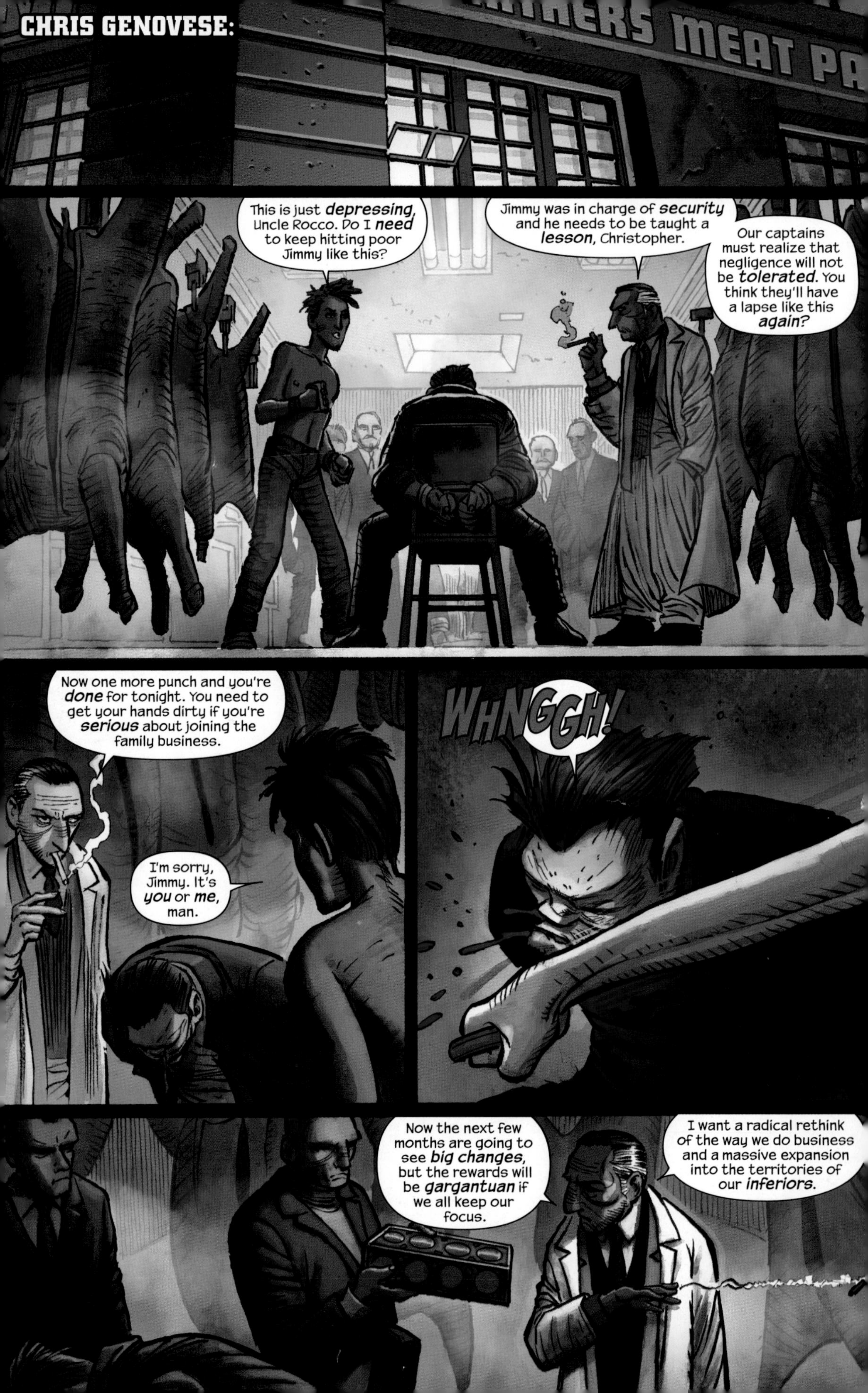
CHRIS GENOVESE:
...THERS MEAT PA...
This is just depressing, Uncle Rocco. Do I need to keep hitting poor Jimmy like this?
Jimmy was in charge of security and he needs to be taught a lesson, Christopher.
Our captains must realize that negligence will not be tolerated. You think they'll have a lapse like this again?
Now one more punch and you're done for tonight. You need to get your hands dirty if you're serious about joining the family business.
I'm sorry, Jimmy. It's you or me, man.
WHNGGH!
Now the next few months are going to see big changes, but the rewards will be gargantuan if we all keep our focus.
I want a radical rethink of the way we do business and a massive expansion into the territories of our inferiors.

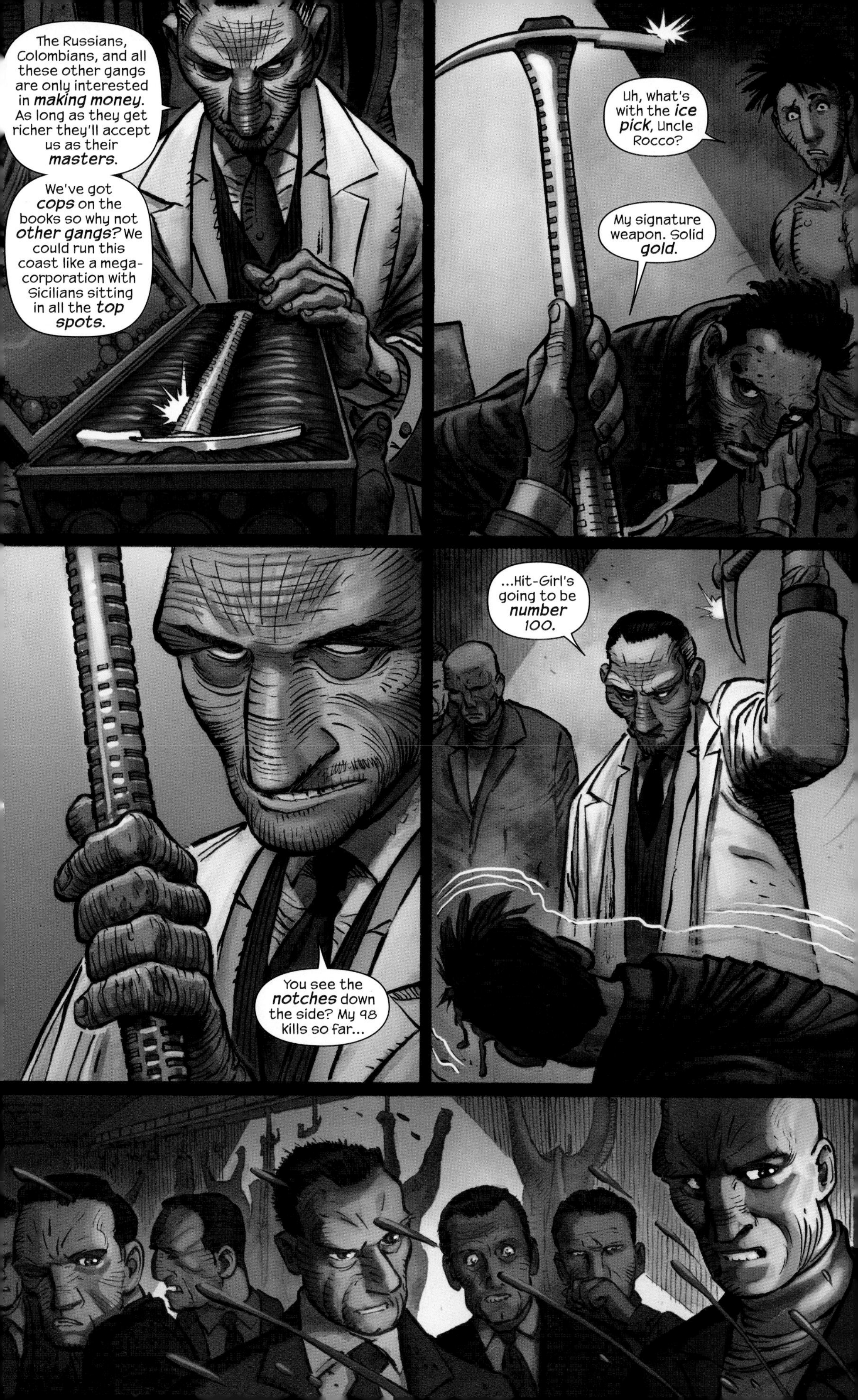

The Russians, Colombians, and all these other gangs are only interested in making money. As long as they get richer they'll accept us as their masters.
We've got cops on the books so why not other gangs? We could run this coast like a mega-corporation with Sicilians sitting in all the top spots.
Uh, what's with the ice pick, Uncle Rocco?
My signature weapon. Solid gold.
You see the notches down the side? My 98 kills so far...
...Hit-Girl's going to be number 100.

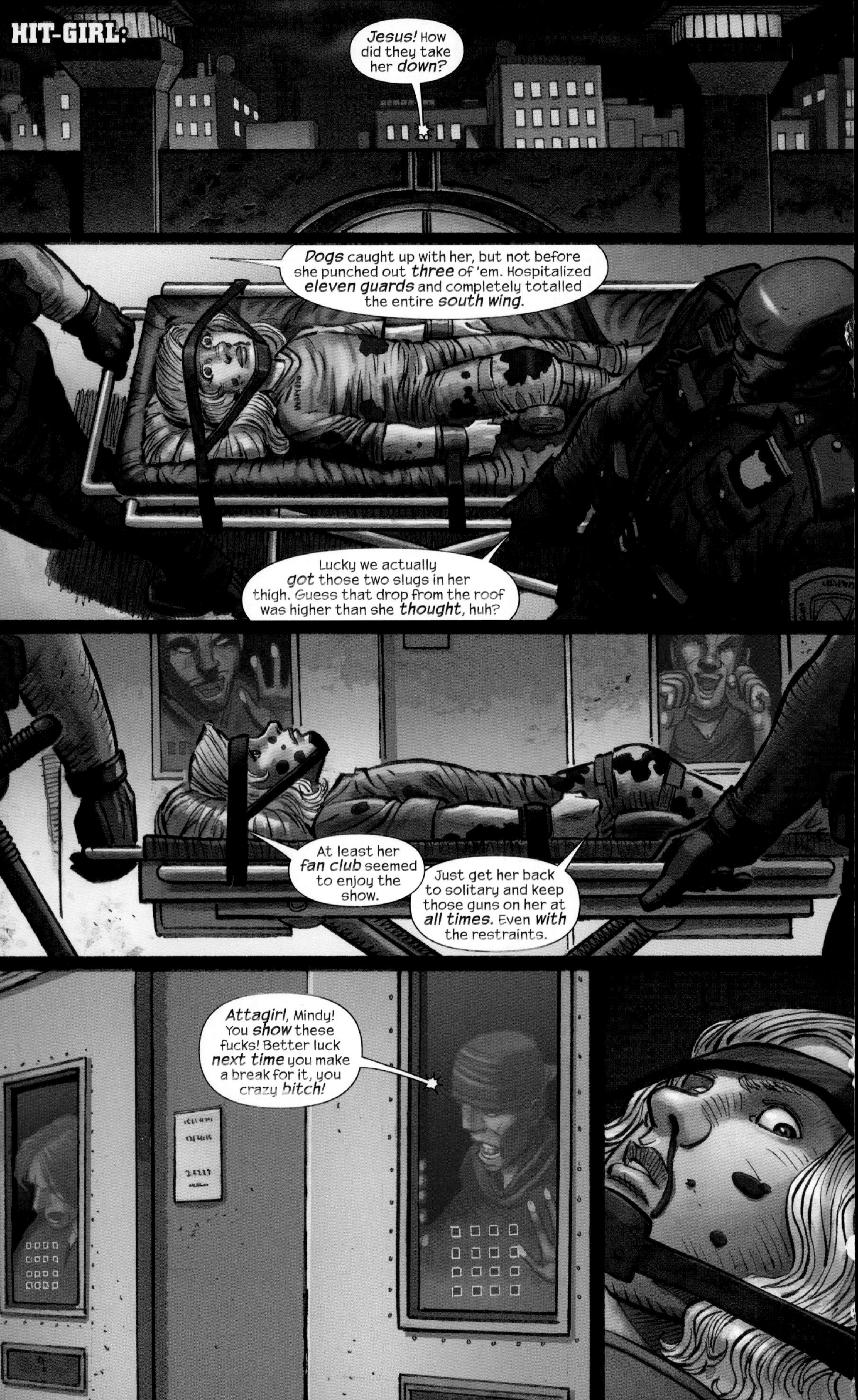
HIT-GIRL:
Jesus! How did they take her down?
Dogs caught up with her, but not before she punched out three of 'em. Hospitalized eleven guards and completely totalled the entire south wing.
Lucky we actually got those two slugs in her thigh. Guess that drop from the roof was higher than she thought, huh?
At least her fan club seemed to enjoy the show.
Just get her back to solitary and keep those guns on her at all times. Even with the restraints.
Attagirl, Mindy! You show these fucks! Better luck next time you make a break for it, you crazy bitch!

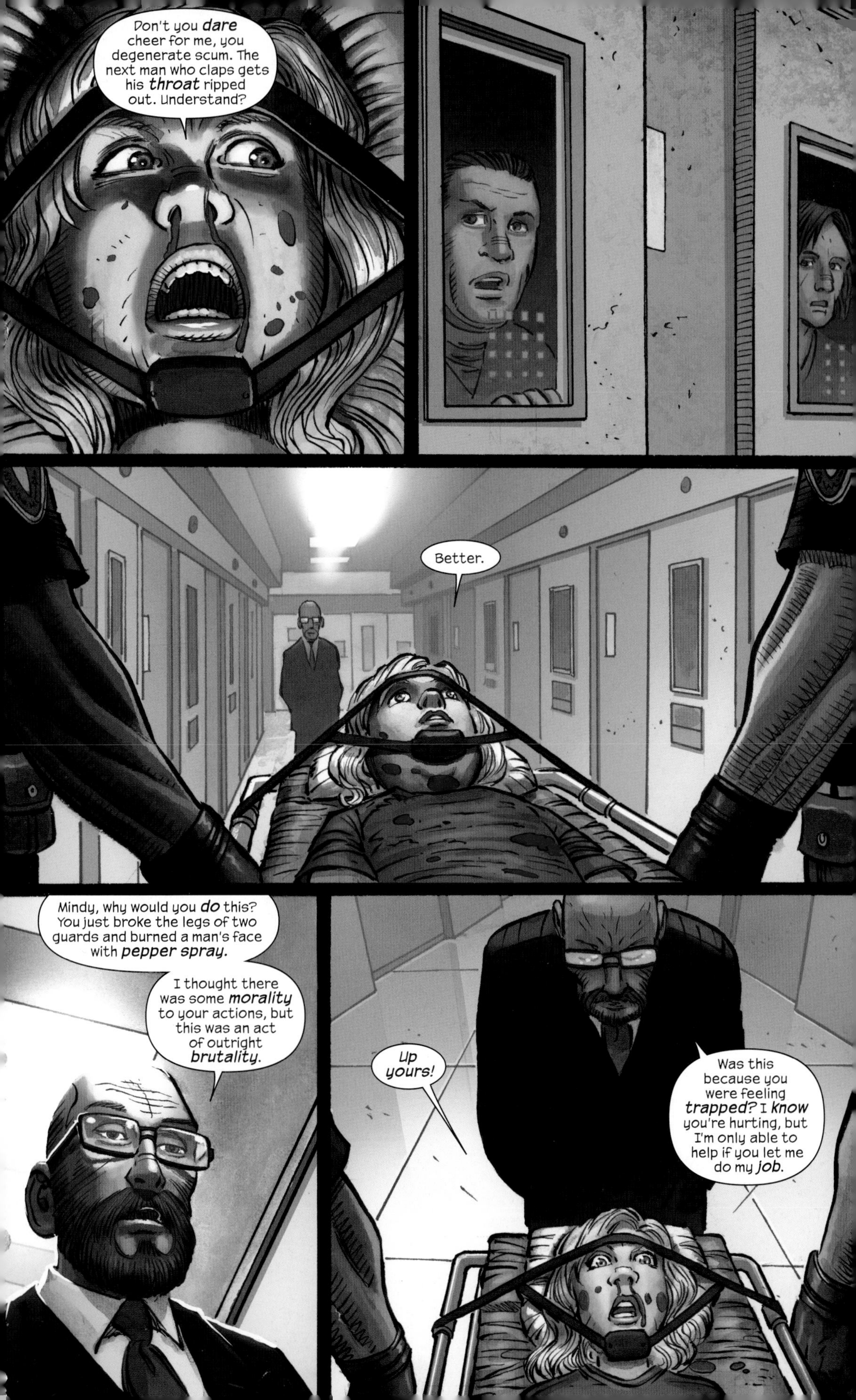
Don't you dare cheer for me, you degenerate scum. The next man who claps gets his throat ripped out. Understand?
Better.
Mindy, why would you do this? You just broke the legs of two guards and burned a man's face with pepper spray.
I thought there was some morality to your actions, but this was an act of outright brutality.
Up yours!
Was this because you were feeling trapped? I know you're hurting, but I'm only able to help if you let me do my job.

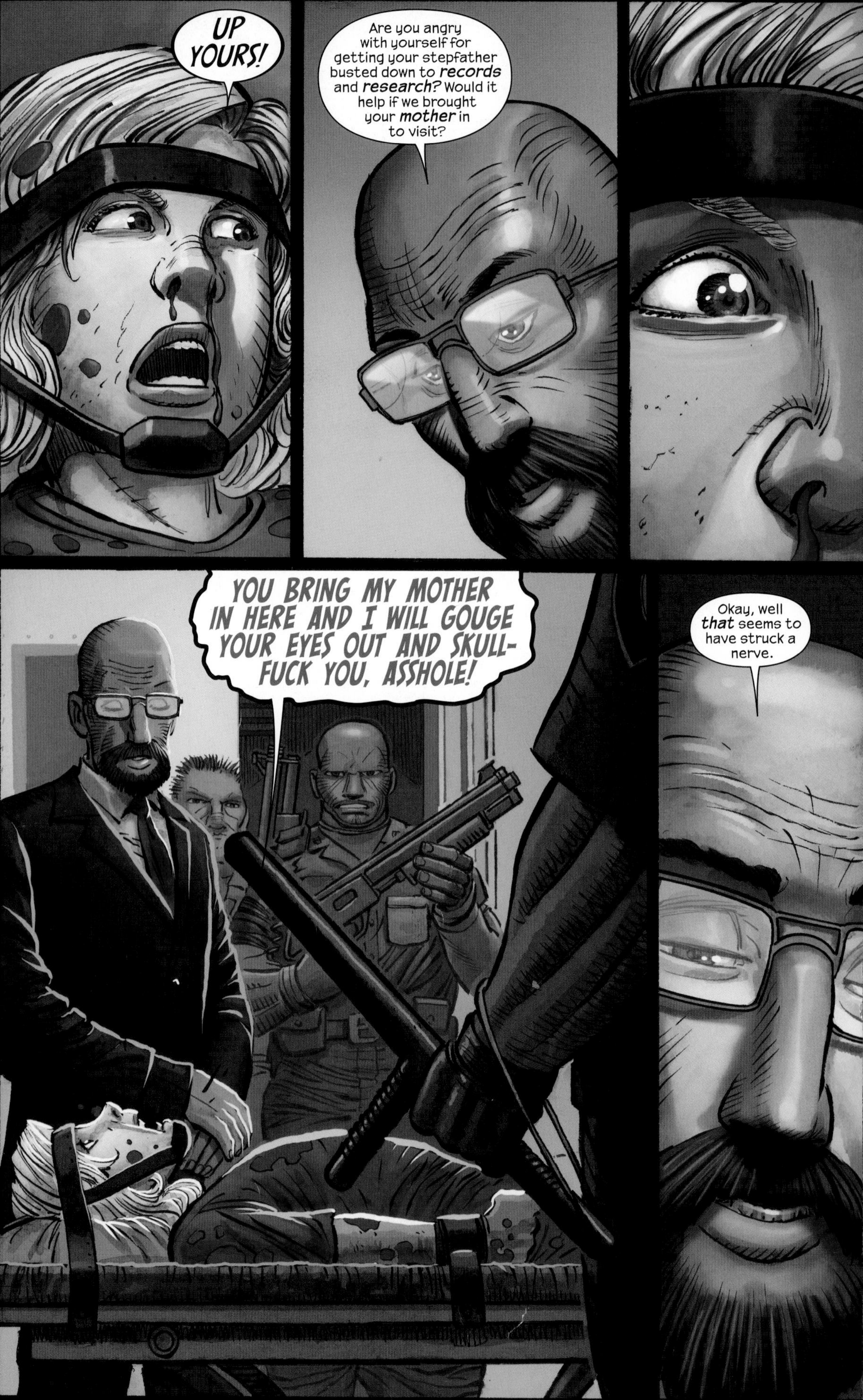
UP YOURS!
Are you angry with yourself for getting your stepfather busted down to records and research? Would it help if we brought your mother in to visit?
YOU BRING MY MOTHER IN HERE AND I WILL GOUGE YOUR EYES OUT AND SKULL-FUCK YOU, ASSHOLE!
Okay, well that seems to have struck a nerve.

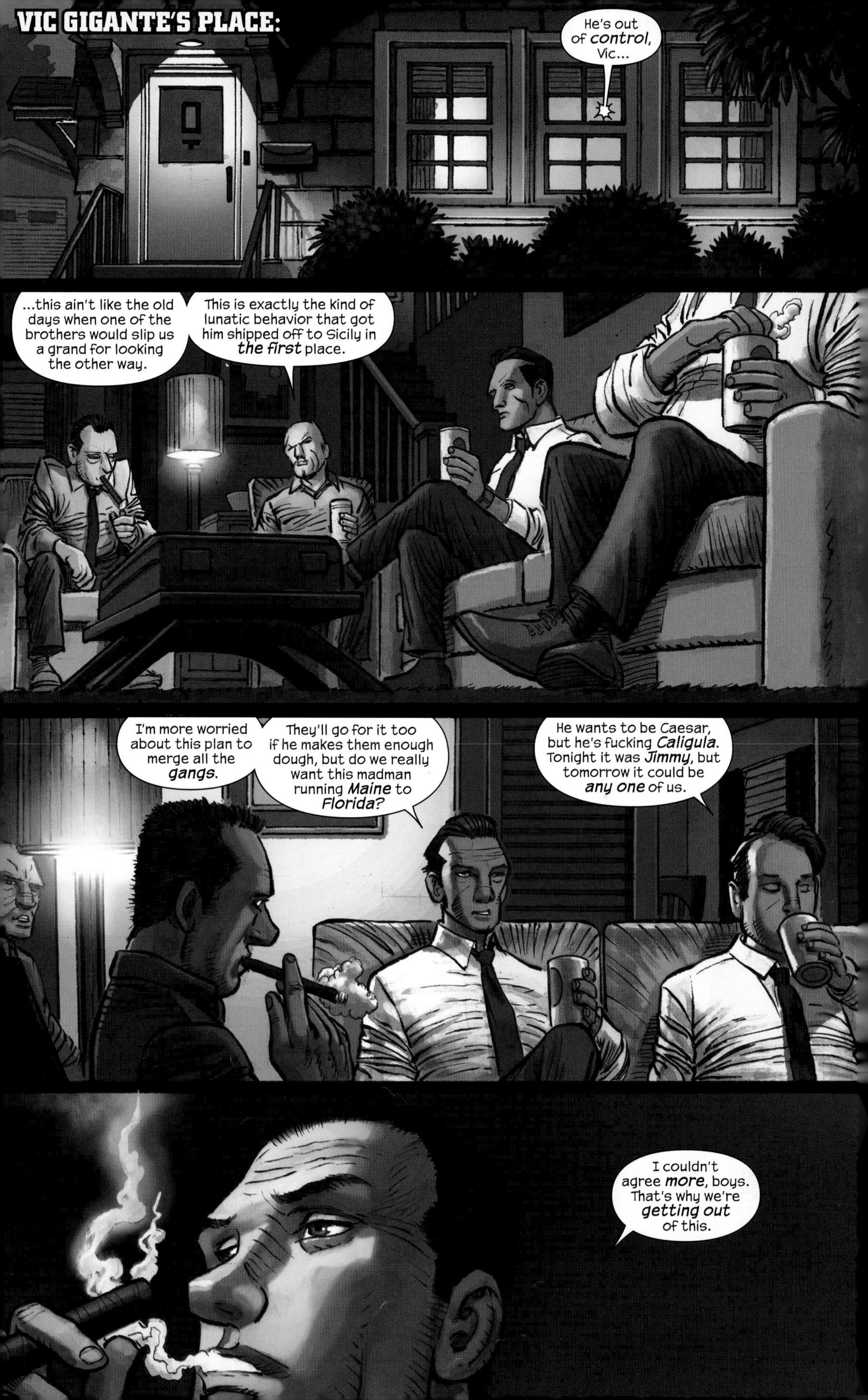
VIC GIGANTE'S PLACE:
He's out of *control*, Vic...
...this ain't like the old days when one of the brothers would slip us a grand for looking the other way.
This is exactly the kind of lunatic behavior that got him shipped off to Sicily in *the first* place.
I'm more worried about this plan to merge all the *gangs*.
They'll go for it too if he makes them enough dough, but do we really want this madman running *Maine* to *Florida*?
He wants to be Caesar, but he's fucking *Caligula*. Tonight it was *Jimmy*, but tomorrow it could be *any one* of us.
I couldn't agree *more*, boys. That's why we're *getting out* of this.

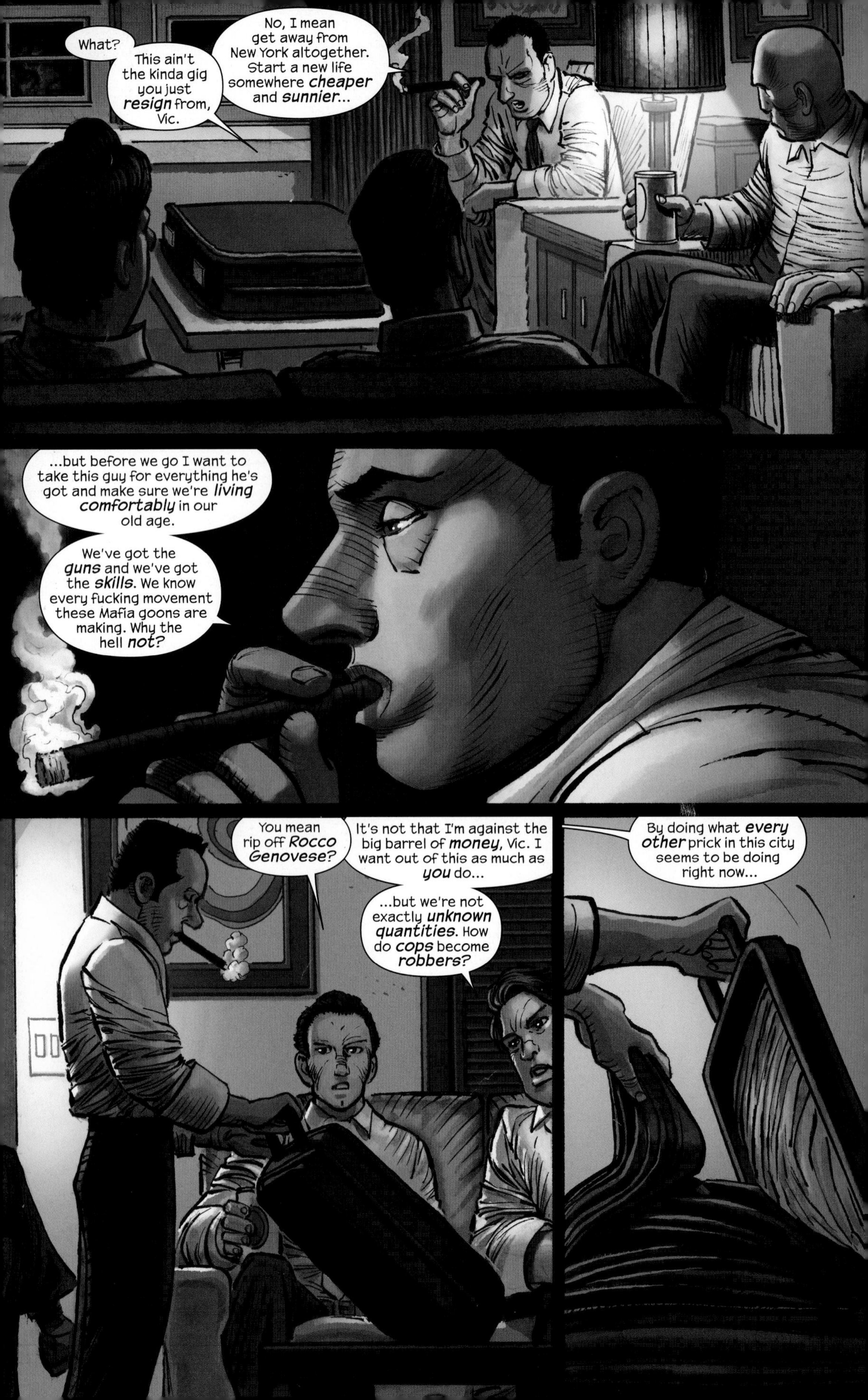
What?
This ain't the kinda gig you just resign from, Vic.
No, I mean get away from New York altogether. Start a new life somewhere cheaper and sunnier...
...but before we go I want to take this guy for everything he's got and make sure we're living comfortably in our old age.
We've got the guns and we've got the skills. We know every fucking movement these Mafia goons are making. Why the hell not?
You mean rip off Rocco Genovese?
It's not that I'm against the big barrel of money, Vic. I want out of this as much as you do...
...but we're not exactly unknown quantities. How do cops become robbers?
By doing what every other prick in this city seems to be doing right now...

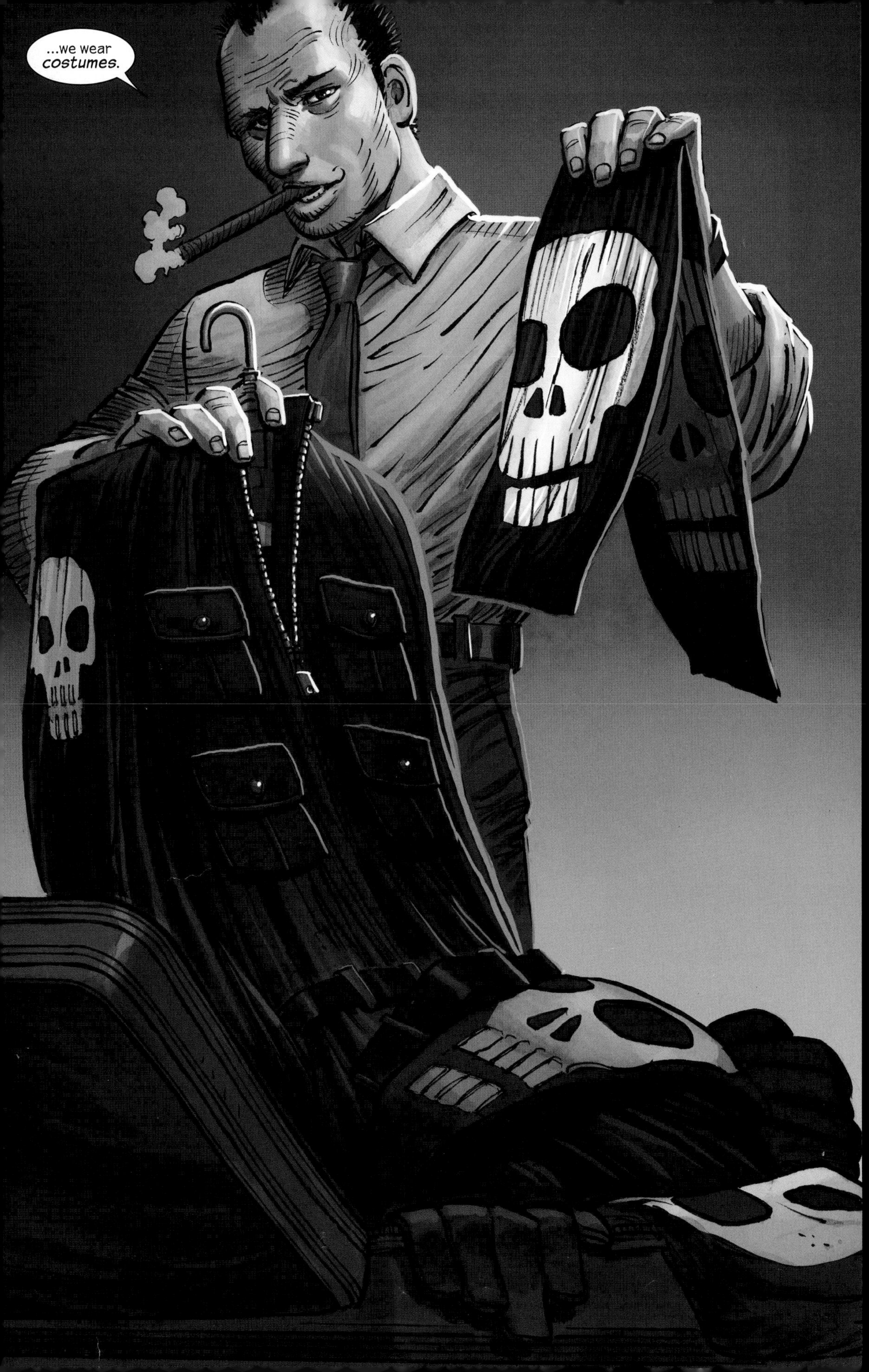
...we wear costumes.

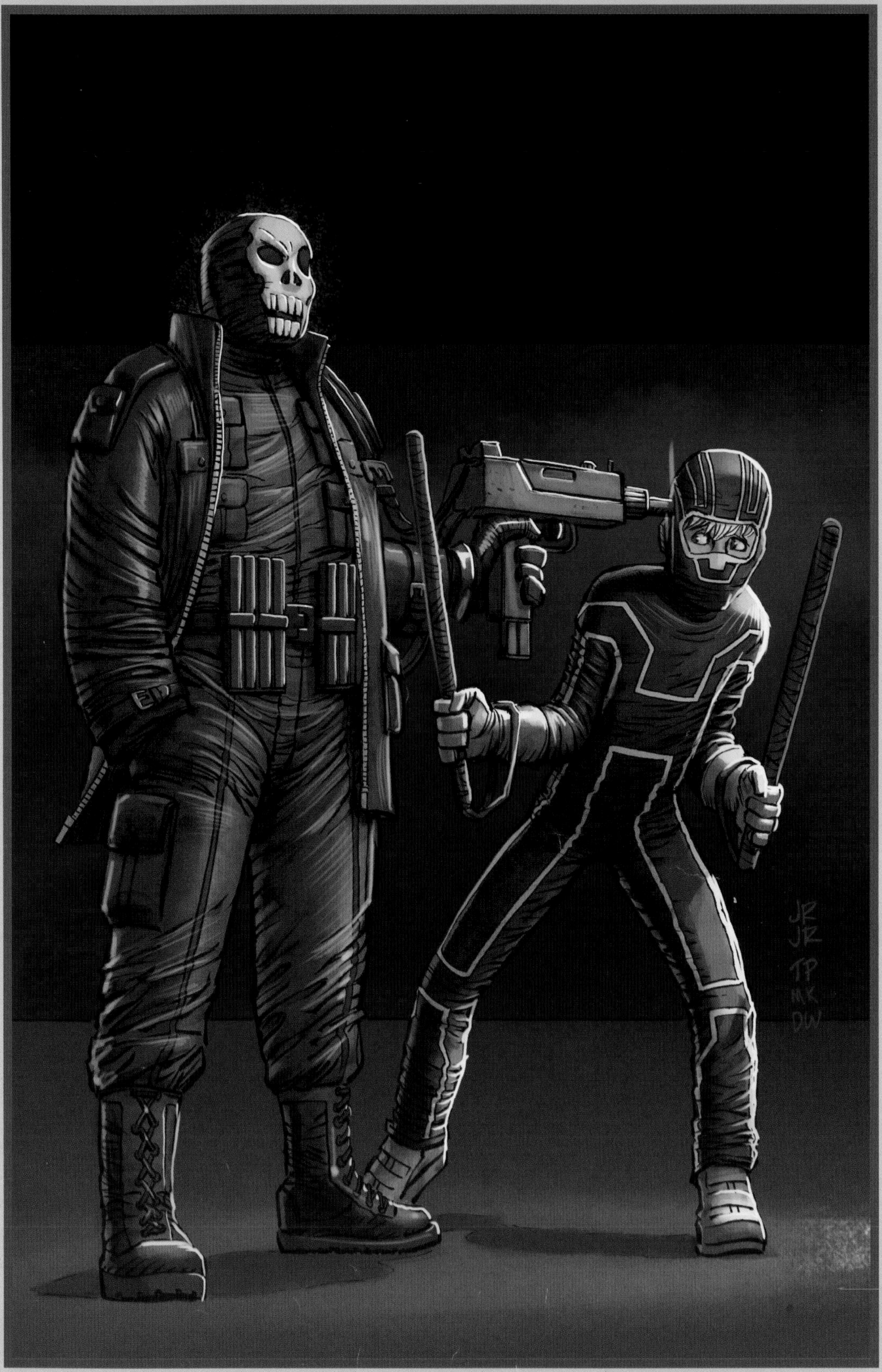
JR
JR
TP
MK
DW

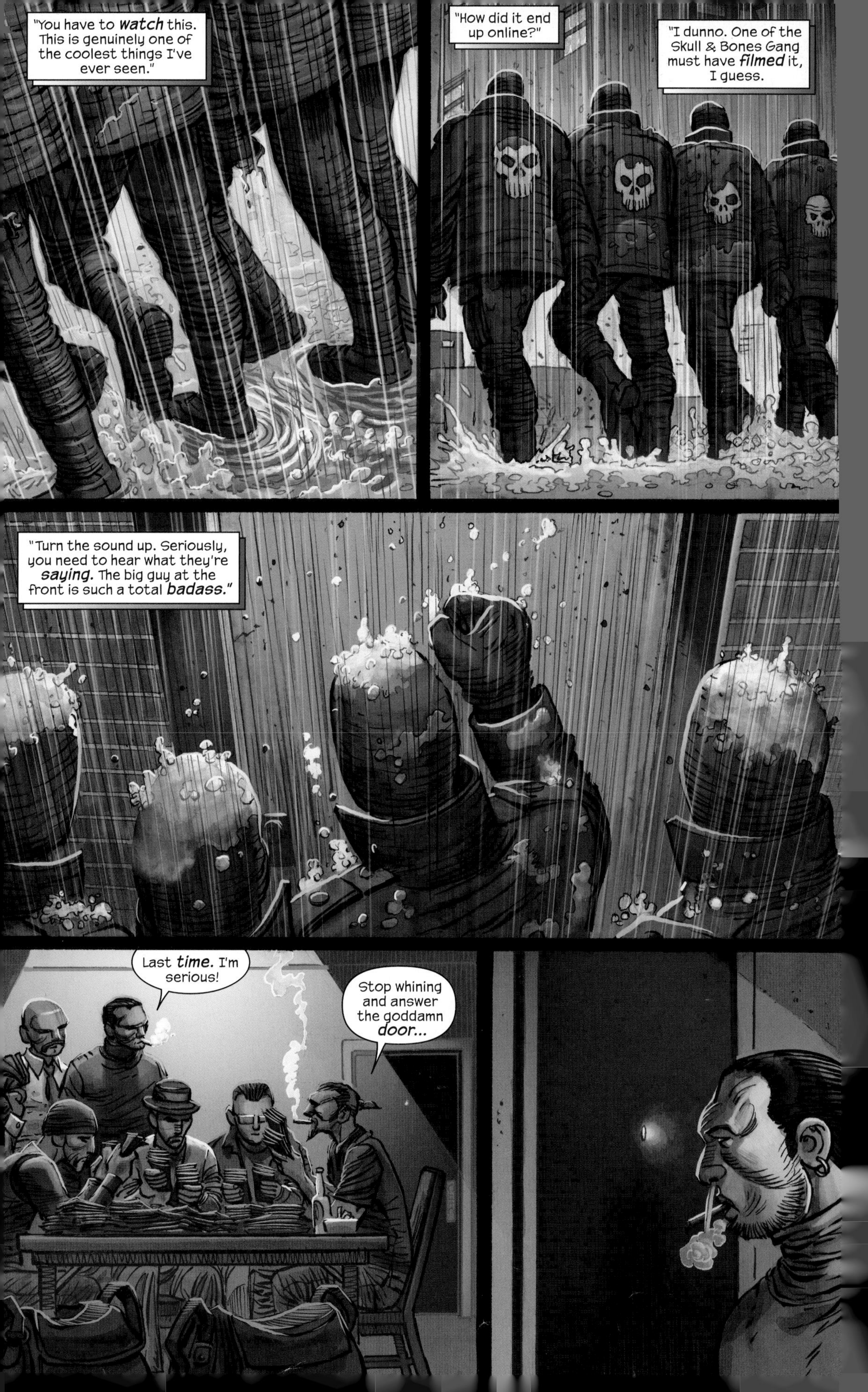
"You have to watch this. This is genuinely one of the coolest things I've ever seen."
"How did it end up online?"
"I dunno. One of the Skull & Bones Gang must have filmed it, I guess.
"Turn the sound up. Seriously, you need to hear what they're saying. The big guy at the front is such a total badass."
Last time. I'm serious!
Stop whining and answer the goddamn door...

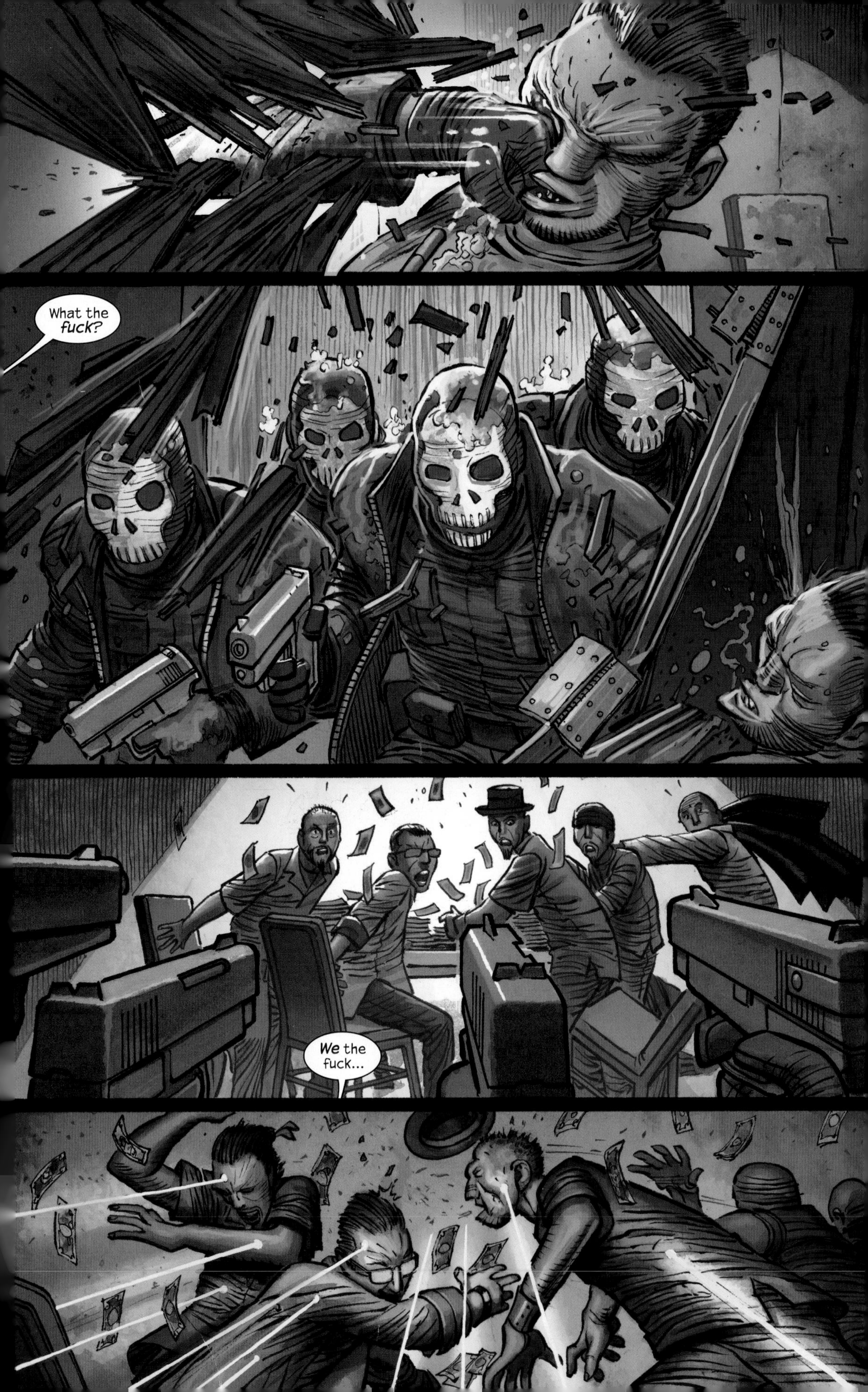
What the *fuck?*
We the fuck...

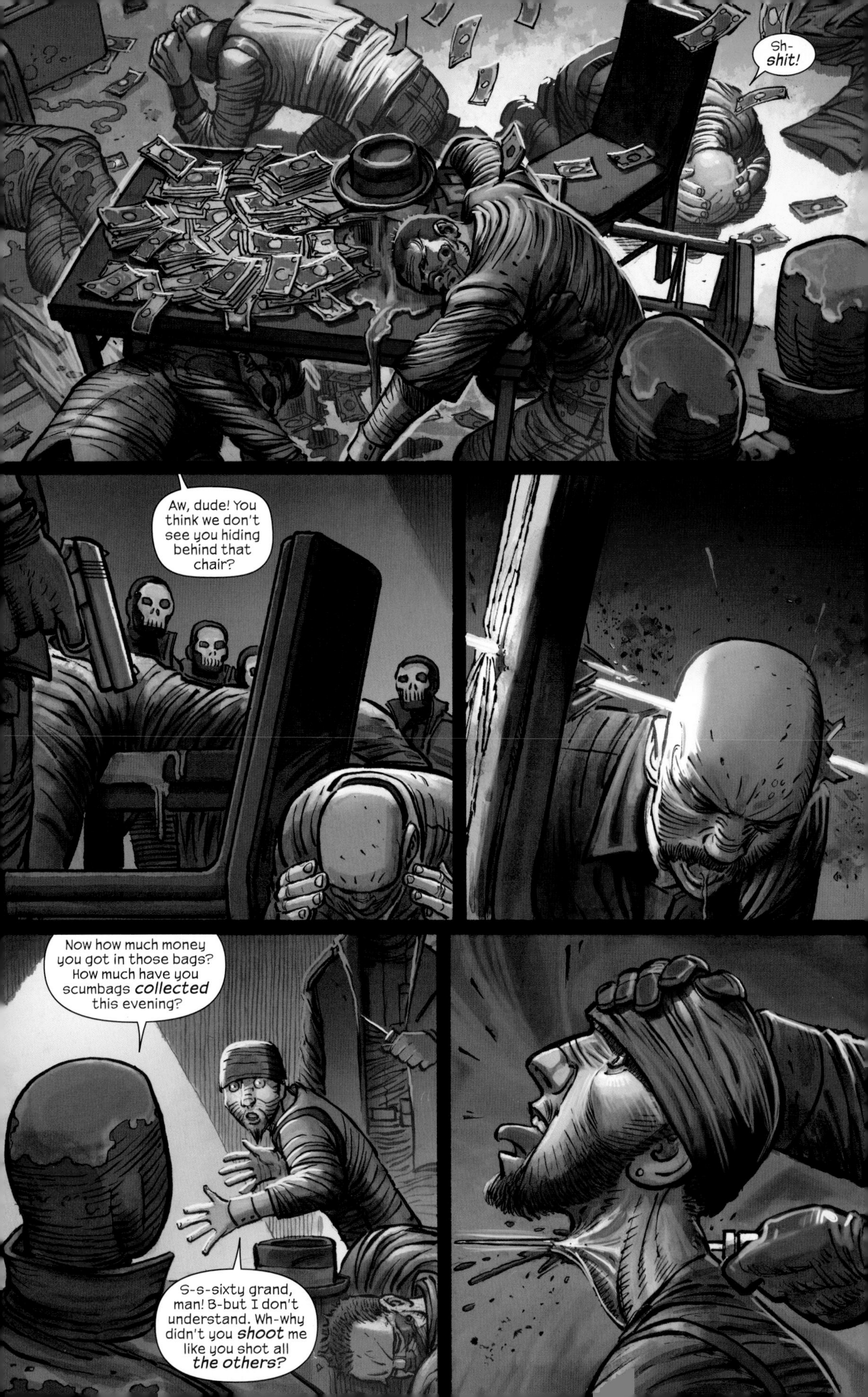
Sh-shit!
Aw, dude! You think we don't see you hiding behind that chair?
Now how much money you got in those bags? How much have you scumbags *collected* this evening?
S-s-sixty grand, man! B-but I don't understand. Wh-why didn't you *shoot* me like you shot all *the others*?

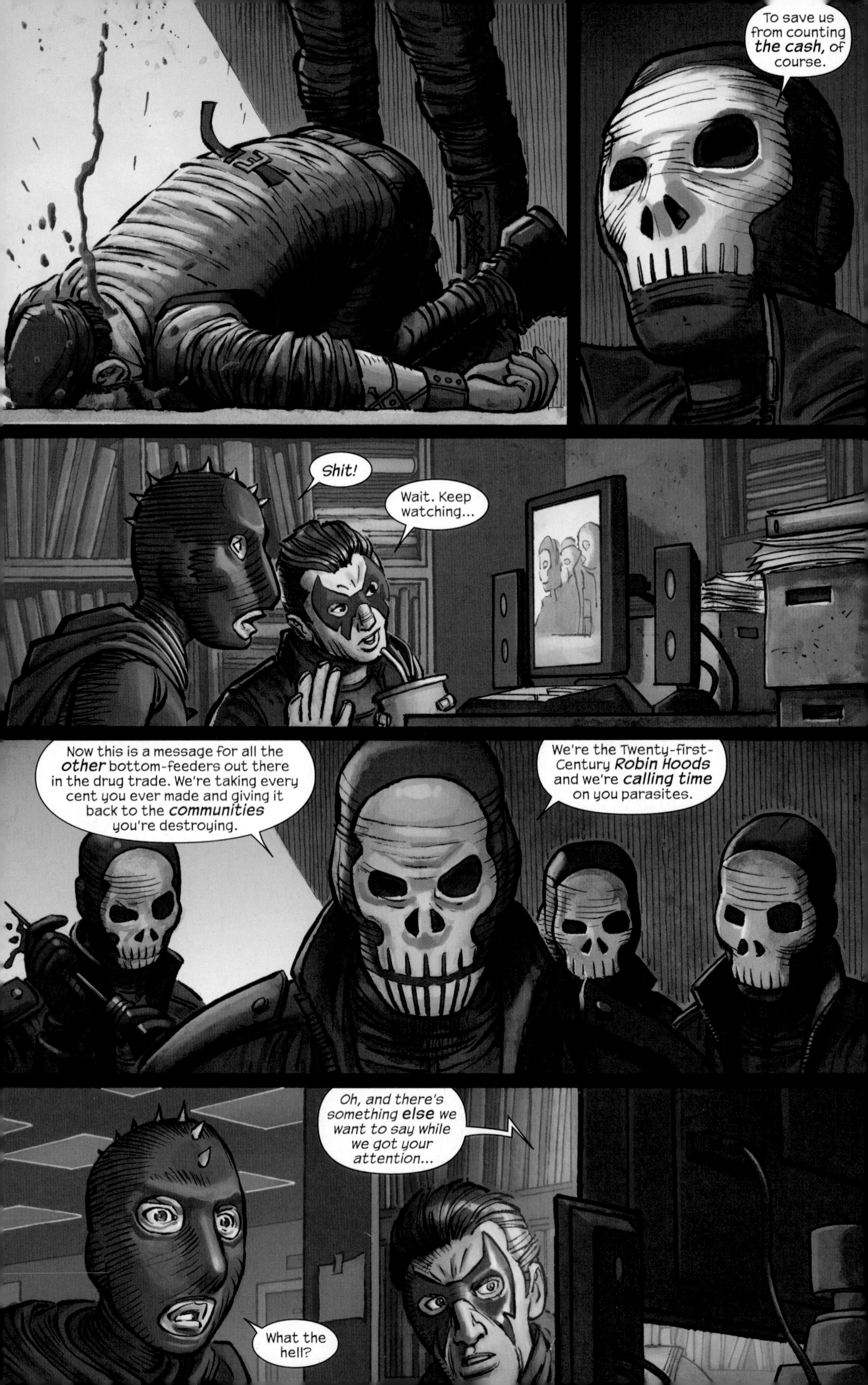
To save us from counting the cash, of course.
Shit!
Wait. Keep watching...
Now this is a message for all the other bottom-feeders out there in the drug trade. We're taking every cent you ever made and giving it back to the communities you're destroying.
We're the Twenty-first-Century Robin Hoods and we're calling time on you parasites.
Oh, and there's something else we want to say while we got your attention...
What the hell?

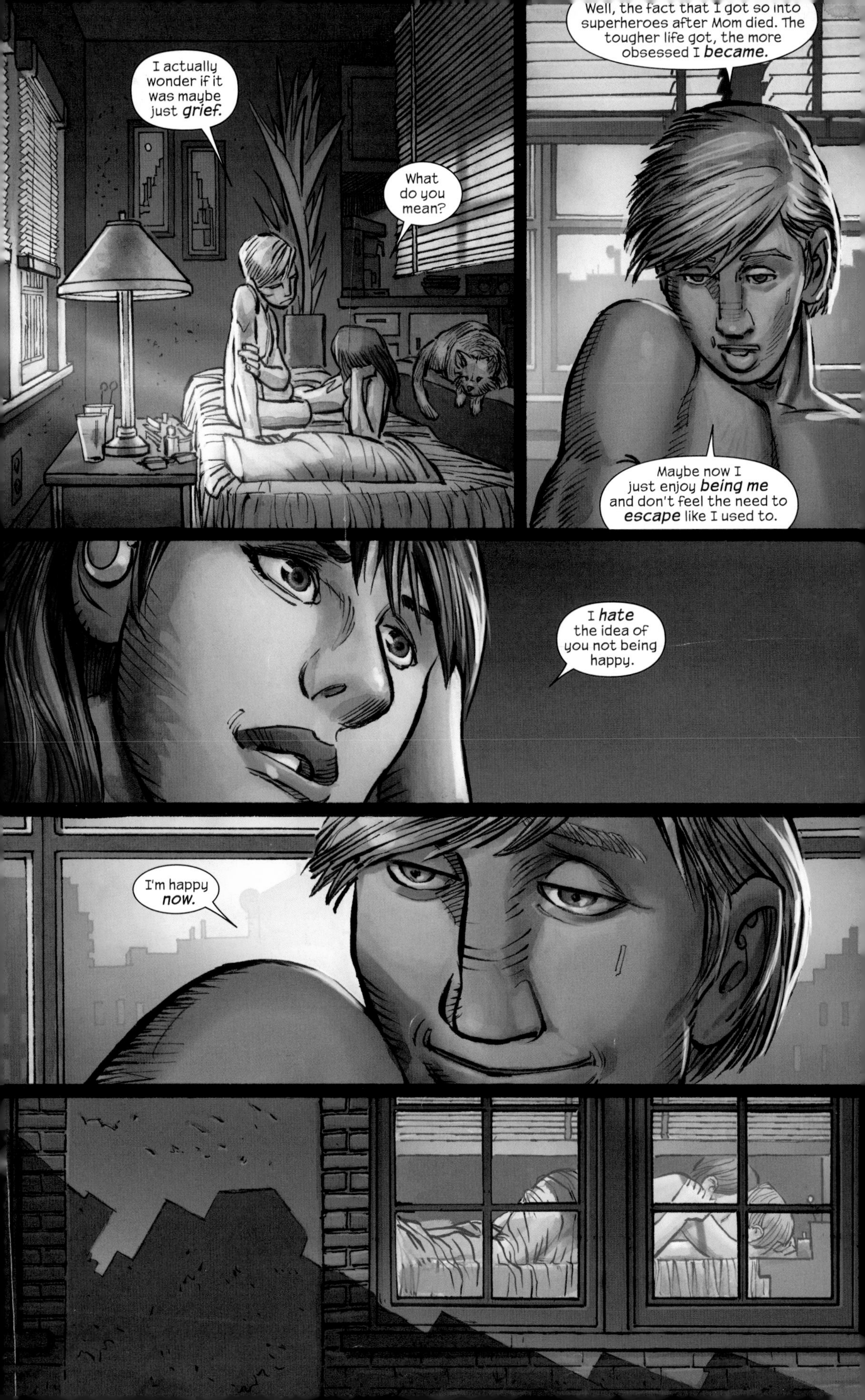
I actually wonder if it was maybe just *grief.*
What do you mean?
Well, the fact that I got so into superheroes after Mom died. The tougher life got, the more obsessed I *became.*
Maybe now I just enjoy *being me* and don't feel the need to *escape* like I used to.
I *hate* the idea of you not being happy.
I'm happy *now.*

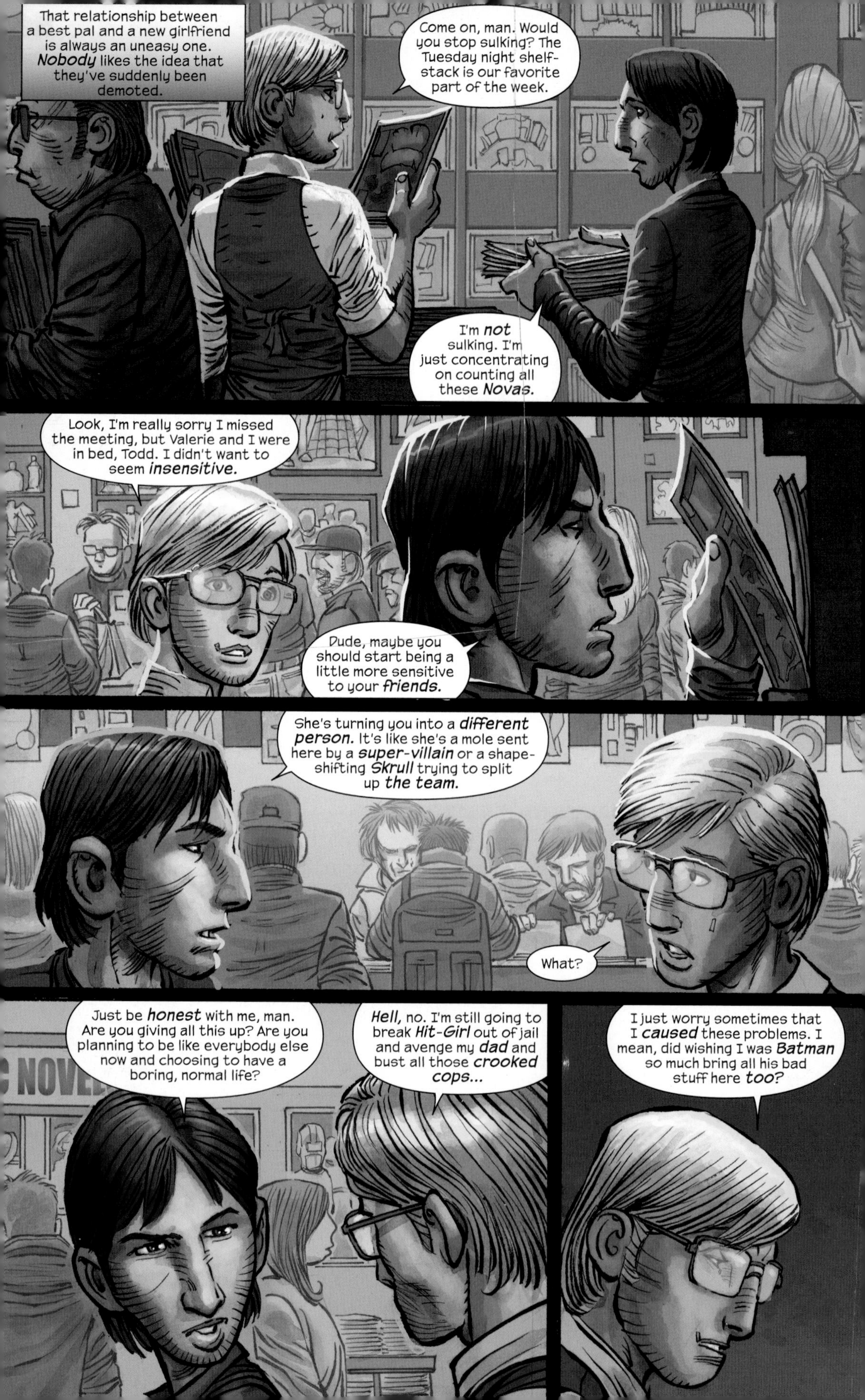
That relationship between a best pal and a new girlfriend is always an uneasy one. *Nobody* likes the idea that they've suddenly been demoted.
Come on, man. Would you stop sulking? The Tuesday night shelf-stack is our favorite part of the week.
I'm *not* sulking. I'm just concentrating on counting all these *Novas.*
Look, I'm really sorry I missed the meeting, but Valerie and I were in bed, Todd. I didn't want to seem *insensitive.*
Dude, maybe you should start being a little more sensitive to your *friends.*
She's turning you into a *different person.* It's like she's a mole sent here by a *super-villain* or a shape-shifting *Skrull* trying to split up *the team.*
What?
Just be *honest* with me, man. Are you giving all this up? Are you planning to be like everybody else now and choosing to have a boring, normal life?
Hell, no. I'm still going to break *Hit-Girl* out of jail and avenge my *dad* and bust all those *crooked cops...*
I just worry sometimes that I *caused* these problems. I mean, did wishing I was *Batman* so much bring all his bad stuff here *too?*

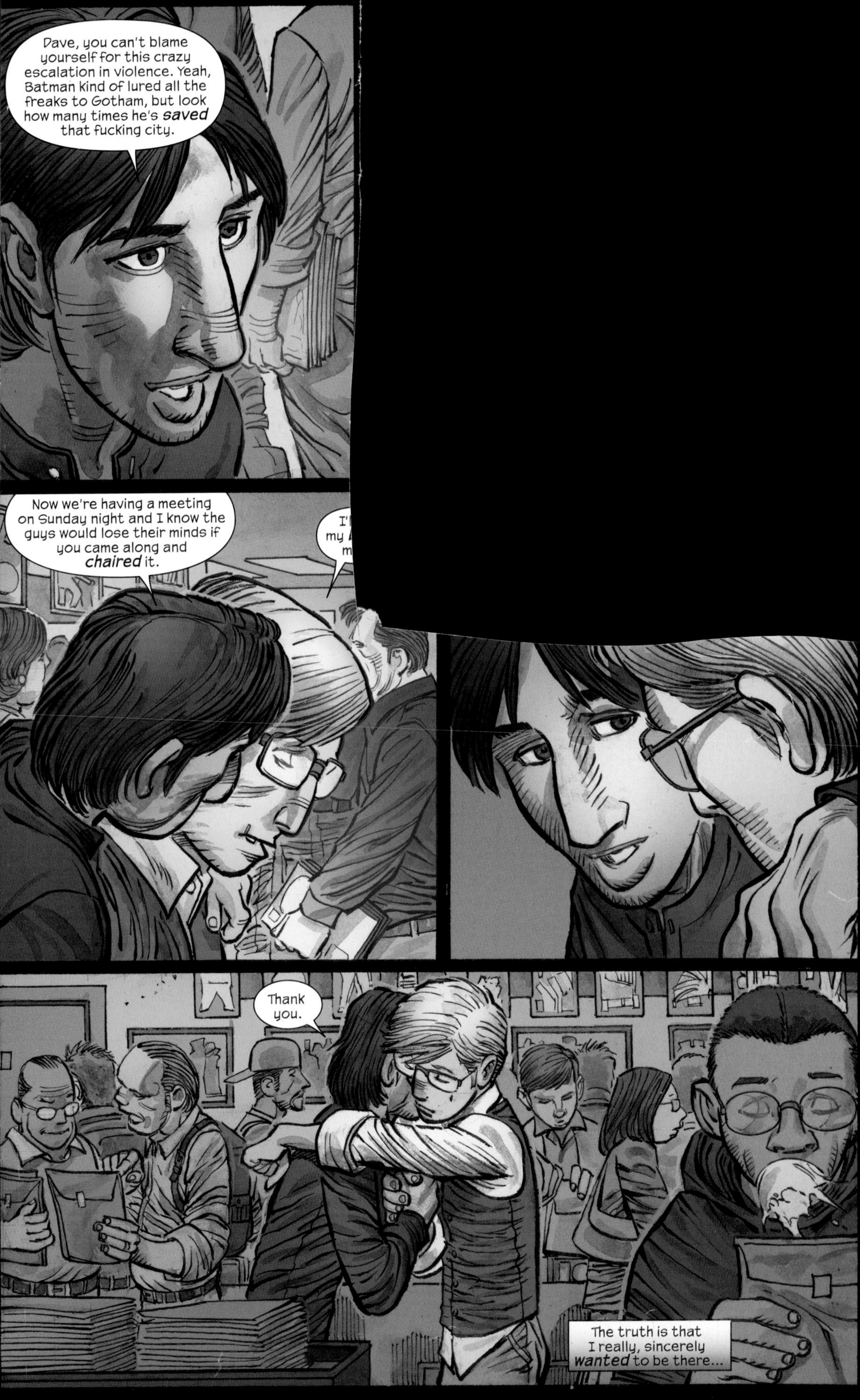
Dave, you can't blame yourself for this crazy escalation in violence. Yeah, Batman kind of lured all the freaks to Gotham, but look how many times he's *saved* that fucking city.
Now we're having a meeting on Sunday night and I know the guys would lose their minds if you came along and *chaired* it.
[redacted]
Thank you.
The truth is that I really, sincerely *wanted* to be there...

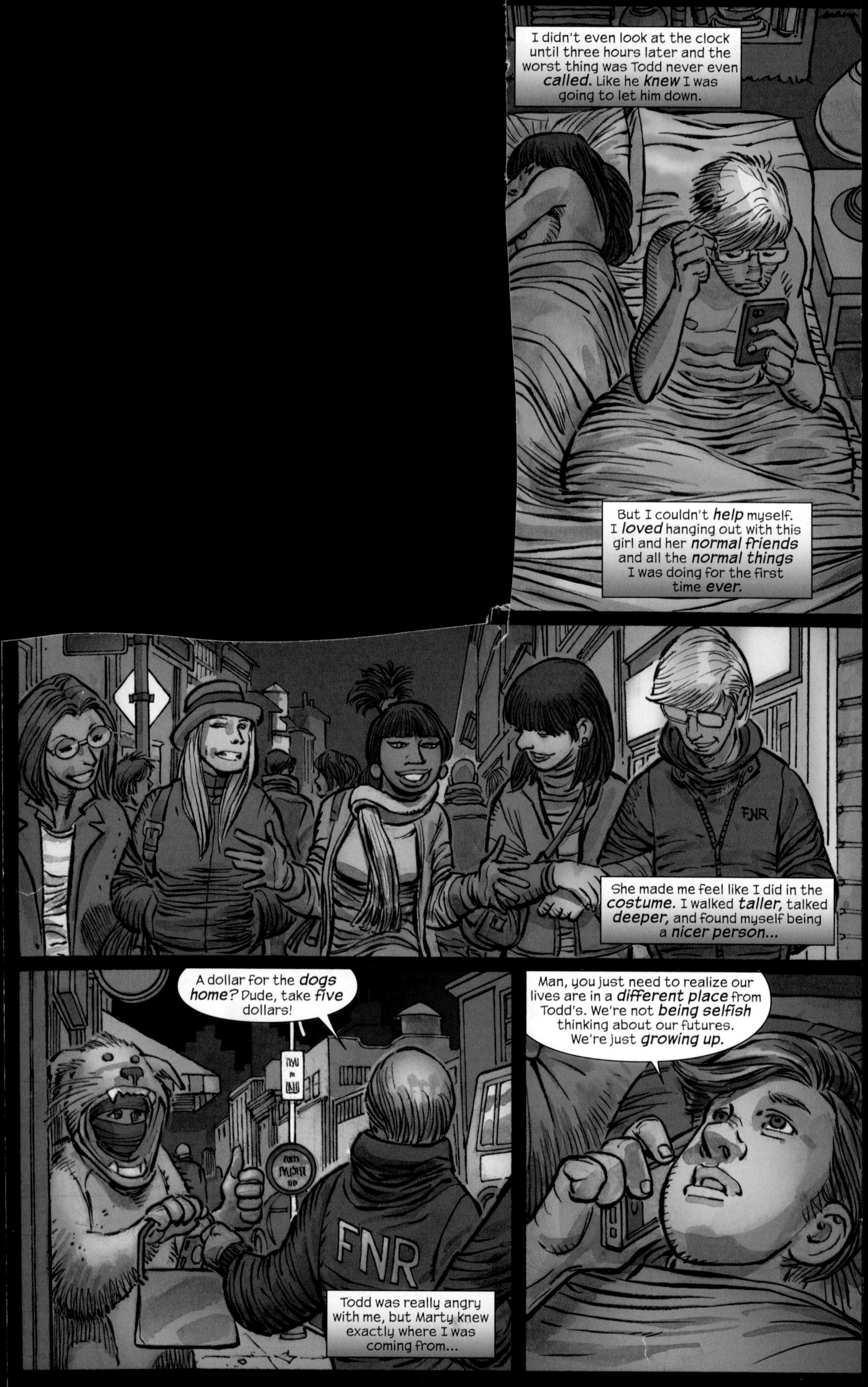
I didn't even look at the clock until three hours later and the worst thing was Todd never even *called.* Like he *knew* I was going to let him down.
But I couldn't *help* myself. I *loved* hanging out with this girl and her *normal friends* and all the *normal things* I was doing for the first time *ever.*
She made me feel like I did in the *costume.* I walked *taller,* talked *deeper,* and found myself being a *nicer person...*
FNR
A dollar for the *dogs home?* Dude, take *five* dollars!
FNR
Todd was really angry with me, but Marty knew exactly where I was coming from...
Man, you just need to realize our lives are in a *different place* from Todd's. We're not *being selfish* thinking about our futures. We're just *growing up.*

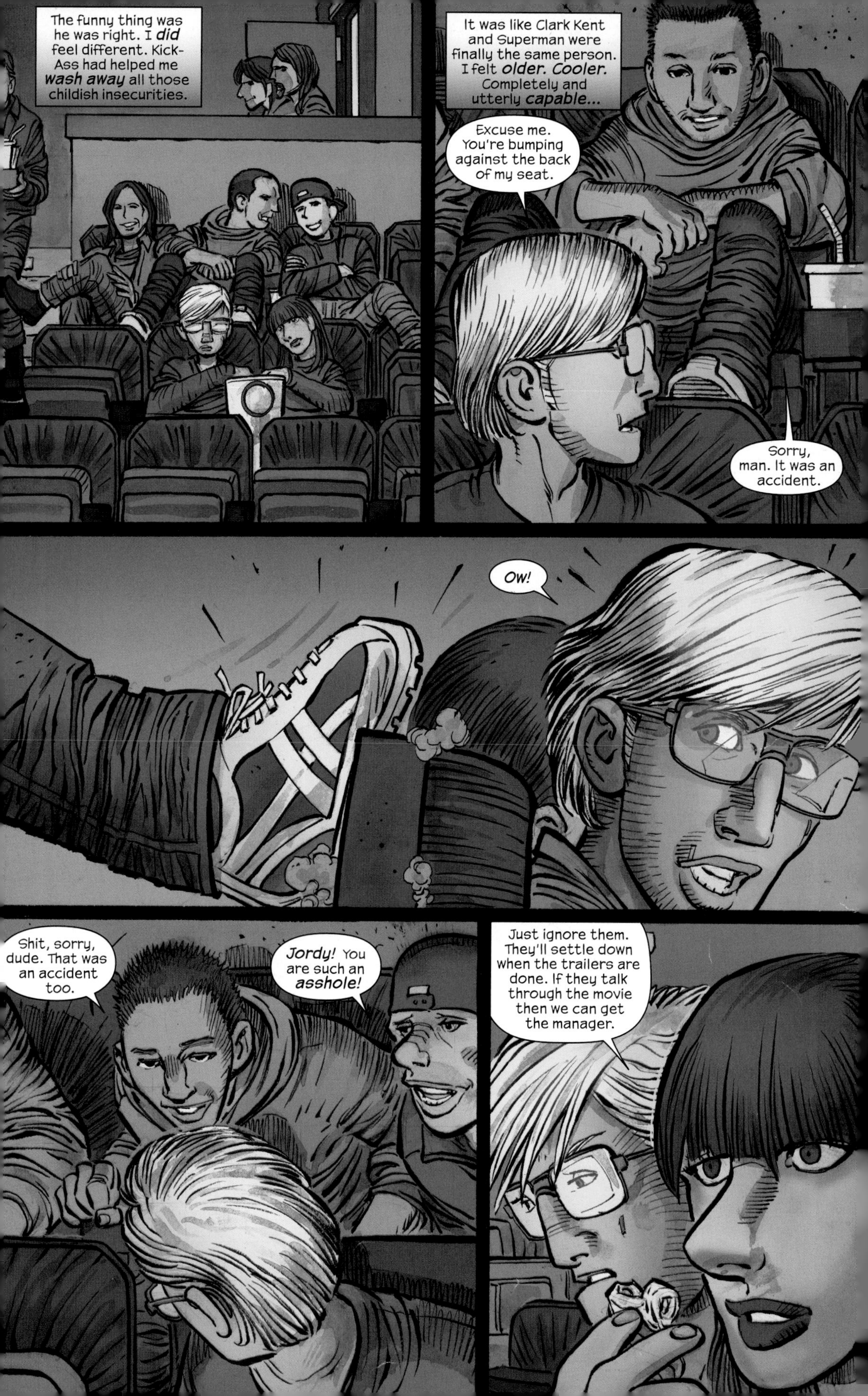
The funny thing was he was right. I *did* feel different. Kick-Ass had helped me ***wash away*** all those childish insecurities.
It was like Clark Kent and Superman were finally the same person. I felt ***older. Cooler.*** Completely and utterly ***capable...***
Excuse me. You're bumping against the back of my seat.
Sorry, man. It was an accident.
Ow!
Shit, sorry, dude. That was an accident too.
Jordy! You are such an ***asshole!***
Just ignore them. They'll settle down when the trailers are done. If they talk through the movie then we can get the manager.

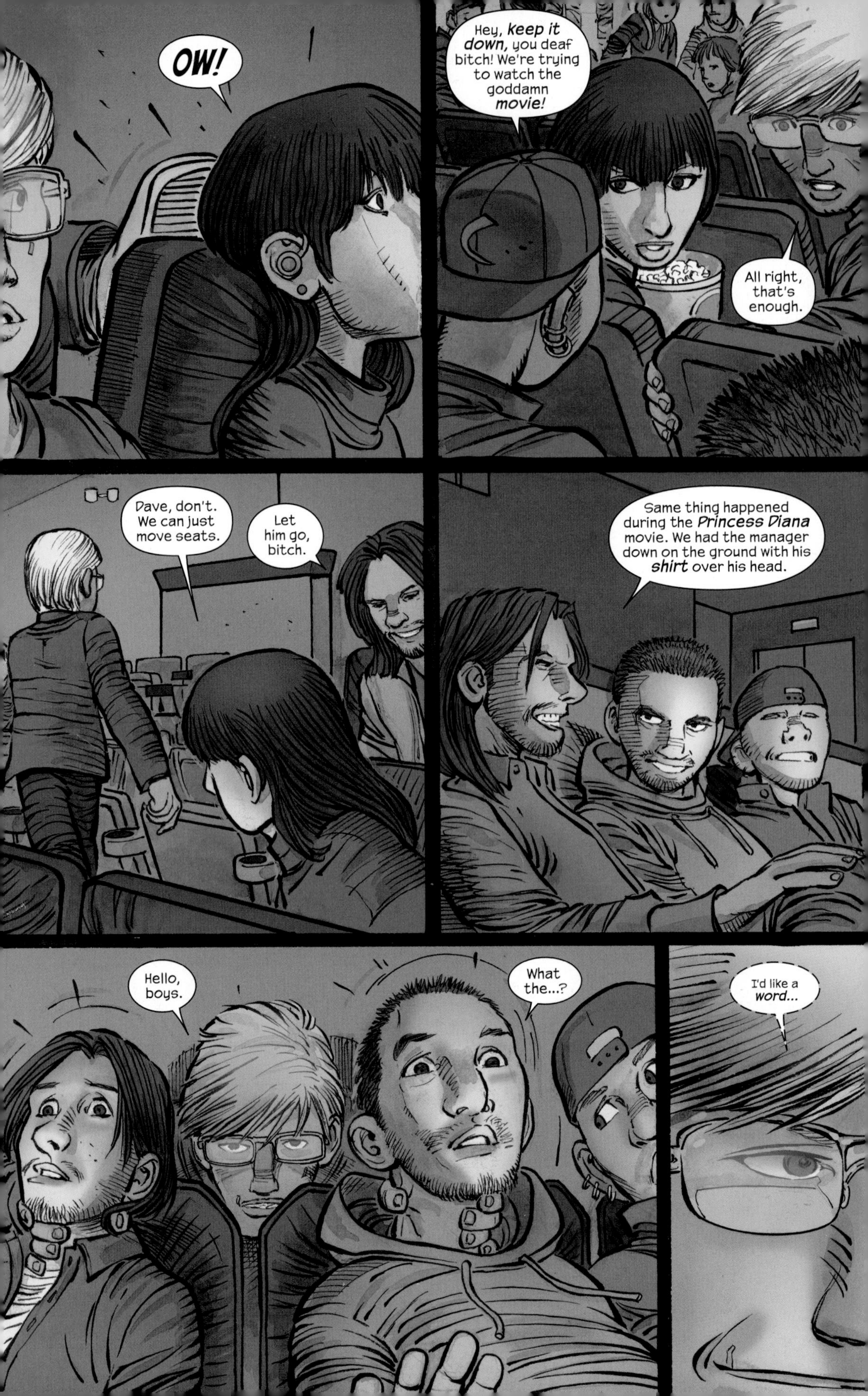
OW!
Hey, keep it down, you deaf bitch! We're trying to watch the goddamn movie!
All right, that's enough.
Dave, don't. We can just move seats.
Let him go, bitch.
Same thing happened during the Princess Diana movie. We had the manager down on the ground with his shirt over his head.
Hello, boys.
What the...?
I'd like a word...

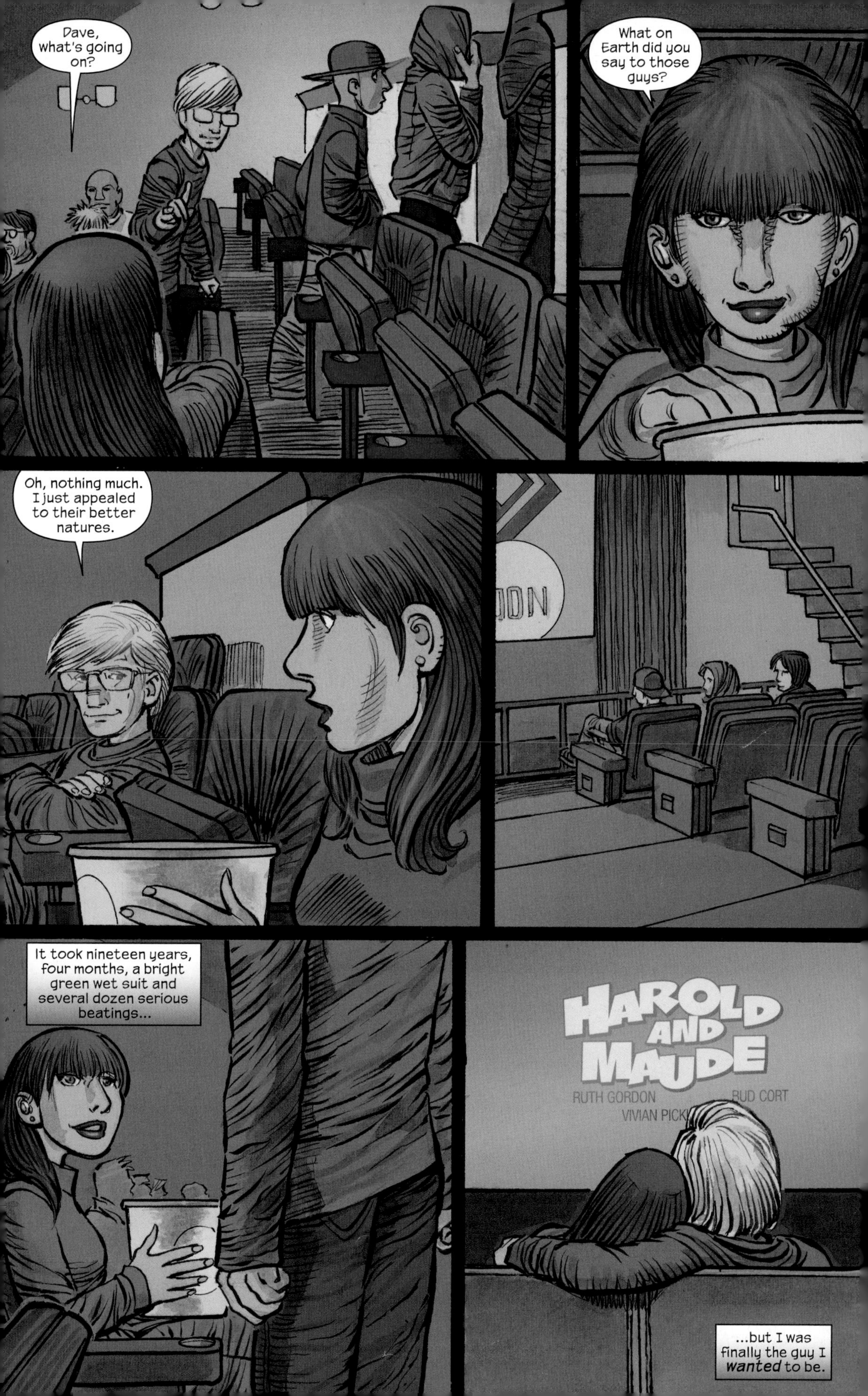
Dave, what's going on?
What on Earth did you say to those guys?
Oh, nothing much. I just appealed to their better natures.
It took nineteen years, four months, a bright green wet suit and several dozen serious beatings...
HAROLD AND MAUDE
RUTH GORDON
BUD CORT
...but I was finally the guy I *wanted* to be.

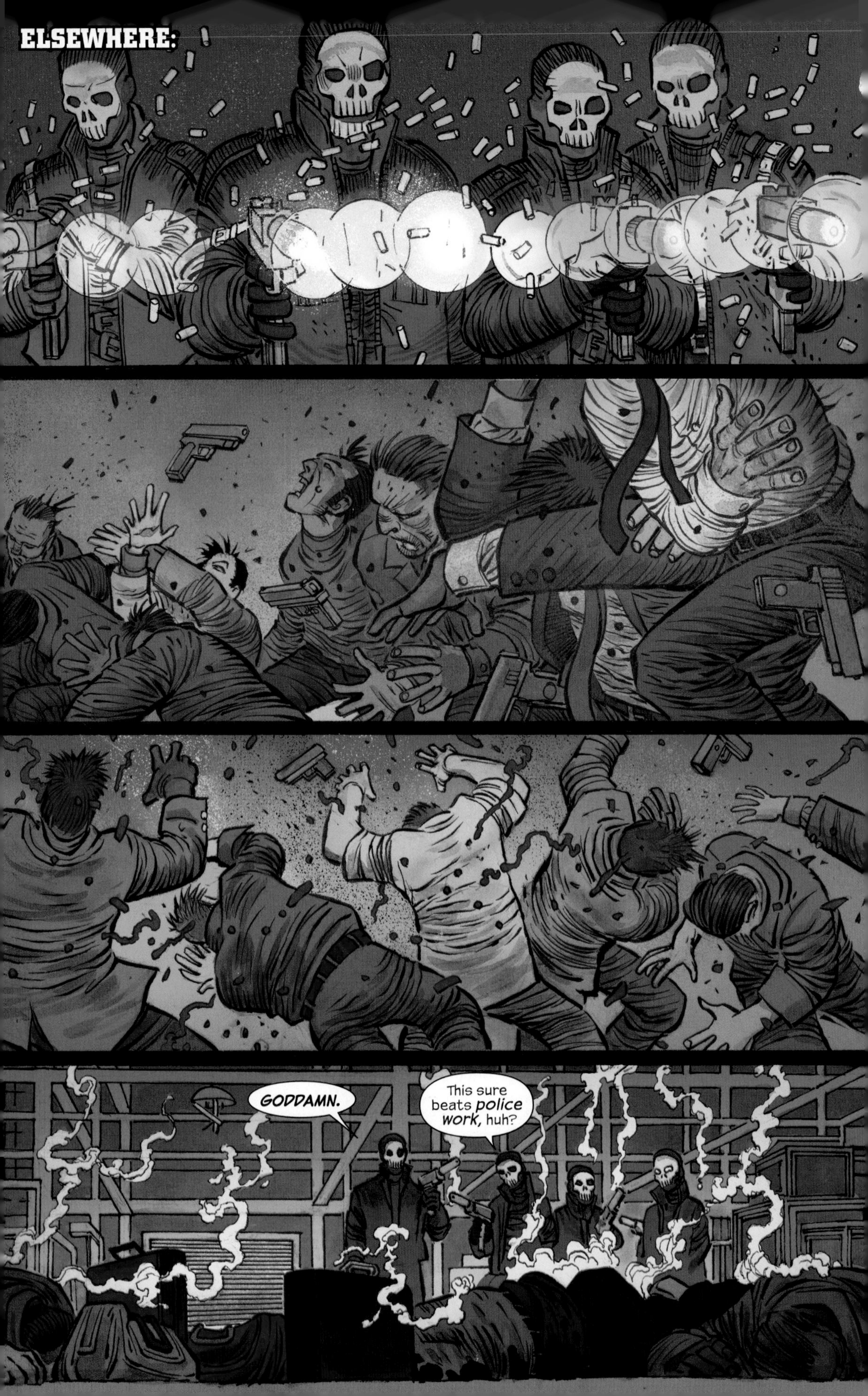
ELSEWHERE:
GODDAMN.
This sure beats police work, huh?

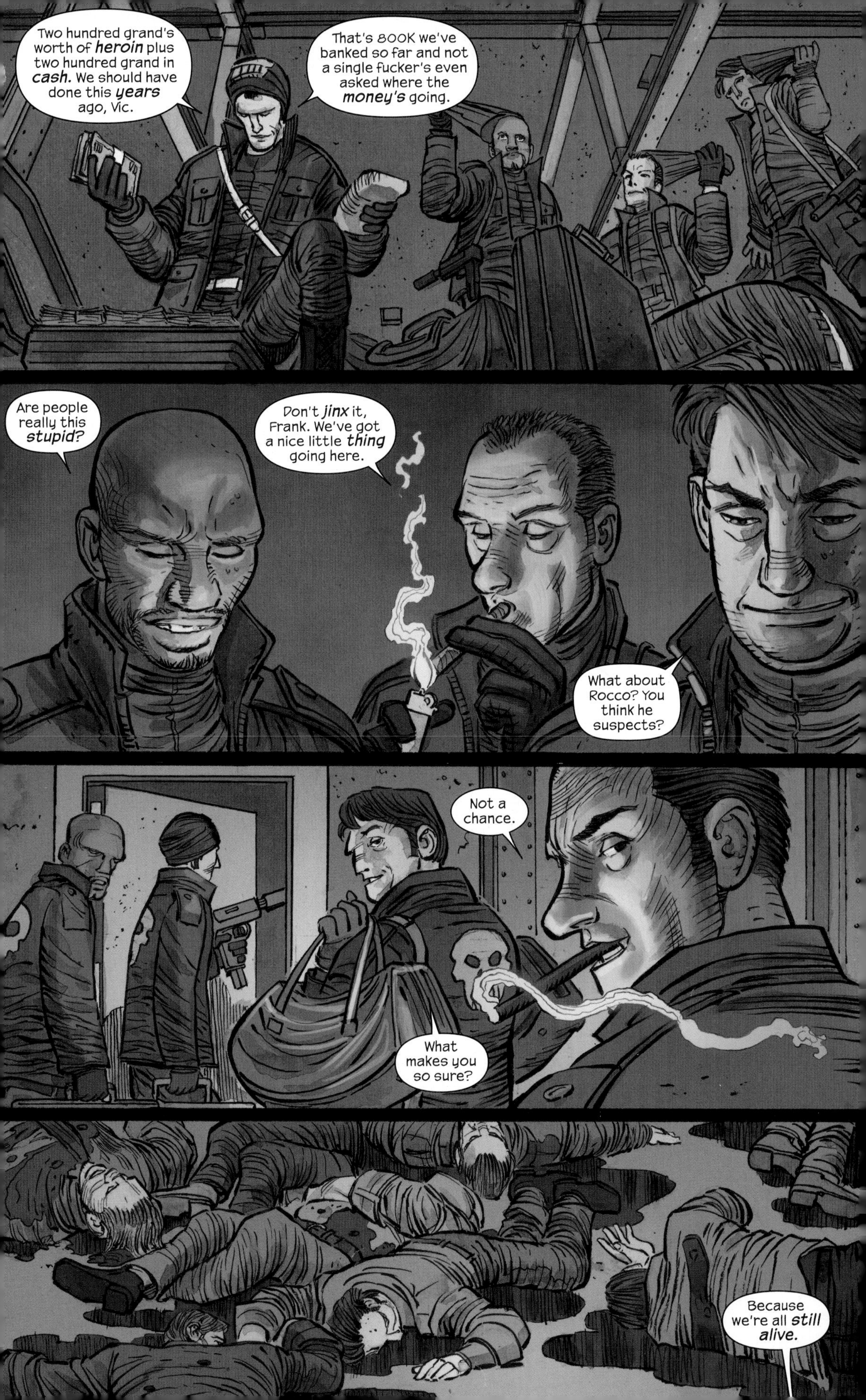
Two hundred grand's worth of heroin plus two hundred grand in cash. We should have done this years ago, Vic.
That's 800K we've banked so far and not a single fucker's even asked where the money's going.
Are people really this stupid?
Don't jinx it, Frank. We've got a nice little thing going here.
What about Rocco? You think he suspects?
Not a chance.
What makes you so sure?
Because we're all still alive.

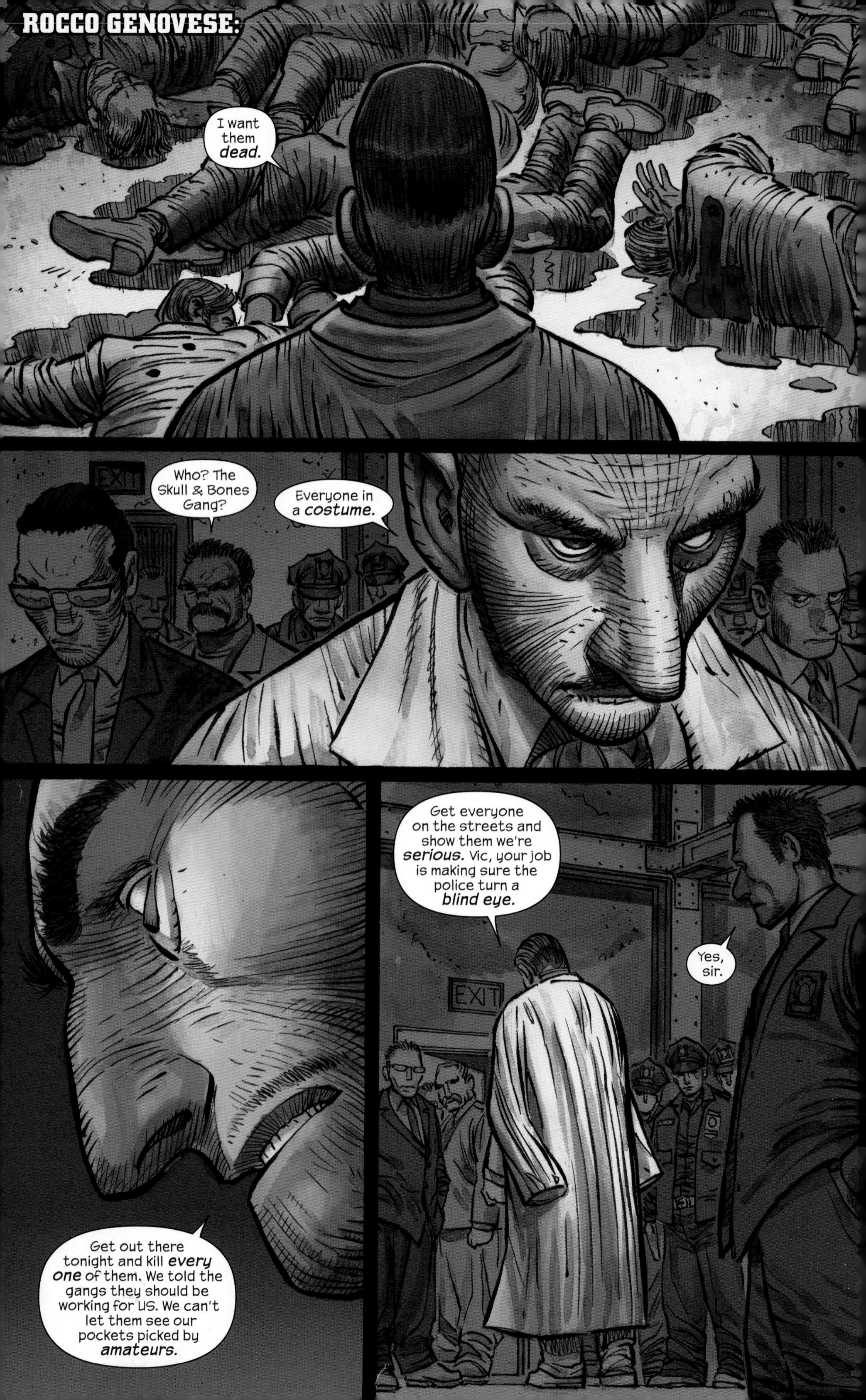
ROCCO GENOVESE:
I want them dead.
Who? The Skull & Bones Gang?
Everyone in a costume.
Get out there tonight and kill every one of them. We told the gangs they should be working for US. We can't let them see our pockets picked by amateurs.
Get everyone on the streets and show them we're serious. Vic, your job is making sure the police turn a blind eye.
Yes, sir.

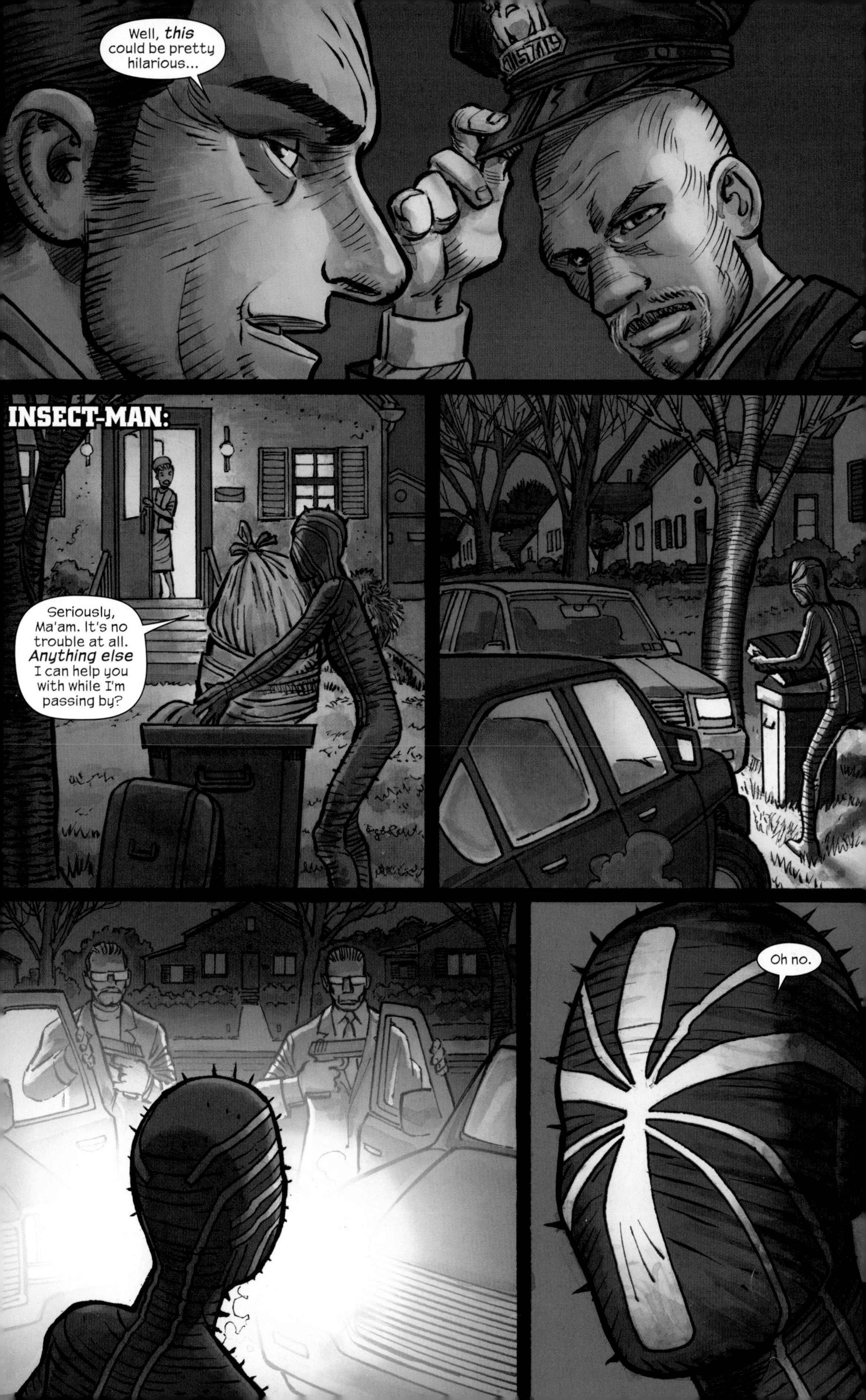
Well, *this* could be pretty hilarious...
INSECT-MAN:
Seriously, Ma'am. It's no trouble at all. *Anything else* I can help you with while I'm passing by?
Oh no.

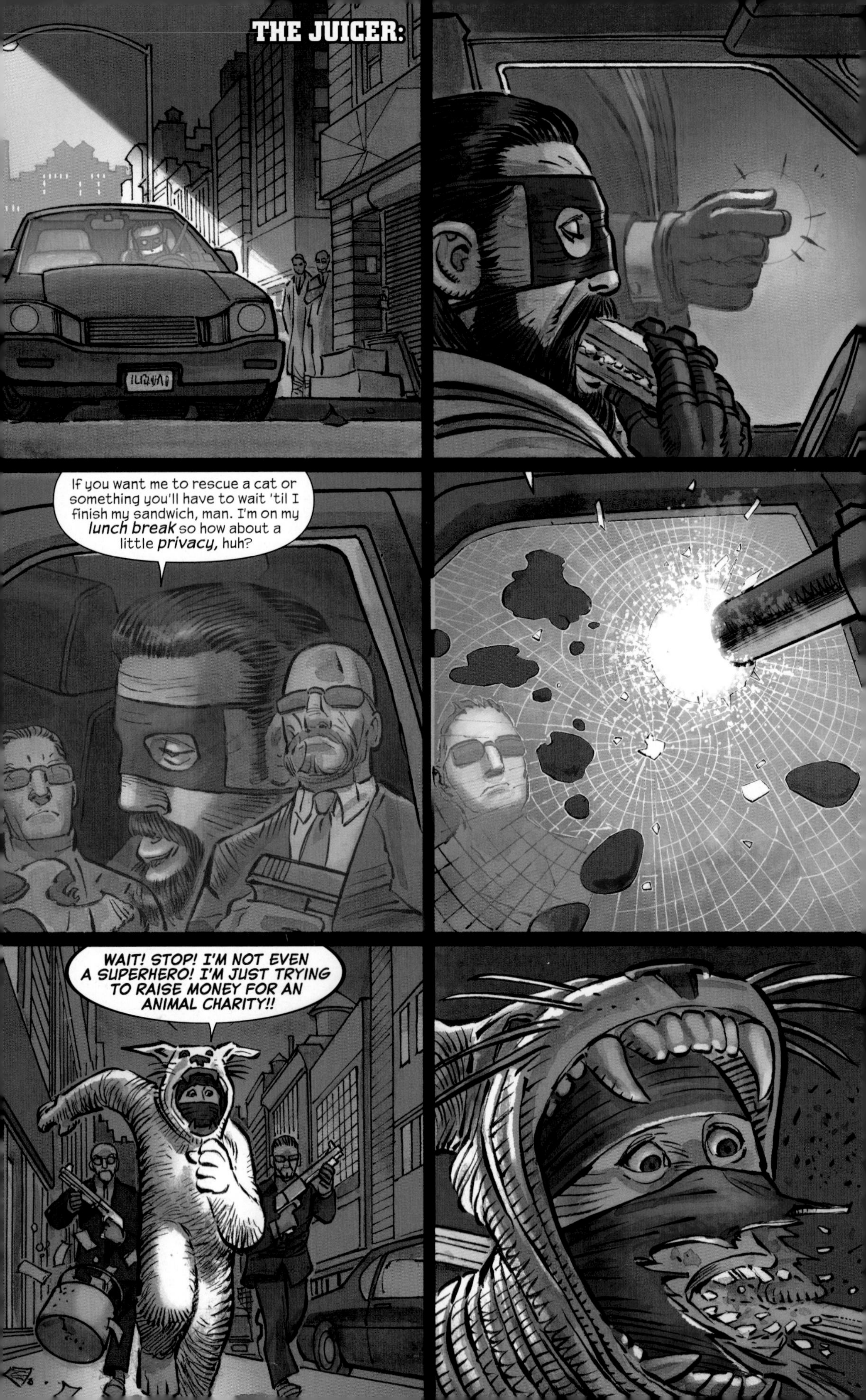
THE JUICER:
If you want me to rescue a cat or something you'll have to wait 'til I finish my sandwich, man. I'm on my *lunch break* so how about a little *privacy*, huh?
WAIT! STOP! I'M NOT EVEN A SUPERHERO! I'M JUST TRYING TO RAISE MONEY FOR AN ANIMAL CHARITY!!

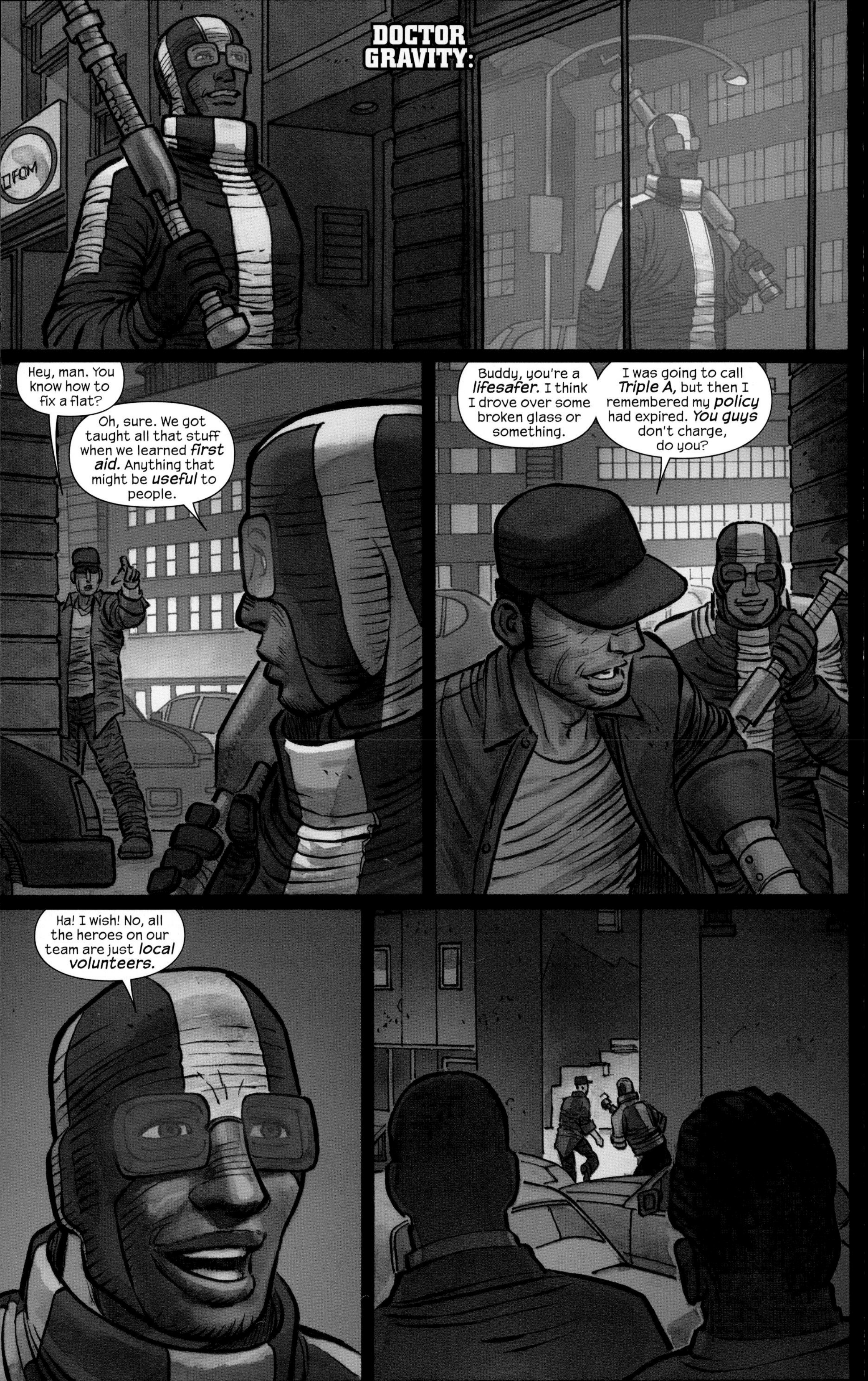
DOCTOR GRAVITY:
Hey, man. You know how to fix a flat?
Oh, sure. We got taught all that stuff when we learned *first aid.* Anything that might be *useful* to people.
Buddy, you're a *lifesafer.* I think I drove over some broken glass or something.
I was going to call *Triple A,* but then I remembered my *policy* had expired. *You guys* don't charge, do you?
Ha! I wish! No, all the heroes on our team are just *local volunteers.*

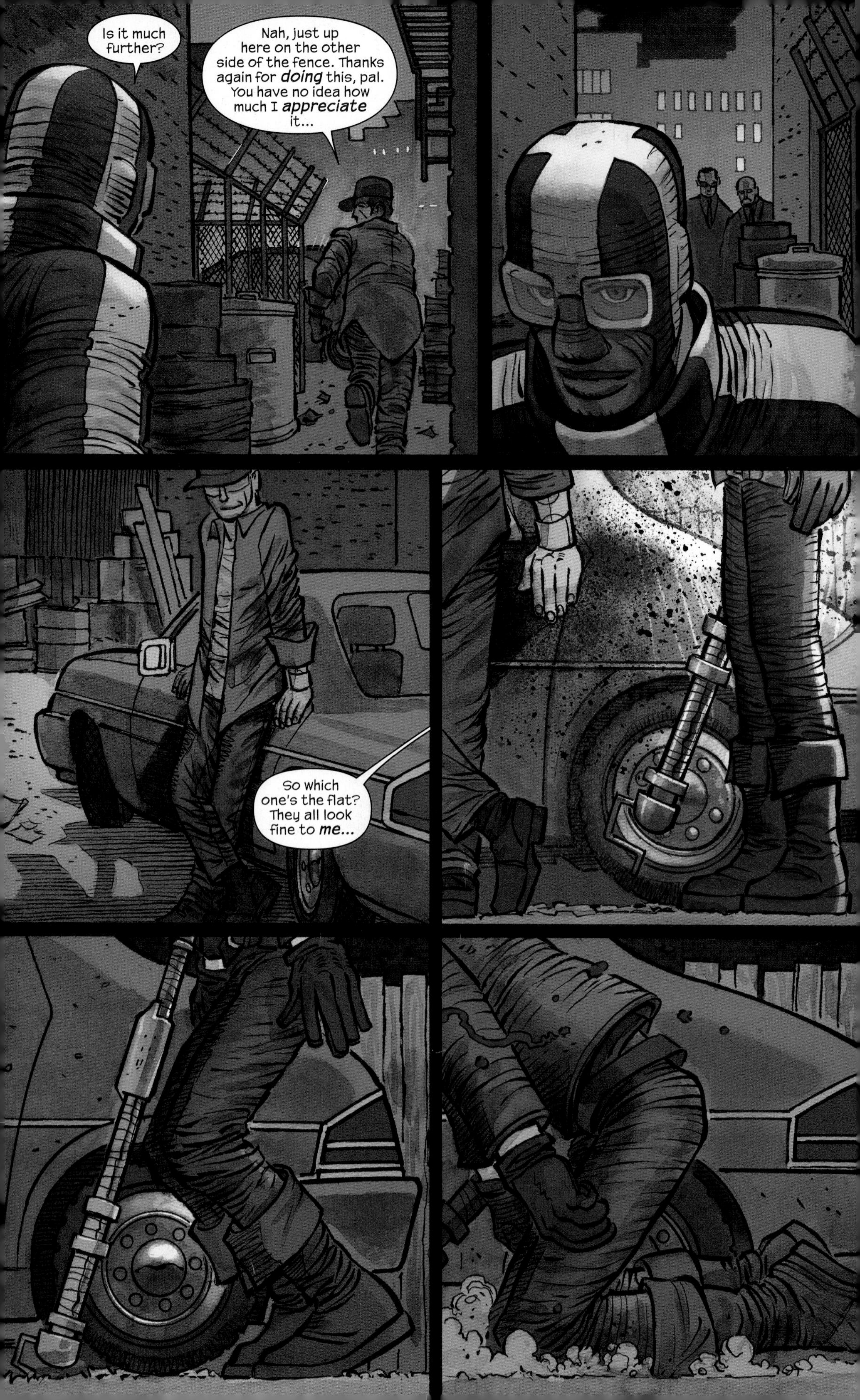
Is it much further?
Nah, just up here on the other side of the fence. Thanks again for *doing* this, pal. You have no idea how much I *appreciate* it...
So which one's the flat? They all look fine to *me*...

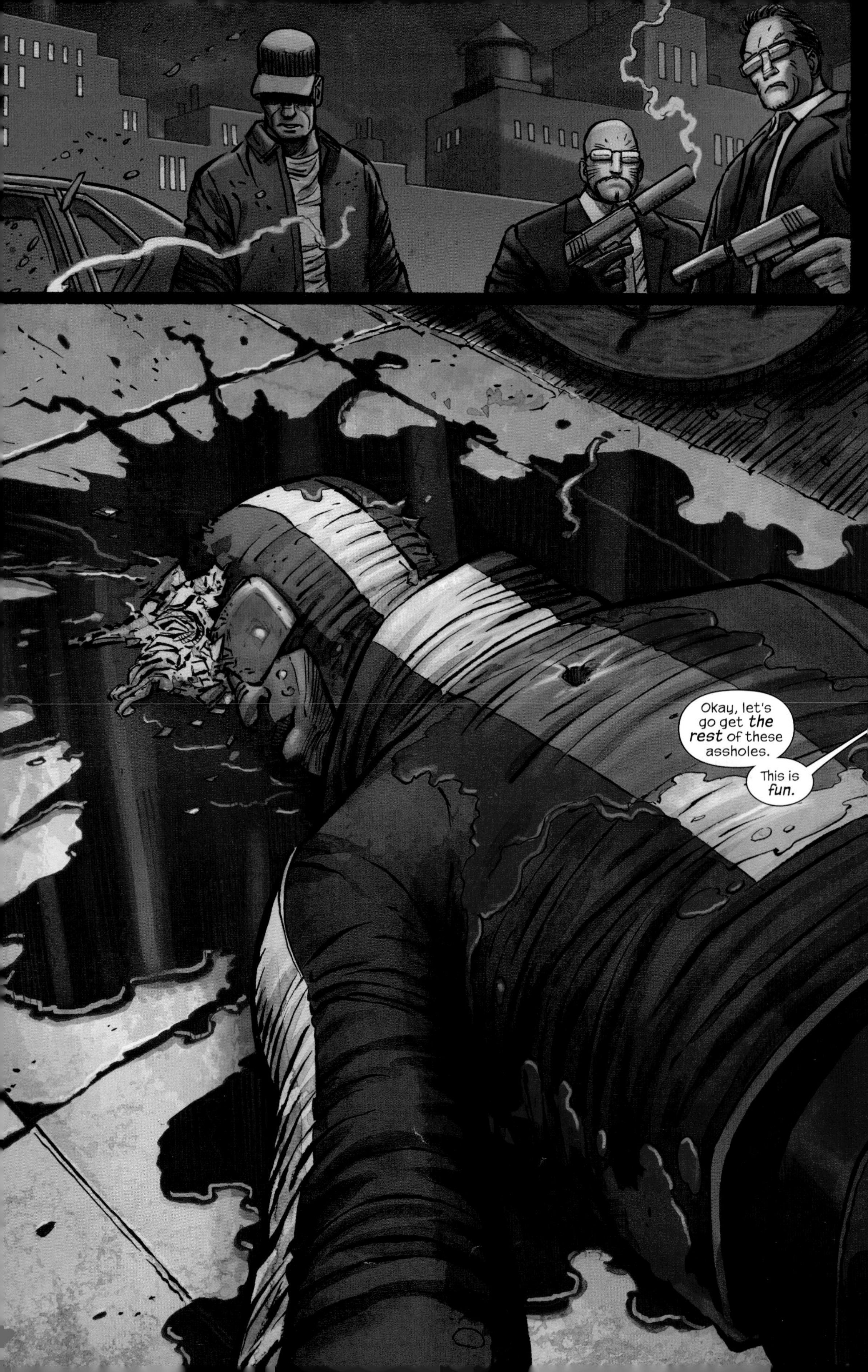
Okay, let's go get the rest of these assholes.
This is fun.

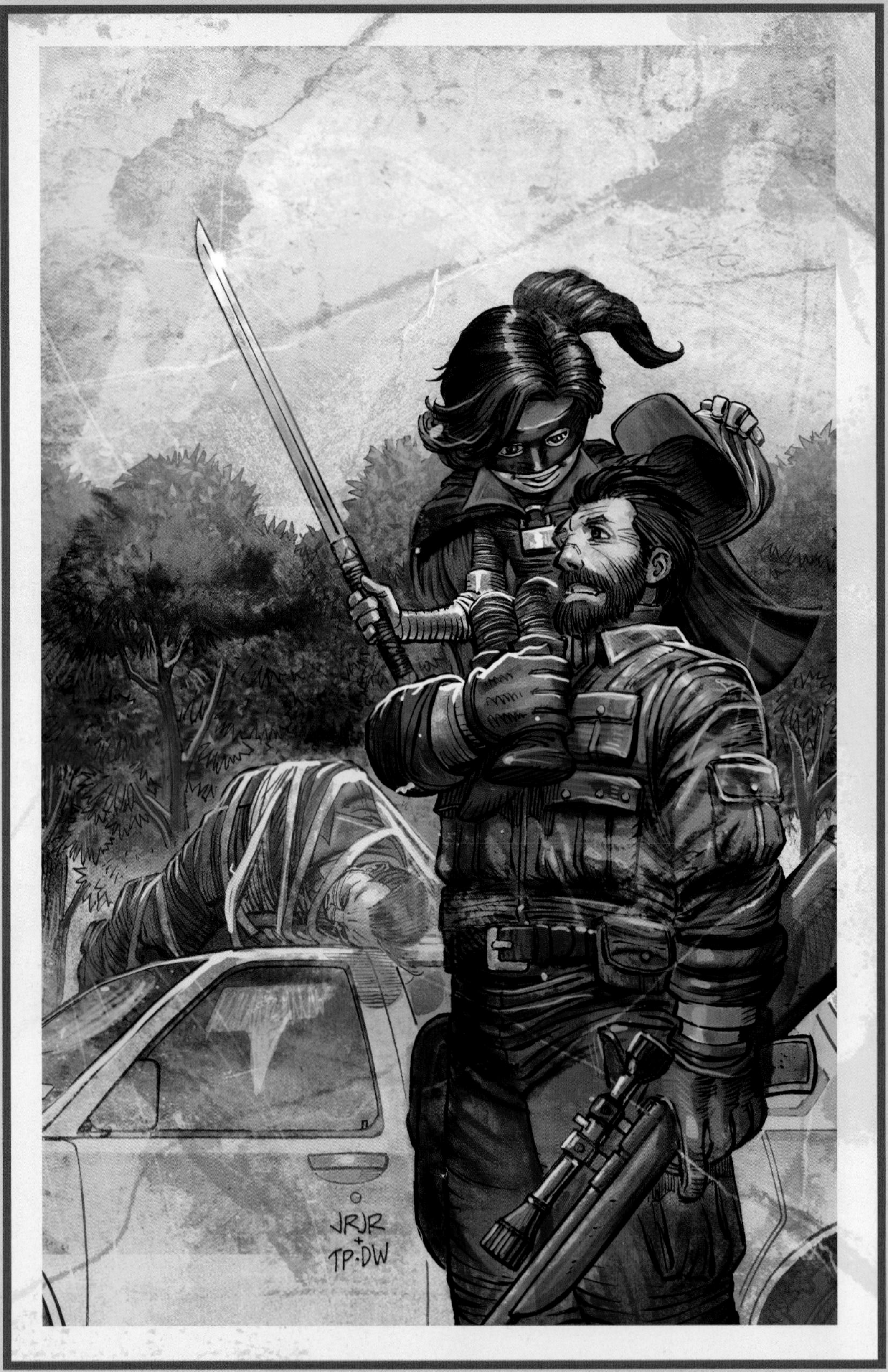
JRJR
+
TP·DW

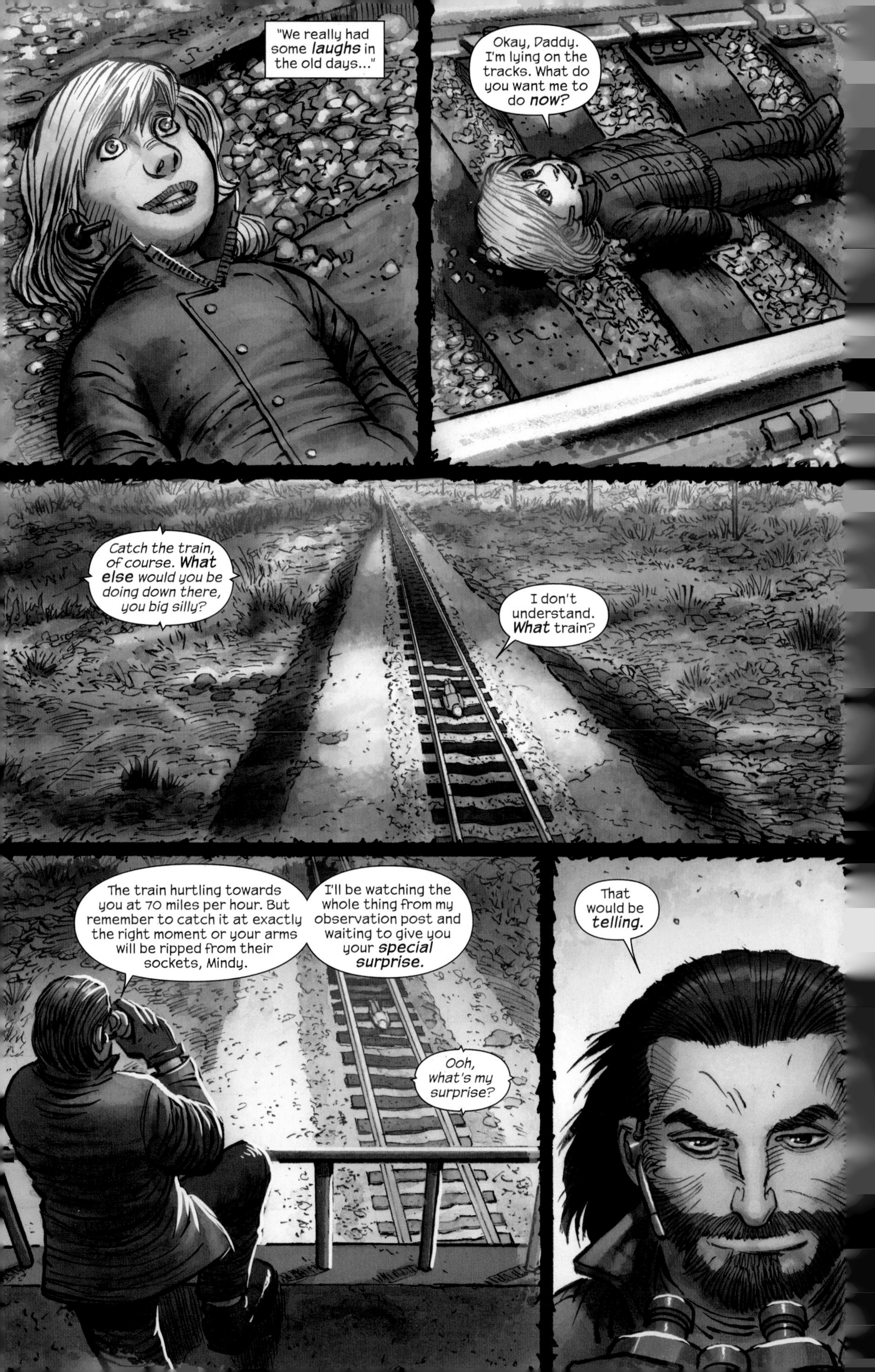
"We really had some laughs in the old days..."
Okay, Daddy. I'm lying on the tracks. What do you want me to do now?
Catch the train, of course. What else would you be doing down there, you big silly?
I don't understand. What train?
The train hurtling towards you at 70 miles per hour. But remember to catch it at exactly the right moment or your arms will be ripped from their sockets, Mindy.
I'll be watching the whole thing from my observation post and waiting to give you your special surprise.
Ooh, what's my surprise?
That would be telling.

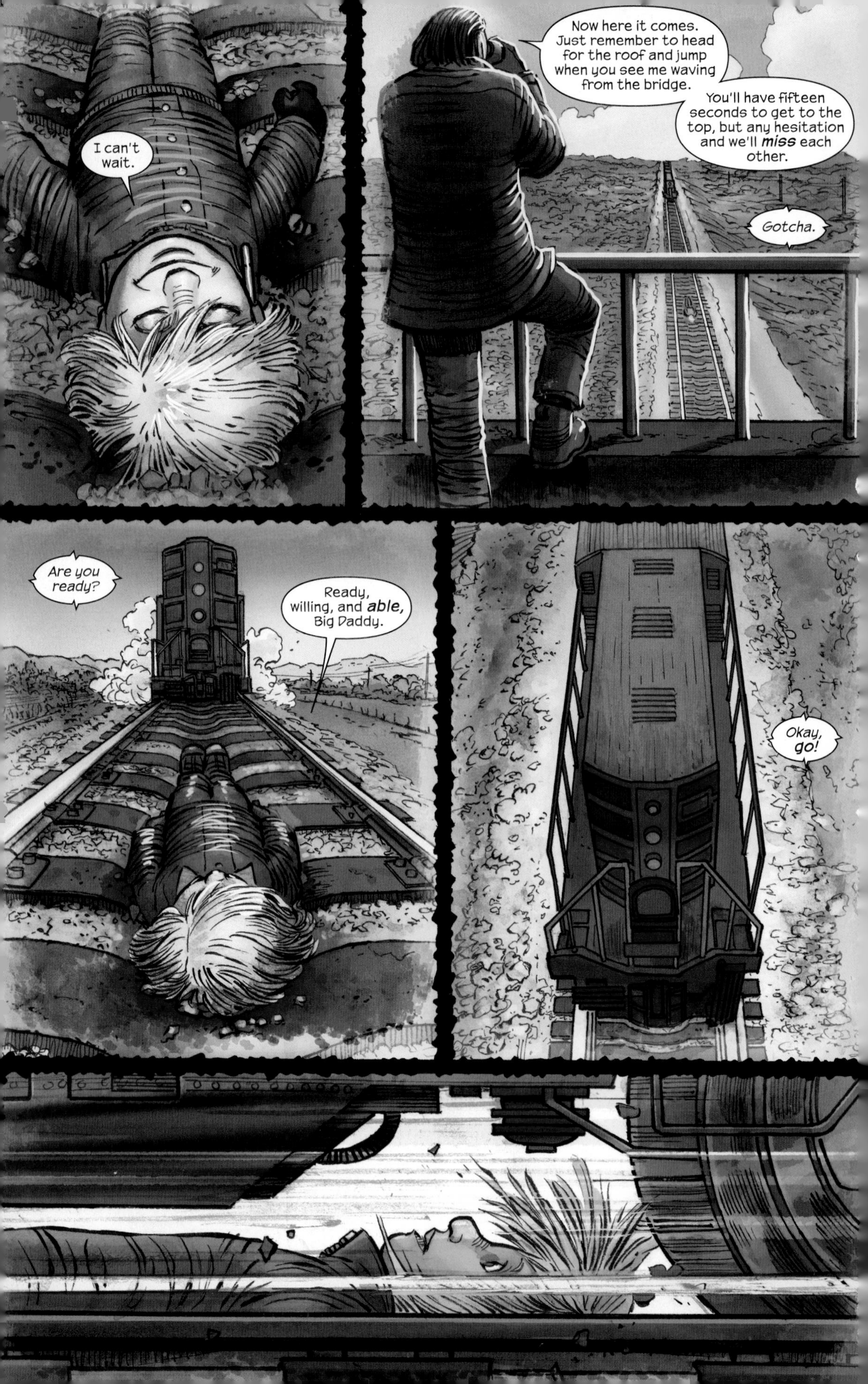

I can't wait.
Now here it comes. Just remember to head for the roof and jump when you see me waving from the bridge.
You'll have fifteen seconds to get to the top, but any hesitation and we'll *miss* each other.
Gotcha.
Are you ready?
Ready, willing, and ***able,*** Big Daddy.
Okay, ***go!***

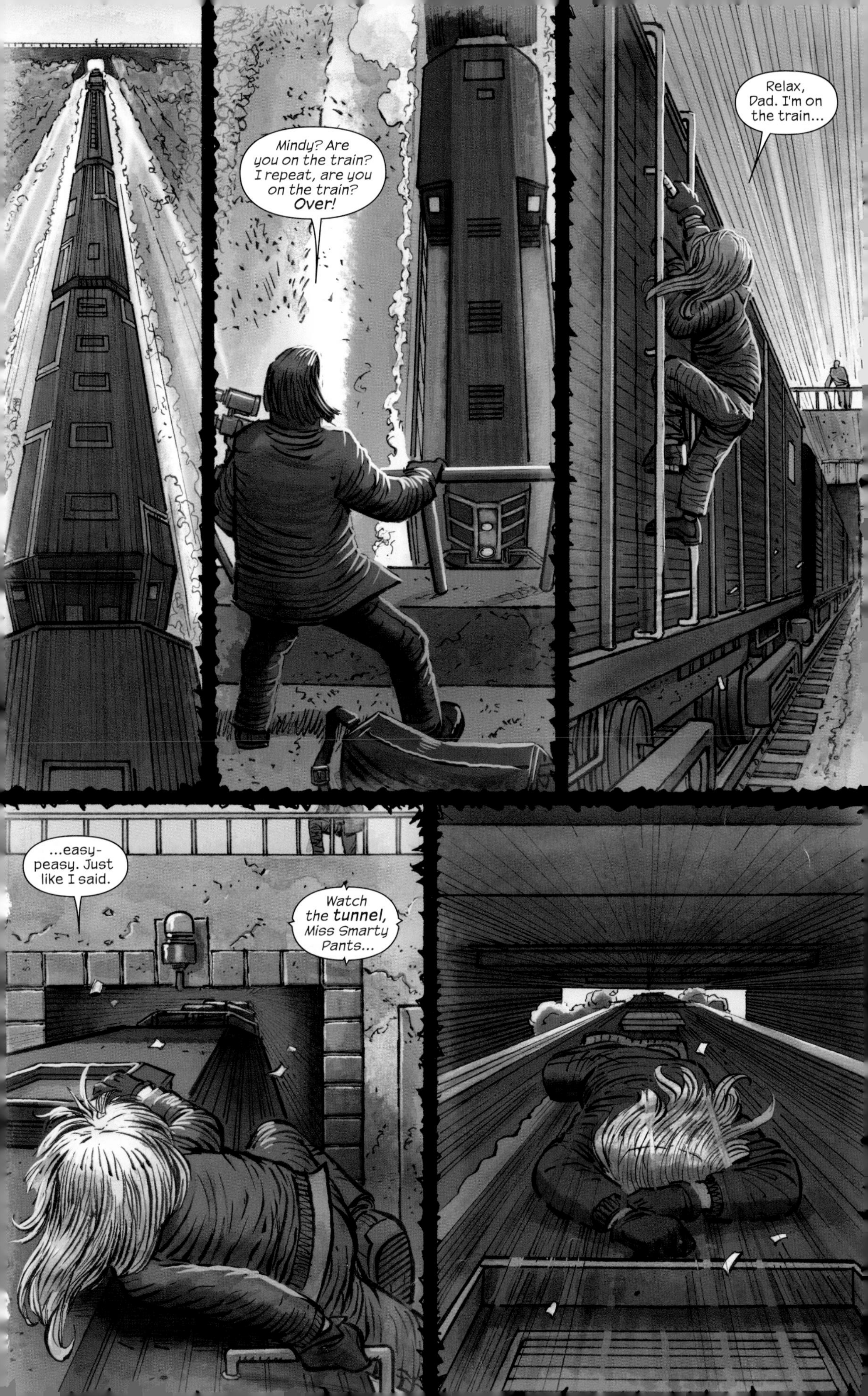
Mindy? Are you on the train? I repeat, are you on the train? Over!
Relax, Dad. I'm on the train...
...easy-peasy. Just like I said.
Watch the tunnel, Miss Smarty Pants...

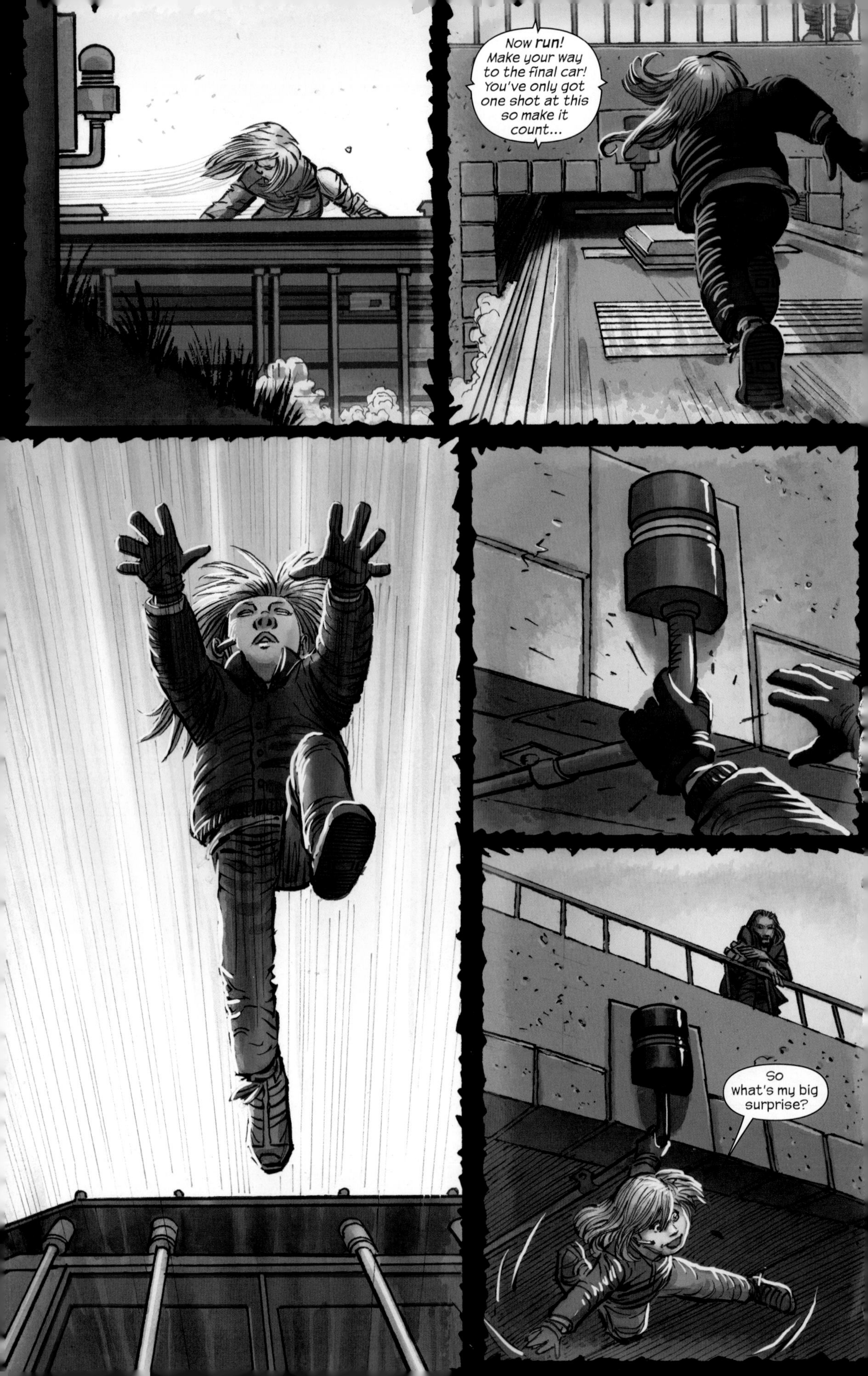
Now run! Make your way to the final car! You've only got one shot at this so make it count...
So what's my big surprise?

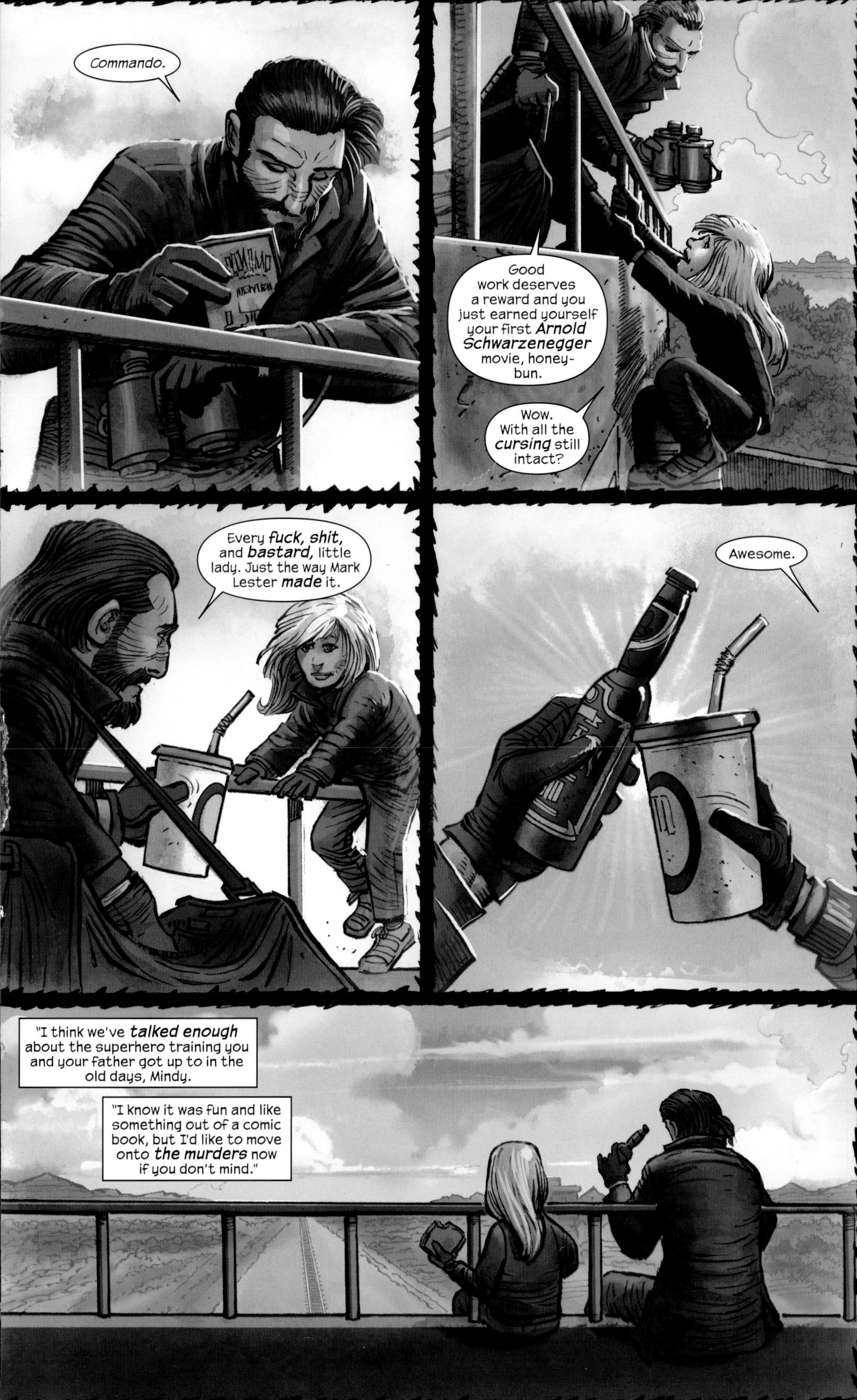
Commando.
Good work deserves a reward and you just earned yourself your first **Arnold Schwarzenegger** movie, honey-bun.
Wow. With all the **cursing** still intact?
Every **fuck, shit,** and **bastard,** little lady. Just the way Mark Lester **made** it.
Awesome.
"I think we've **talked enough** about the superhero training you and your father got up to in the old days, Mindy.
"I know it was fun and like something out of a comic book, but I'd like to move onto **the murders** now if you don't mind."

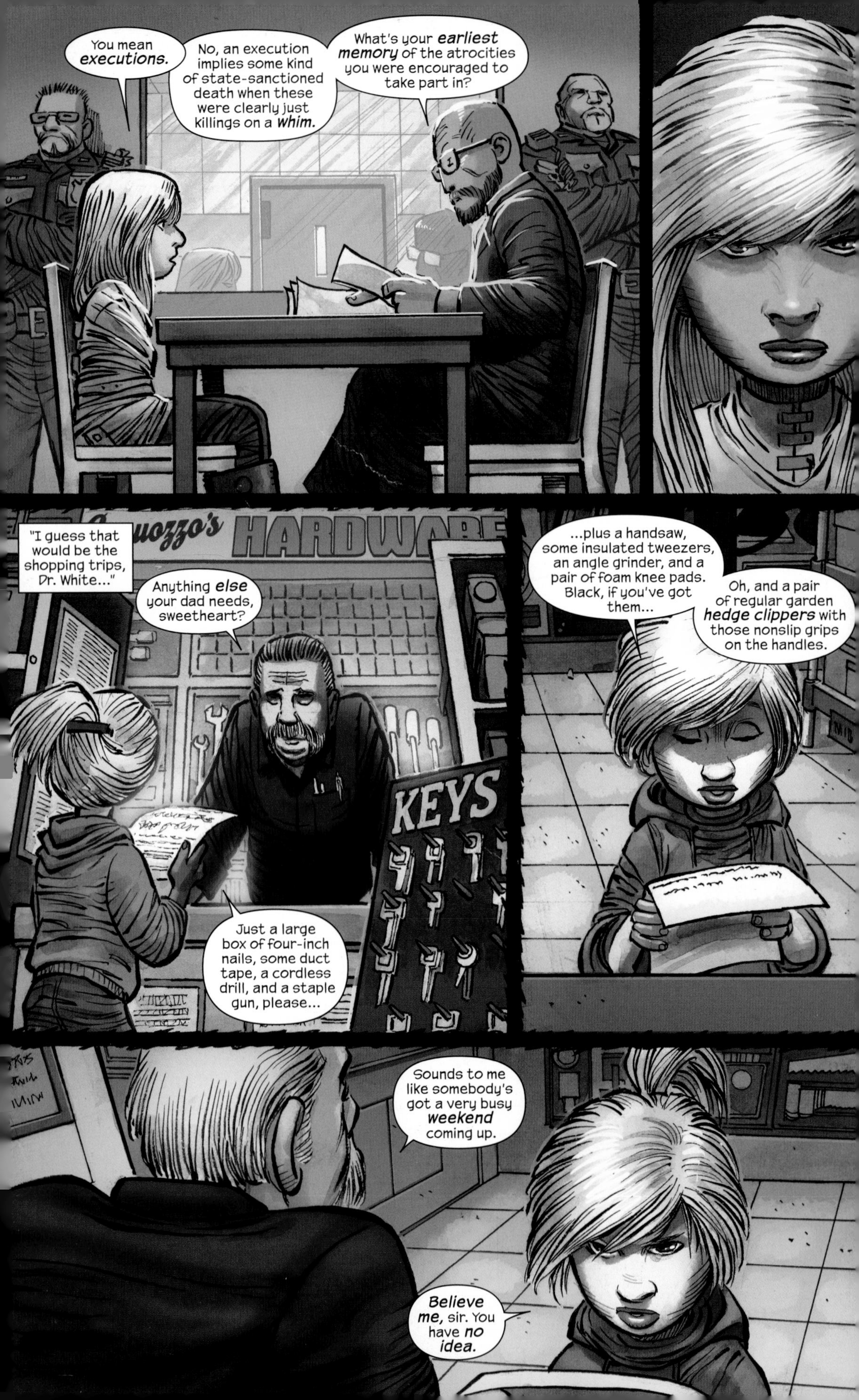
You mean executions.
No, an execution implies some kind of state-sanctioned death when these were clearly just killings on a whim.
What's your earliest memory of the atrocities you were encouraged to take part in?
"I guess that would be the shopping trips, Dr. White..."
HARDWARE
Anything else your dad needs, sweetheart?
KEYS
Just a large box of four-inch nails, some duct tape, a cordless drill, and a staple gun, please...
...plus a handsaw, some insulated tweezers, an angle grinder, and a pair of foam knee pads. Black, if you've got them...
Oh, and a pair of regular garden hedge clippers with those nonslip grips on the handles.
Sounds to me like somebody's got a very busy weekend coming up.
Believe me, sir. You have no idea.

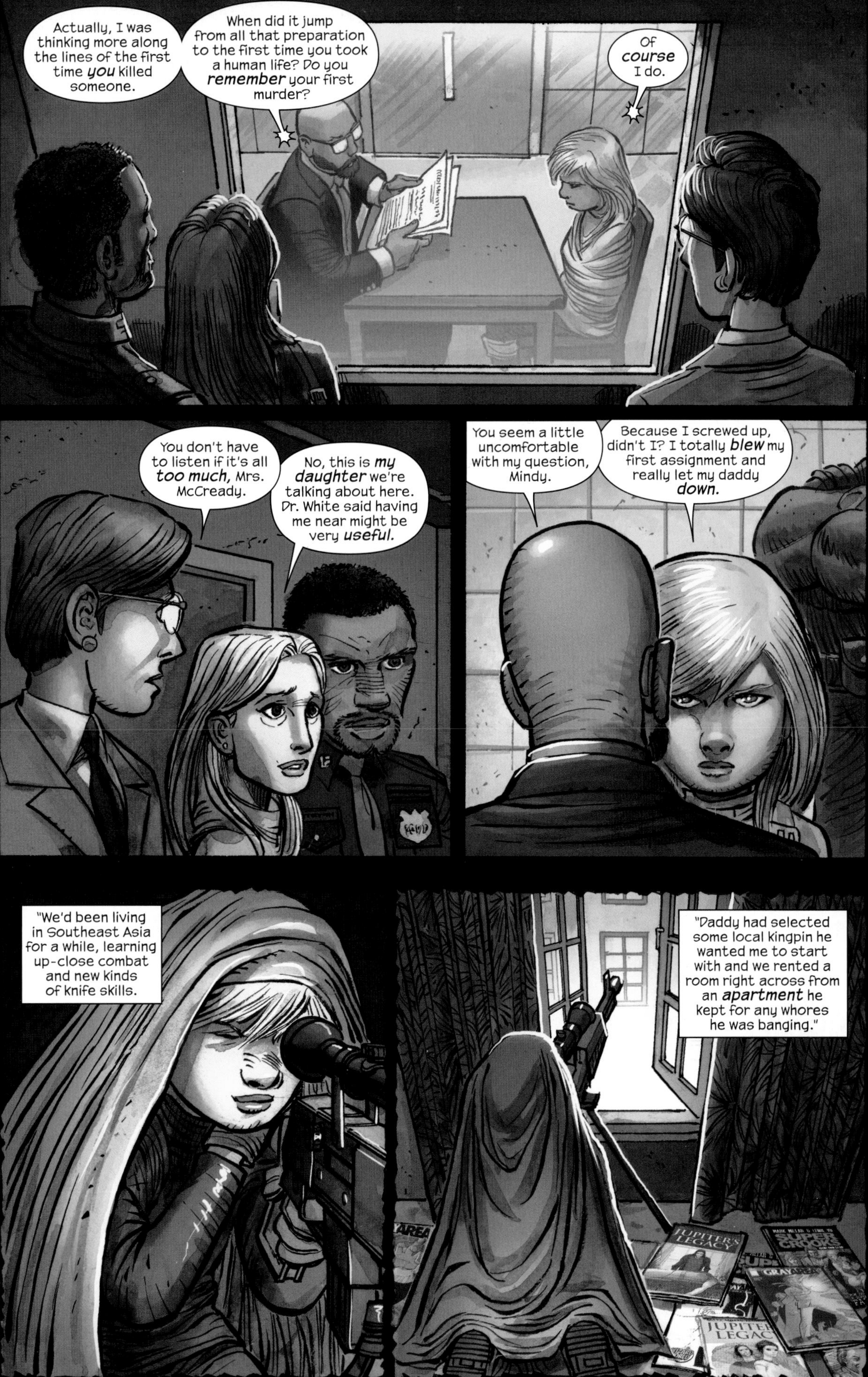
Actually, I was thinking more along the lines of the first time *you* killed someone.
When did it jump from all that preparation to the first time you took a human life? Do you *remember* your first murder?
Of *course* I do.
You don't have to listen if it's all *too much*, Mrs. McCready.
No, this is *my daughter* we're talking about here. Dr. White said having me near might be very *useful.*
You seem a little uncomfortable with my question, Mindy.
Because I screwed up, didn't I? I totally *blew* my first assignment and really let my daddy *down.*
"We'd been living in Southeast Asia for a while, learning up-close combat and new kinds of knife skills.
"Daddy had selected some local kingpin he wanted me to start with and we rented a room right across from an *apartment* he kept for any whores he was banging."
AREA
JUPITER'S LEGACY
SUPER CROOKS
GRAY AREA
JUPITER'S LEGACY

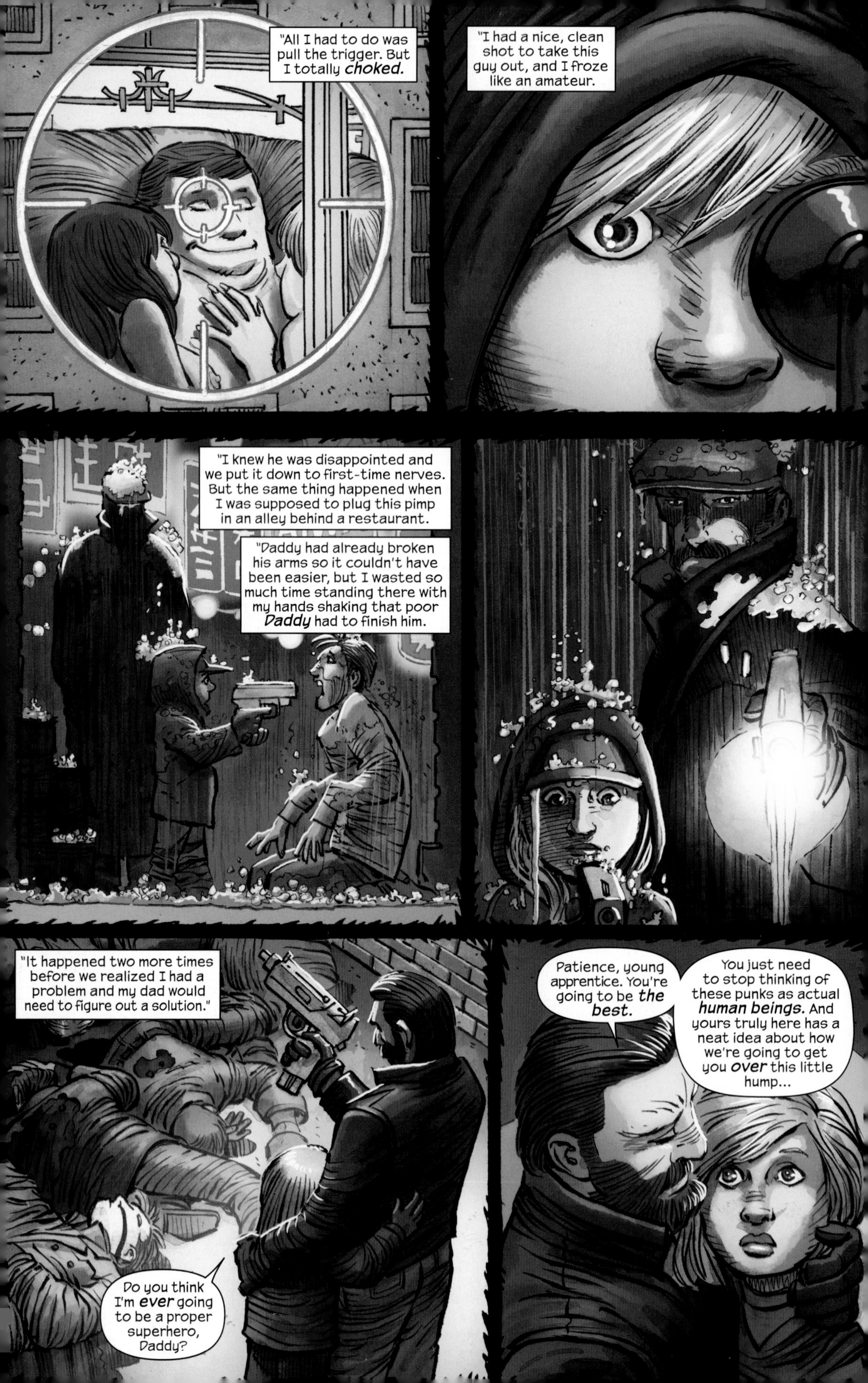
"All I had to do was pull the trigger. But I totally *choked.*
"I had a nice, clean shot to take this guy out, and I froze like an amateur.
"I knew he was disappointed and we put it down to first-time nerves. But the same thing happened when I was supposed to plug this pimp in an alley behind a restaurant.
"Daddy had already broken his arms so it couldn't have been easier, but I wasted so much time standing there with my hands shaking that poor *Daddy* had to finish him.
"It happened two more times before we realized I had a problem and my dad would need to figure out a solution."
Do you think I'm *ever* going to be a proper superhero, Daddy?
Patience, young apprentice. You're going to be *the best.*
You just need to stop thinking of these punks as actual *human beings.* And yours truly here has a neat idea about how we're going to get you *over* this little hump...

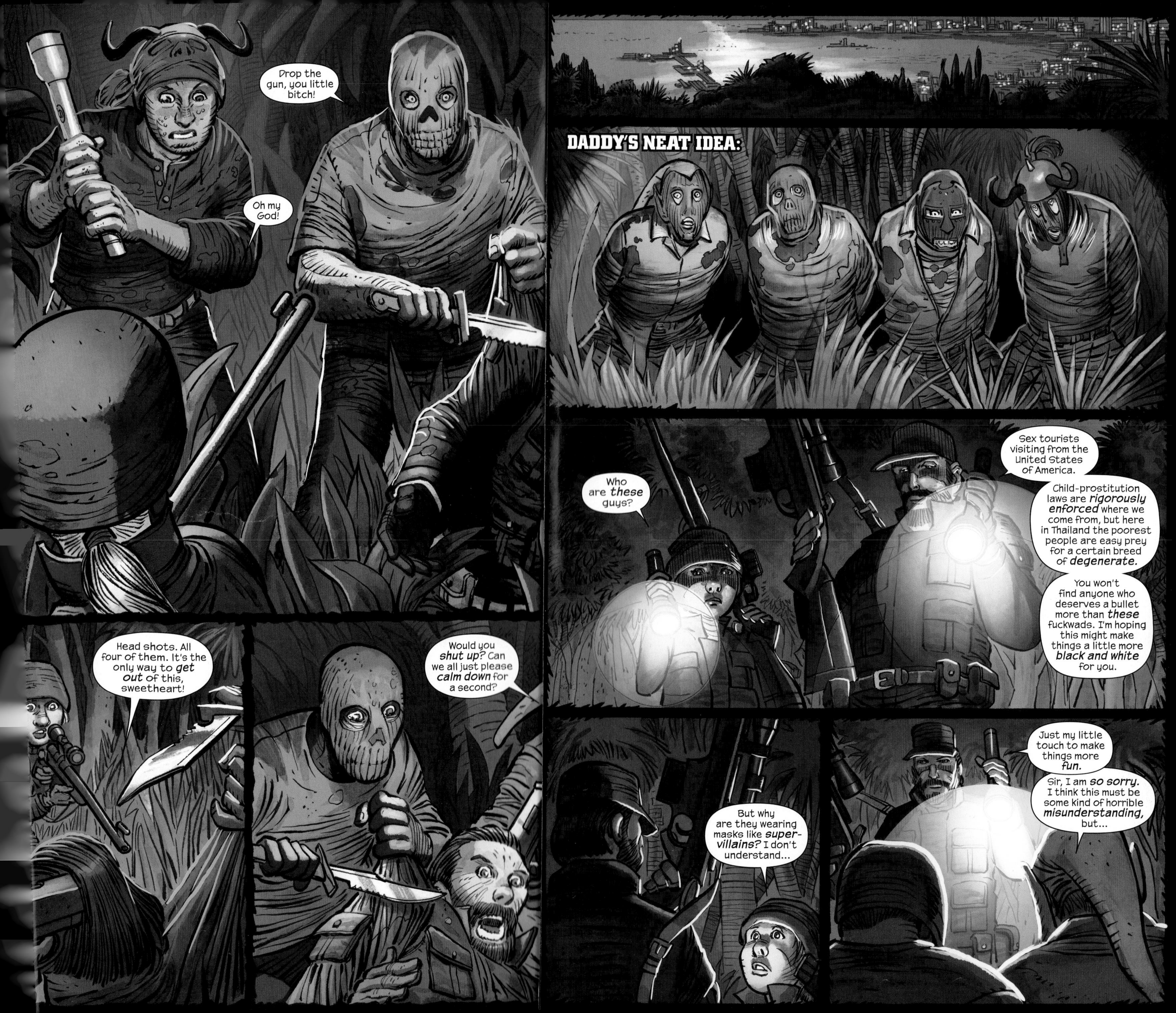

Drop the gun, you little bitch!
Oh my God!
Head shots. All four of them. It's the only way to get out of this, sweetheart!
Would you shut up? Can we all just please calm down for a second?
DADDY'S NEAT IDEA:
Who are these guys?
Sex tourists visiting from the United States of America.
Child-prostitution laws are rigorously enforced where we come from, but here in Thailand the poorest people are easy prey for a certain breed of degenerate.
You won't find anyone who deserves a bullet more than these fuckwads. I'm hoping this might make things a little more black and white for you.
But why are they wearing masks like super-villains? I don't understand...
Just my little touch to make things more fun.
Sir, I am so sorry. I think this must be some kind of horrible misunderstanding, but...

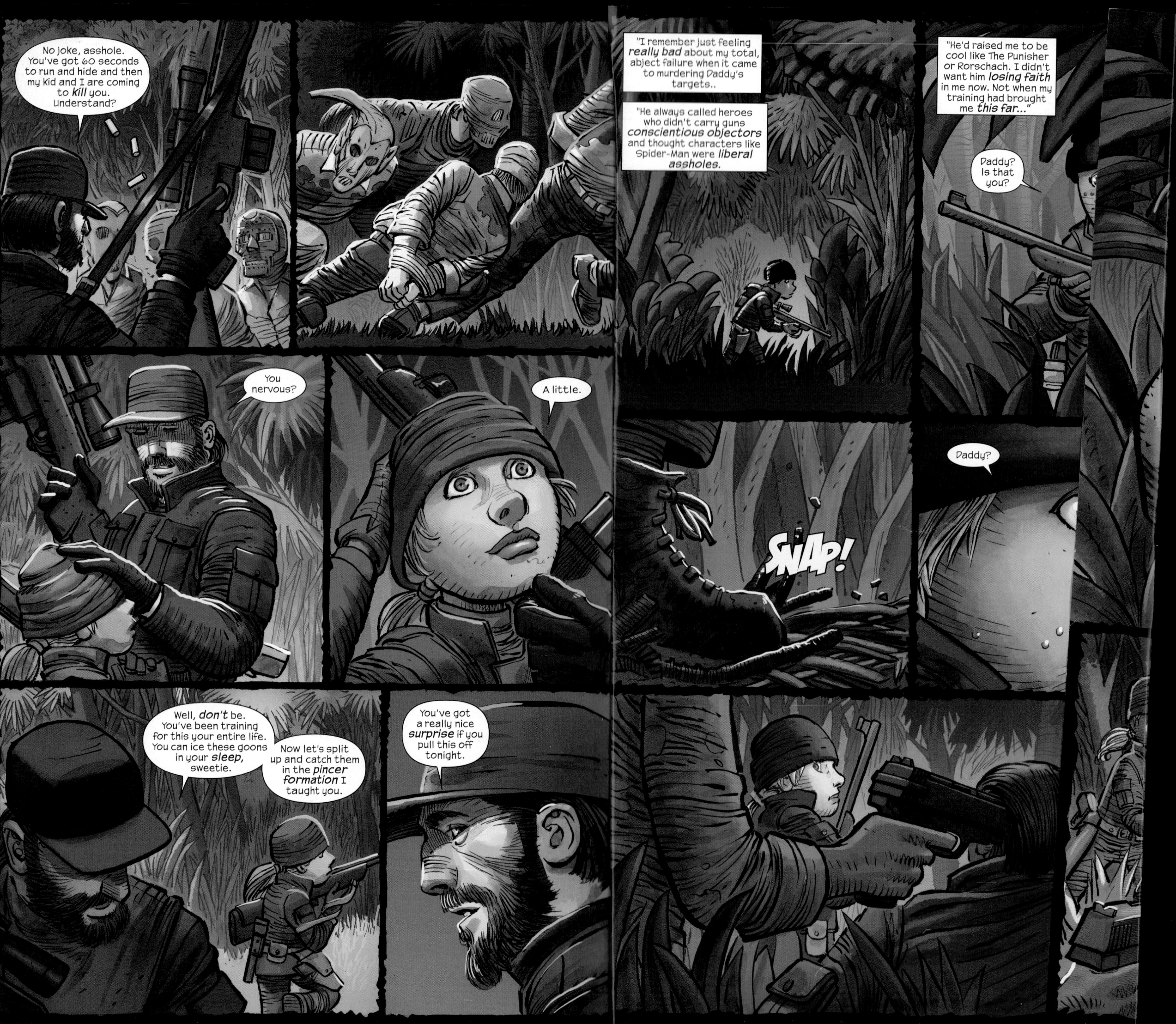

No joke, asshole. You've got 60 seconds to run and hide and then my kid and I are coming to *kill* you. Understand?
You nervous?
A little.
Well, *don't* be. You've been training for this your entire life. You can ice these goons in your *sleep,* sweetie.
Now let's split up and catch them in the *pincer formation* I taught you.
You've got a really nice *surprise* if you pull this off tonight.
"I remember just feeling *really bad* about my total, abject failure when it came to murdering Daddy's targets..
"He always called heroes who didn't carry guns *conscientious objectors* and thought characters like Spider-Man were *liberal assholes.*
"He'd raised me to be cool like The Punisher or Rorschach. I didn't want him *losing faith* in me now. Not when my training had brought me *this far...*"
Daddy? Is that you?
SNAP!
Daddy?

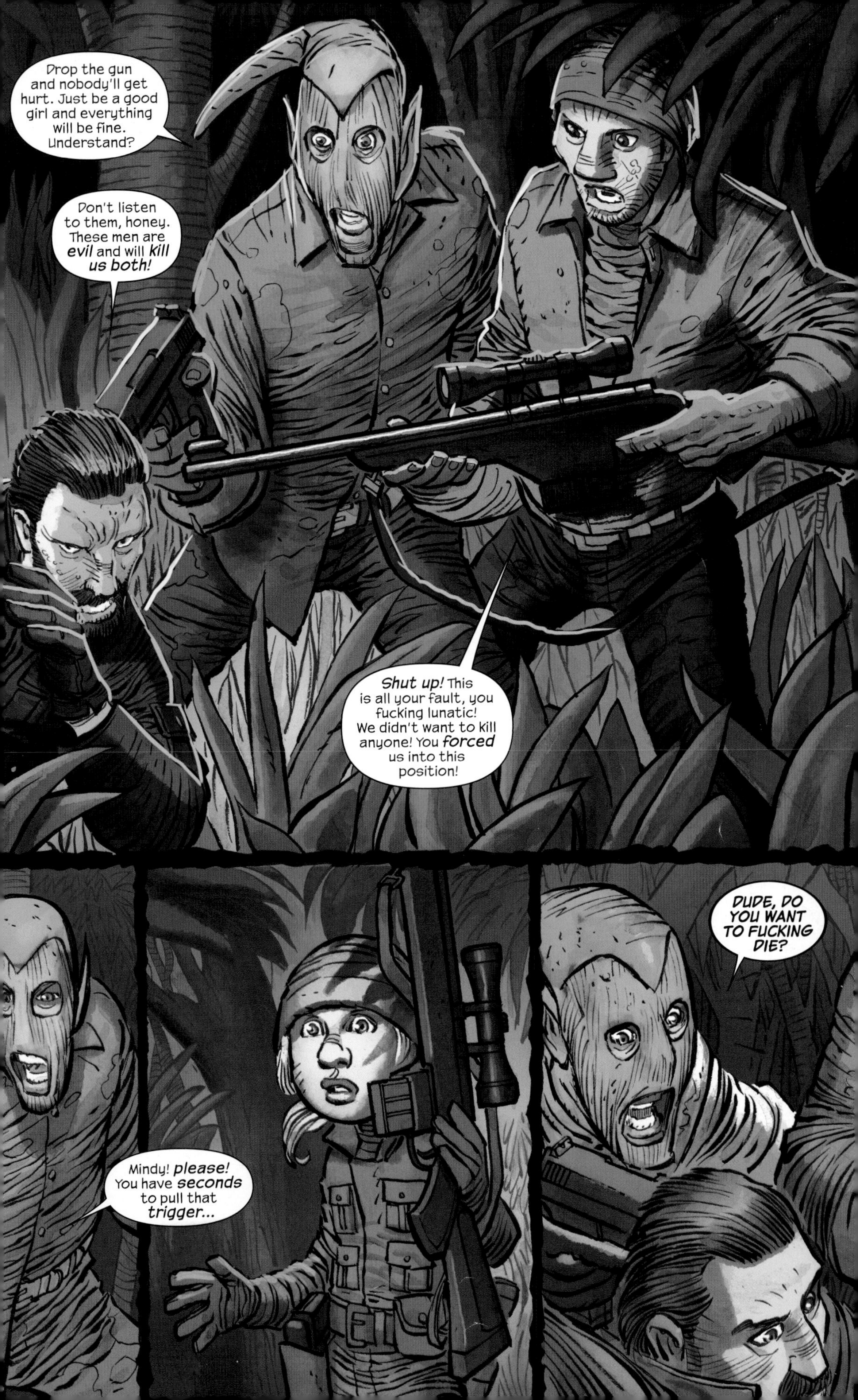
Drop the gun and nobody'll get hurt. Just be a good girl and everything will be fine. Understand?
Don't listen to them, honey. These men are *evil* and will *kill us both!*
Shut up! This is all your fault, you fucking lunatic! We didn't want to kill anyone! You *forced* us into this position!
Mindy! *please!* You have *seconds* to pull that *trigger...*
DUDE, DO YOU WANT TO FUCKING DIE?

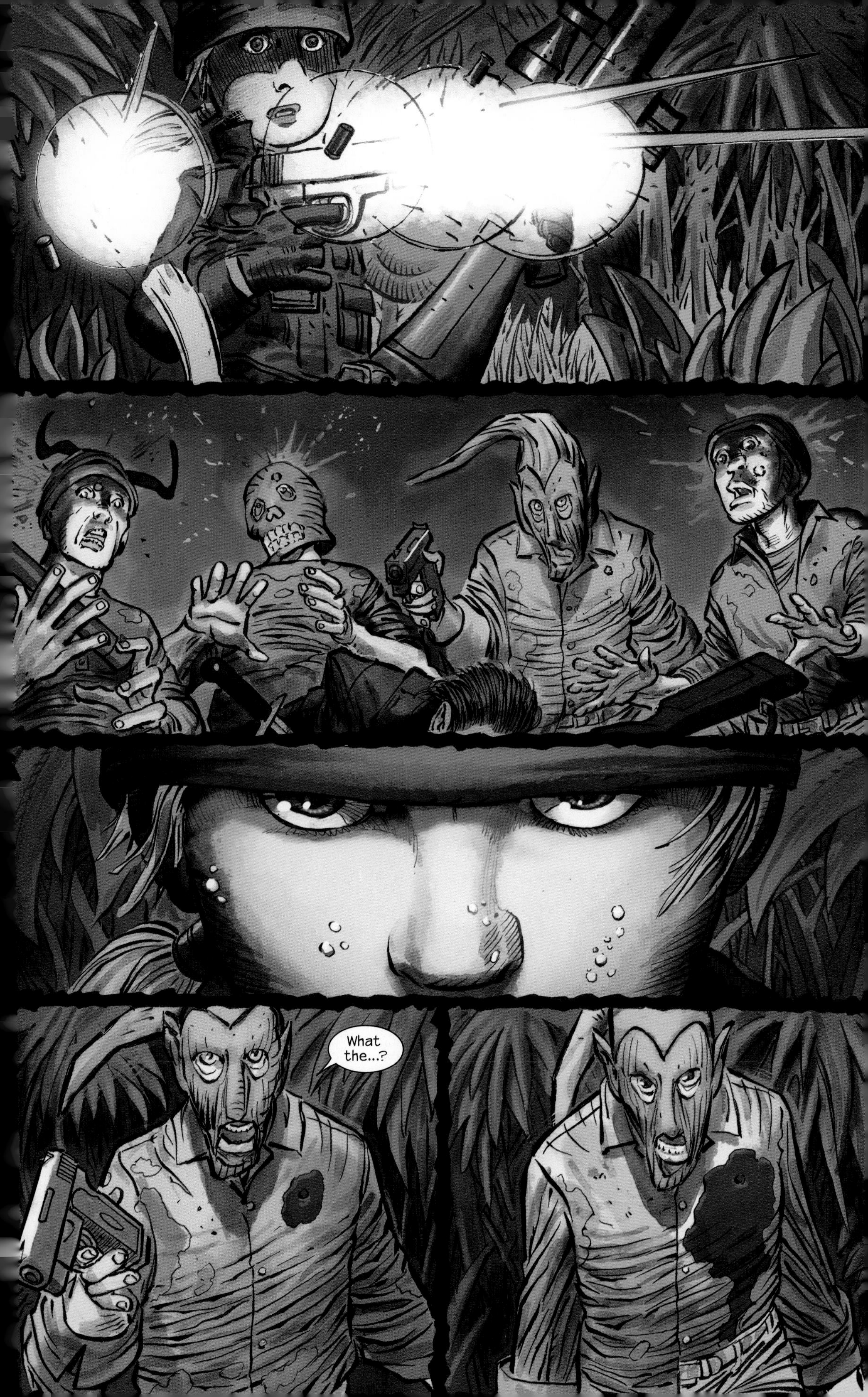
What the...?

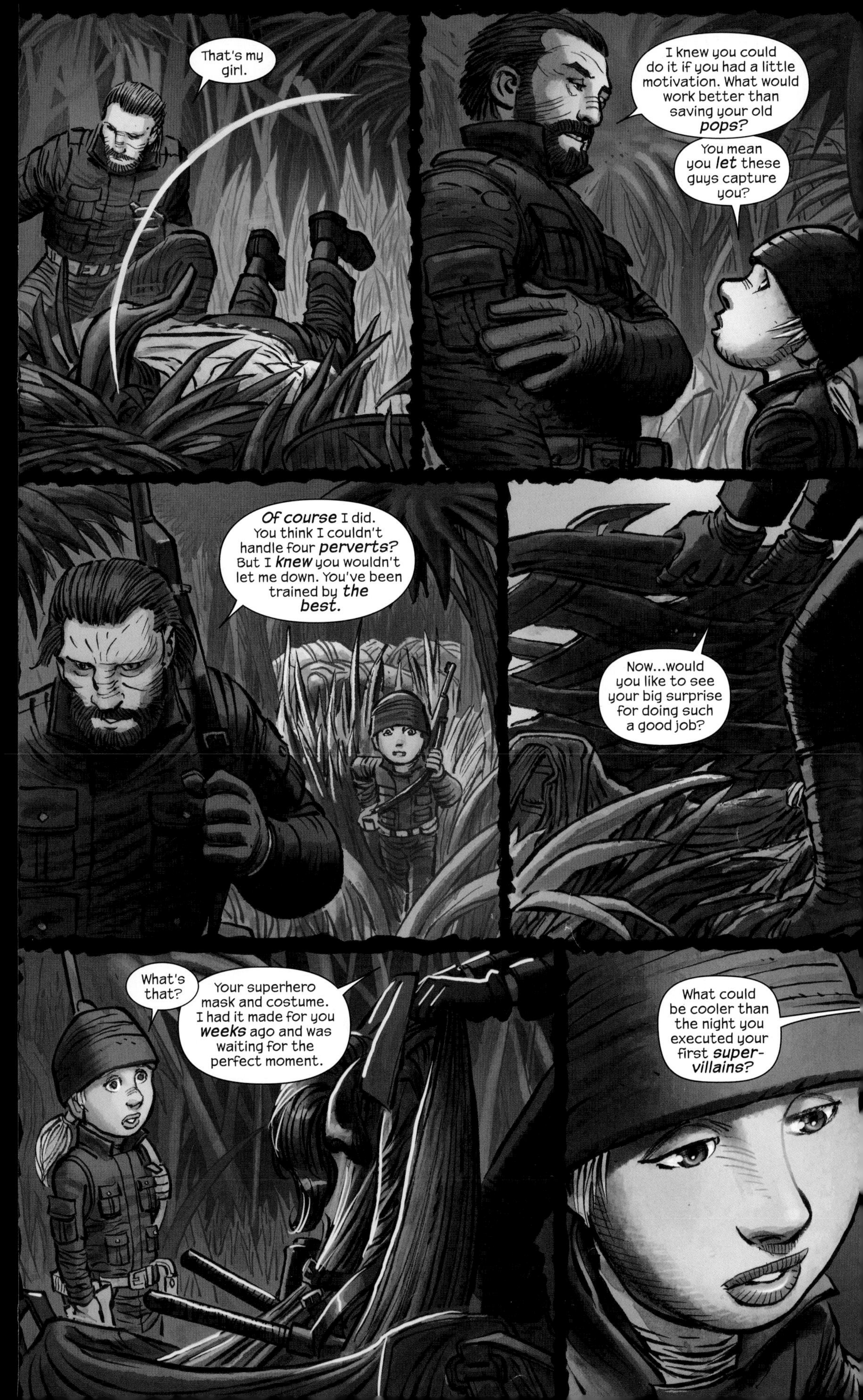

That's my girl.
I knew you could do it if you had a little motivation. What would work better than saving your old pops?
You mean you let these guys capture you?
Of course I did. You think I couldn't handle four perverts? But I knew you wouldn't let me down. You've been trained by the best.
Now...would you like to see your big surprise for doing such a good job?
What's that?
Your superhero mask and costume. I had it made for you weeks ago and was waiting for the perfect moment.
What could be cooler than the night you executed your first super-villains?

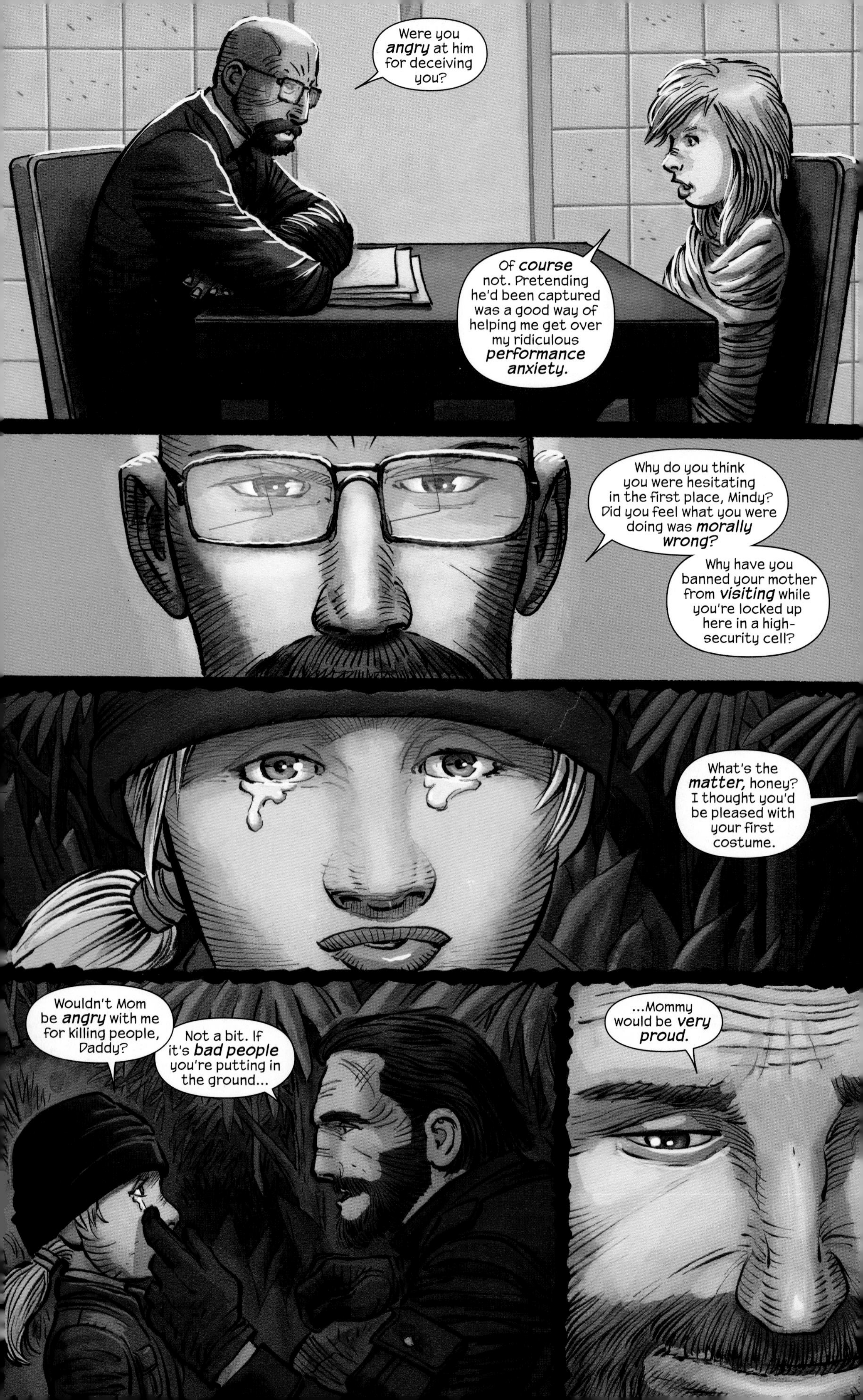

Were you angry at him for deceiving you?
Of course not. Pretending he'd been captured was a good way of helping me get over my ridiculous performance anxiety.
Why do you think you were hesitating in the first place, Mindy? Did you feel what you were doing was morally wrong?
Why have you banned your mother from visiting while you're locked up here in a high-security cell?
What's the matter, honey? I thought you'd be pleased with your first costume.
Wouldn't Mom be angry with me for killing people, Daddy?
Not a bit. If it's bad people you're putting in the ground...
...Mommy would be very proud.

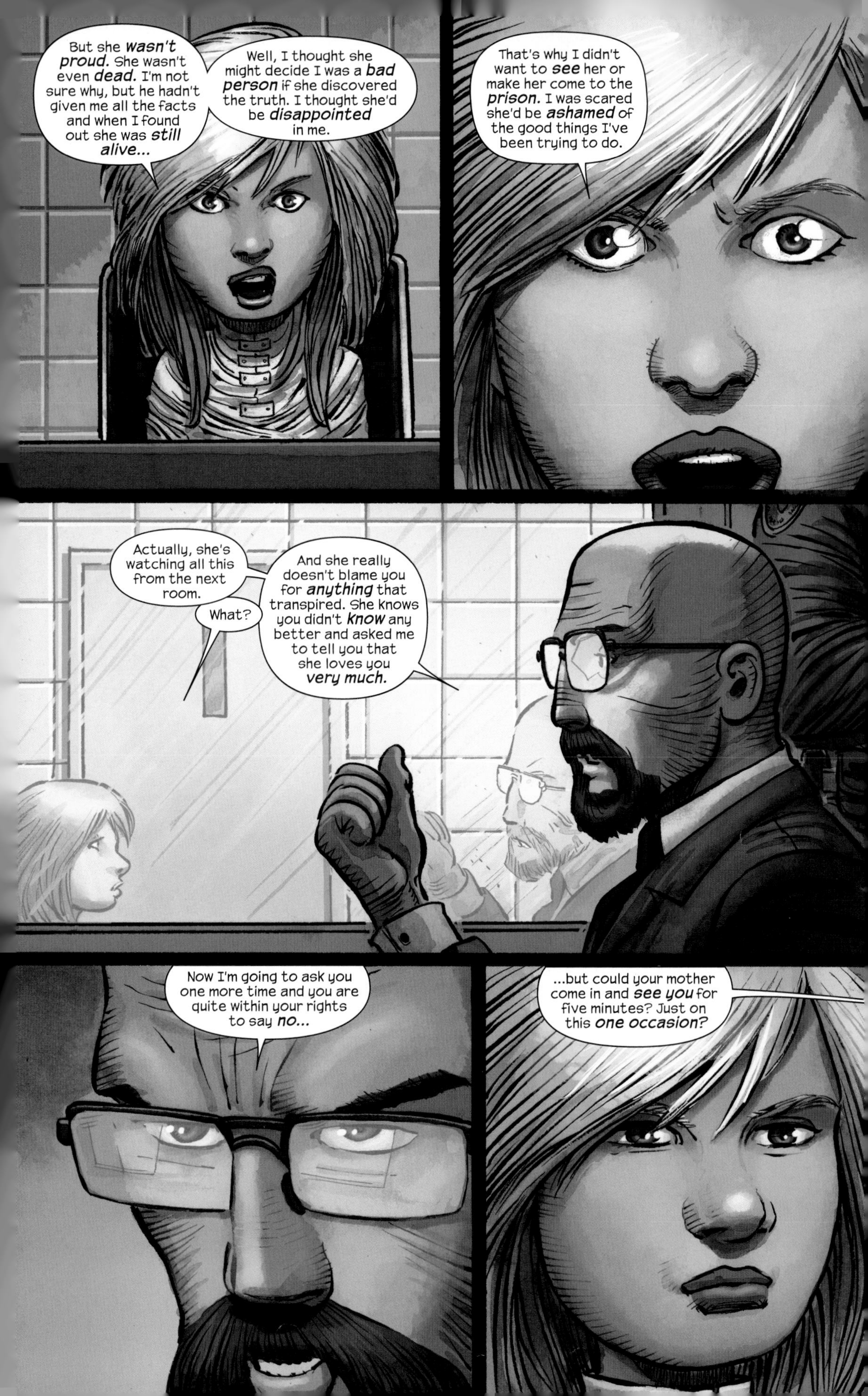

But she wasn't proud. She wasn't even dead. I'm not sure why, but he hadn't given me all the facts and when I found out she was still alive...
Well, I thought she might decide I was a bad person if she discovered the truth. I thought she'd be disappointed in me.
That's why I didn't want to see her or make her come to the prison. I was scared she'd be ashamed of the good things I've been trying to do.
Actually, she's watching all this from the next room.
What?
And she really doesn't blame you for anything that transpired. She knows you didn't know any better and asked me to tell you that she loves you very much.
Now I'm going to ask you one more time and you are quite within your rights to say no...
...but could your mother come in and see you for five minutes? Just on this one occasion?

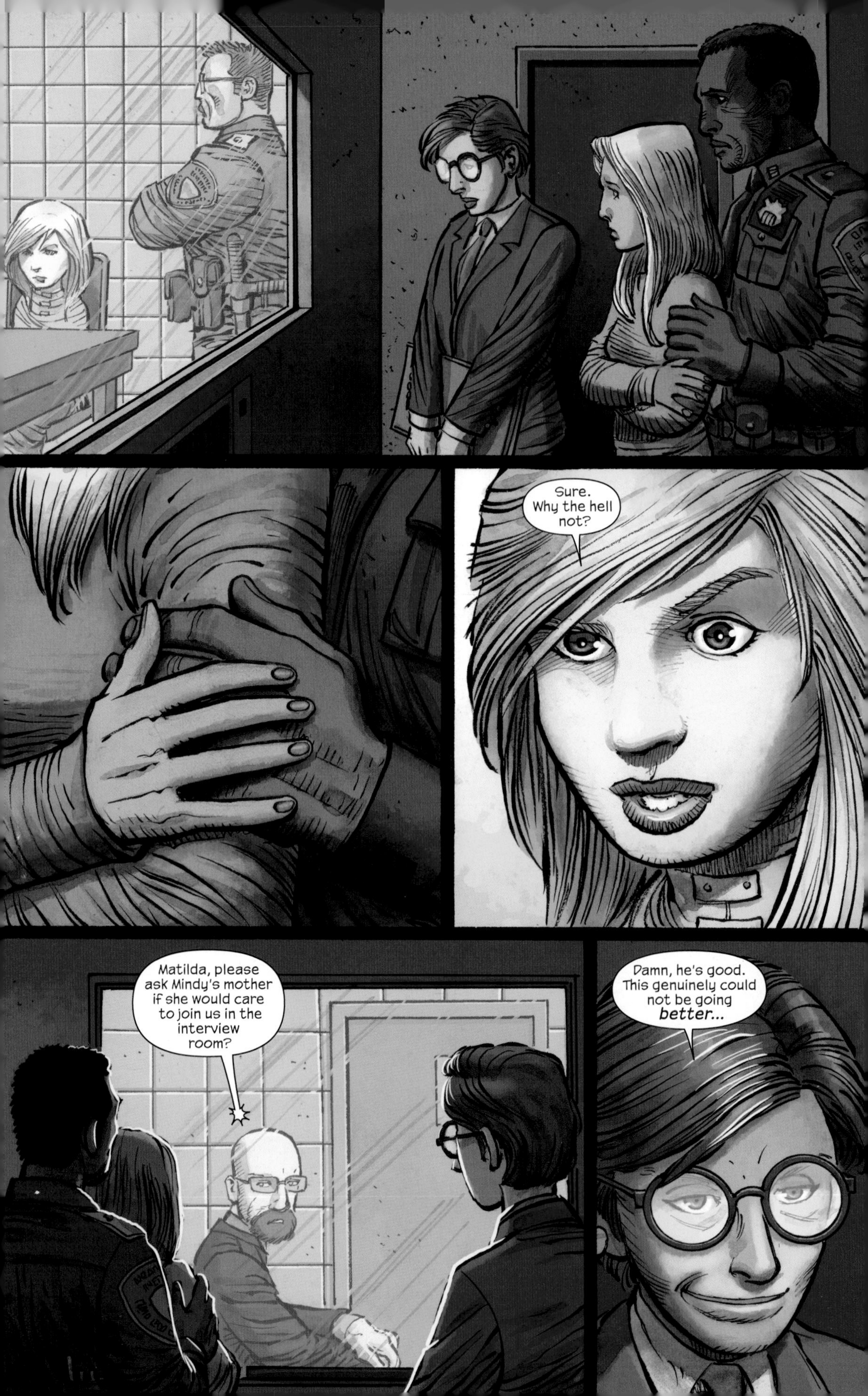
Sure. Why the hell not?
Matilda, please ask Mindy's mother if she would care to join us in the interview room?
Damn, he's good. This genuinely could not be going *better...*

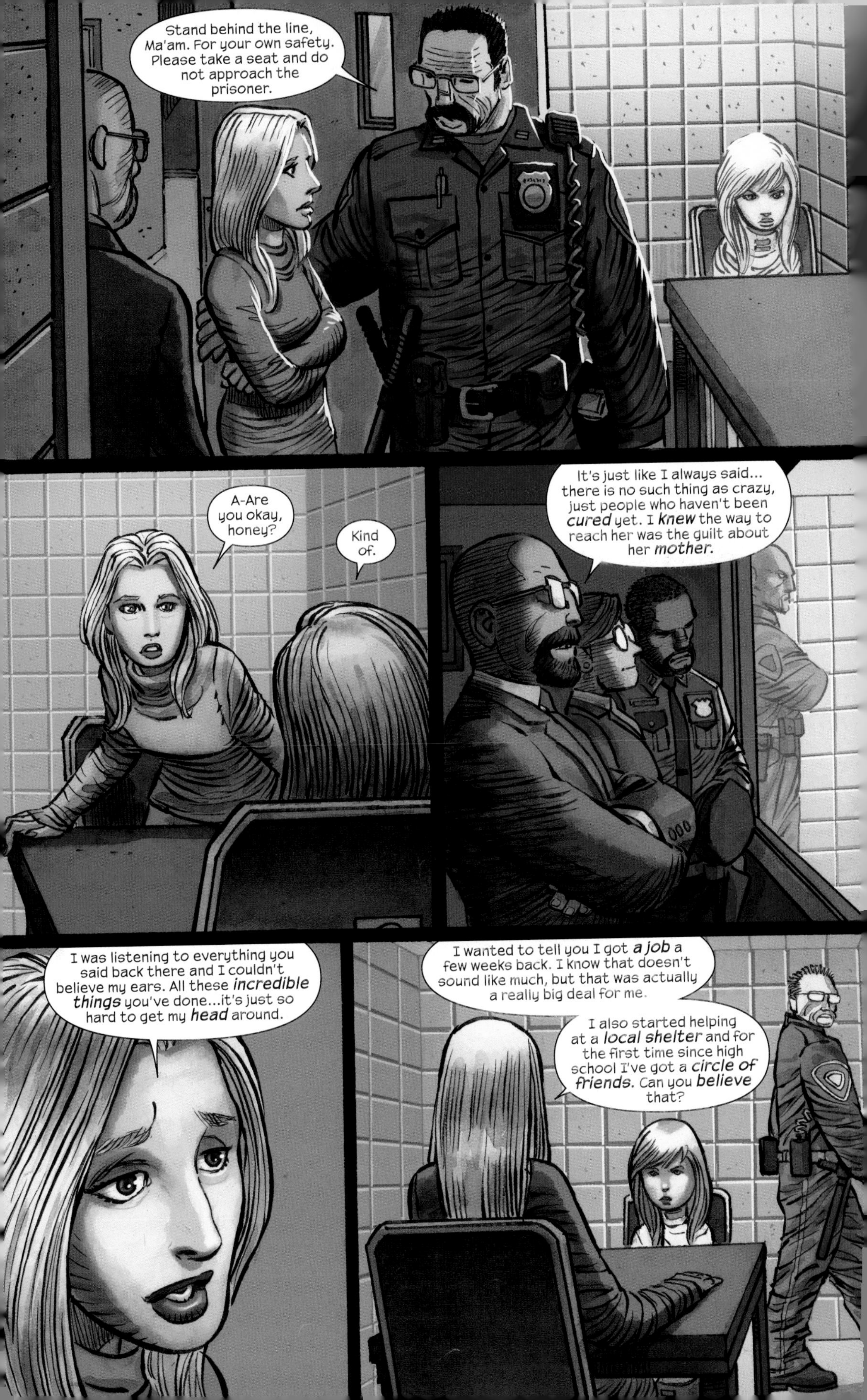
Stand behind the line, Ma'am. For your own safety. Please take a seat and do not approach the prisoner.
A-Are you okay, honey?
Kind of.
It's just like I always said... there is no such thing as crazy, just people who haven't been *cured* yet. I *knew* the way to reach her was the guilt about her *mother*.
I was listening to everything you said back there and I couldn't believe my ears. All these *incredible things* you've done...it's just so hard to get my *head* around.
I wanted to tell you I got *a job* a few weeks back. I know that doesn't sound like much, but that was actually a really big deal for me.
I also started helping at a *local shelter* and for the first time since high school I've got a *circle of friends*. Can you *believe* that?

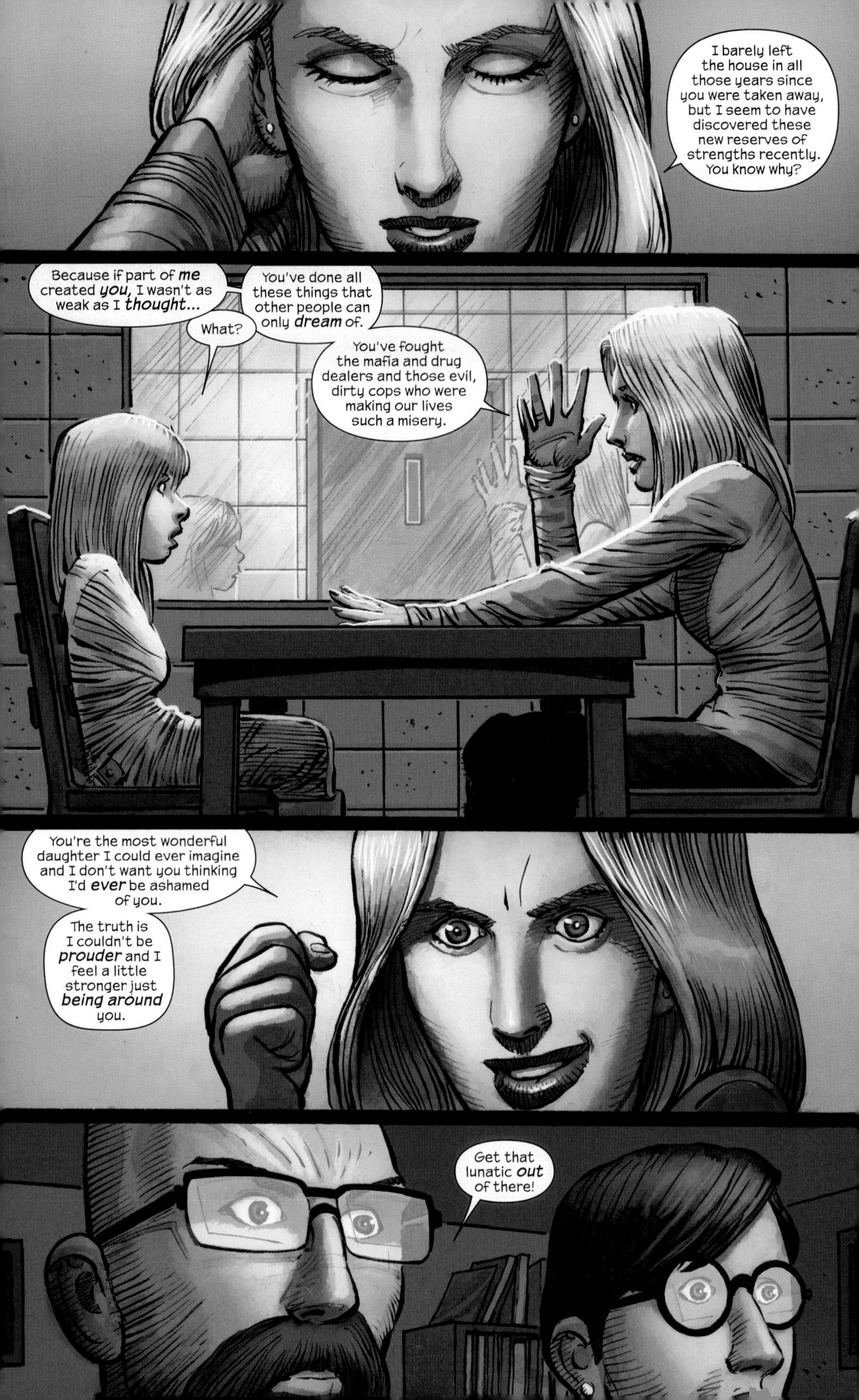
I barely left the house in all those years since you were taken away, but I seem to have discovered these new reserves of strengths recently. You know why?
Because if part of me created you, I wasn't as weak as I thought...
What?
You've done all these things that other people can only dream of.
You've fought the mafia and drug dealers and those evil, dirty cops who were making our lives such a misery.
You're the most wonderful daughter I could ever imagine and I don't want you thinking I'd ever be ashamed of you.
The truth is I couldn't be prouder and I feel a little stronger just being around you.
Get that lunatic out of there!

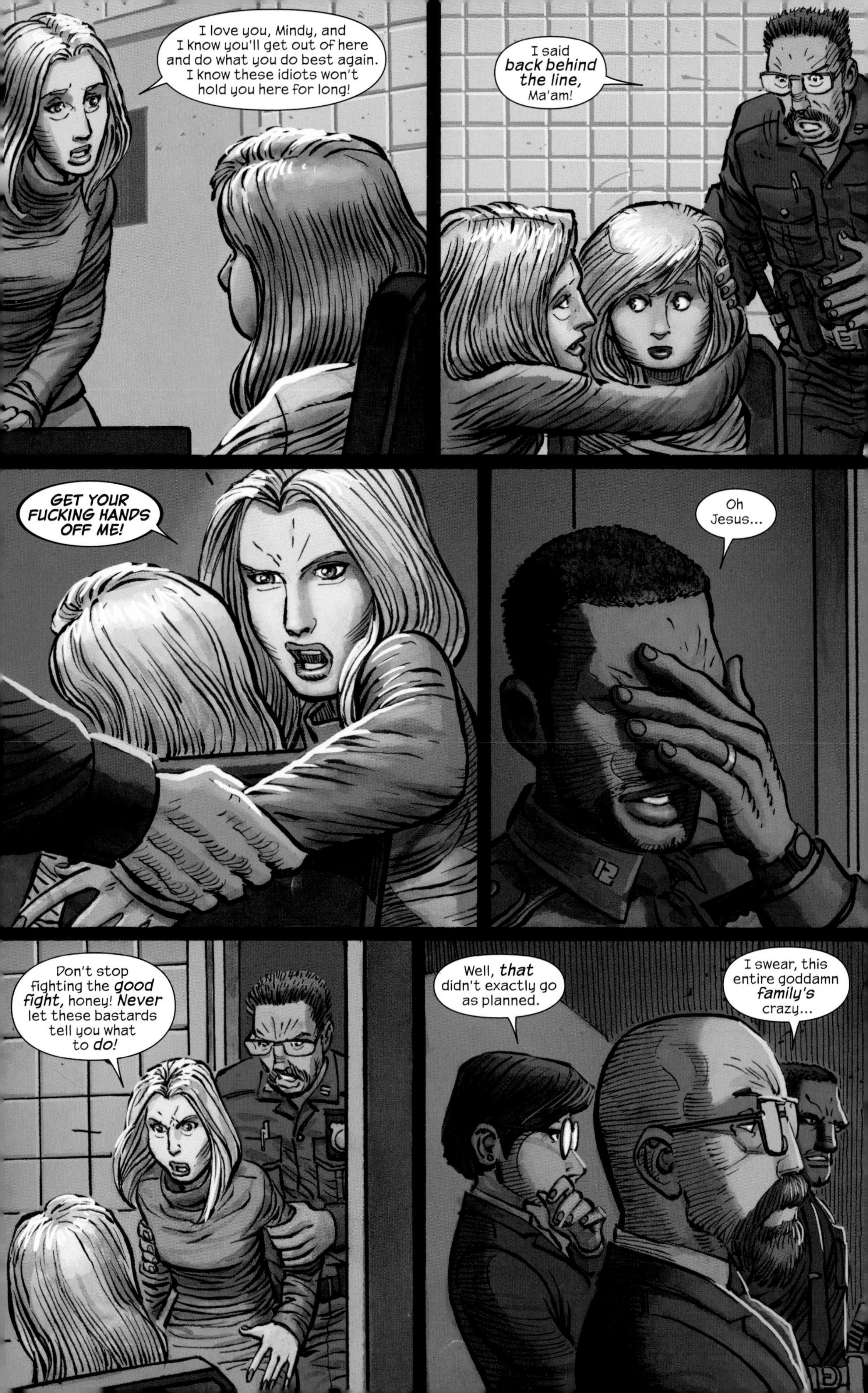
I love you, Mindy, and I know you'll get out of here and do what you do best again. I know these idiots won't hold you here for long!
I said *back behind the line,* Ma'am!
GET YOUR FUCKING HANDS OFF ME!
Oh Jesus...
Don't stop fighting the *good fight,* honey! *Never* let these bastards tell you what to *do!*
Well, *that* didn't exactly go as planned.
I swear, this entire goddamn *family's* crazy...

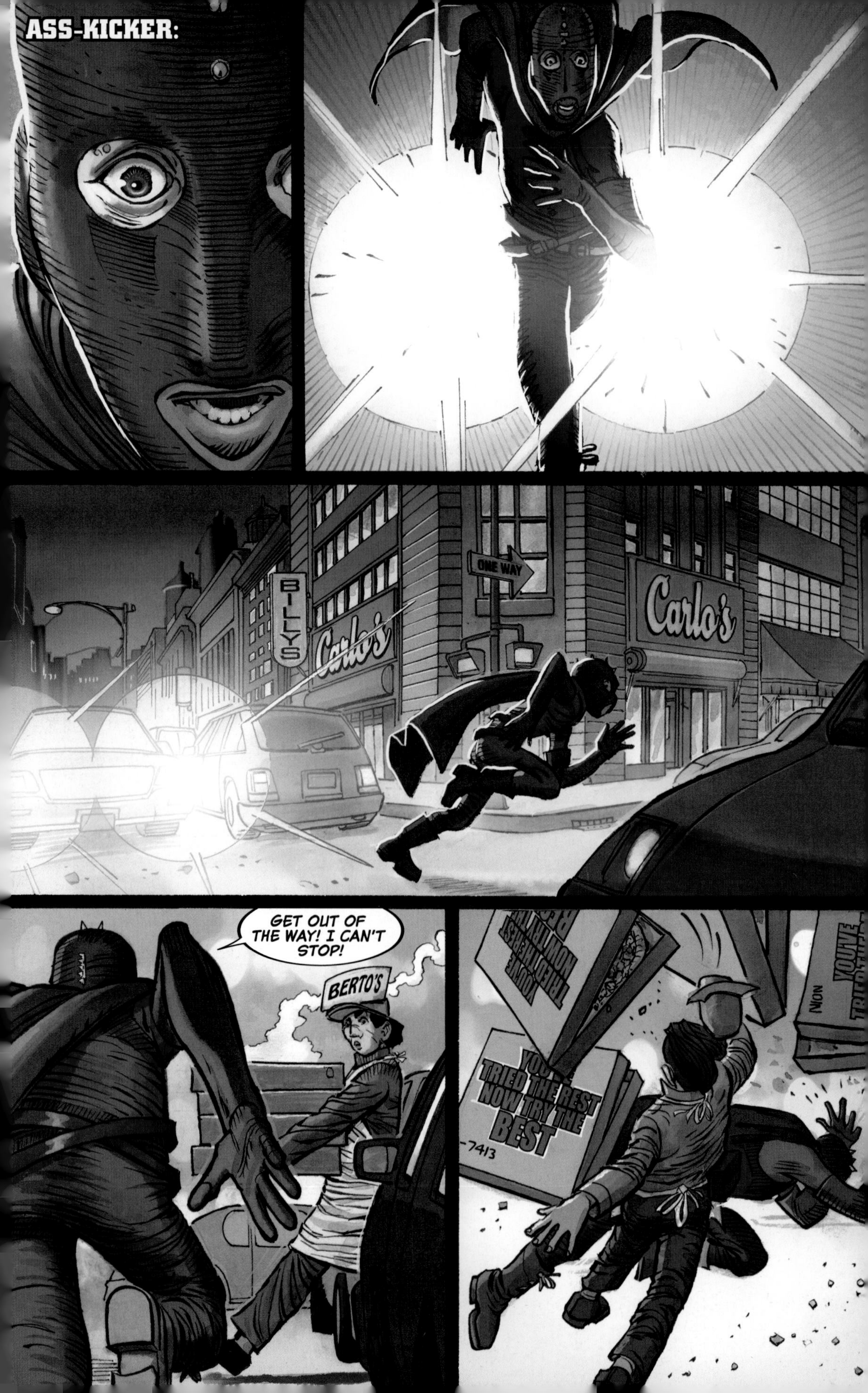
ASS-KICKER:
BILLYS
ONE WAY
Carlo's
Carlo's
GET OUT OF THE WAY! I CAN'T STOP!
BERTO'S
YOU'VE TRIED THE REST NOW TRY THE BEST
-7413

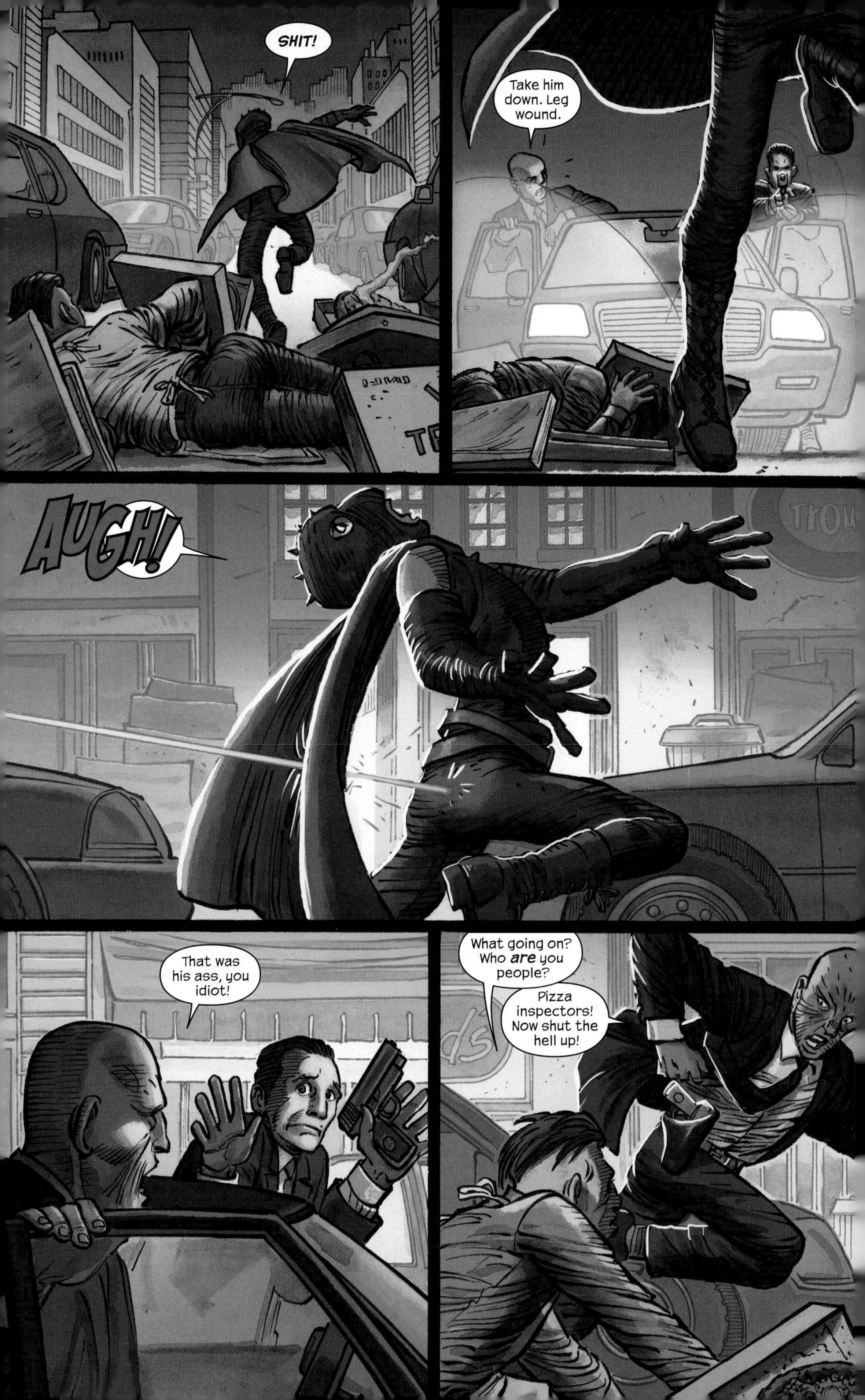

SHIT!
Take him down. Leg wound.
AUGH!
That was his ass, you idiot!
What going on? Who *are* you people?
Pizza inspectors! Now shut the hell up!

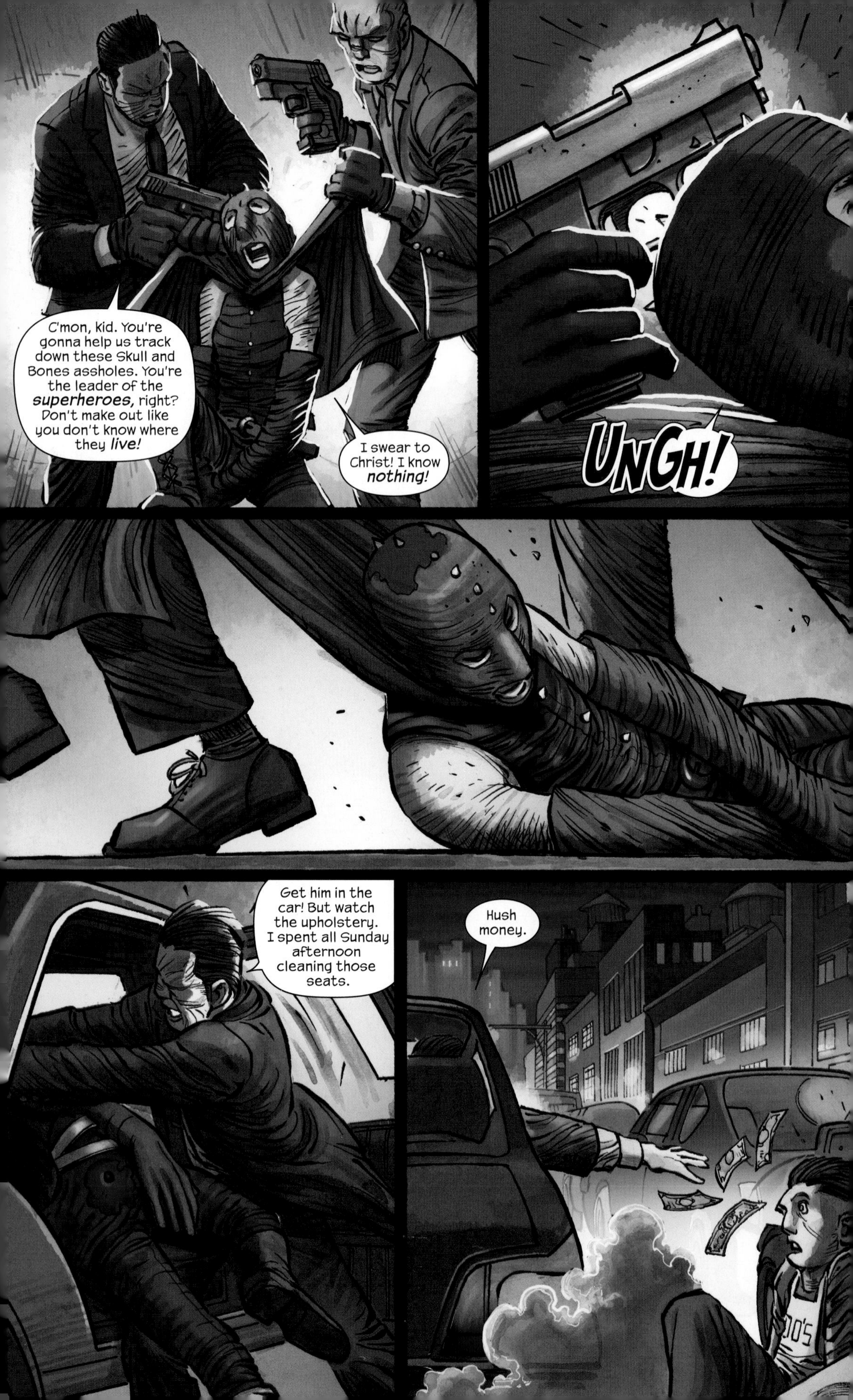
C'mon, kid. You're gonna help us track down these Skull and Bones assholes. You're the leader of the **superheroes,** right? Don't make out like you don't know where they *live!*
I swear to Christ! I know ***nothing!***
UNGH!
Get him in the car! But watch the upholstery. I spent all Sunday afternoon cleaning those seats.
Hush money.

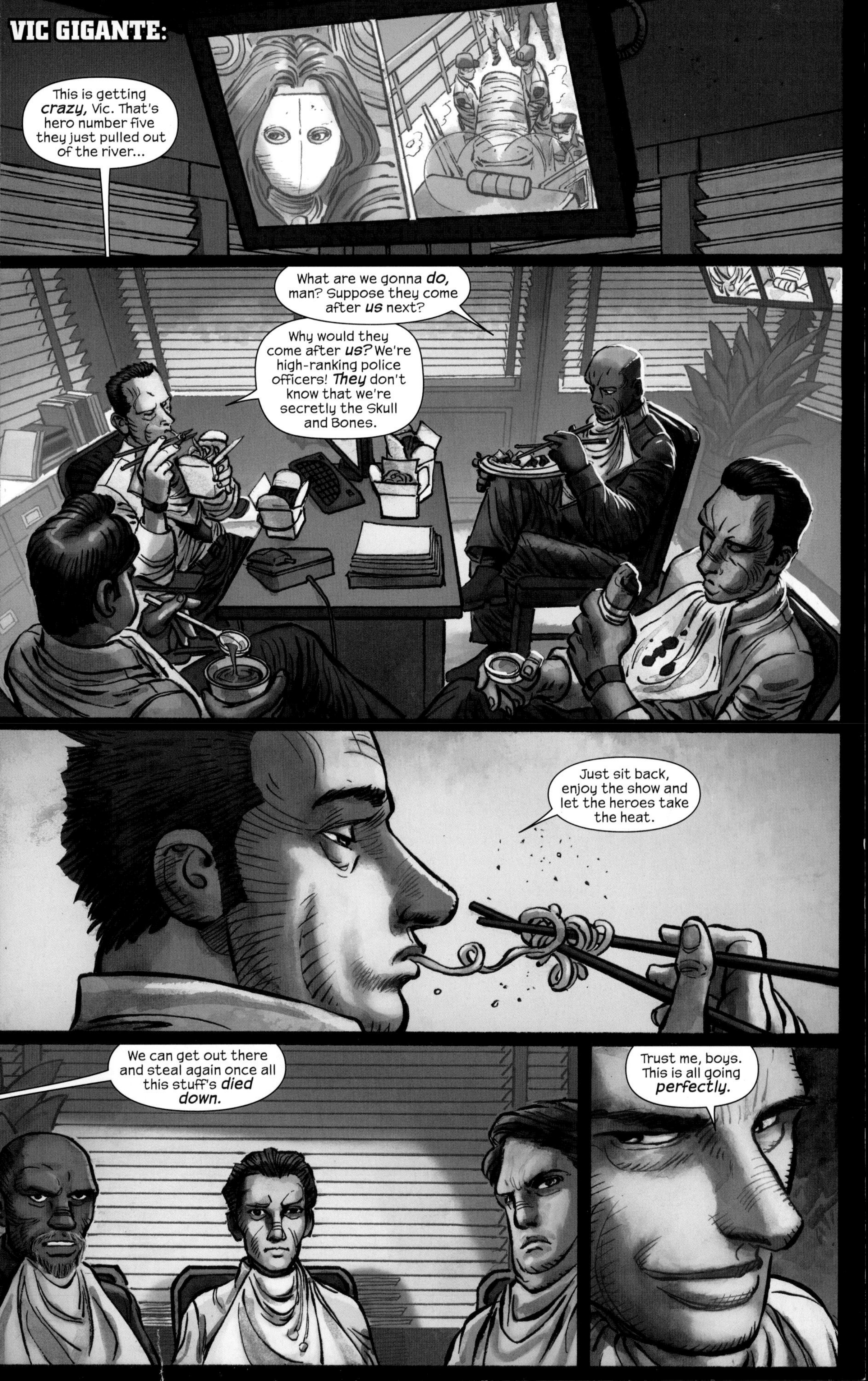
VIC GIGANTE:
This is getting *crazy,* Vic. That's hero number five they just pulled out of the river...
What are we gonna *do,* man? Suppose they come after *us* next?
Why would they come after *us?* We're high-ranking police officers! *They* don't know that we're secretly the Skull and Bones.
Just sit back, enjoy the show and let the heroes take the heat.
We can get out there and steal again once all this stuff's *died down.*
Trust me, boys. This is all going *perfectly.*

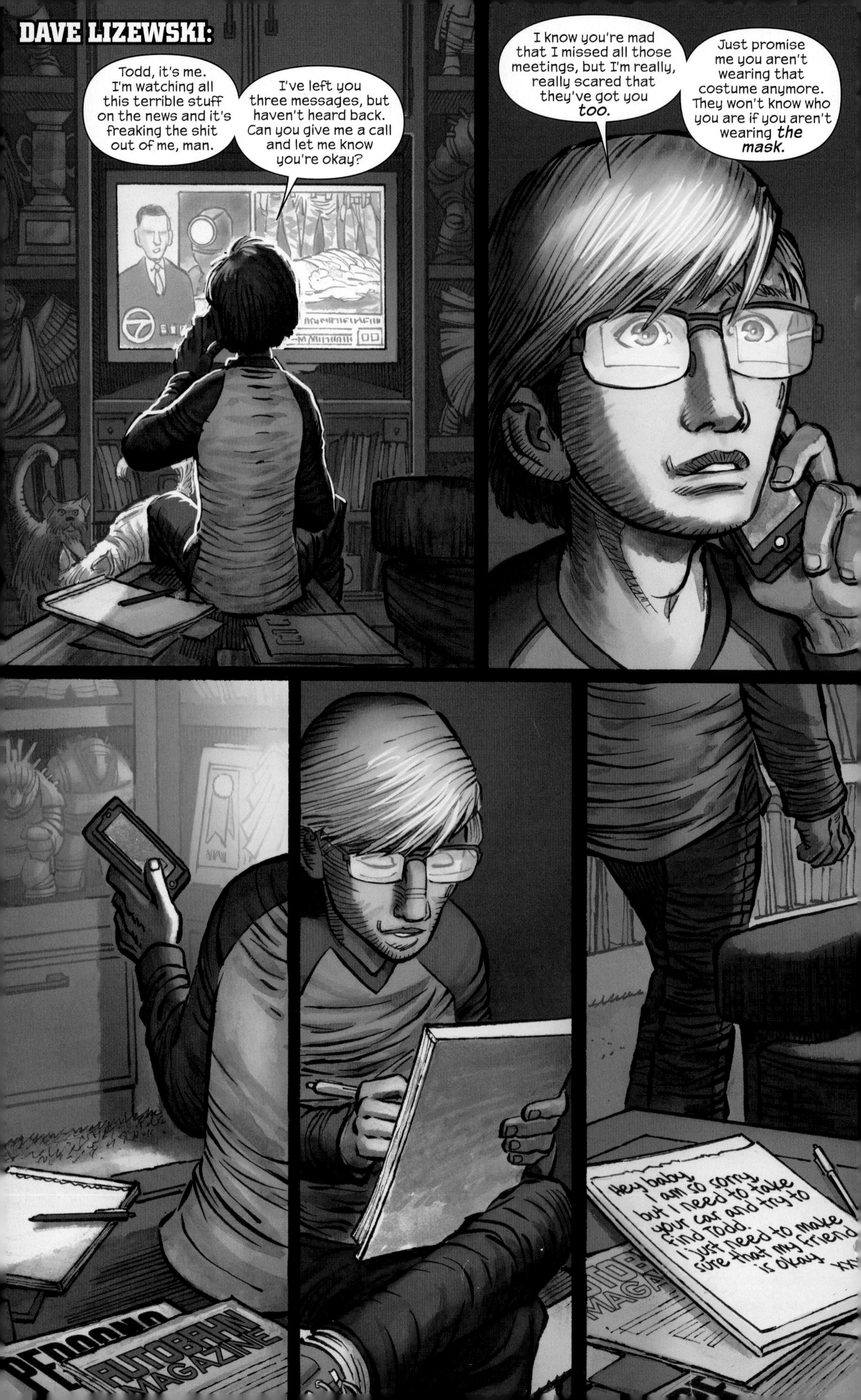
DAVE LIZEWSKI:
Todd, it's me. I'm watching all this terrible stuff on the news and it's freaking the shit out of me, man.
I've left you three messages, but haven't heard back. Can you give me a call and let me know you're okay?
I know you're mad that I missed all those meetings, but I'm really, really scared that they've got you *too.*
Just promise me you aren't wearing that costume anymore. They won't know who you are if you aren't wearing *the mask.*
AUTOBAHN MAGAZINE
Hey baby, I am so sorry, but I need to take your car and try to find Todd. I just need to make sure that my friend is okay. xx

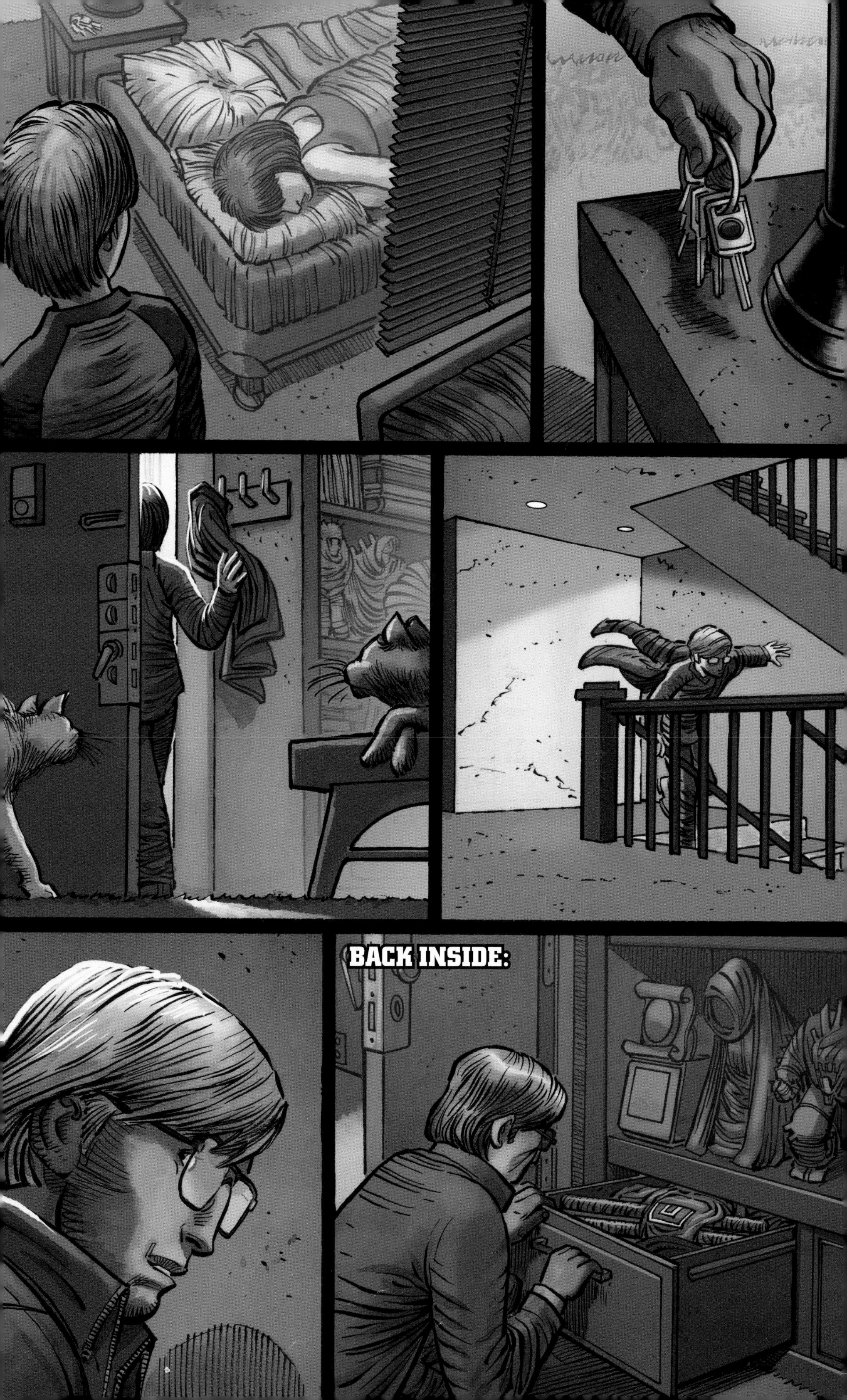
BACK INSIDE:

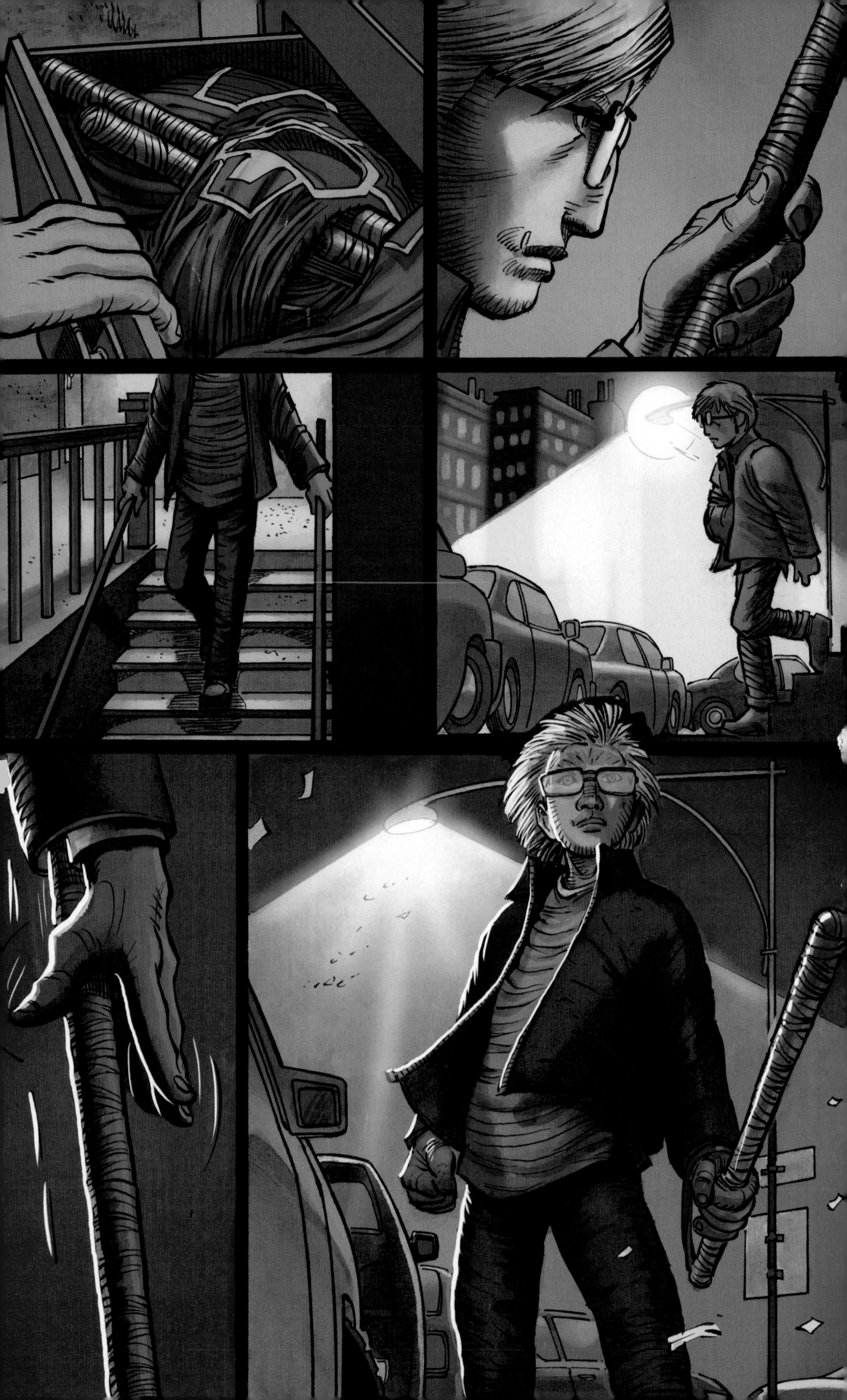

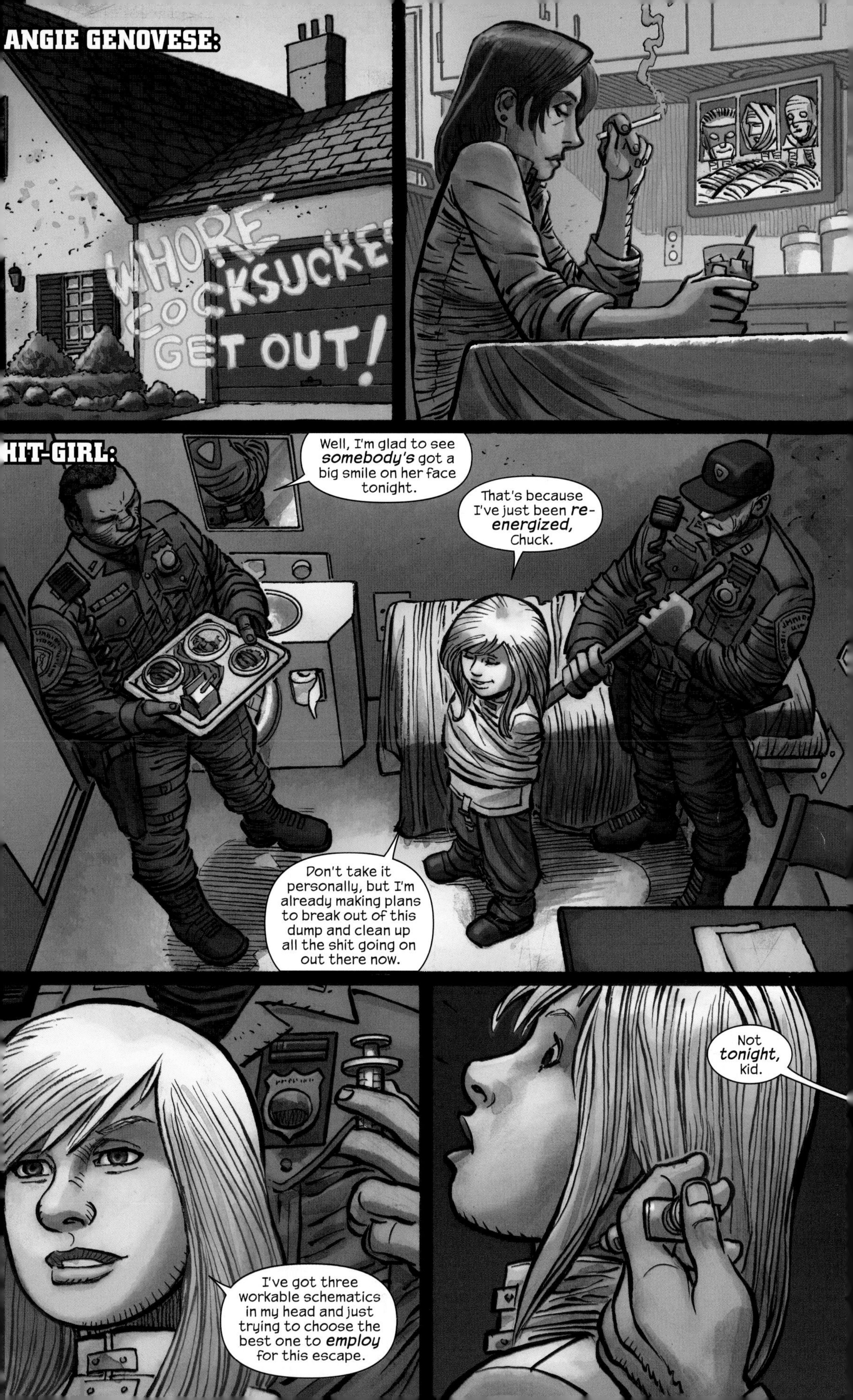
ANGIE GENOVESE:
WHORE
COCKSUCKE
GET OUT!
HIT-GIRL:
Well, I'm glad to see somebody's got a big smile on her face tonight.
That's because I've just been re-energized, Chuck.
Don't take it personally, but I'm already making plans to break out of this dump and clean up all the shit going on out there now.
I've got three workable schematics in my head and just trying to choose the best one to employ for this escape.
Not tonight, kid.

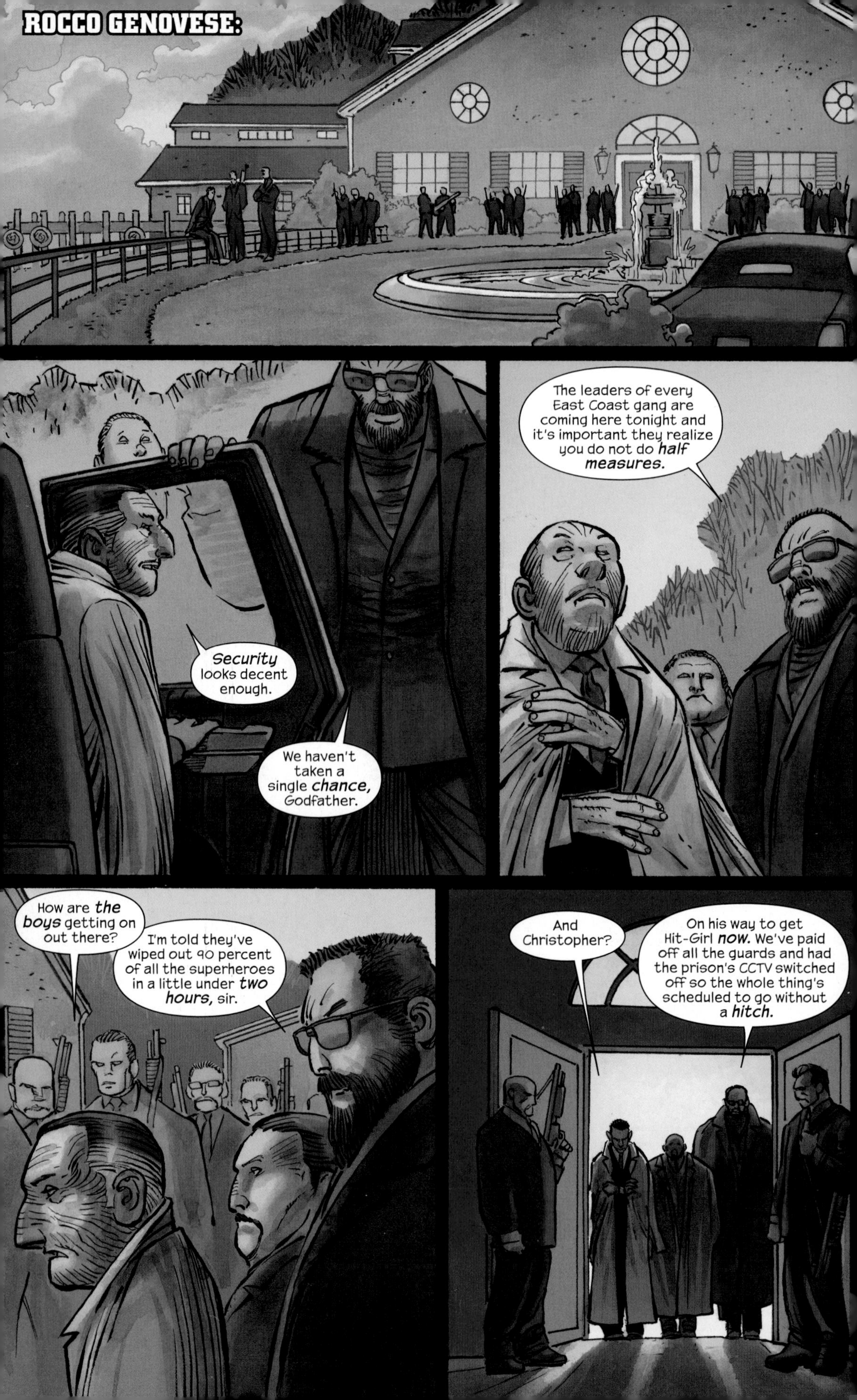
ROCCO GENOVESE:
Security looks decent enough.
We haven't taken a single chance, Godfather.
The leaders of every East Coast gang are coming here tonight and it's important they realize you do not do half measures.
How are the boys getting on out there?
I'm told they've wiped out 90 percent of all the superheroes in a little under two hours, sir.
And Christopher?
On his way to get Hit-Girl now. We've paid off all the guards and had the prison's CCTV switched off so the whole thing's scheduled to go without a hitch.

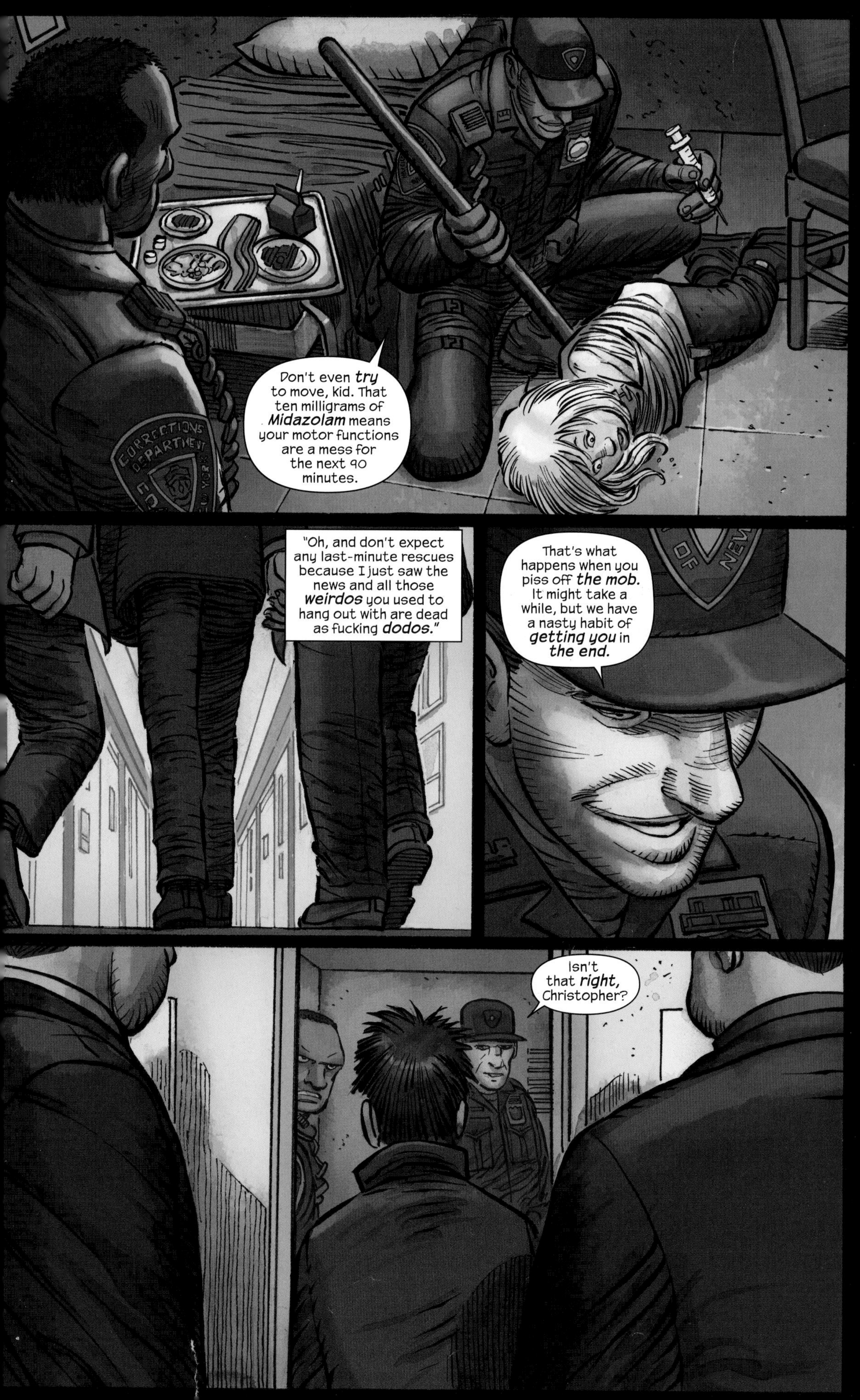
Don't even try to move, kid. That ten milligrams of Midazolam means your motor functions are a mess for the next 90 minutes.
CORRECTIONS DEPARTMENT
"Oh, and don't expect any last-minute rescues because I just saw the news and all those weirdos you used to hang out with are dead as fucking dodos."
That's what happens when you piss off the mob. It might take a while, but we have a nasty habit of getting you in the end.
Isn't that right, Christopher?

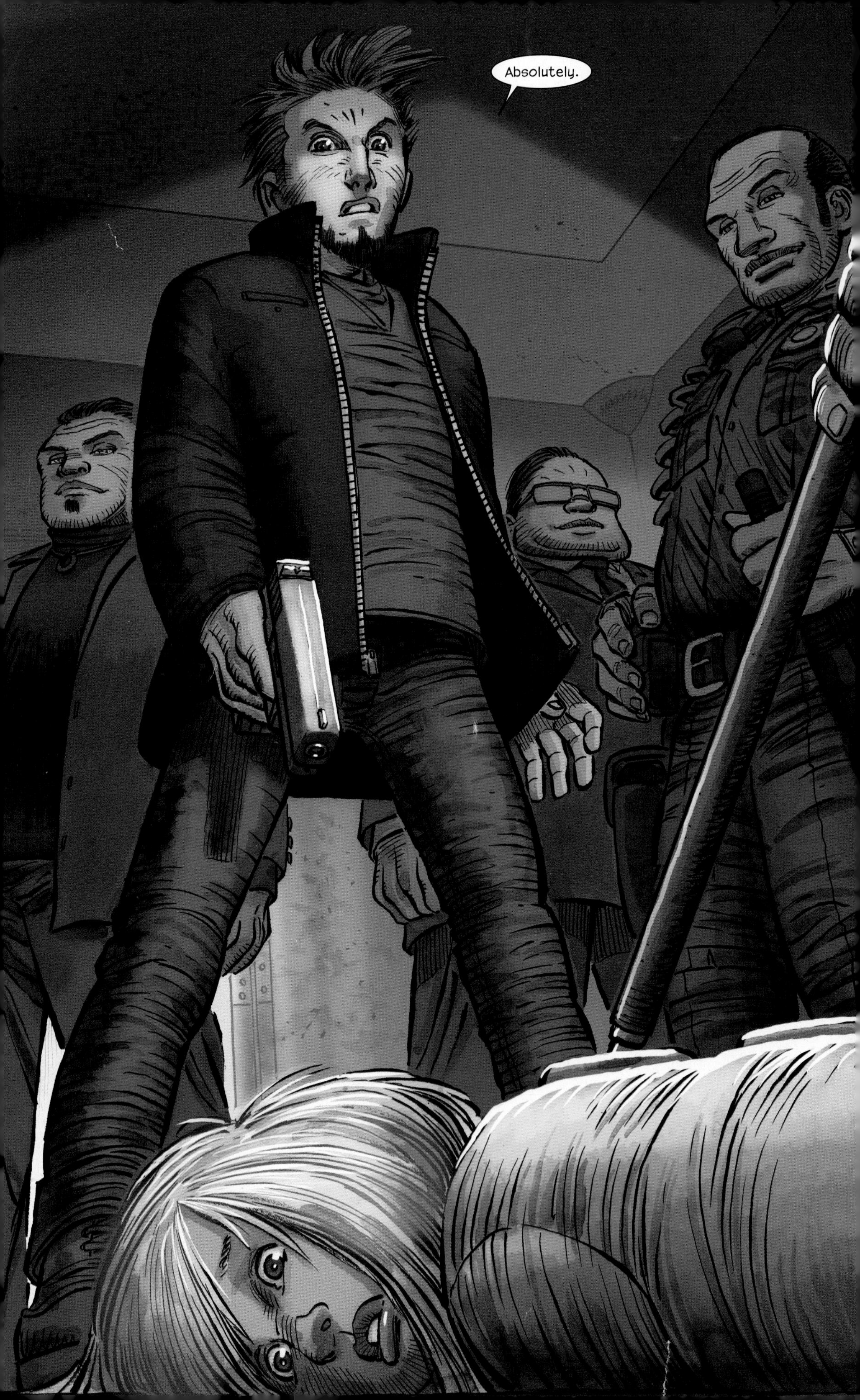
Absolutely.

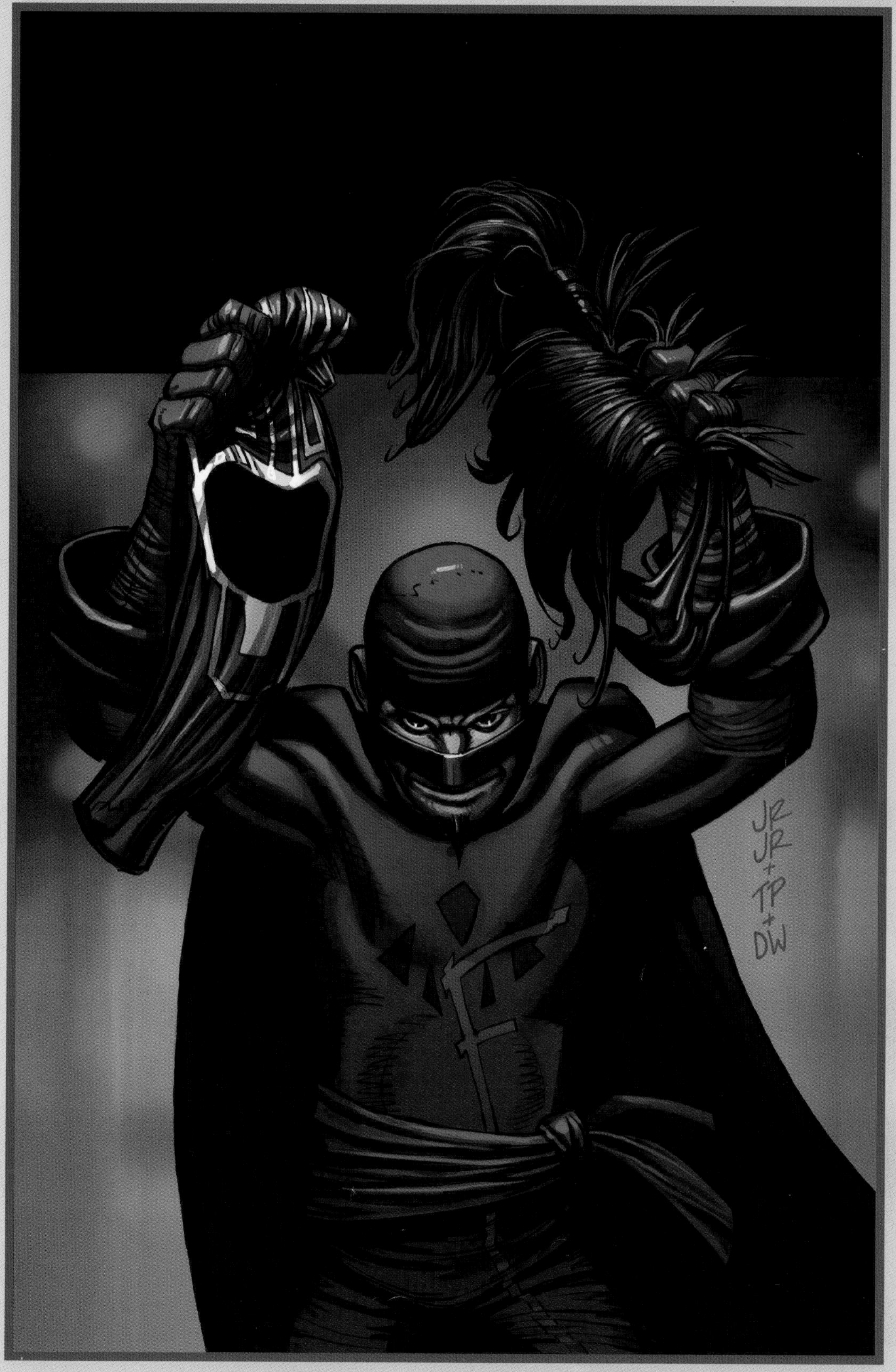
JR
JR
+
TP
+
DW

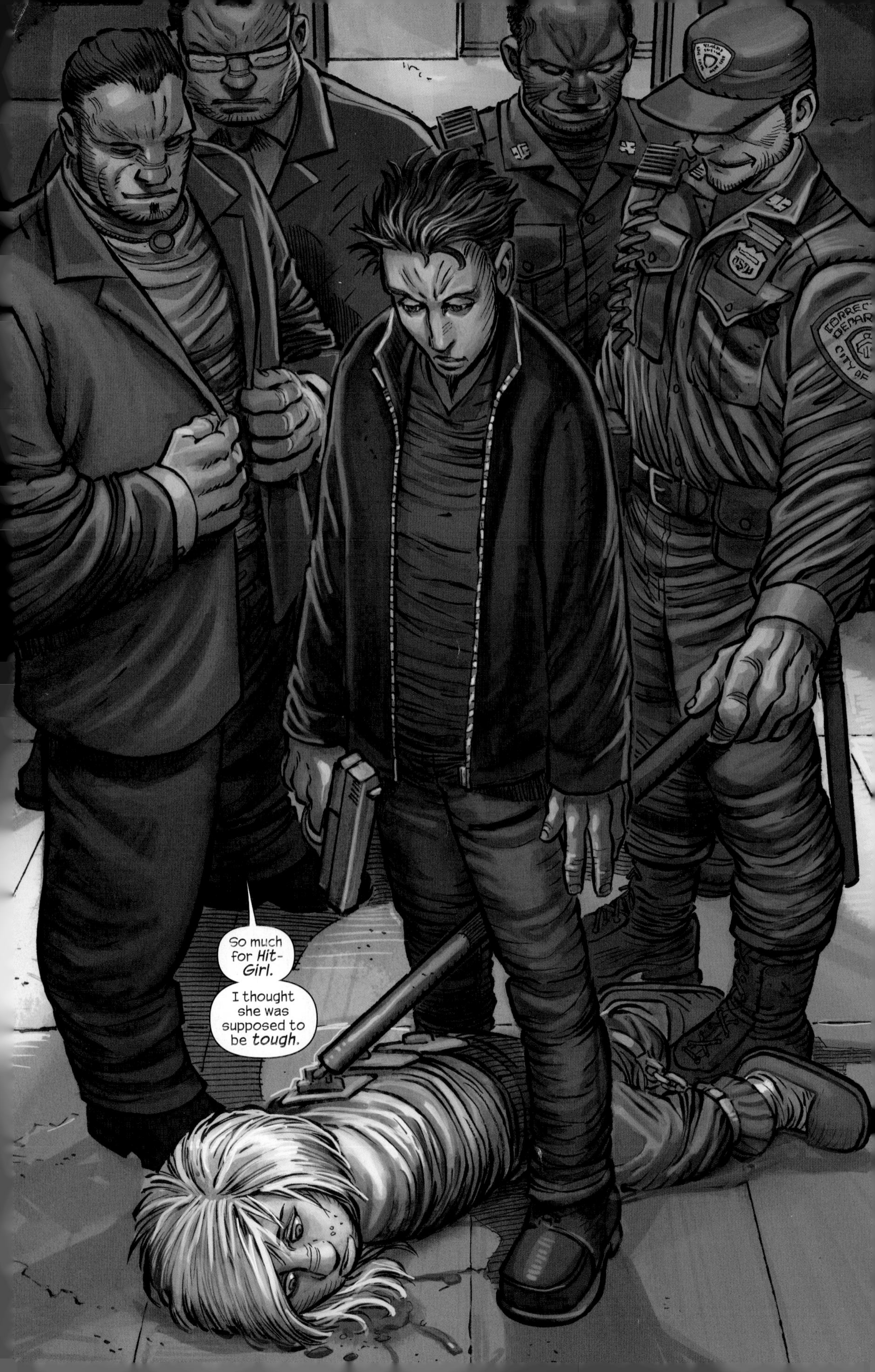
So much for *Hit-Girl.*
I thought she was supposed to be ***tough.***

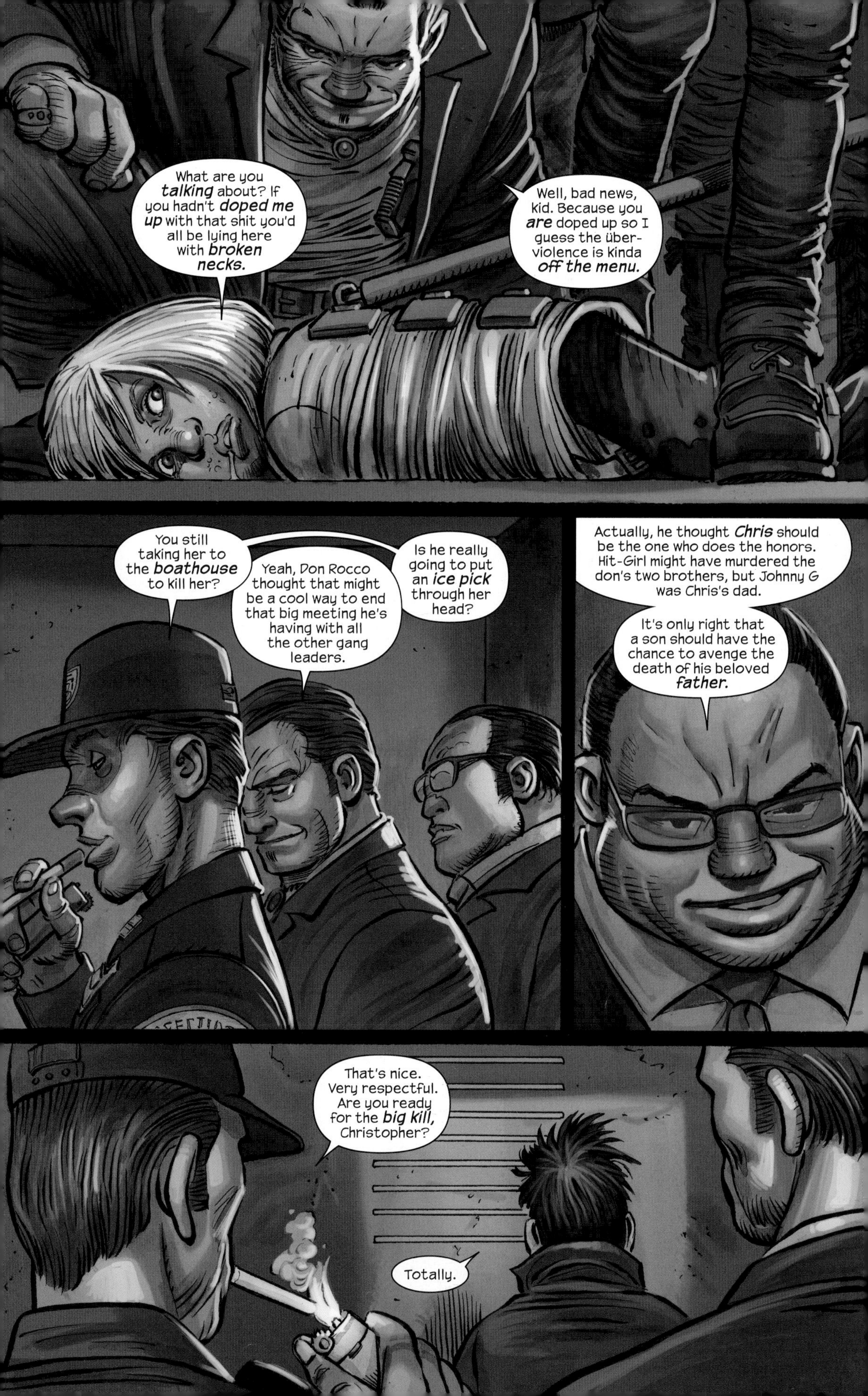

What are you *talking* about? If you hadn't *doped me up* with that shit you'd all be lying here with *broken necks.*
Well, bad news, kid. Because you *are* doped up so I guess the über-violence is kinda *off the menu.*
You still taking her to the *boathouse* to kill her?
Yeah, Don Rocco thought that might be a cool way to end that big meeting he's having with all the other gang leaders.
Is he really going to put an *ice pick* through her head?
Actually, he thought *Chris* should be the one who does the honors. Hit-Girl might have murdered the don's two brothers, but Johnny G was Chris's dad.
It's only right that a son should have the chance to avenge the death of his beloved *father.*
That's nice. Very respectful. Are you ready for the *big kill,* Christopher?
Totally.

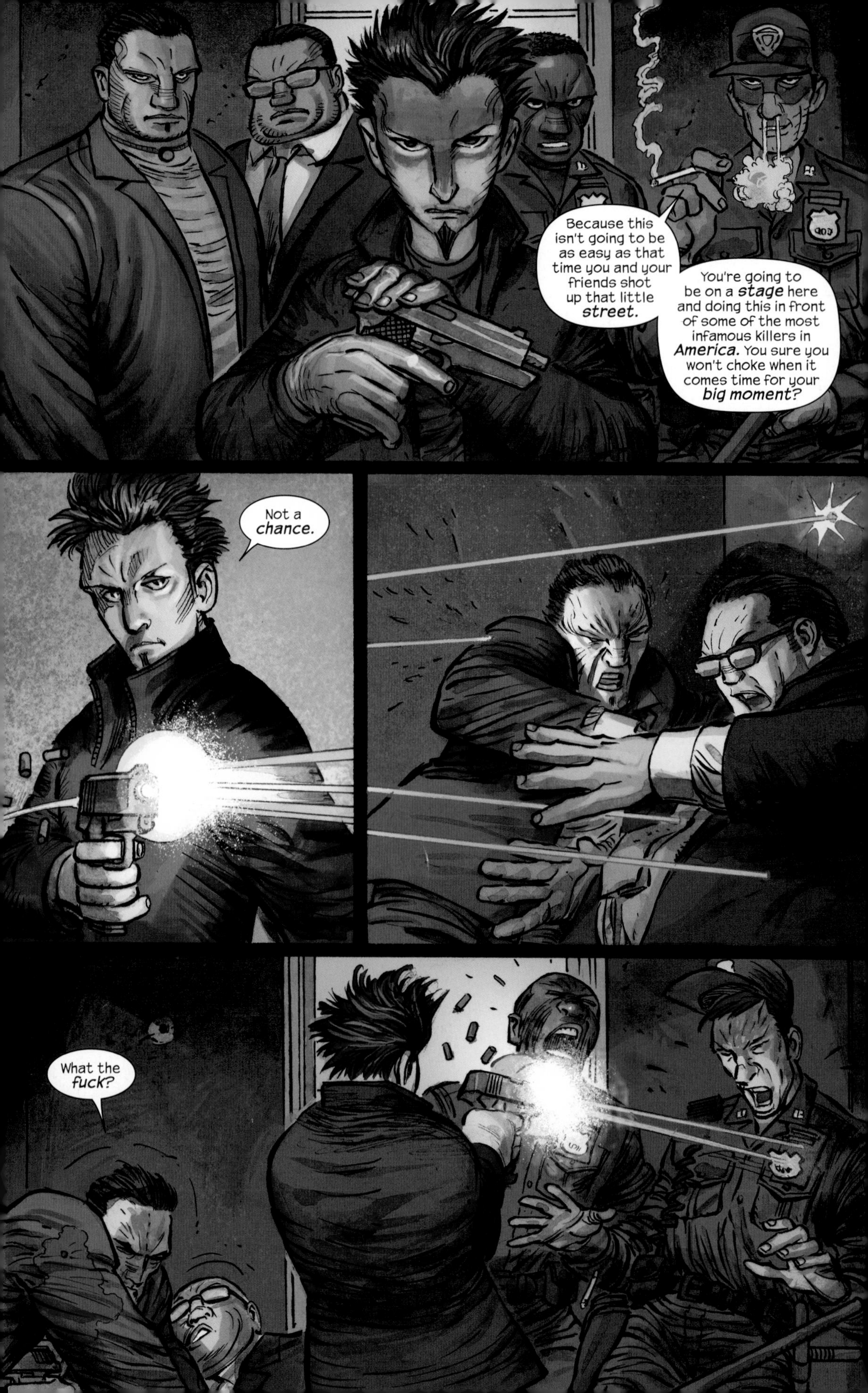
Because this isn't going to be as easy as that time you and your friends shot up that little *street.*
You're going to be on a *stage* here and doing this in front of some of the most infamous killers in *America.* You sure you won't choke when it comes time for your *big moment?*
Not a *chance.*
What the *fuck?*

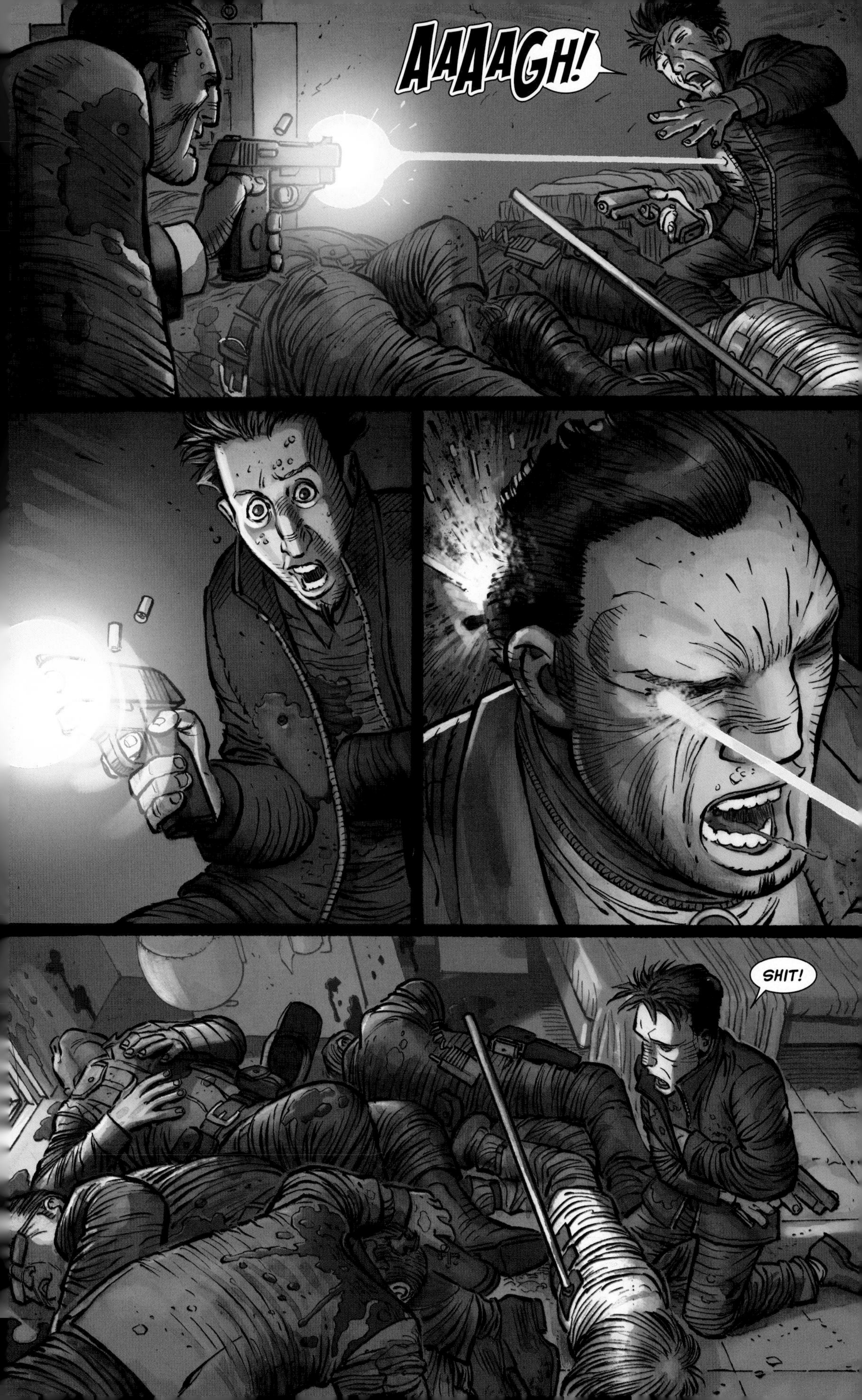
AAAAGH!
SHIT!

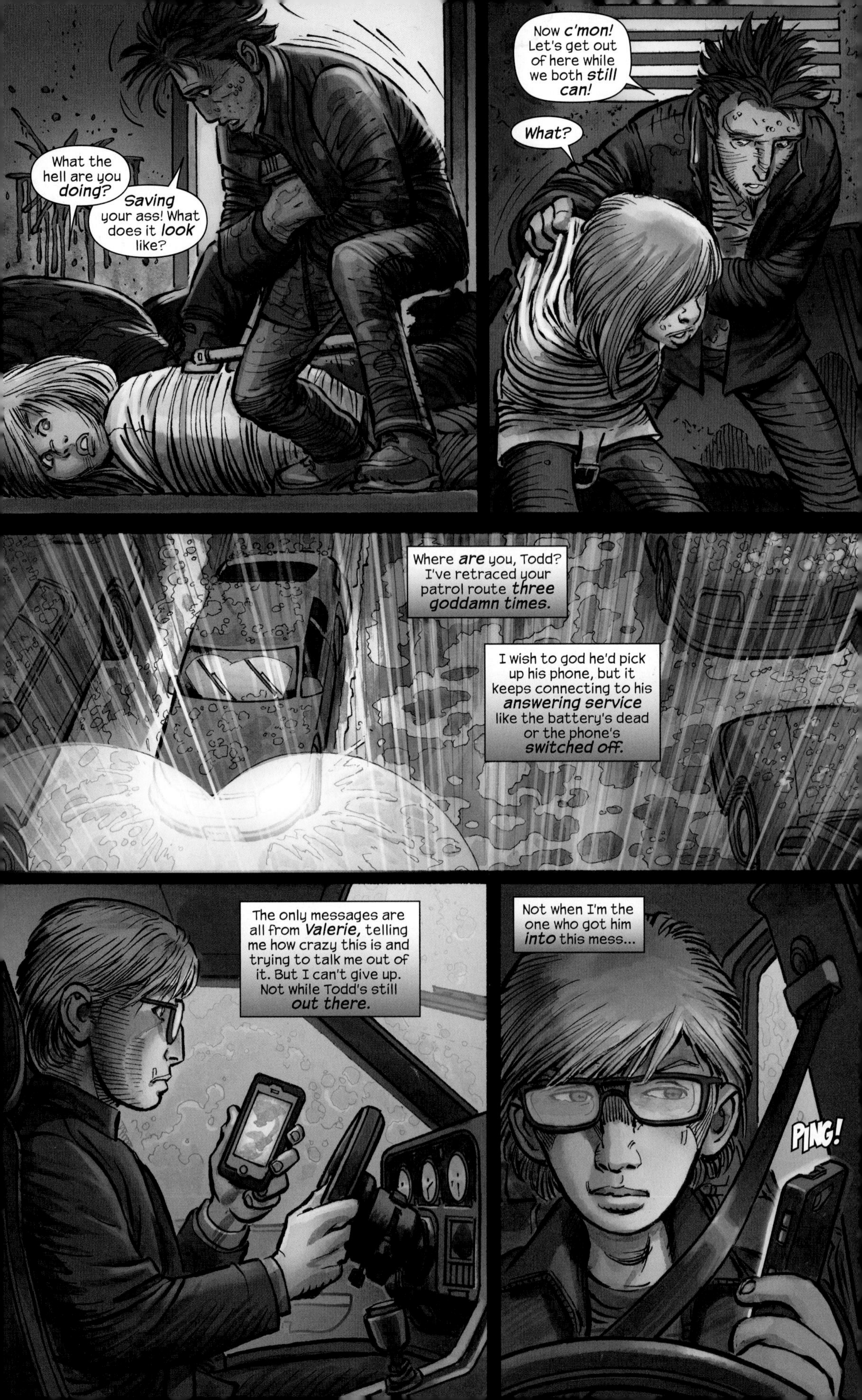
What the hell are you doing?
Saving your ass! What does it look like?
Now c'mon! Let's get out of here while we both still can!
What?
Where are you, Todd? I've retraced your patrol route three goddamn times.
I wish to god he'd pick up his phone, but it keeps connecting to his answering service like the battery's dead or the phone's switched off.
The only messages are all from Valerie, telling me how crazy this is and trying to talk me out of it. But I can't give up. Not while Todd's still out there.
Not when I'm the one who got him into this mess...
PING!

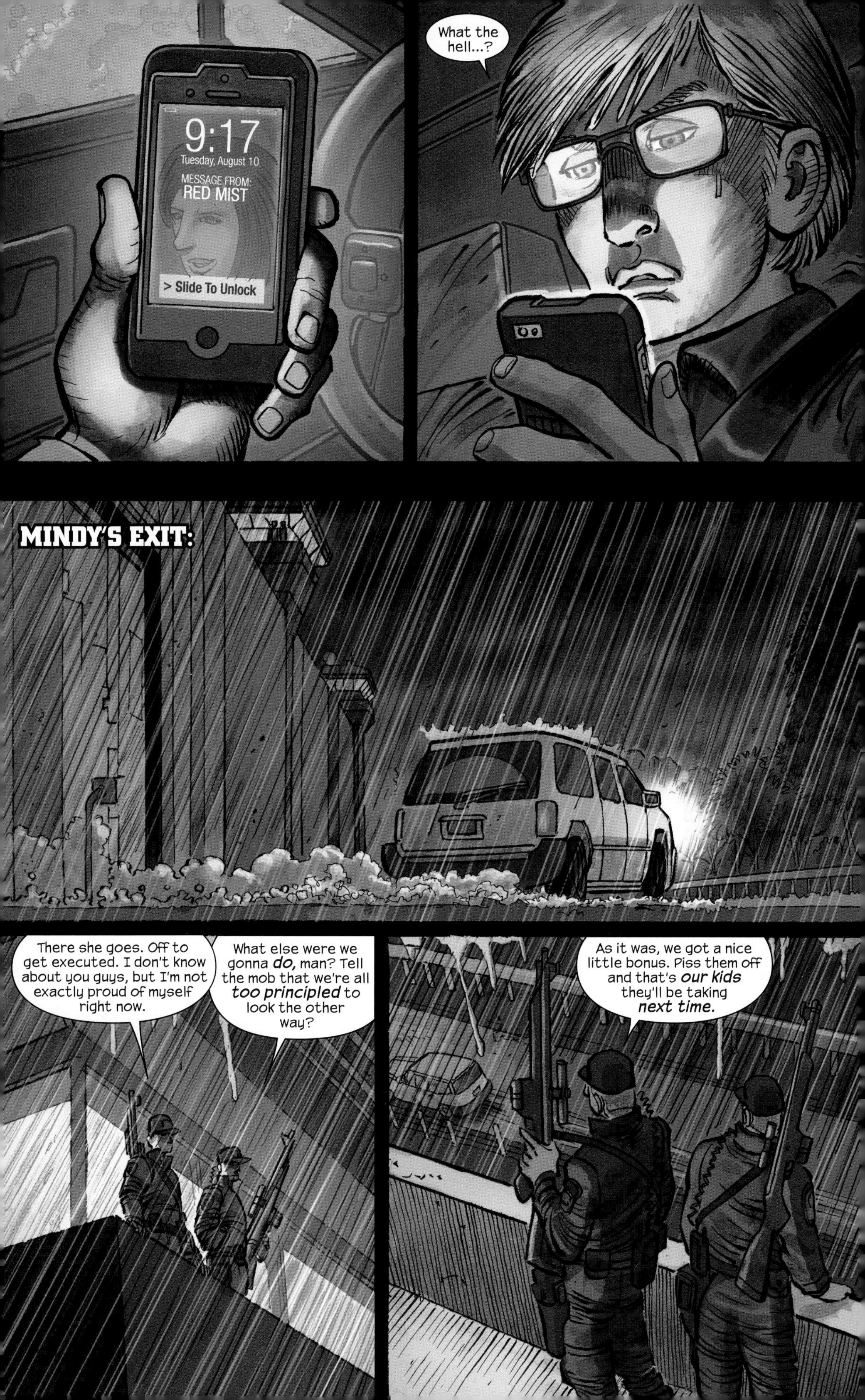
9:17
Tuesday, August 10
MESSAGE FROM:
RED MIST
> Slide To Unlock
What the hell...?
MINDY'S EXIT:
There she goes. Off to get executed. I don't know about you guys, but I'm not exactly proud of myself right now.
What else were we gonna *do,* man? Tell the mob that we're all *too principled* to look the other way?
As it was, we got a nice little bonus. Piss them off and that's *our kids* they'll be taking *next time.*

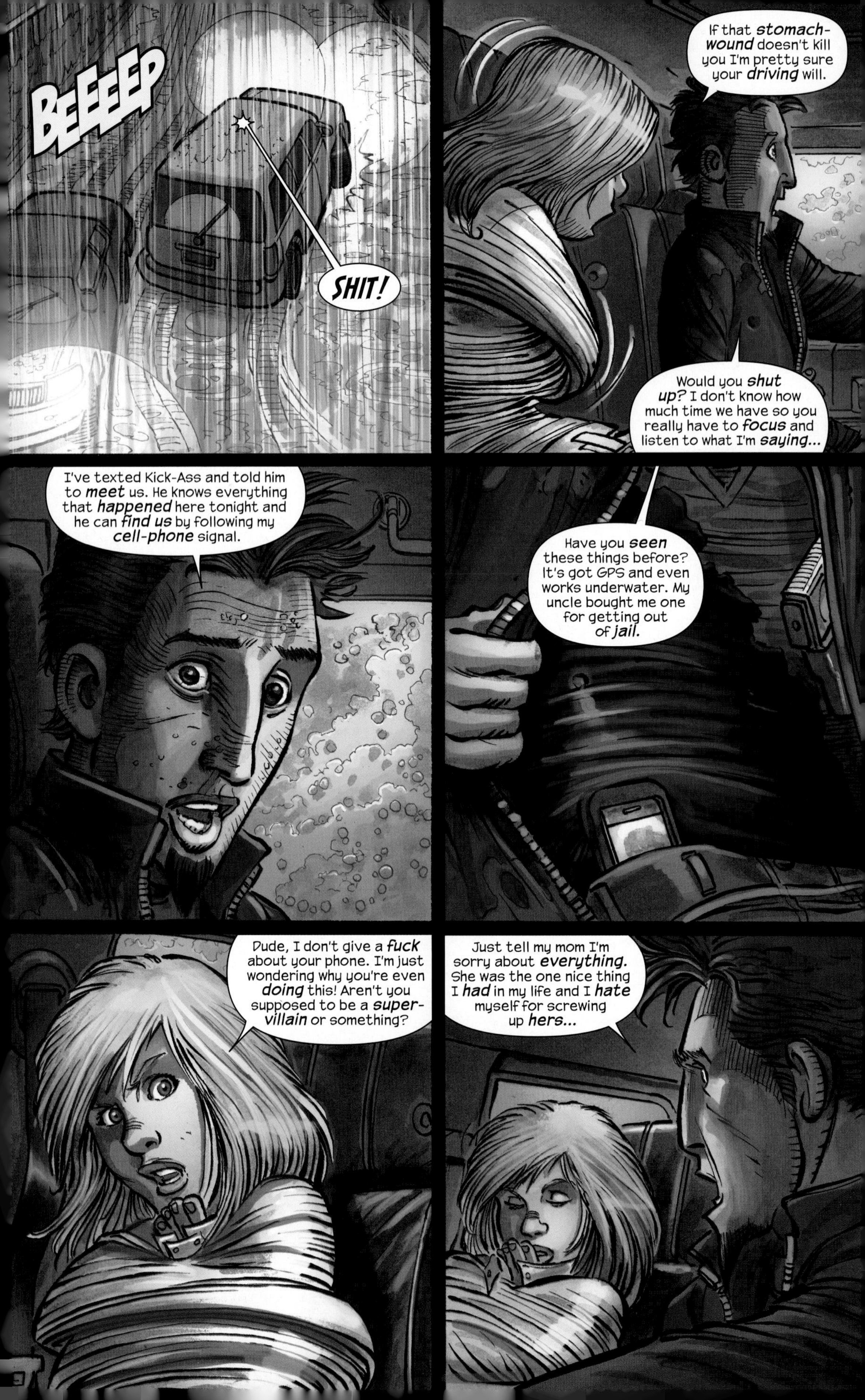
BEEEEP
SHIT!
If that stomach-wound doesn't kill you I'm pretty sure your driving will.
Would you shut up? I don't know how much time we have so you really have to focus and listen to what I'm saying...
I've texted Kick-Ass and told him to meet us. He knows everything that happened here tonight and he can find us by following my cell-phone signal.
Have you seen these things before? It's got GPS and even works underwater. My uncle bought me one for getting out of jail.
Dude, I don't give a fuck about your phone. I'm just wondering why you're even doing this! Aren't you supposed to be a super-villain or something?
Just tell my mom I'm sorry about everything. She was the one nice thing I had in my life and I hate myself for screwing up hers...

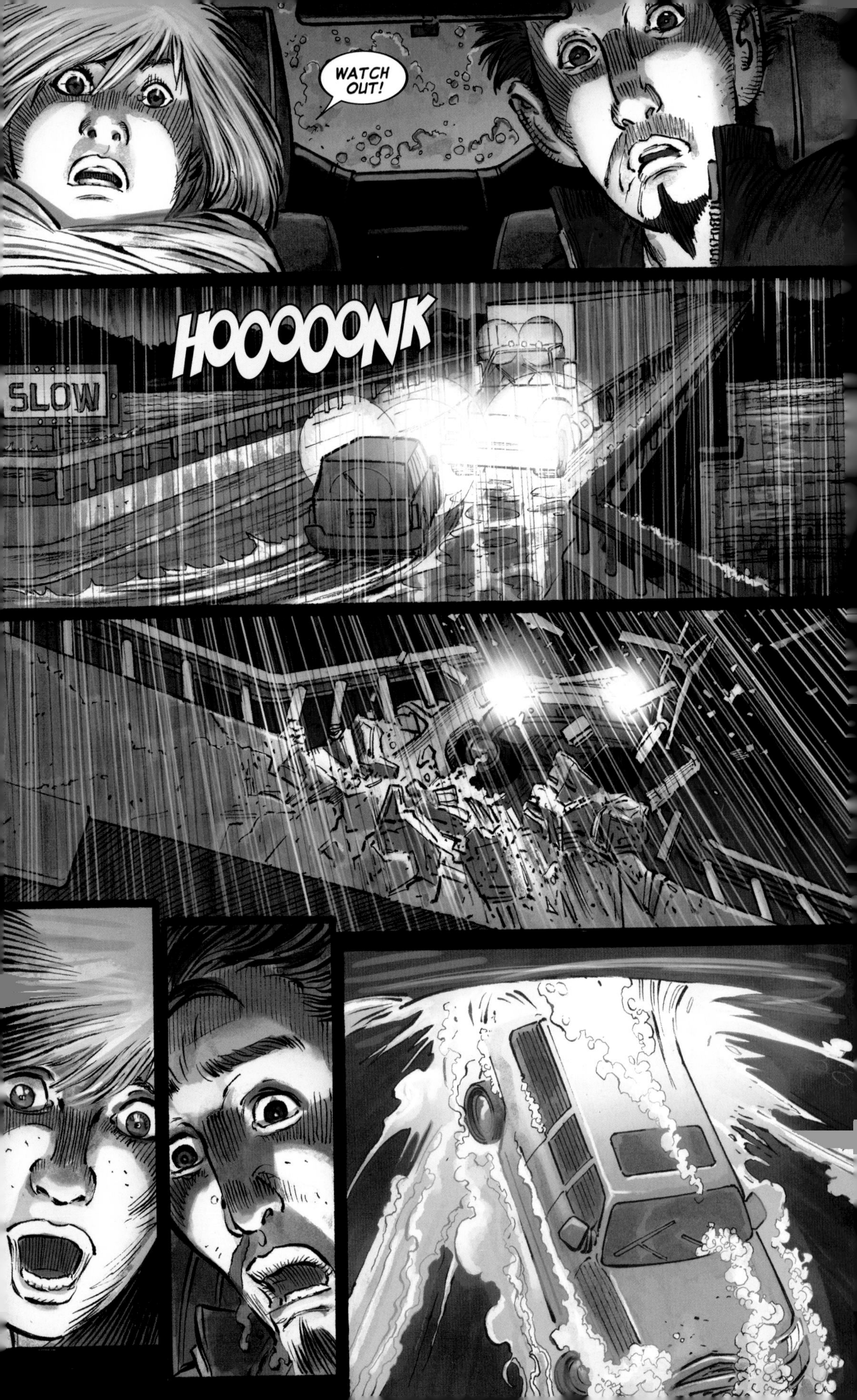
WATCH OUT!
HOOOOONK
SLOW

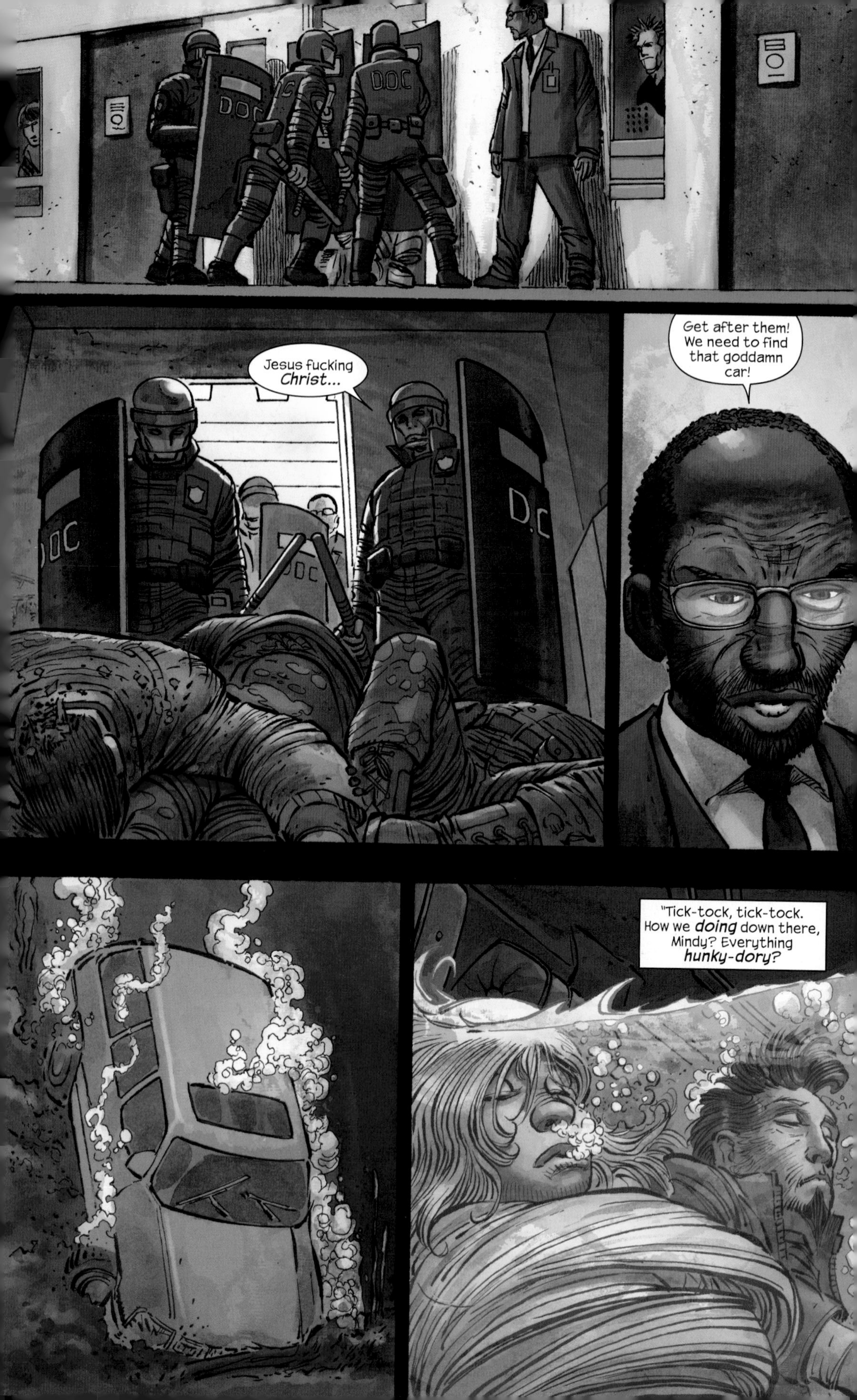

Jesus fucking Christ...
Get after them! We need to find that goddamn car!
"Tick-tock, tick-tock. How we doing down there, Mindy? Everything hunky-dory?

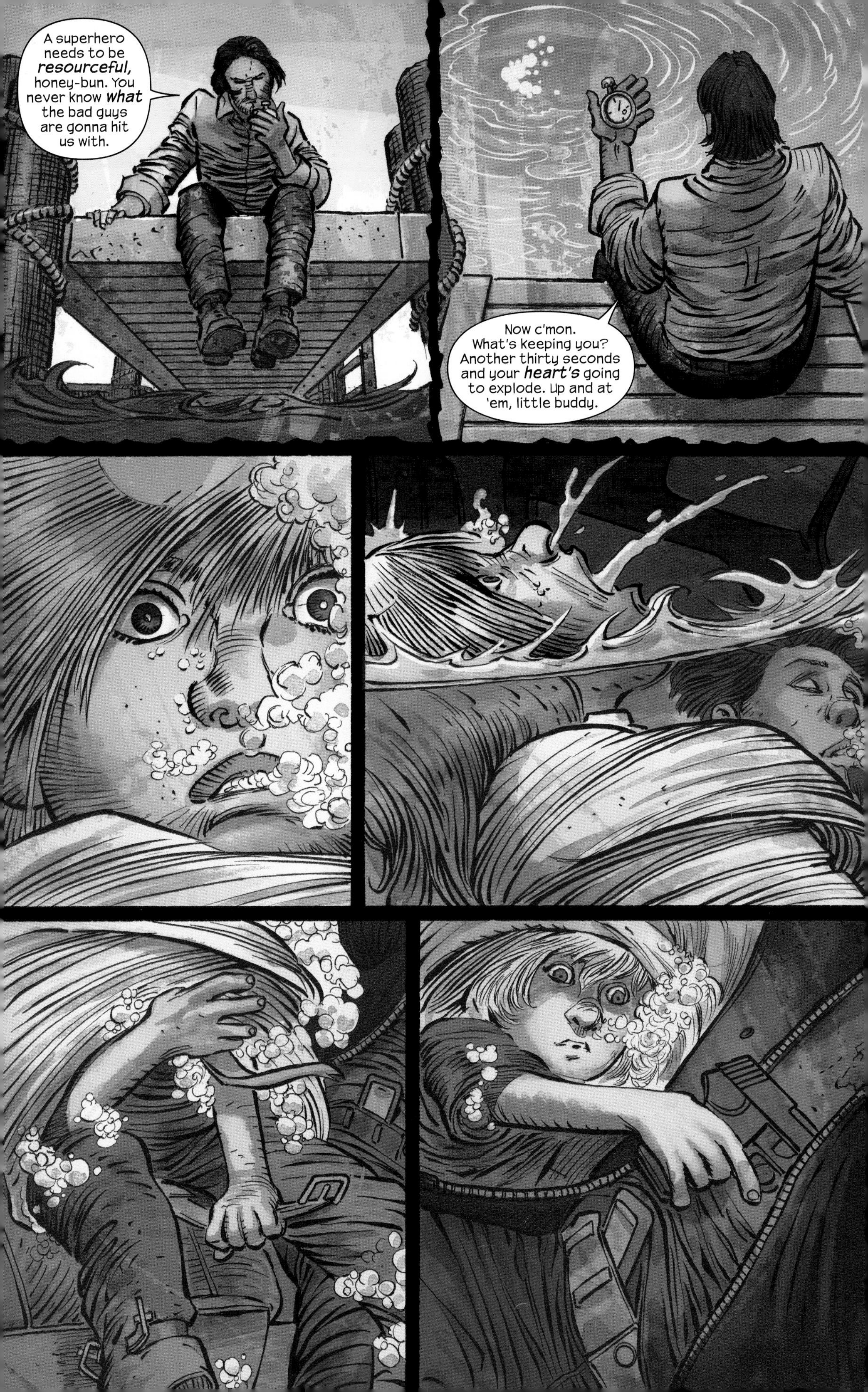
A superhero needs to be **resourceful,** honey-bun. You never know ***what*** the bad guys are gonna hit us with.
Now c'mon. What's keeping you? Another thirty seconds and your ***heart's*** going to explode. Up and at 'em, little buddy.

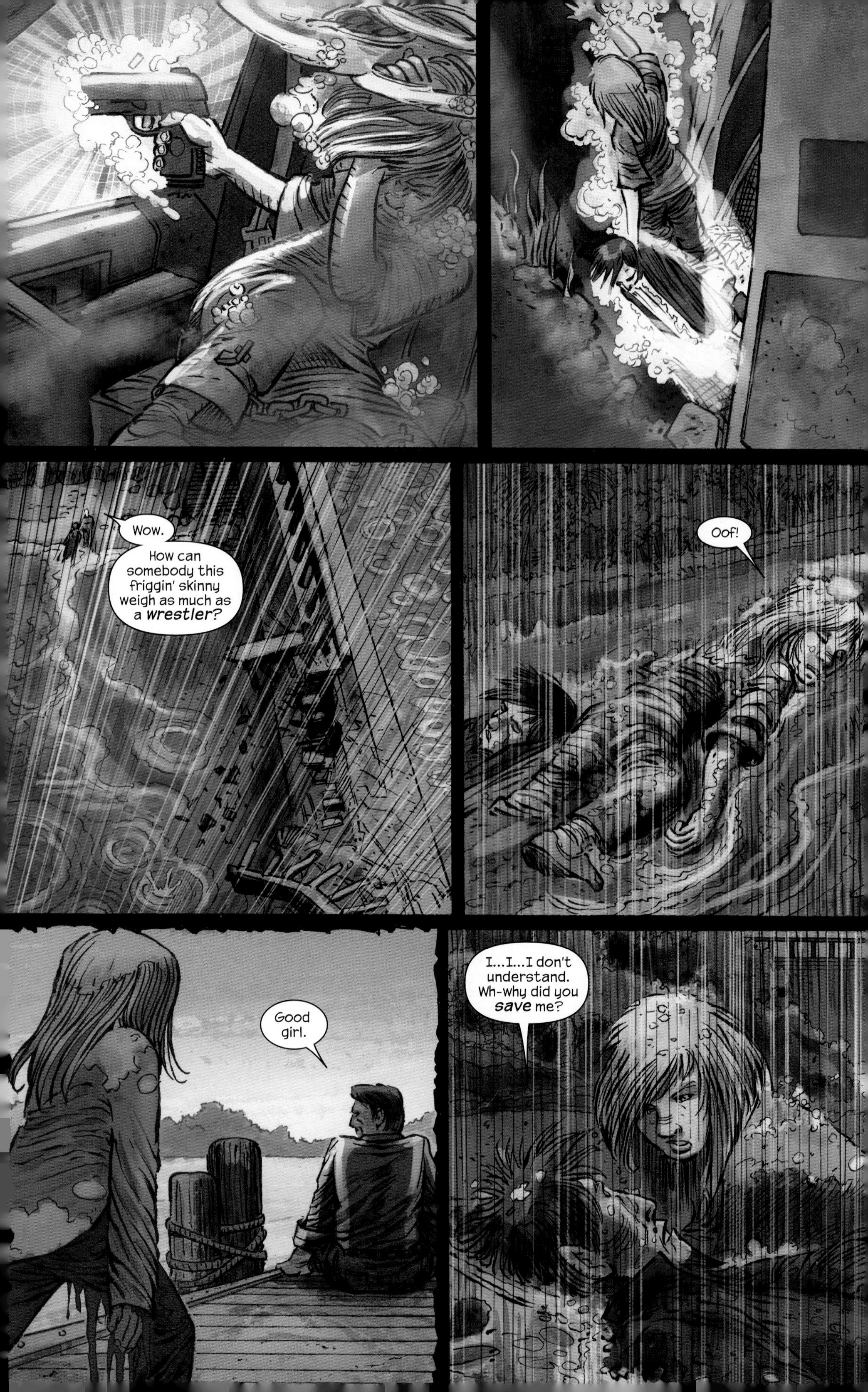
Wow.
How can somebody this friggin' skinny weigh as much as a *wrestler?*
Oof!
Good girl.
I...I...I don't understand. Wh-why did you *save* me?

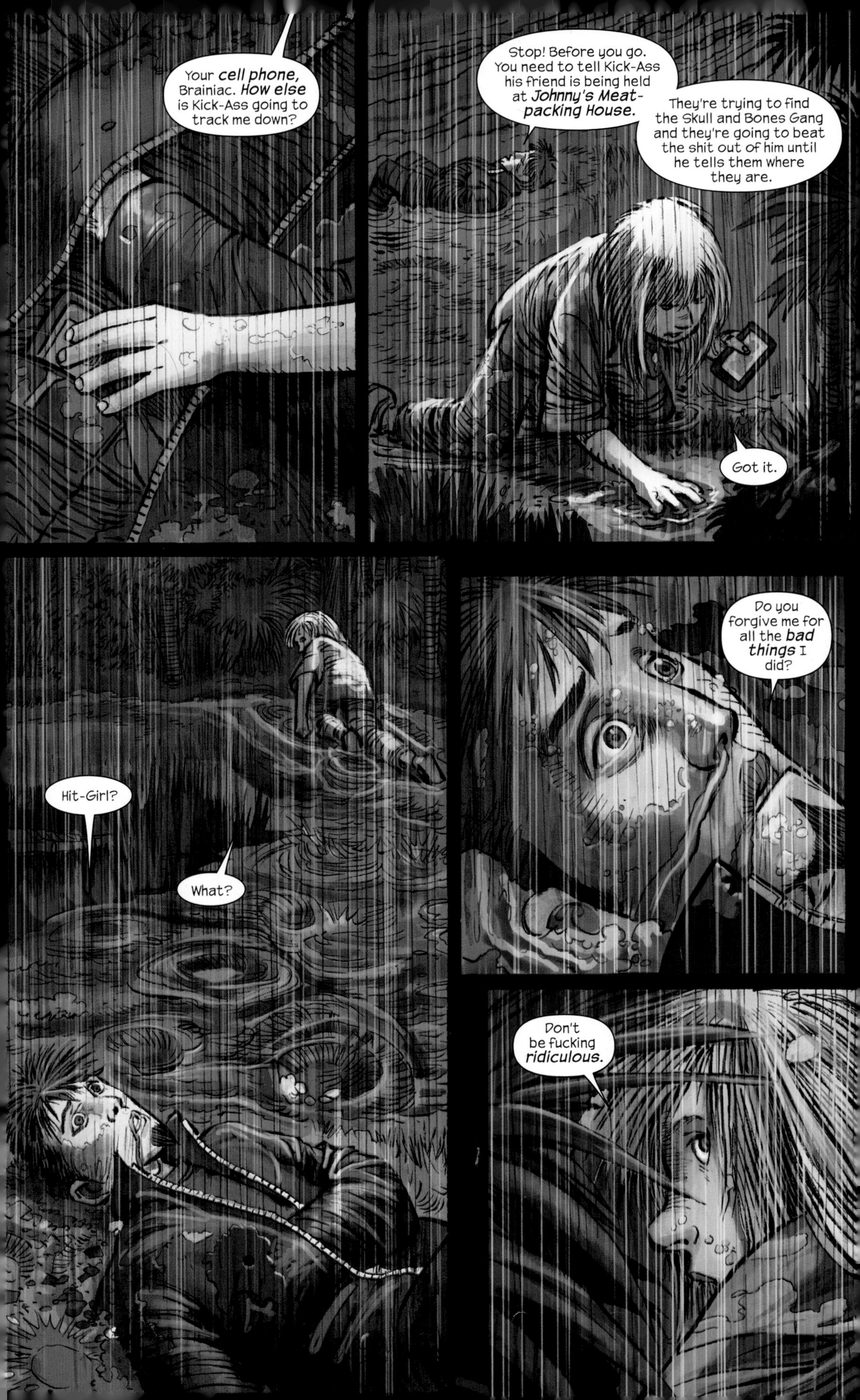
Your *cell phone,* Brainiac. *How else* is Kick-Ass going to track me down?
Stop! Before you go. You need to tell Kick-Ass his friend is being held at *Johnny's Meat-packing House.*
They're trying to find the Skull and Bones Gang and they're going to beat the shit out of him until he tells them where they are.
Got it.
Hit-Girl?
What?
Do you forgive me for all the *bad things* I did?
Don't be fucking *ridiculous.*

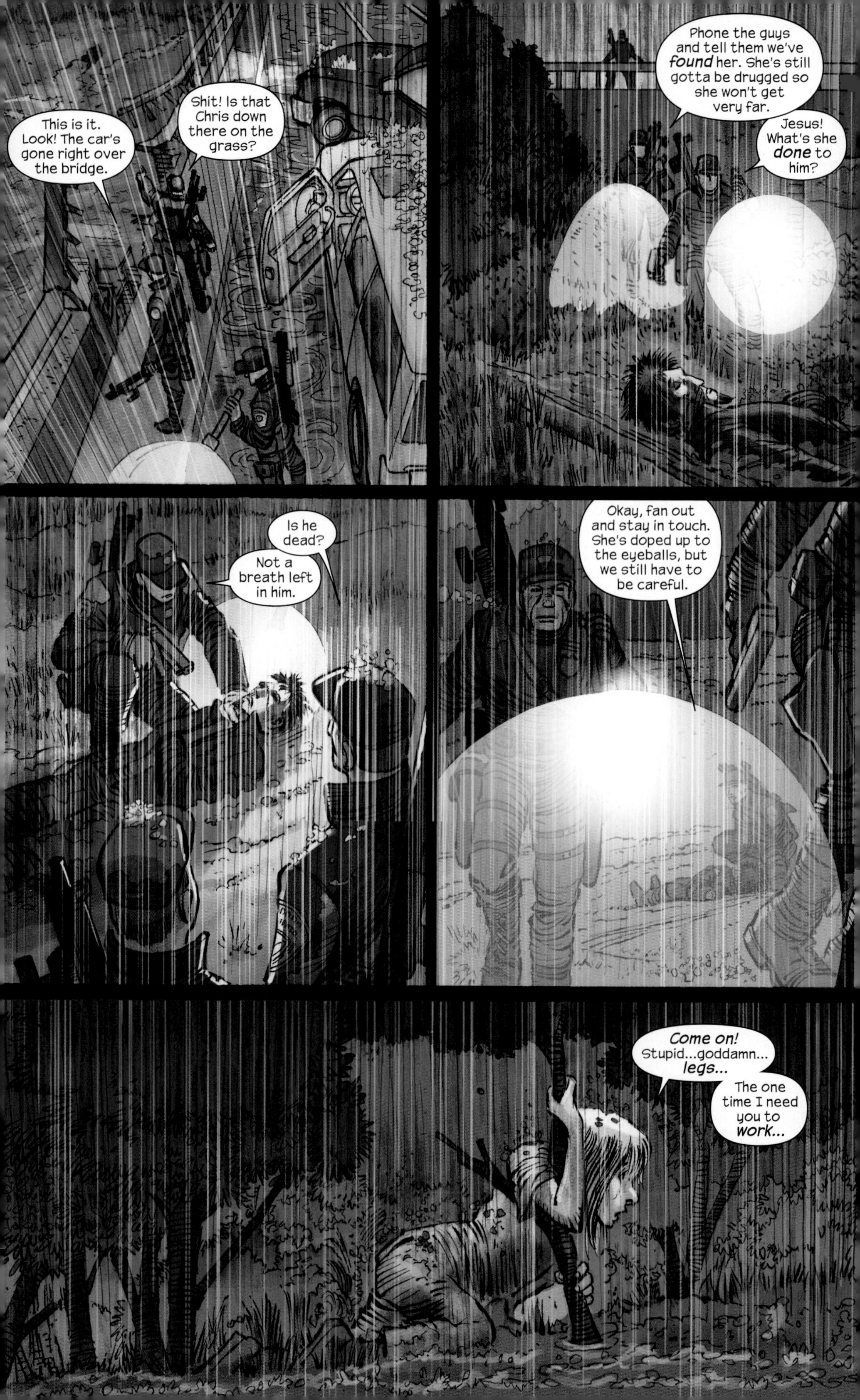
This is it. Look! The car's gone right over the bridge.
Shit! Is that Chris down there on the grass?
Phone the guys and tell them we've *found* her. She's still gotta be drugged so she won't get very far.
Jesus! What's she *done* to him?
Is he dead?
Not a breath left in him.
Okay, fan out and stay in touch. She's doped up to the eyeballs, but we still have to be careful.
Come on! Stupid...goddamn... *legs...*
The one time I need you to *work...*

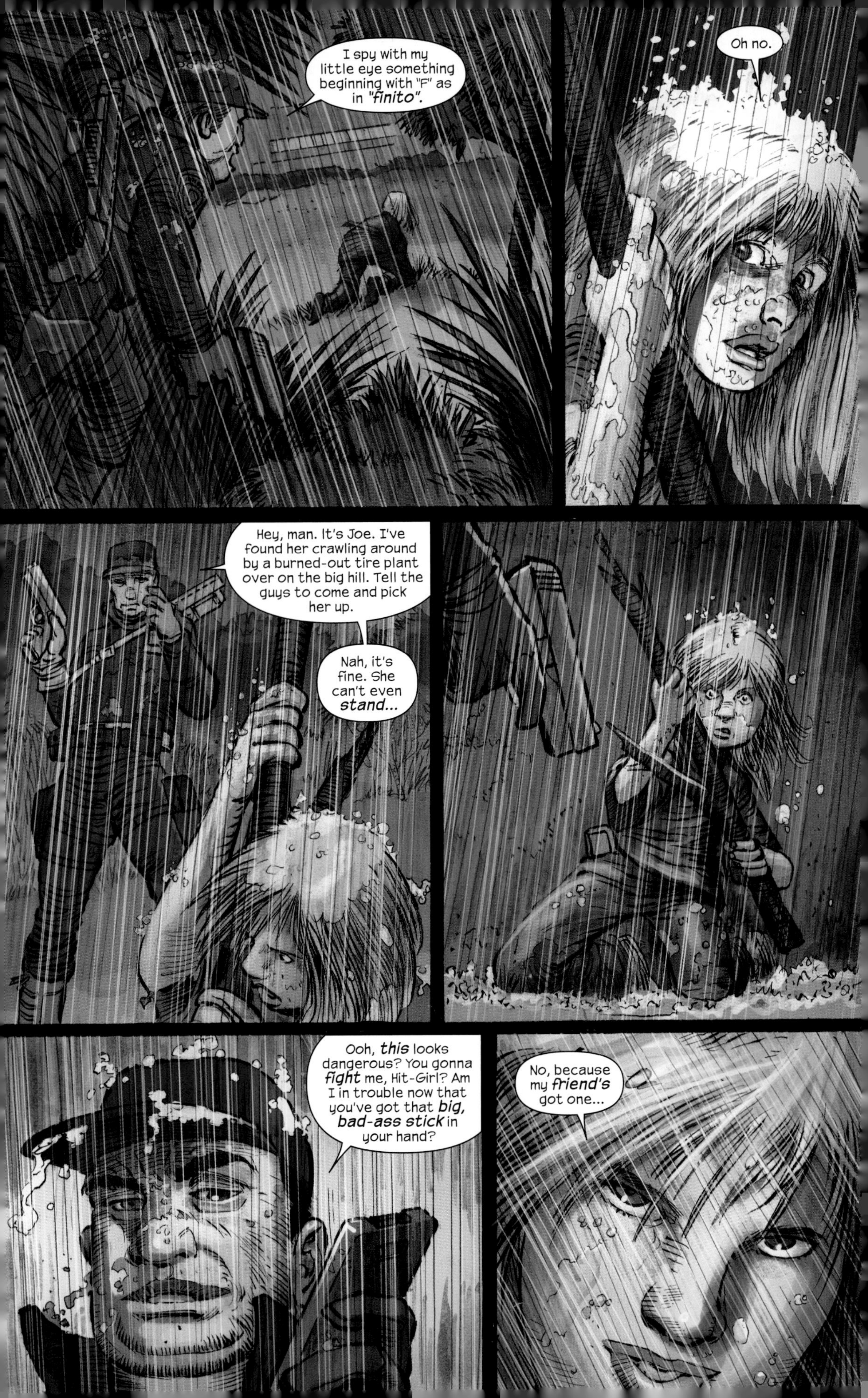
I spy with my little eye something beginning with "F" as in "*finito*".
Oh no.
Hey, man. It's Joe. I've found her crawling around by a burned-out tire plant over on the big hill. Tell the guys to come and pick her up.
Nah, it's fine. She can't even *stand...*
Ooh, *this* looks dangerous? You gonna *fight* me, Hit-Girl? Am I in trouble now that you've got that *big, bad-ass stick* in your hand?
No, because my *friend's* got one...

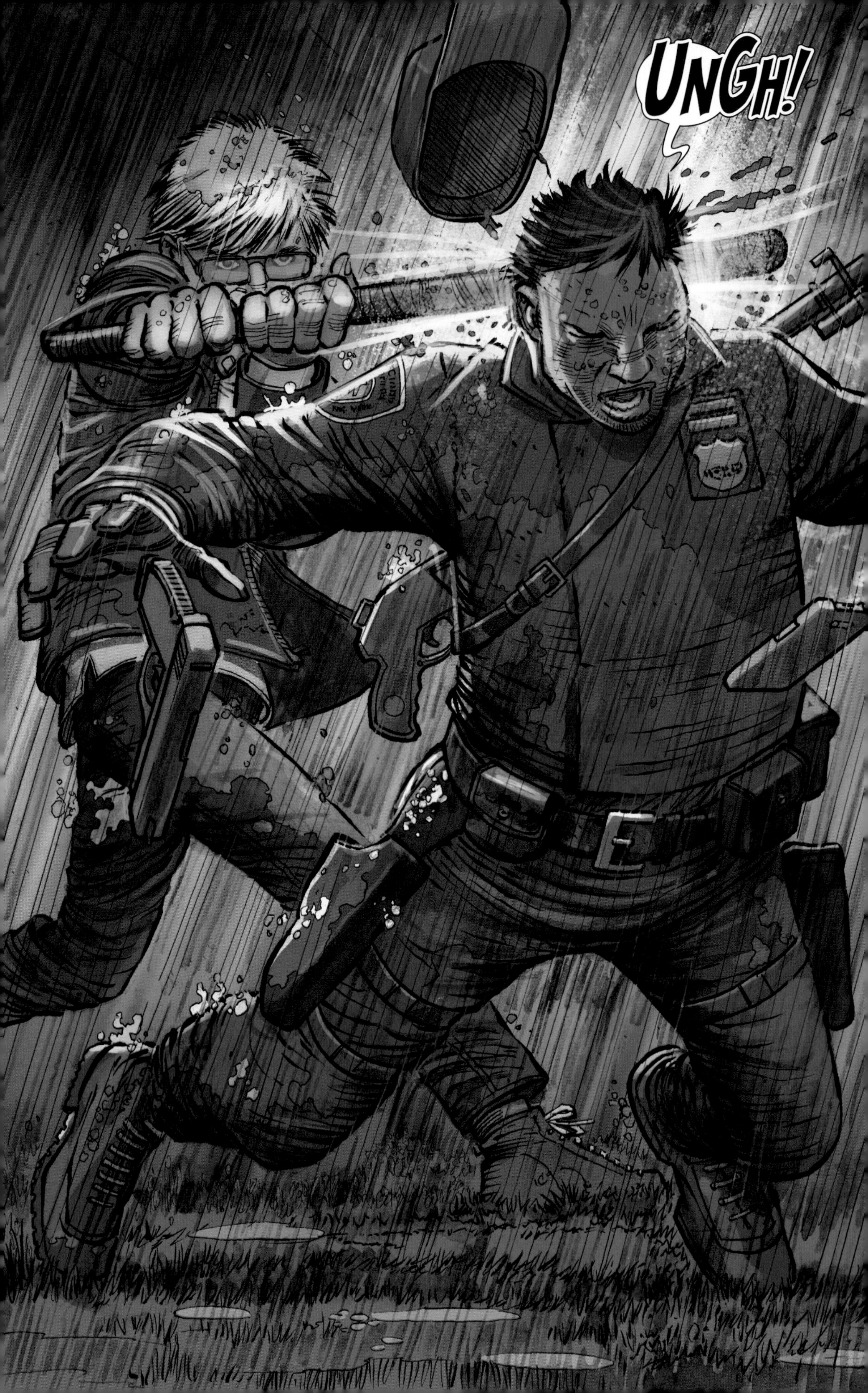
UNGH!

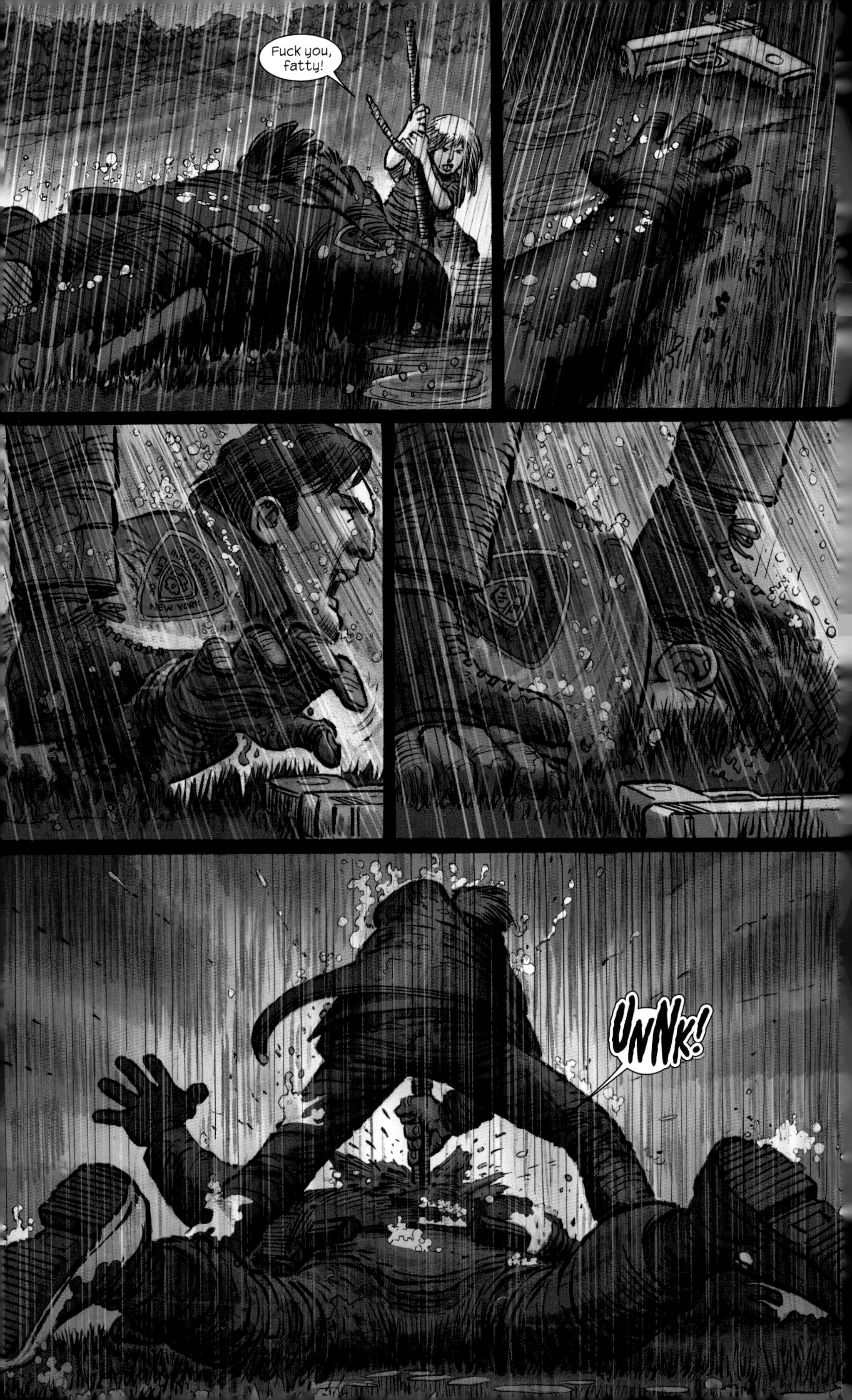
Fuck you, fatty!
NEW YORK
UNNK!

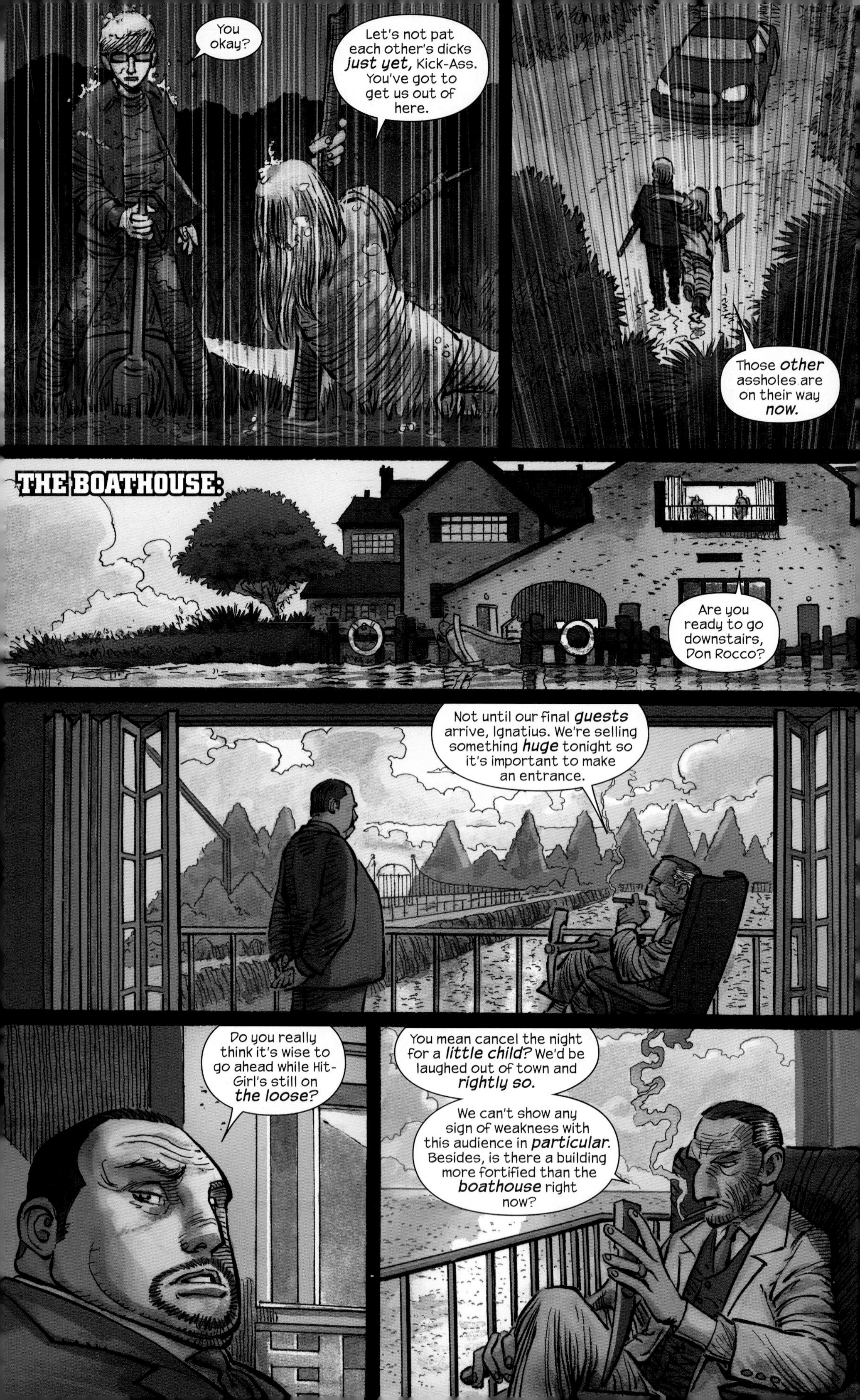
You okay?
Let's not pat each other's dicks just yet, Kick-Ass. You've got to get us out of here.
Those other assholes are on their way now.
THE BOATHOUSE:
Are you ready to go downstairs, Don Rocco?
Not until our final guests arrive, Ignatius. We're selling something huge tonight so it's important to make an entrance.
Do you really think it's wise to go ahead while Hit-Girl's still on the loose?
You mean cancel the night for a little child? We'd be laughed out of town and rightly so.
We can't show any sign of weakness with this audience in particular. Besides, is there a building more fortified than the boathouse right now?

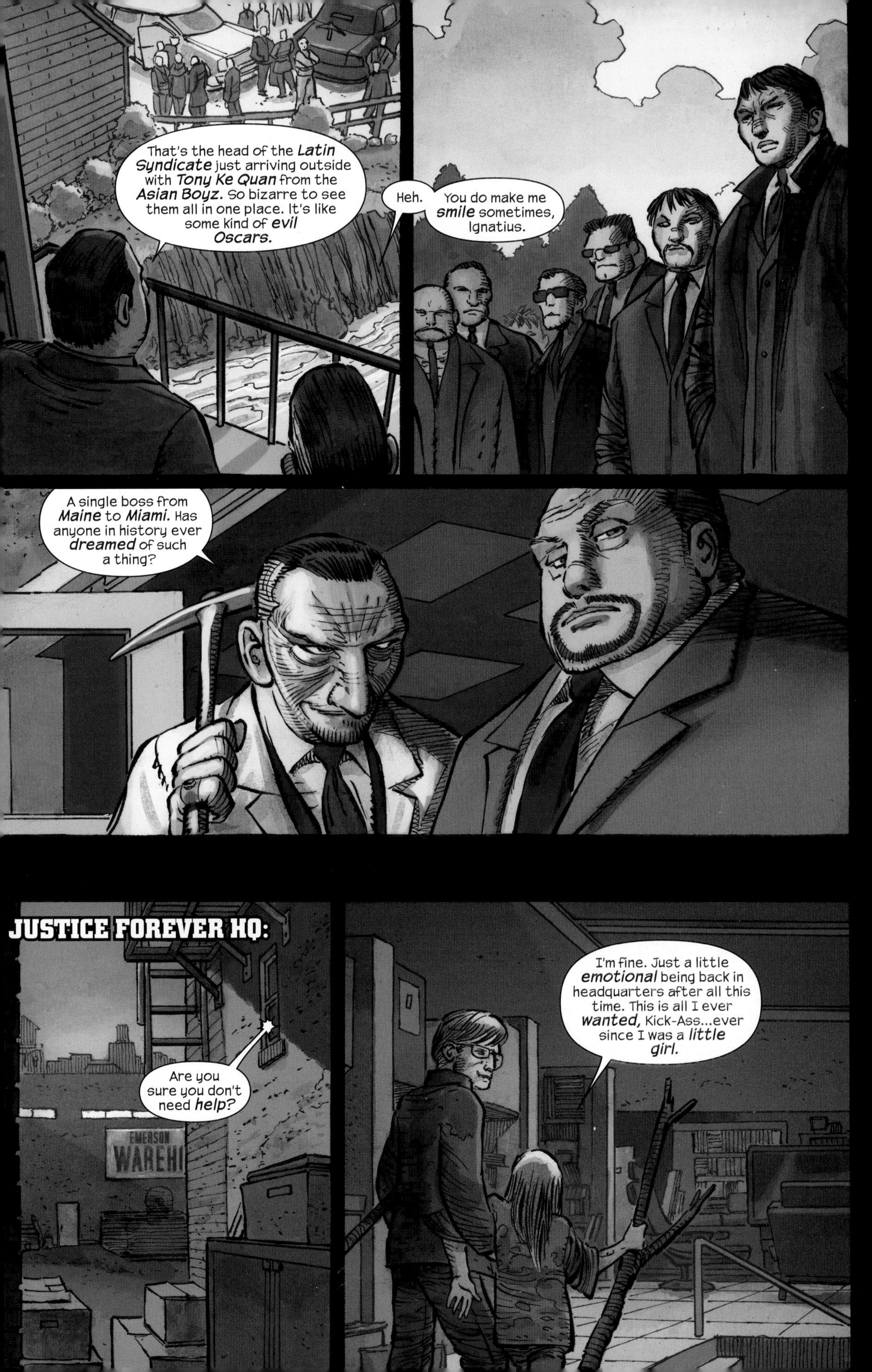

That's the head of the Latin Syndicate just arriving outside with Tony Ke Quan from the Asian Boyz. So bizarre to see them all in one place. It's like some kind of evil Oscars.
Heh.
You do make me smile sometimes, Ignatius.
A single boss from Maine to Miami. Has anyone in history ever dreamed of such a thing?
JUSTICE FOREVER HQ:
Are you sure you don't need help?
EMERSON WAREH
I'm fine. Just a little emotional being back in headquarters after all this time. This is all I ever wanted, Kick-Ass...ever since I was a little girl.

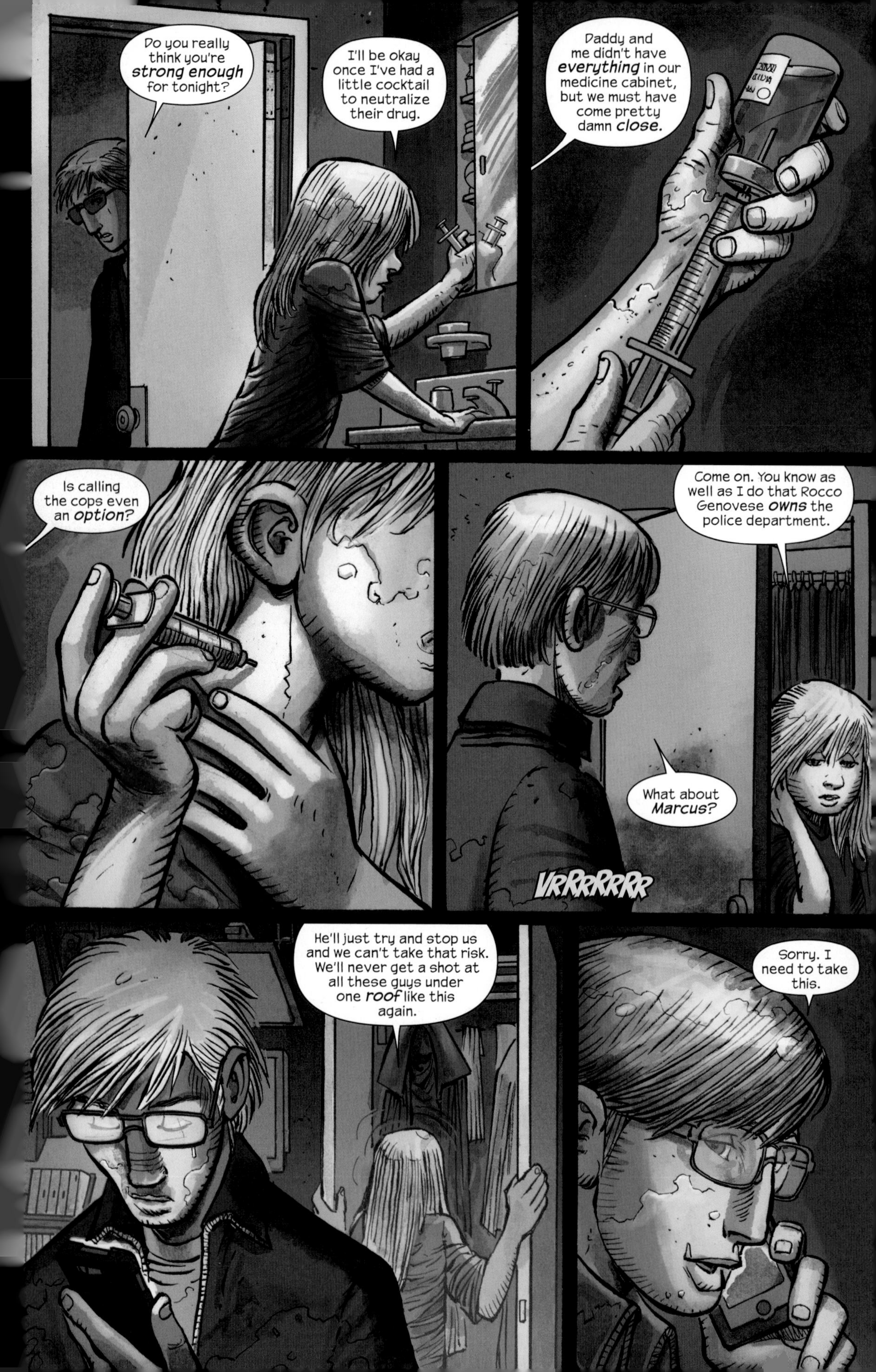
Do you really think you're *strong enough* for tonight?
I'll be okay once I've had a little cocktail to neutralize their drug.
Daddy and me didn't have *everything* in our medicine cabinet, but we must have come pretty damn *close.*
Is calling the cops even an *option*?
Come on. You know as well as I do that Rocco Genovese *owns* the police department.
What about *Marcus?*
VRRRRRRR
He'll just try and stop us and we can't take that risk. We'll never get a shot at all these guys under one *roof* like this again.
Sorry. I need to take this.

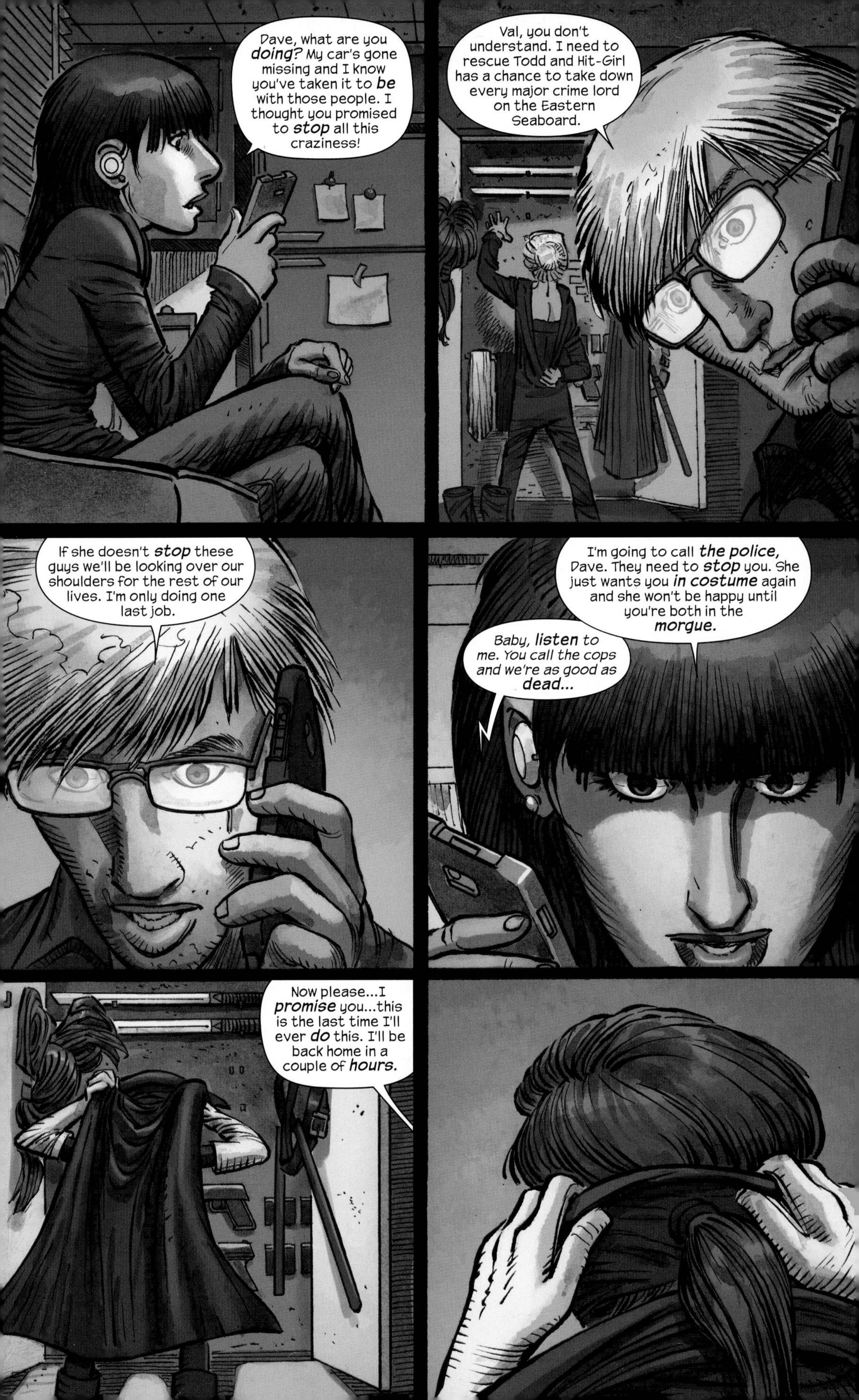
Dave, what are you *doing?* My car's gone missing and I know you've taken it to *be* with those people. I thought you promised to *stop* all this craziness!
Val, you don't understand. I need to rescue Todd and Hit-Girl has a chance to take down every major crime lord on the Eastern Seaboard.
If she doesn't *stop* these guys we'll be looking over our shoulders for the rest of our lives. I'm only doing one last job.
I'm going to call *the police,* Dave. They need to *stop* you. She just wants you *in costume* again and she won't be happy until you're both in the *morgue.*
Baby, *listen* to me. You call the cops and we're as good as *dead...*
Now please...I *promise* you...this is the last time I'll ever *do* this. I'll be back home in a couple of *hours.*

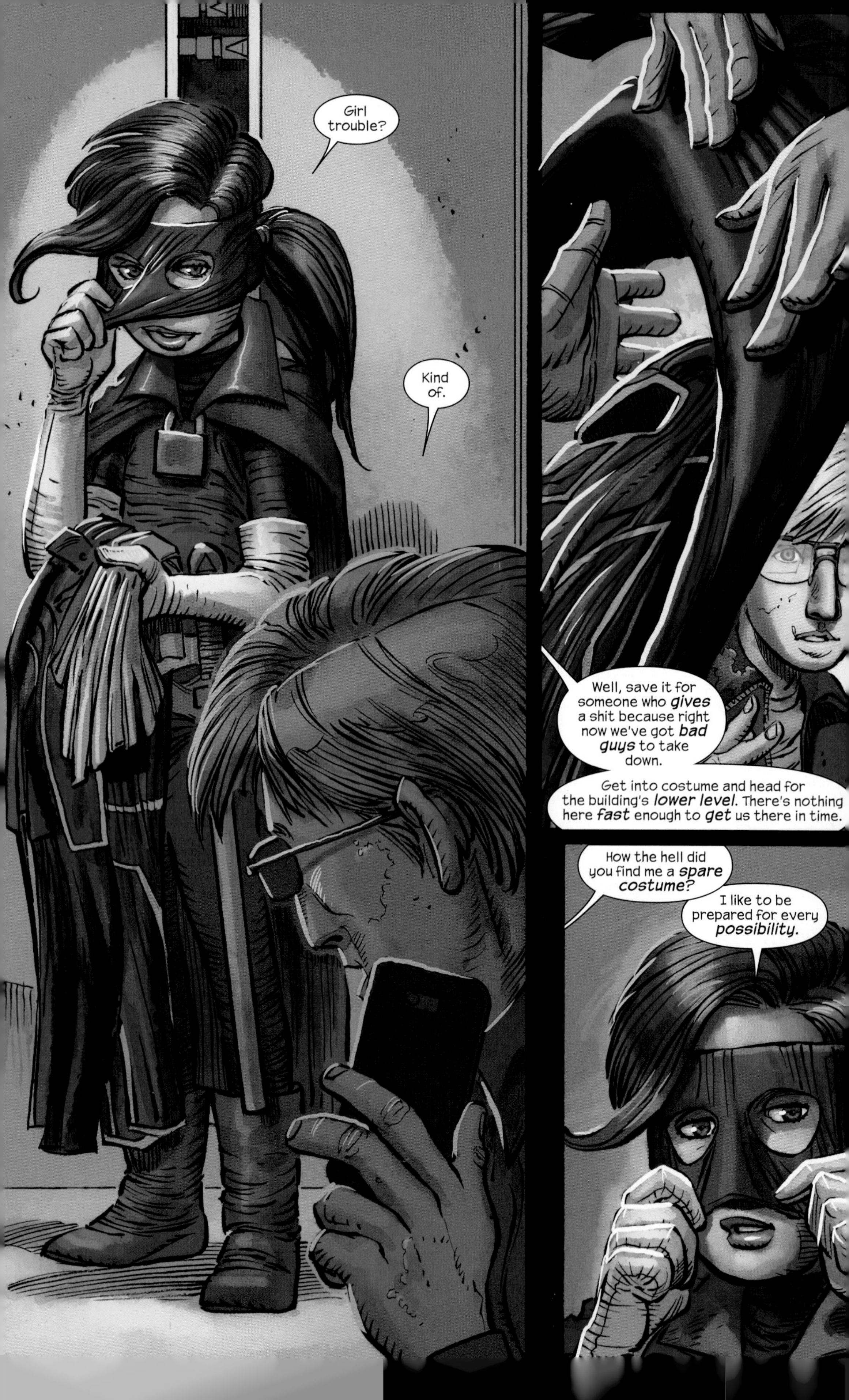
Girl trouble?
Kind of.
Well, save it for someone who *gives* a shit because right now we've got *bad guys* to take down.
Get into costume and head for the building's *lower level*. There's nothing here *fast* enough to *get* us there in time.
How the hell did you find me a *spare costume*?
I like to be prepared for every *possibility*.

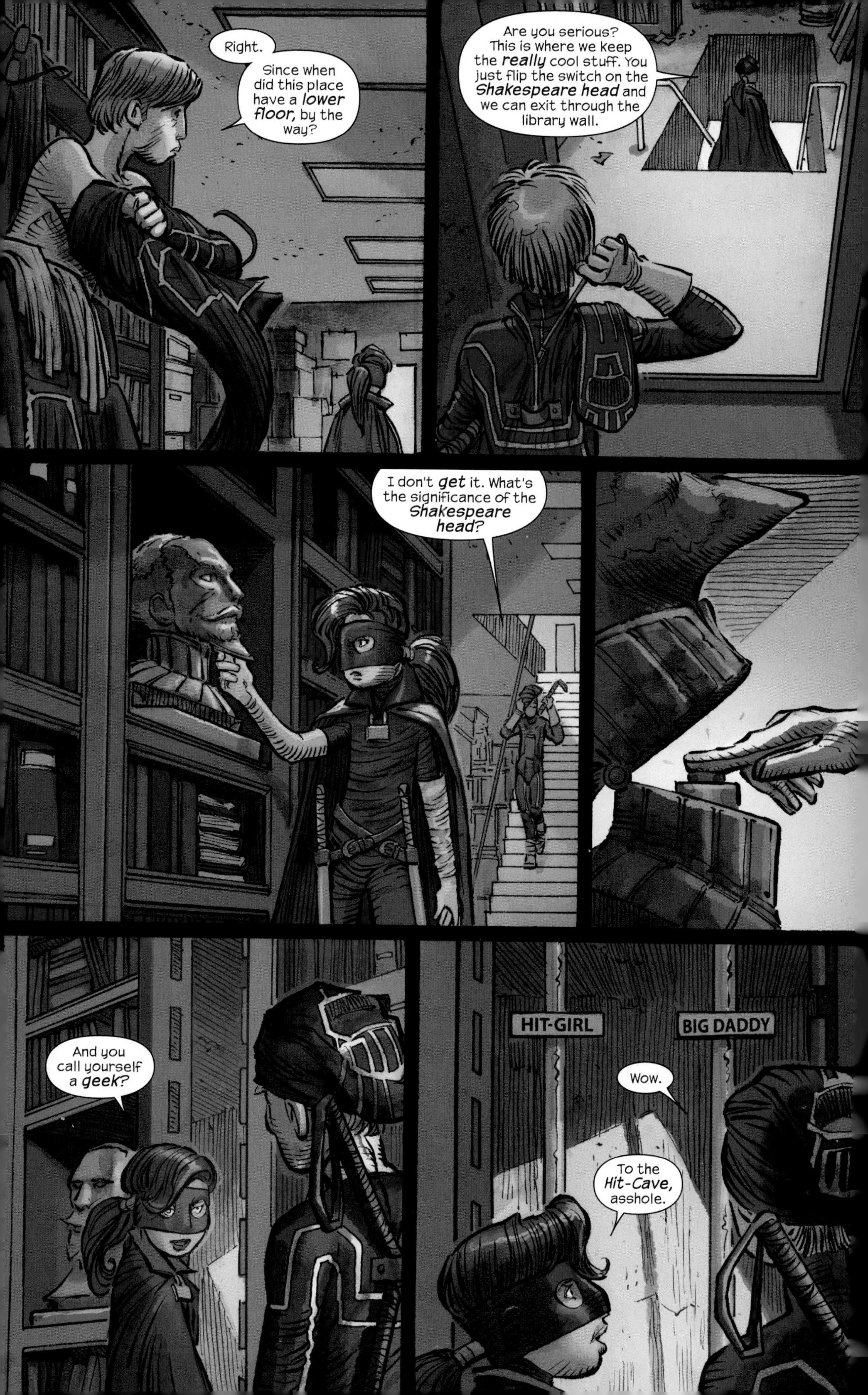
Right.
Since when did this place have a *lower floor,* by the way?
Are you serious? This is where we keep the *really* cool stuff. You just flip the switch on the *Shakespeare head* and we can exit through the library wall.
I don't *get* it. What's the significance of the *Shakespeare head?*
And you call yourself a *geek?*
HIT-GIRL
BIG DADDY
Wow.
To the *Hit-Cave,* asshole.

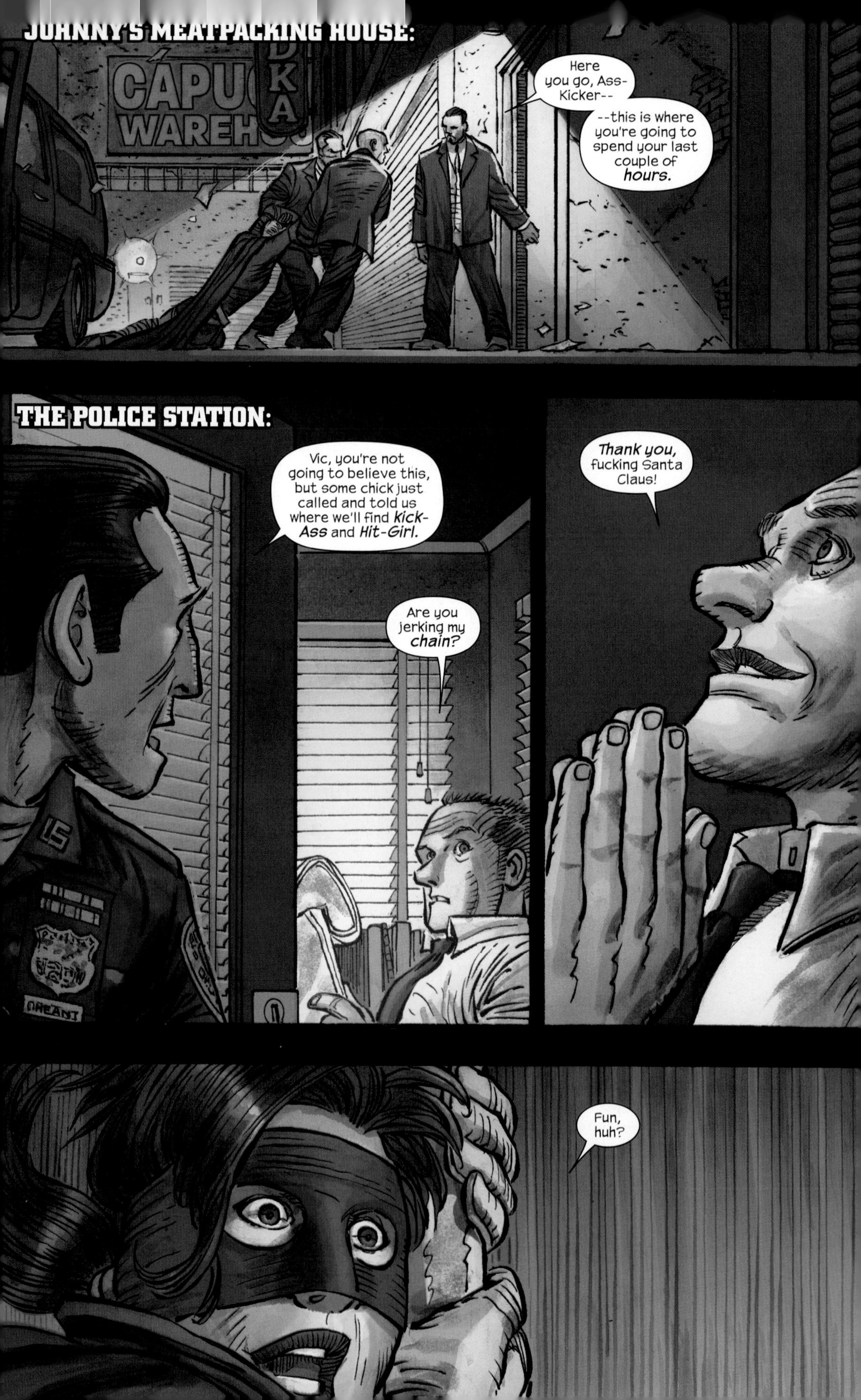
JOHNNY'S MEATPACKING HOUSE:
CAPUC
WAREHOU
DKA
Here you go, Ass-Kicker--
--this is where you're going to spend your last couple of *hours.*
THE POLICE STATION:
Vic, you're not going to believe this, but some chick just called and told us where we'll find *Kick-Ass* and *Hit-Girl.*
Are you jerking my *chain?*
Thank you, fucking Santa Claus!
Fun, huh?

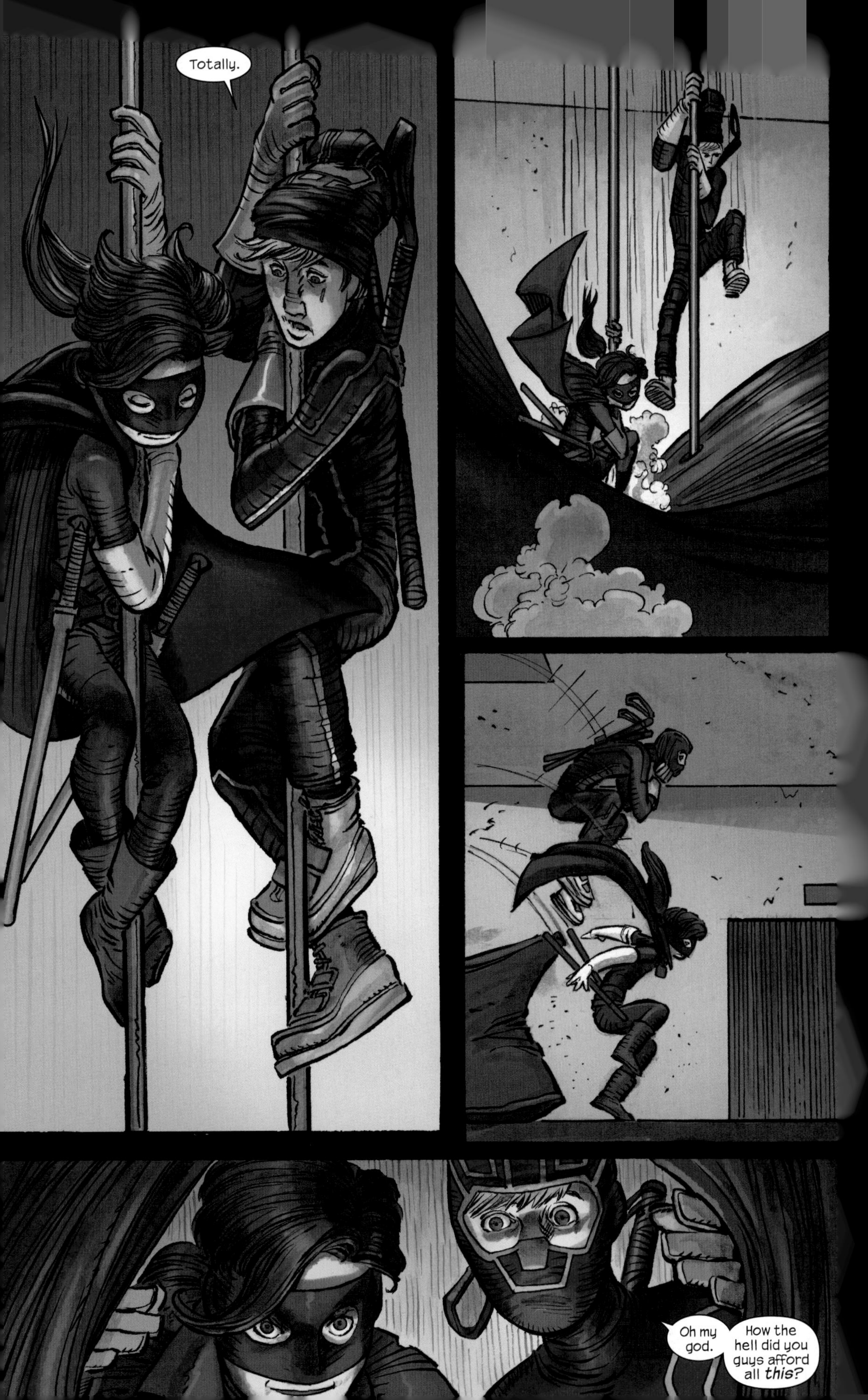
Totally.
Oh my god.
How the hell did you guys afford all *this*?

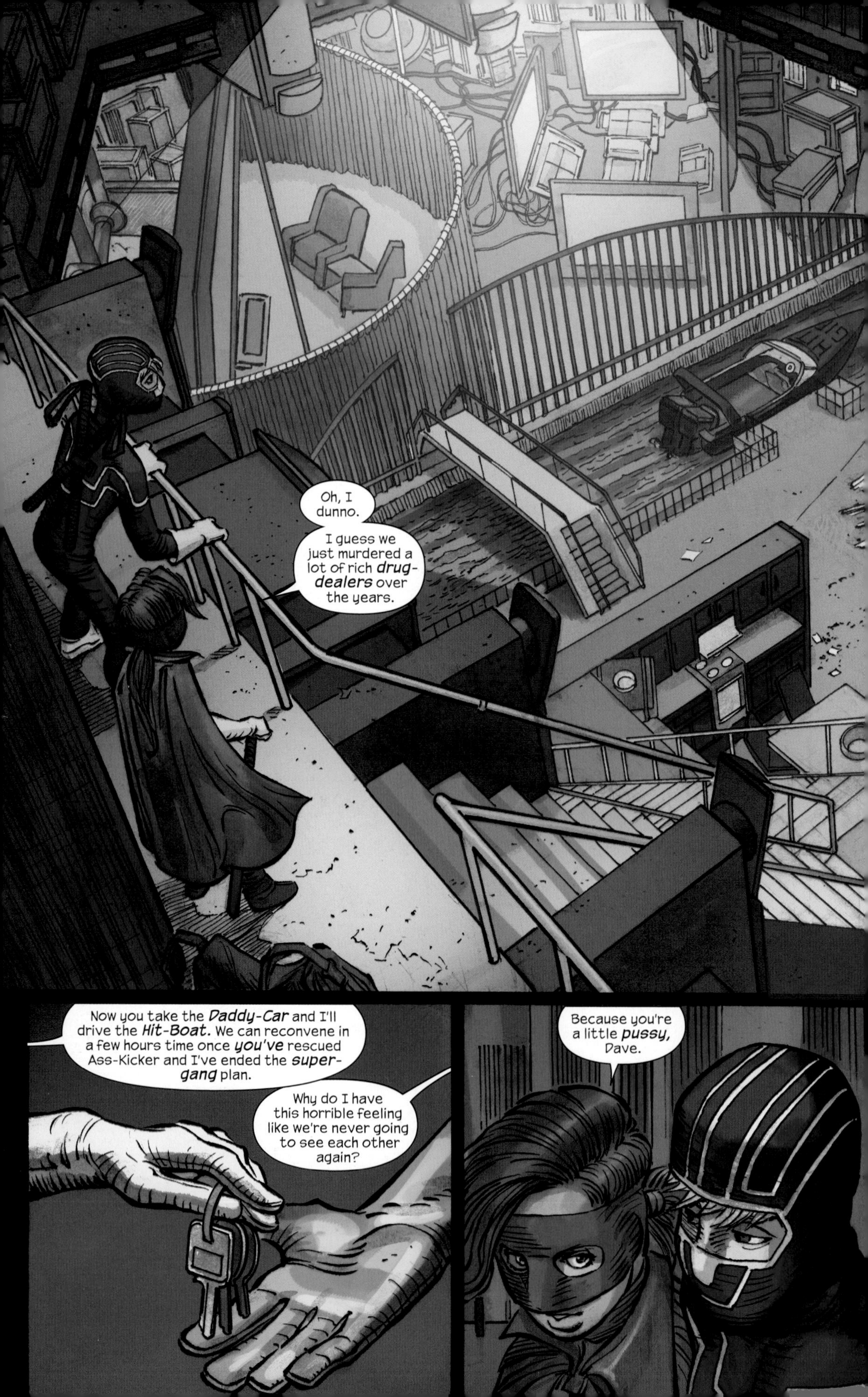
Oh, I dunno.
I guess we just murdered a lot of rich drug-dealers over the years.
Now you take the Daddy-Car and I'll drive the Hit-Boat. We can reconvene in a few hours time once you've rescued Ass-Kicker and I've ended the super-gang plan.
Why do I have this horrible feeling like we're never going to see each other again?
Because you're a little pussy, Dave.

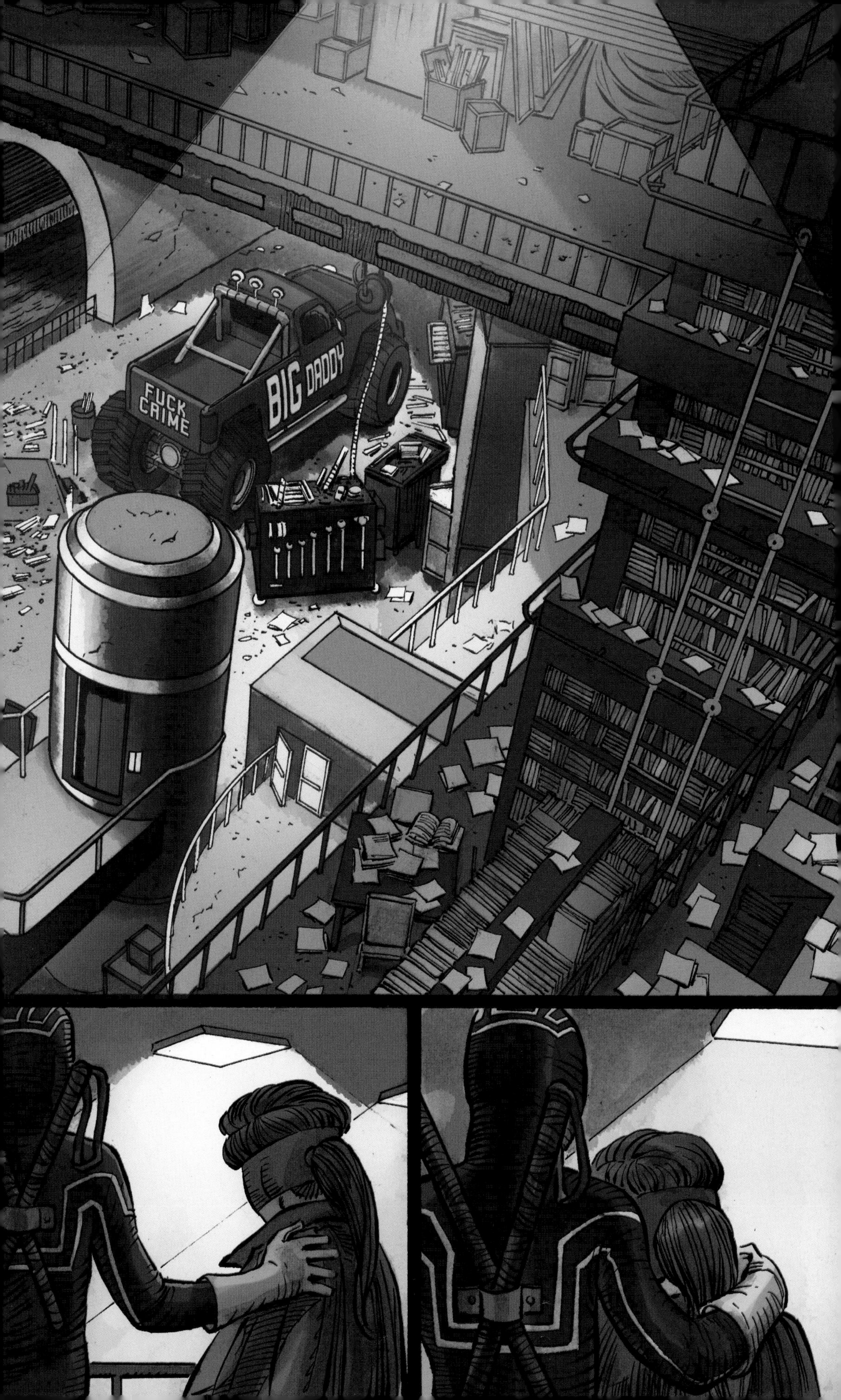
FUCK CRIME
BIG DADDY

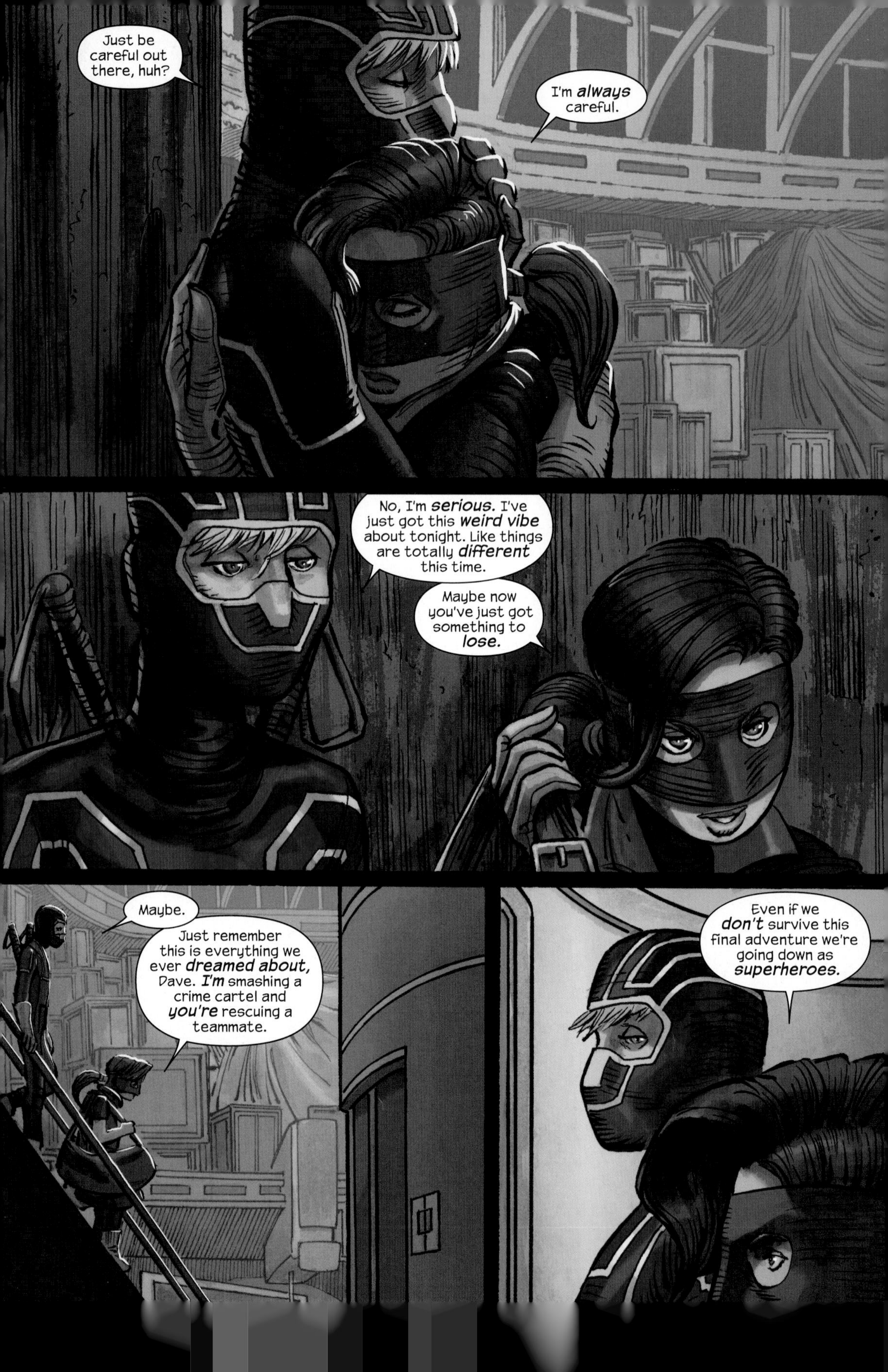
Just be careful out there, huh?
I'm always careful.
No, I'm serious. I've just got this weird vibe about tonight. Like things are totally different this time.
Maybe now you've just got something to lose.
Maybe.
Just remember this is everything we ever dreamed about, Dave. I'm smashing a crime cartel and you're rescuing a teammate.
Even if we don't survive this final adventure we're going down as superheroes.

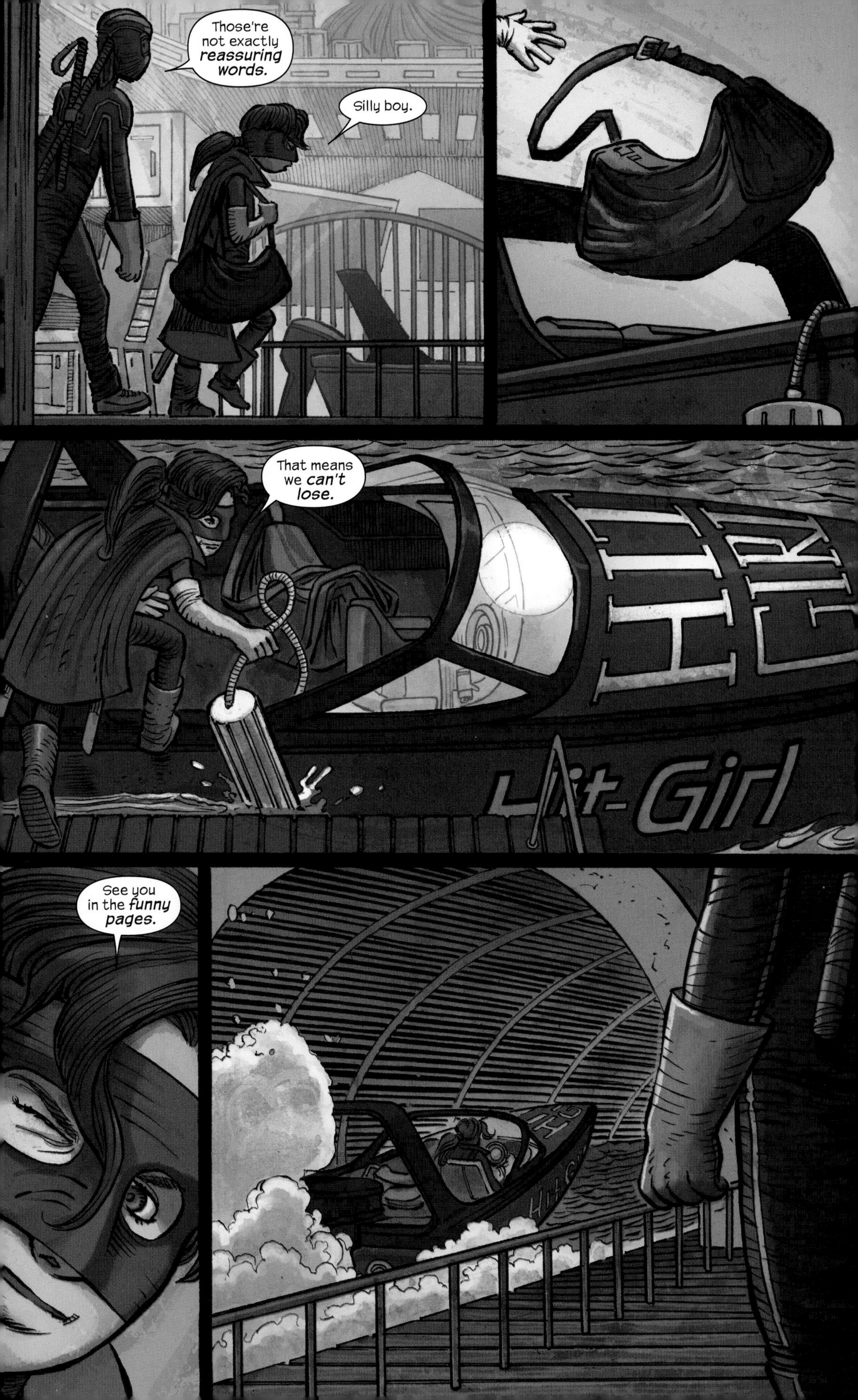

Those're not exactly reassuring words.
Silly boy.
That means we can't lose.
Hit-Girl
See you in the funny pages.

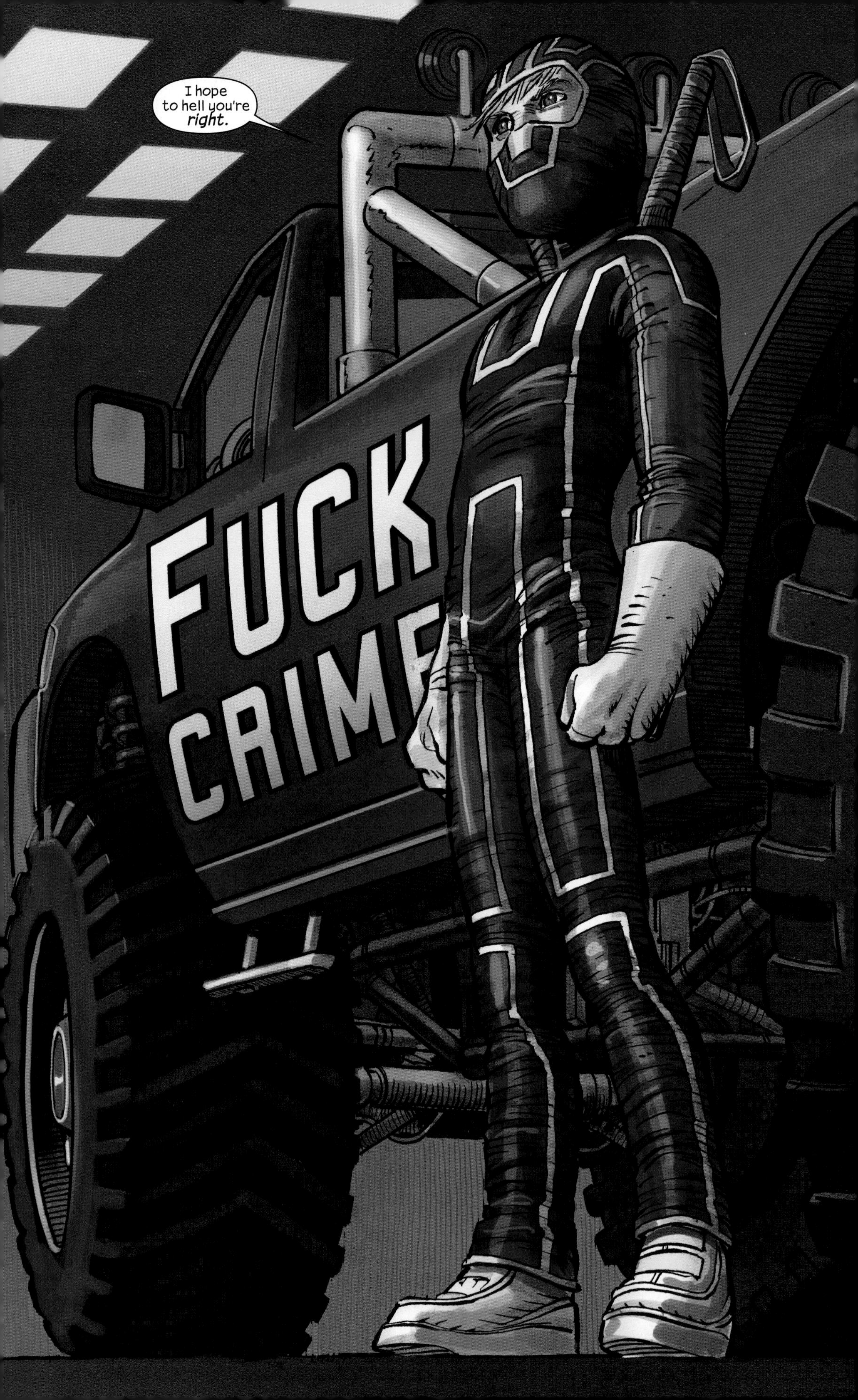
I hope to hell you're *right*.
FUCK CRIME

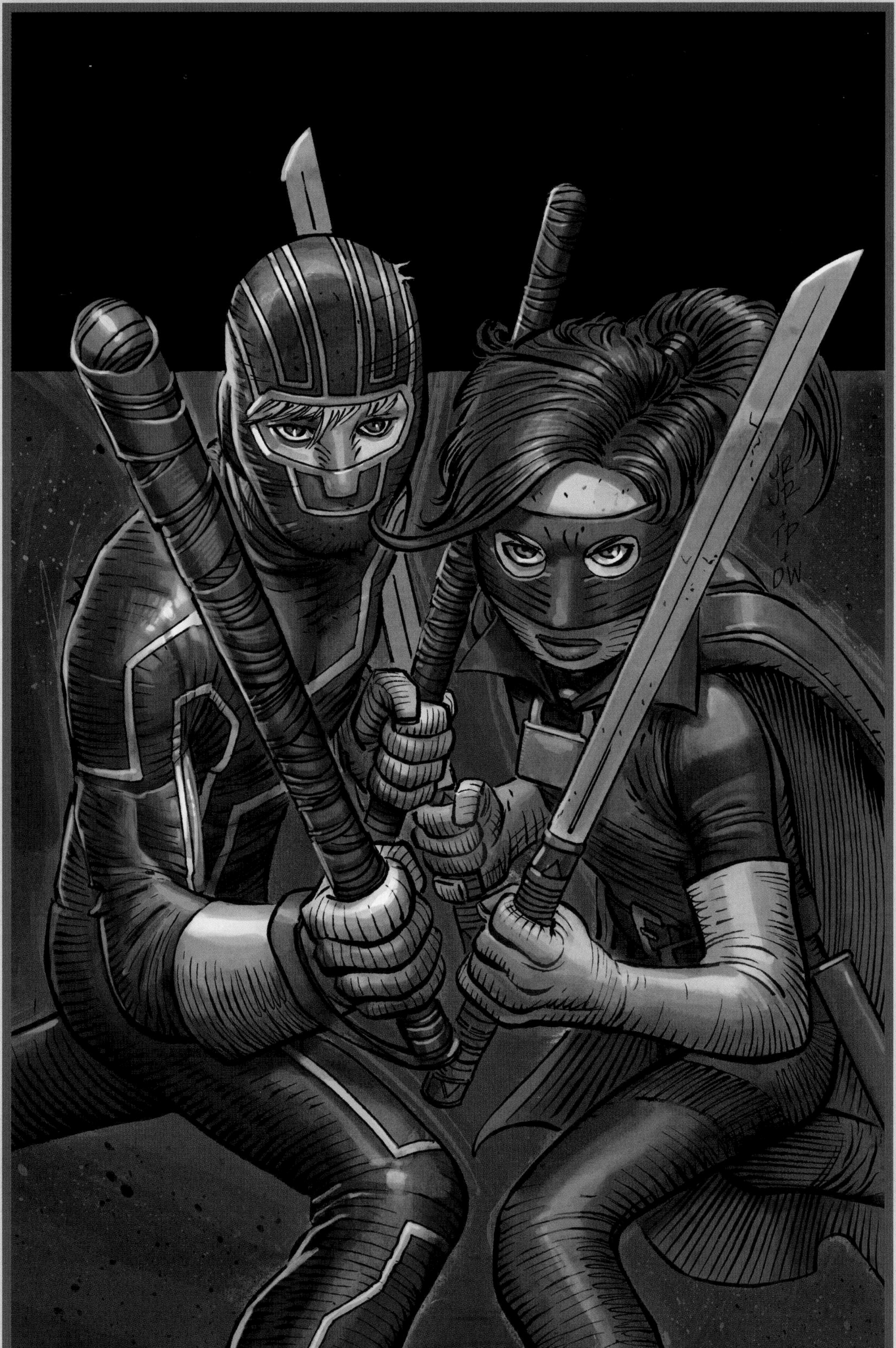

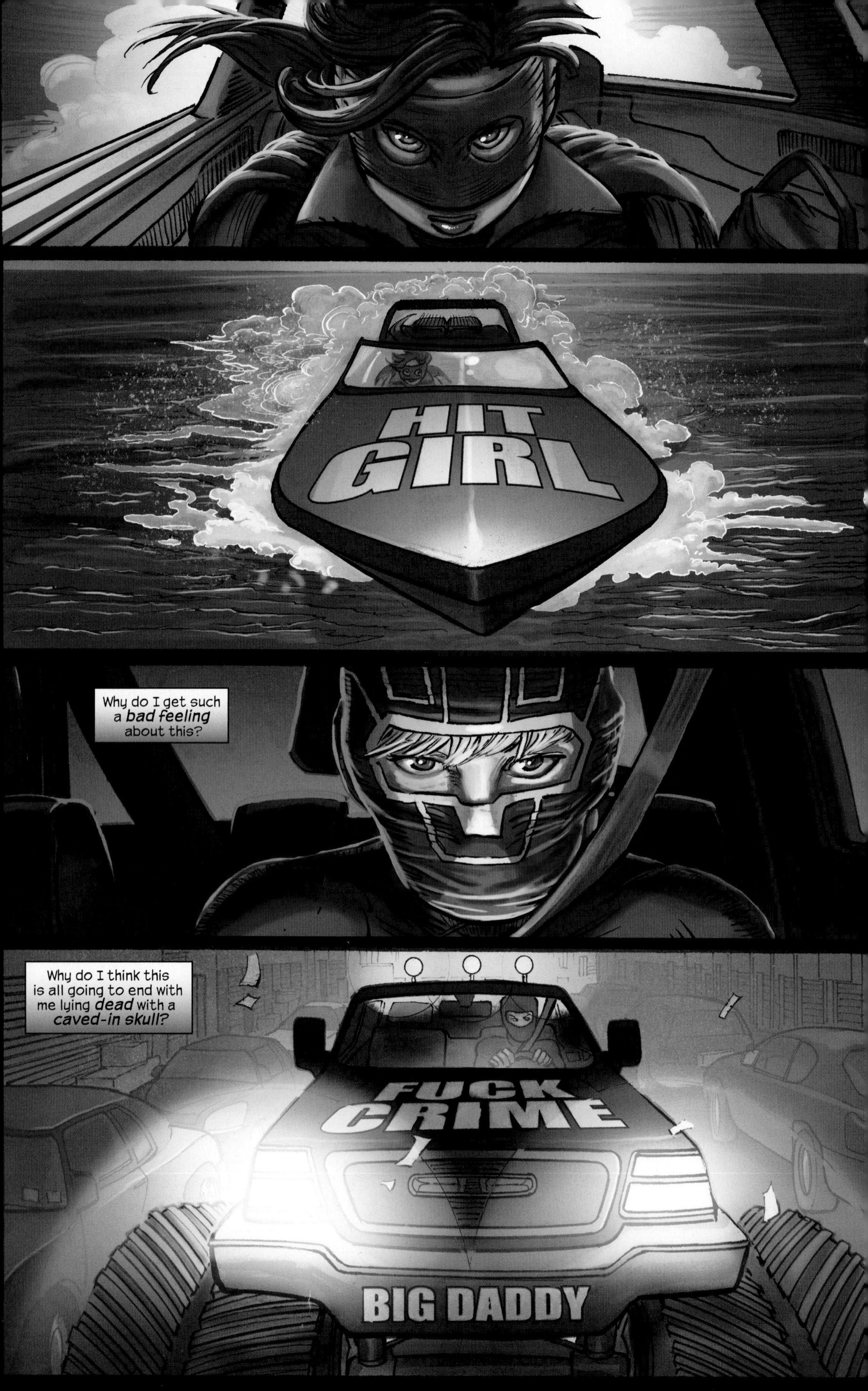
HIT GIRL
Why do I get such a bad feeling about this?
Why do I think this is all going to end with me lying dead with a caved-in skull?
FUCK CRIME
BIG DADDY

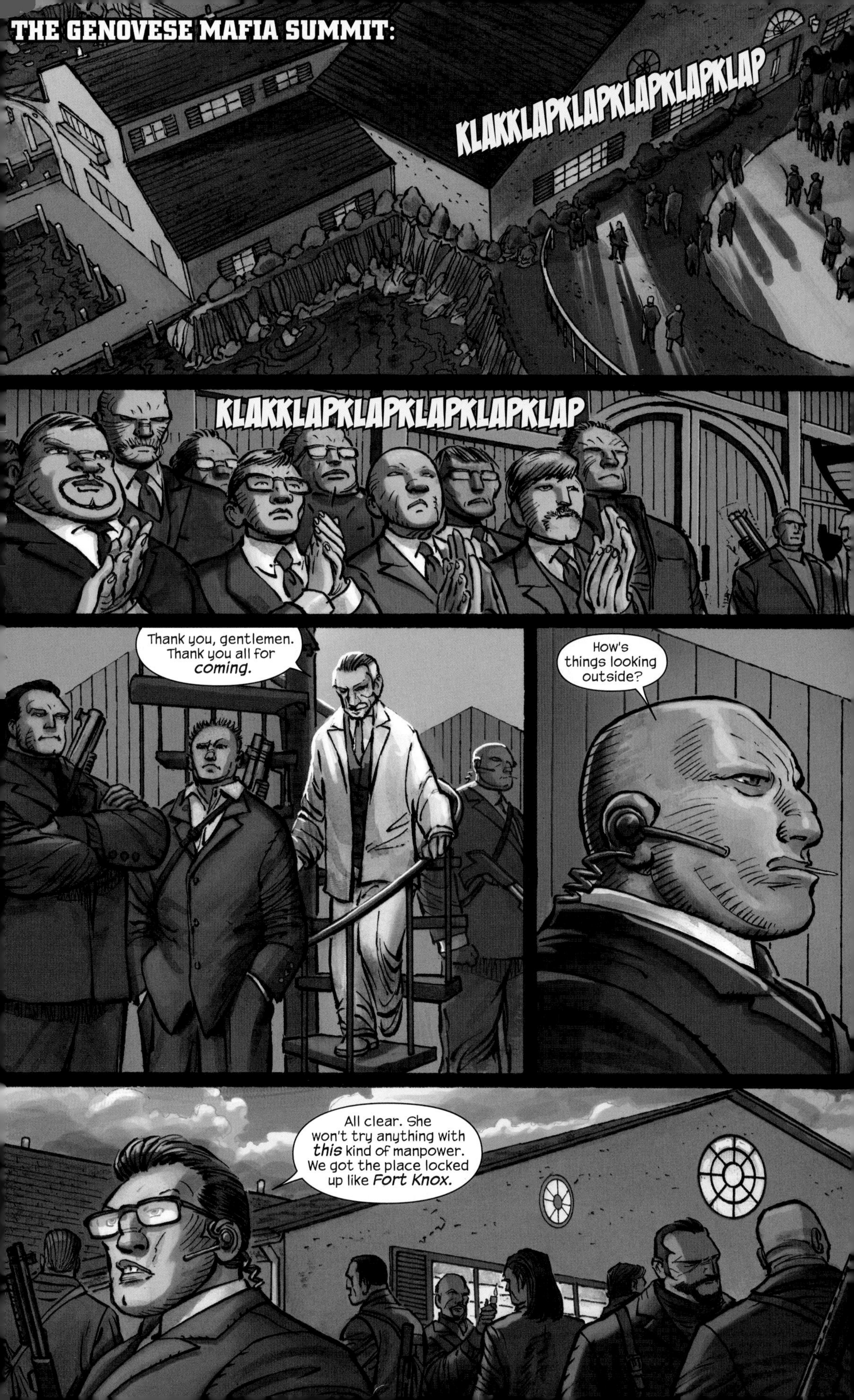
THE GENOVESE MAFIA SUMMIT:
KLAKKLAPKLAPKLAPKLAP
KLAKKLAPKLAPKLAPKLAPKLAP
Thank you, gentlemen. Thank you all for coming.
How's things looking outside?
All clear. She won't try anything with this kind of manpower. We got the place locked up like Fort Knox.

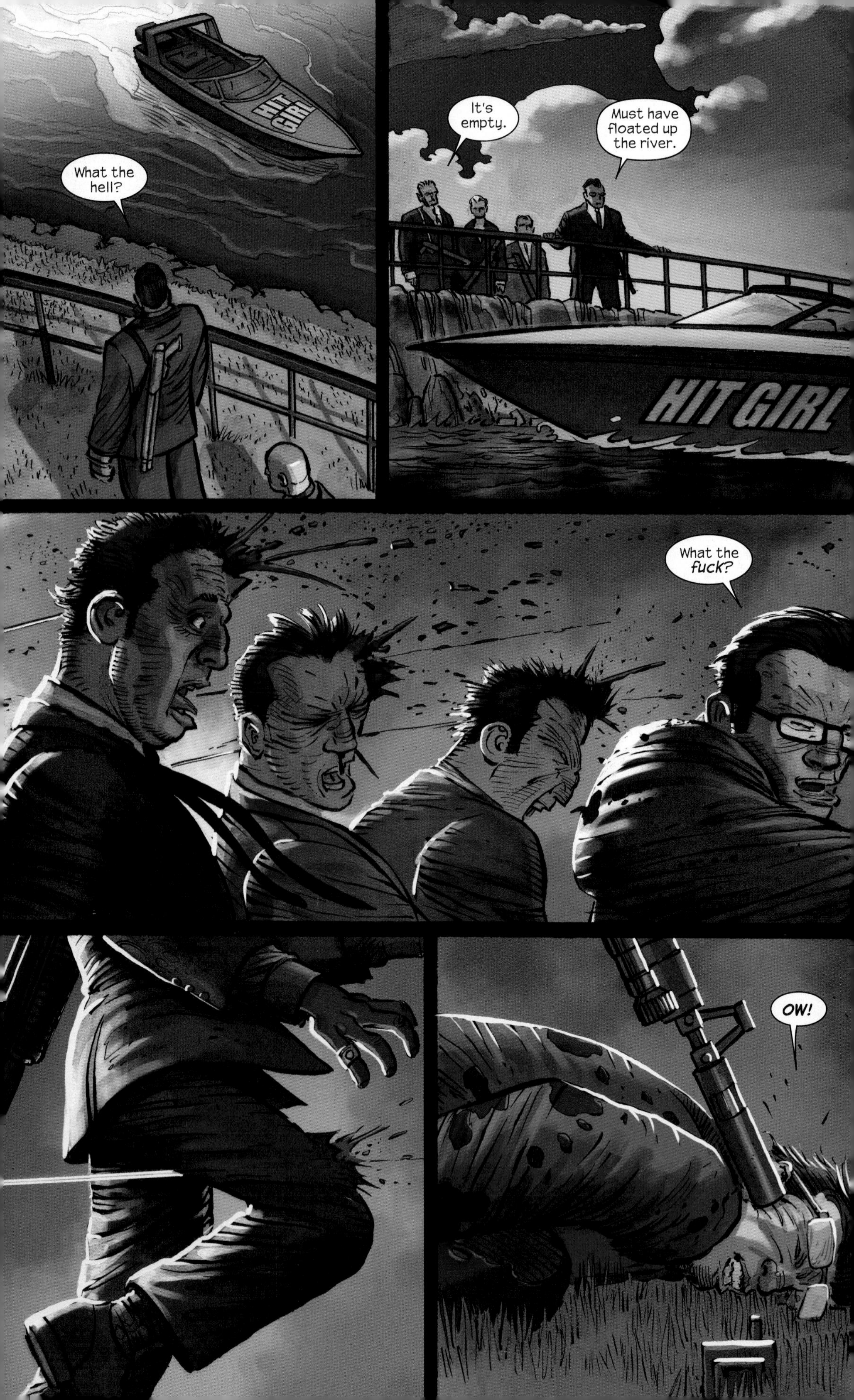
What the hell?
It's empty.
Must have floated up the river.
HIT GIRL
What the *fuck?*
OW!

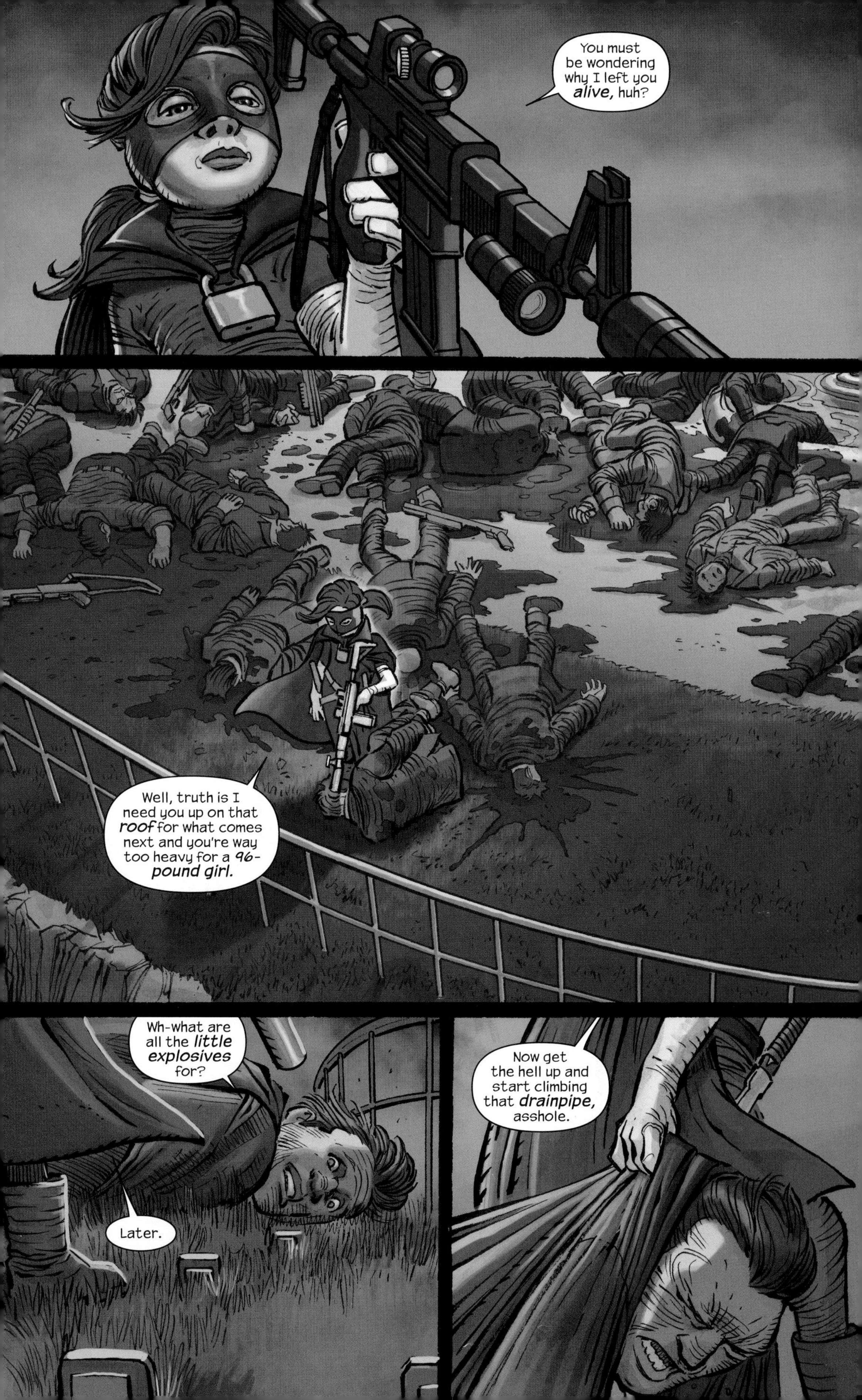

You must be wondering why I left you *alive,* huh?
Well, truth is I need you up on that *roof* for what comes next and you're way too heavy for a 96-pound girl.
Wh-what are all the *little explosives* for?
Later.
Now get the hell up and start climbing that *drainpipe,* asshole.

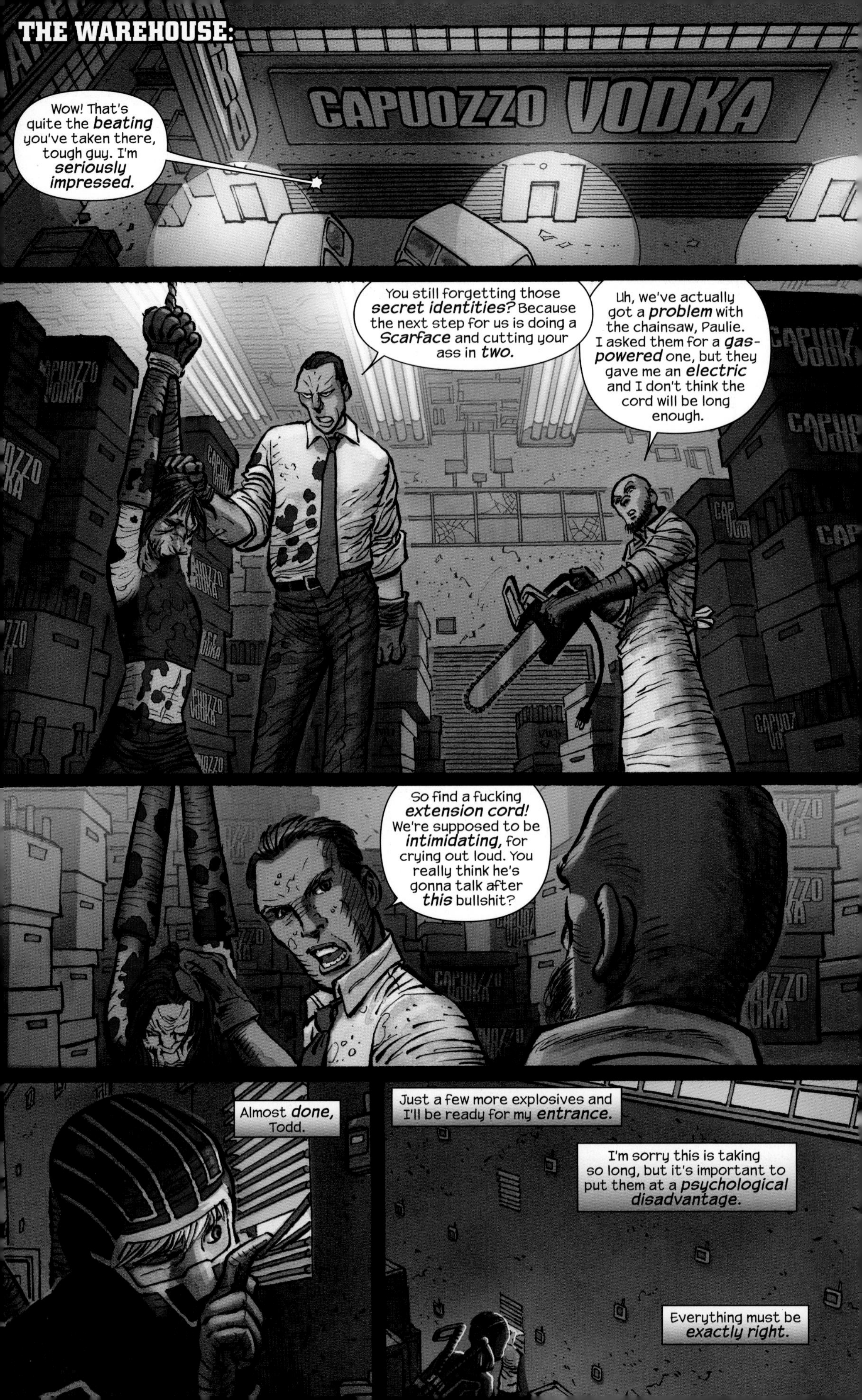
THE WAREHOUSE:
CAPUOZZO VODKA
Wow! That's quite the beating you've taken there, tough guy. I'm seriously impressed.
You still forgetting those secret identities? Because the next step for us is doing a Scarface and cutting your ass in two.
Uh, we've actually got a problem with the chainsaw, Paulie. I asked them for a gas-powered one, but they gave me an electric and I don't think the cord will be long enough.
So find a fucking extension cord! We're supposed to be intimidating, for crying out loud. You really think he's gonna talk after this bullshit?
Almost done, Todd.
Just a few more explosives and I'll be ready for my entrance.
I'm sorry this is taking so long, but it's important to put them at a psychological disadvantage.
Everything must be exactly right.

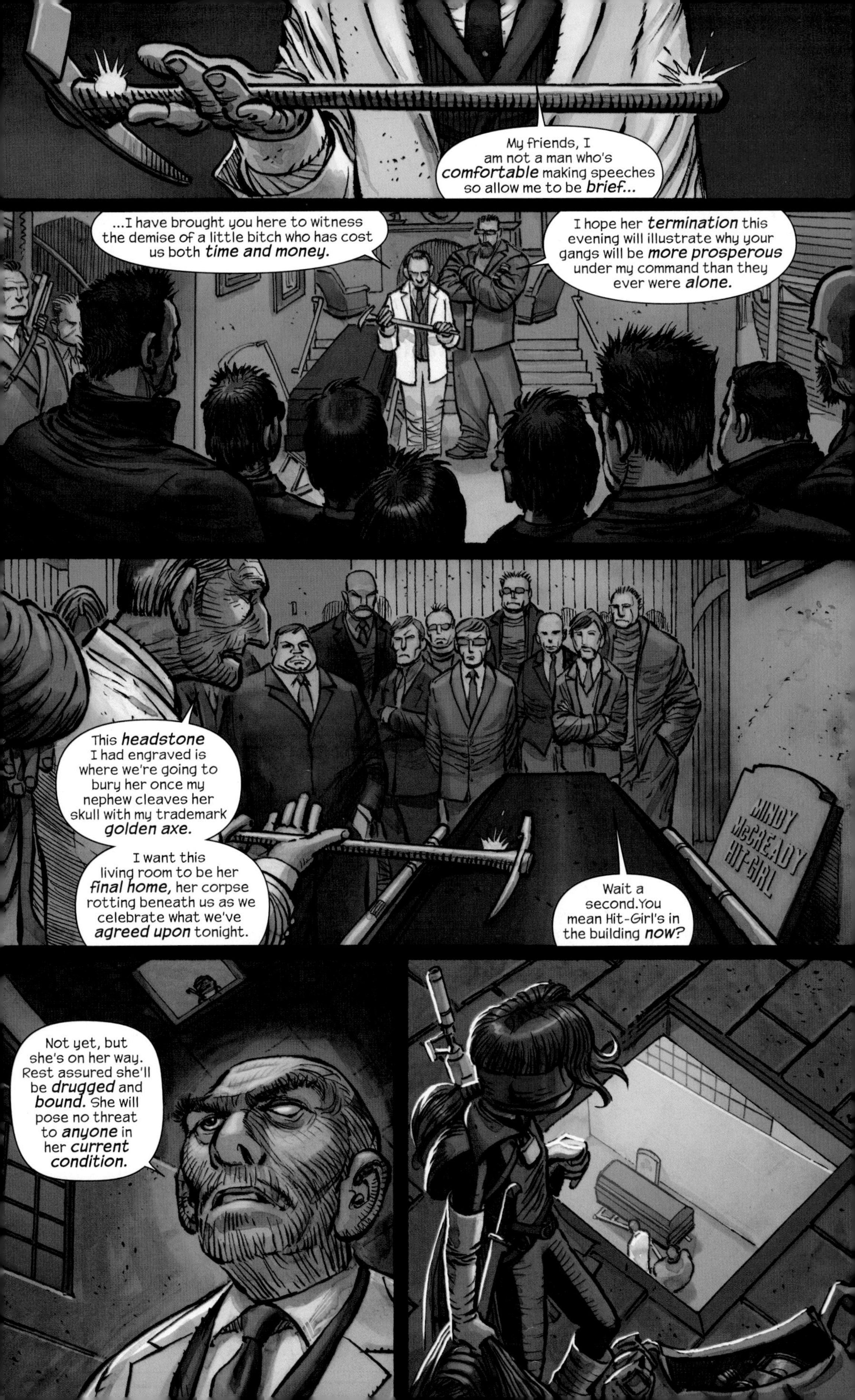

My friends, I am not a man who's comfortable making speeches so allow me to be brief...
...I have brought you here to witness the demise of a little bitch who has cost us both time and money.
I hope her termination this evening will illustrate why your gangs will be more prosperous under my command than they ever were alone.
This headstone I had engraved is where we're going to bury her once my nephew cleaves her skull with my trademark golden axe.
I want this living room to be her final home, her corpse rotting beneath us as we celebrate what we've agreed upon tonight.
MINDY McCREADY HIT-GIRL
Wait a second. You mean Hit-Girl's in the building now?
Not yet, but she's on her way. Rest assured she'll be drugged and bound. She will pose no threat to anyone in her current condition.

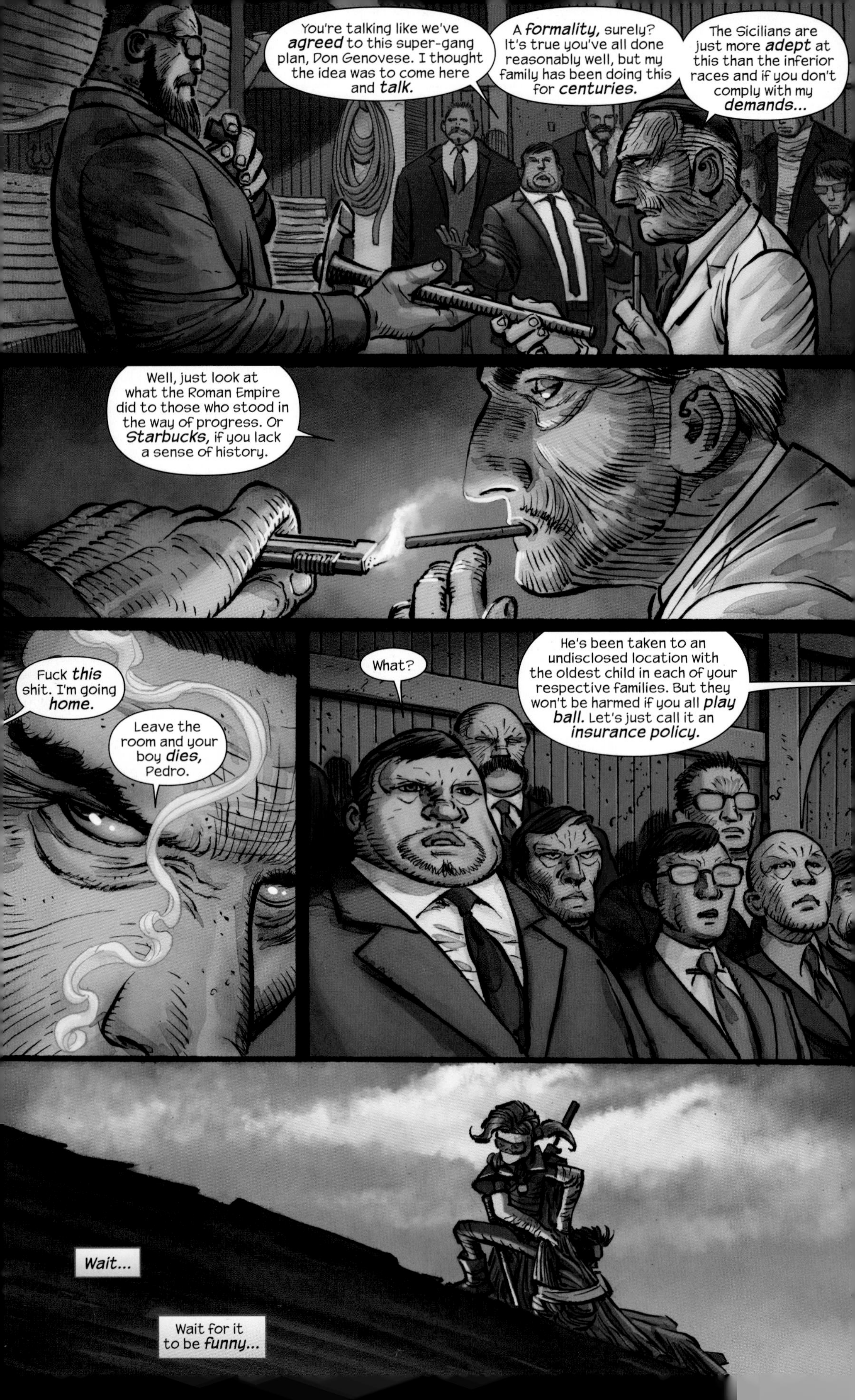
You're talking like we've agreed to this super-gang plan, Don Genovese. I thought the idea was to come here and talk.
A formality, surely? It's true you've all done reasonably well, but my family has been doing this for centuries.
The Sicilians are just more adept at this than the inferior races and if you don't comply with my demands...
Well, just look at what the Roman Empire did to those who stood in the way of progress. Or Starbucks, if you lack a sense of history.
Fuck this shit. I'm going home.
Leave the room and your boy dies, Pedro.
What?
He's been taken to an undisclosed location with the oldest child in each of your respective families. But they won't be harmed if you all play ball. Let's just call it an insurance policy.
Wait...
Wait for it to be funny...

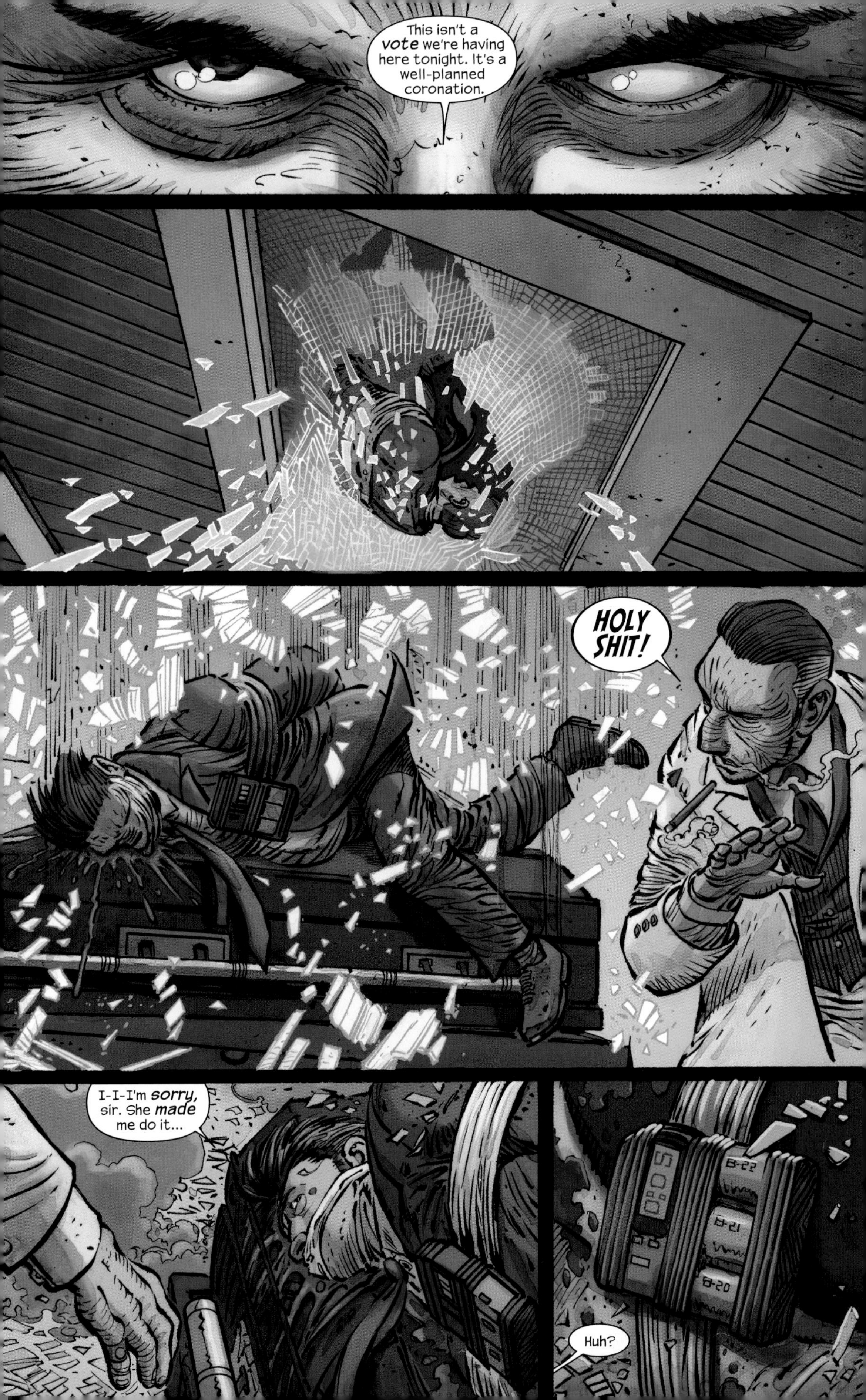

This isn't a vote we're having here tonight. It's a well-planned coronation.
HOLY SHIT!
I-I-I'm sorry, sir. She made me do it...
Huh?

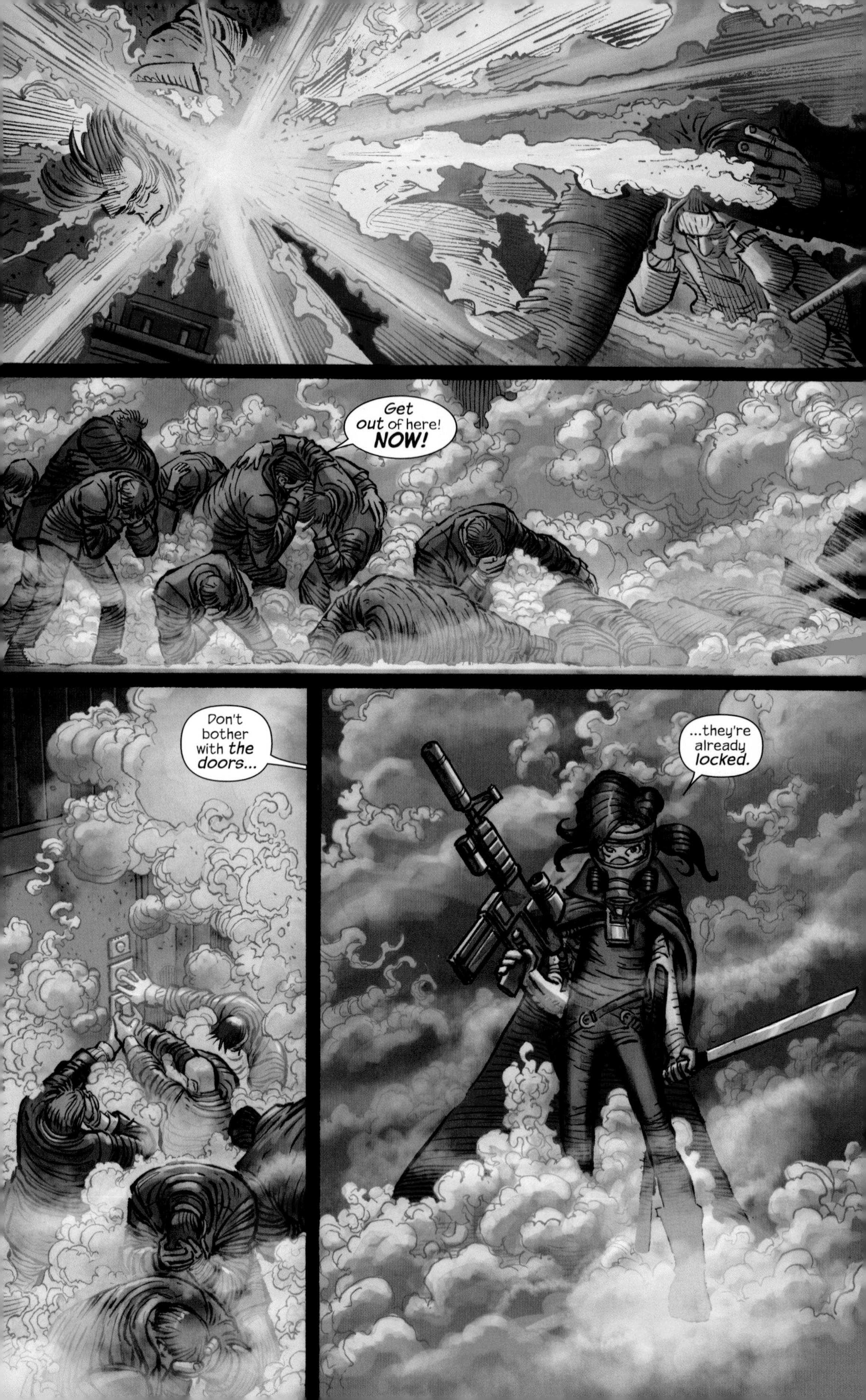
Get out of here! NOW!
Don't bother with the doors...
...they're already locked.

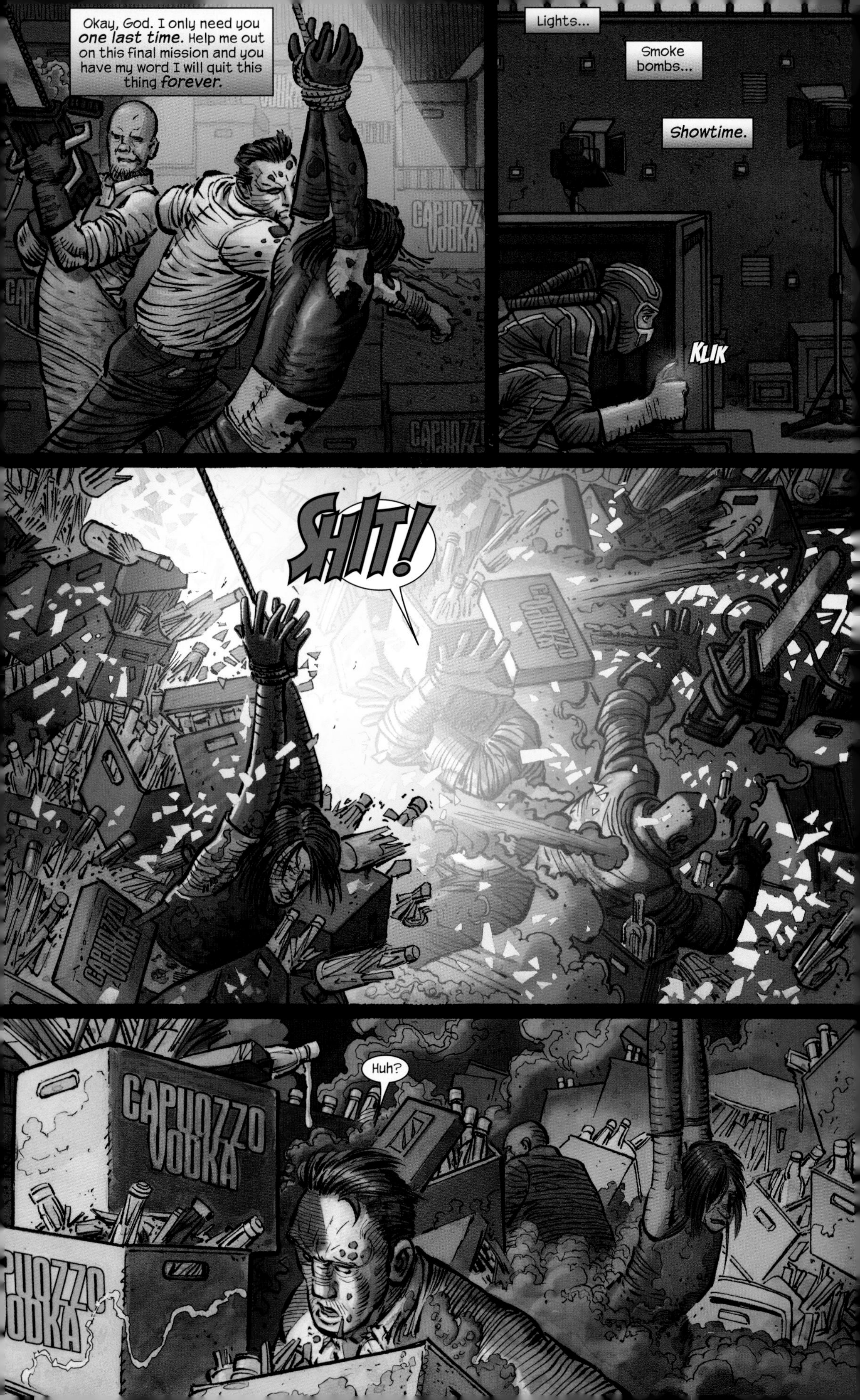

Okay, God. I only need you one last time. Help me out on this final mission and you have my word I will quit this thing forever.
Lights...
Smoke bombs...
Showtime.
KLIK
SHIT!
Huh?

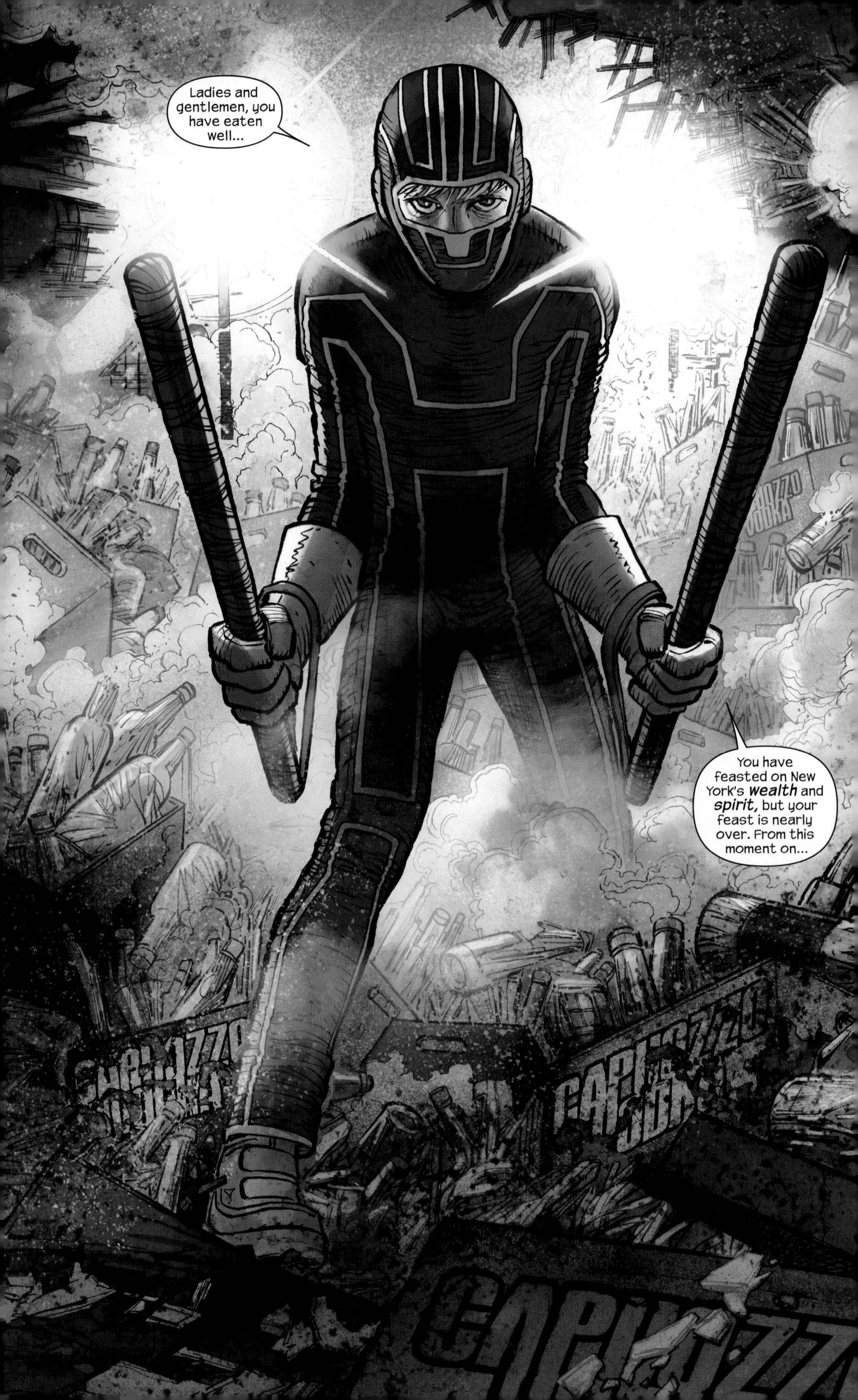
Ladies and gentlemen, you have eaten well...
You have feasted on New York's ***wealth*** and ***spirit,*** but your feast is nearly over. From this moment on...

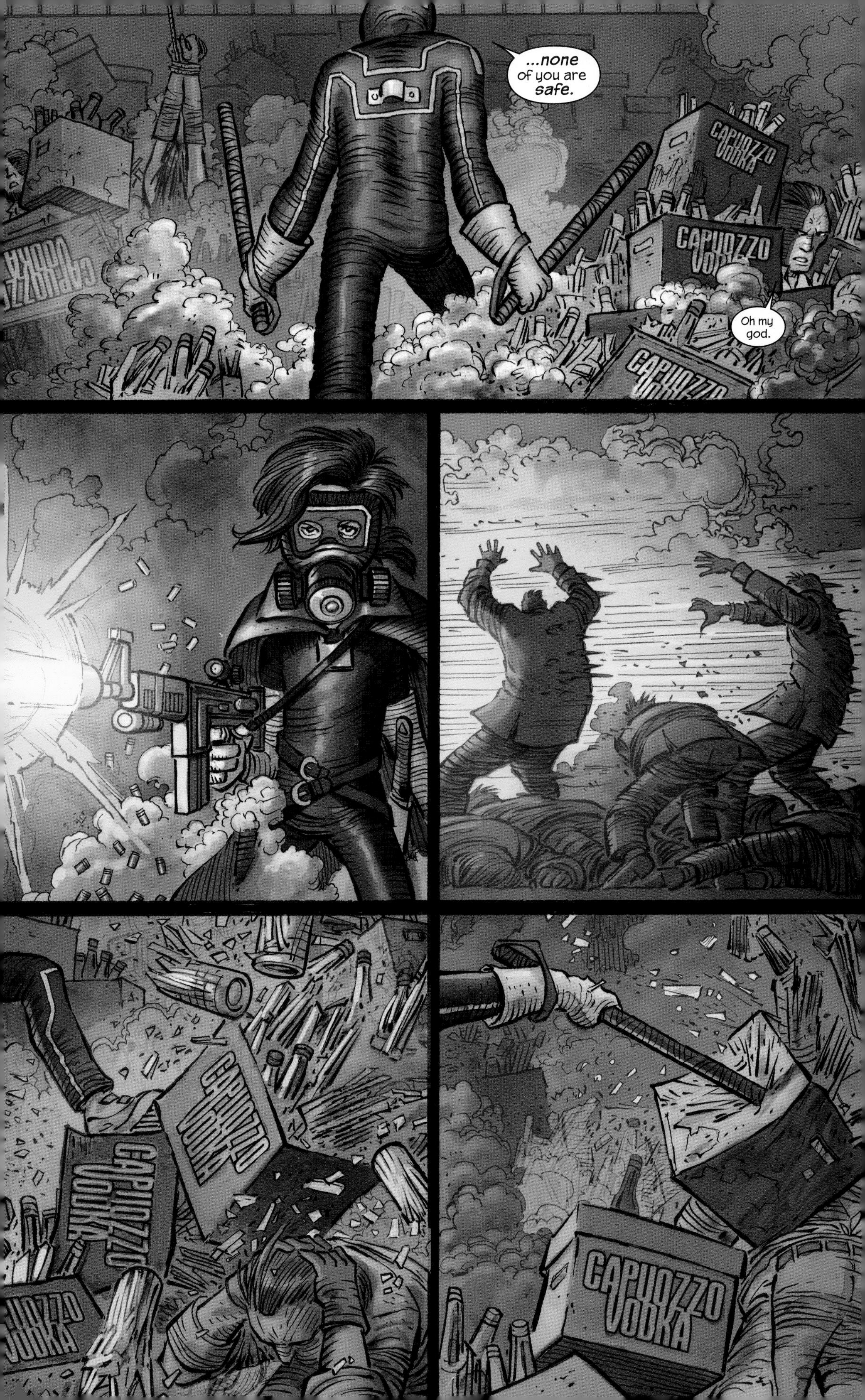
...none of you are safe.
CAPUOZZO VODKA
Oh my god.
CAPUOZZO VODKA

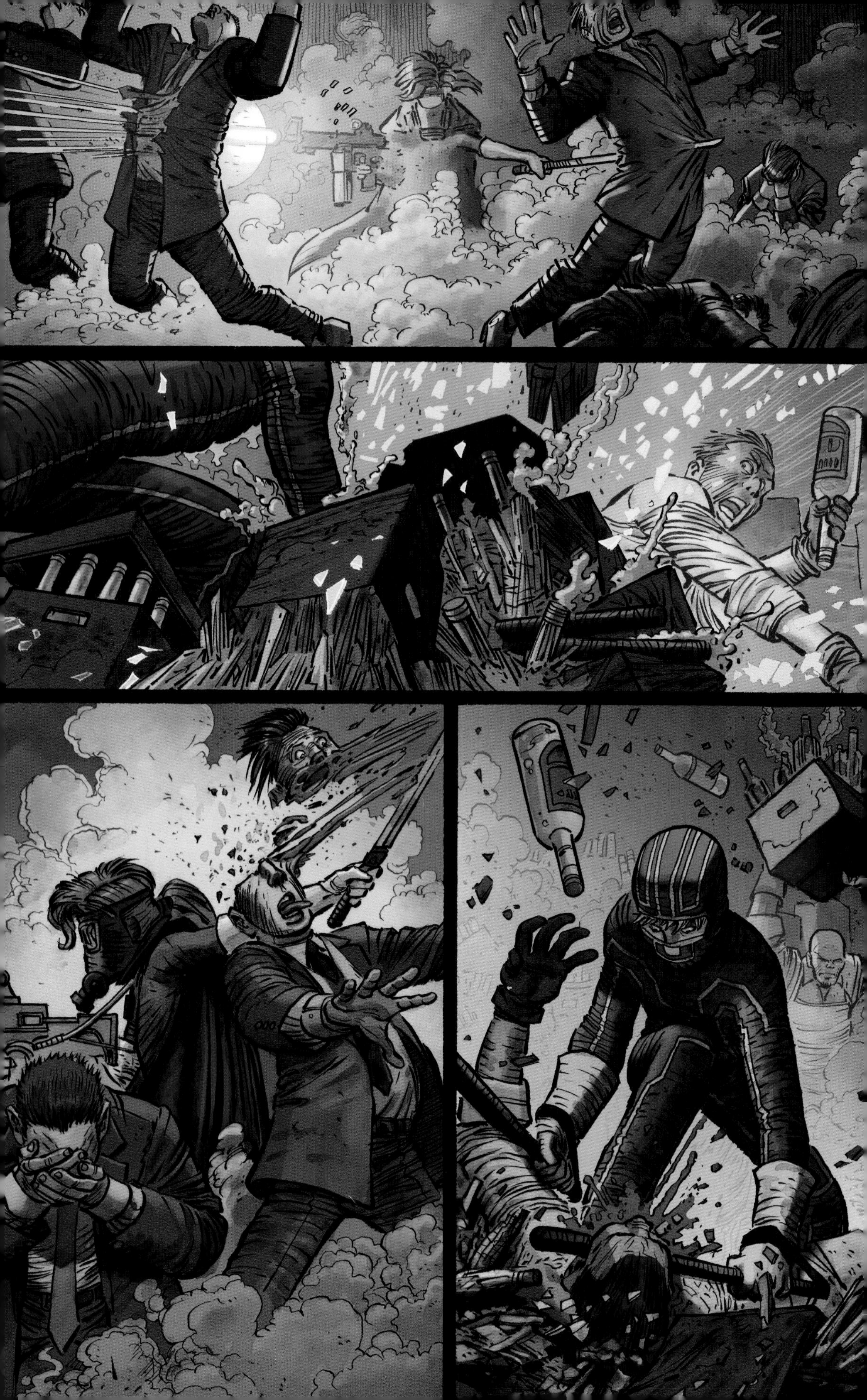

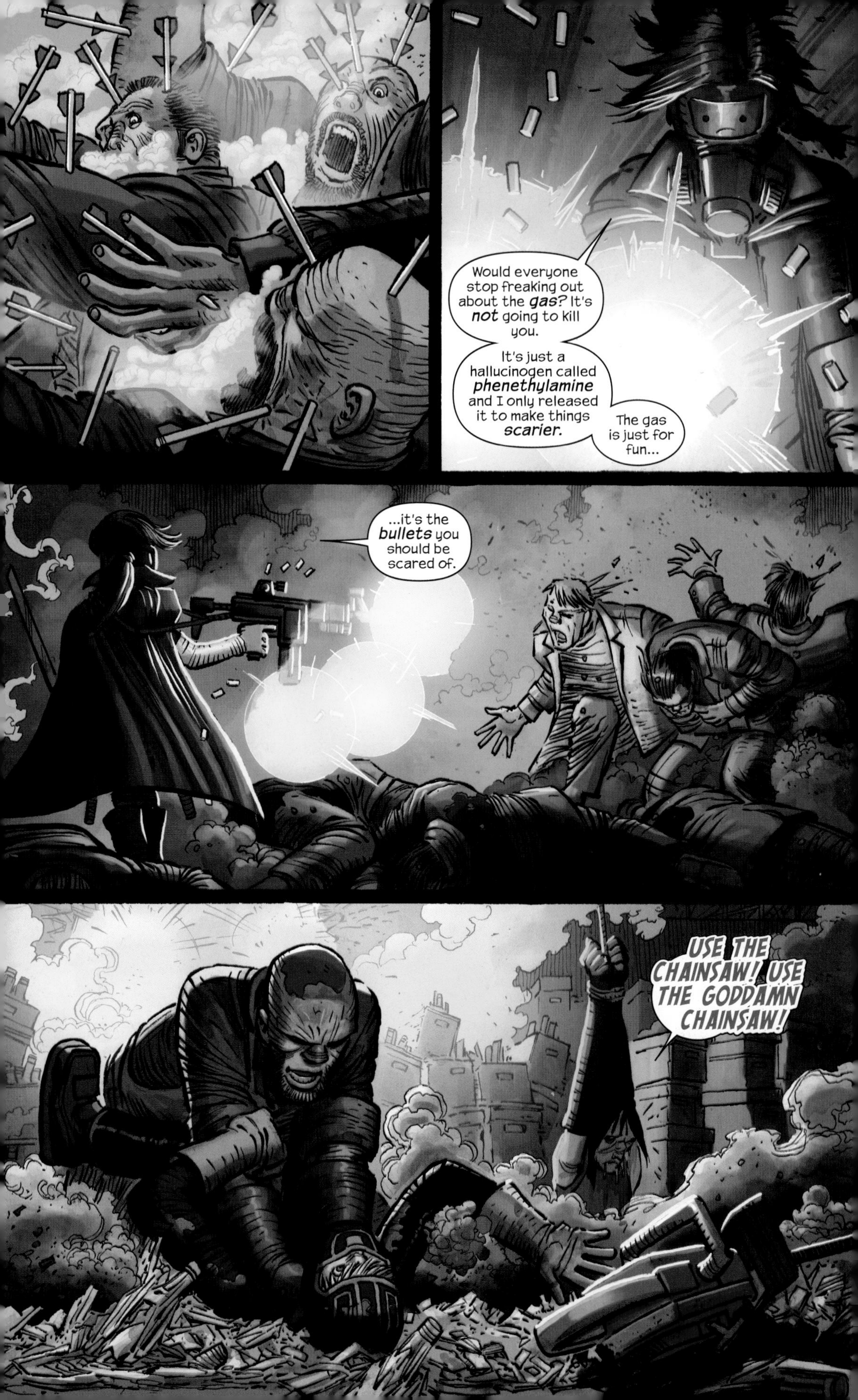
Would everyone stop freaking out about the *gas?* It's *not* going to kill you.
It's just a hallucinogen called *phenethylamine* and I only released it to make things *scarier.*
The gas is just for fun...
...it's the *bullets* you should be scared of.
USE THE CHAINSAW! USE THE GODDAMN CHAINSAW!

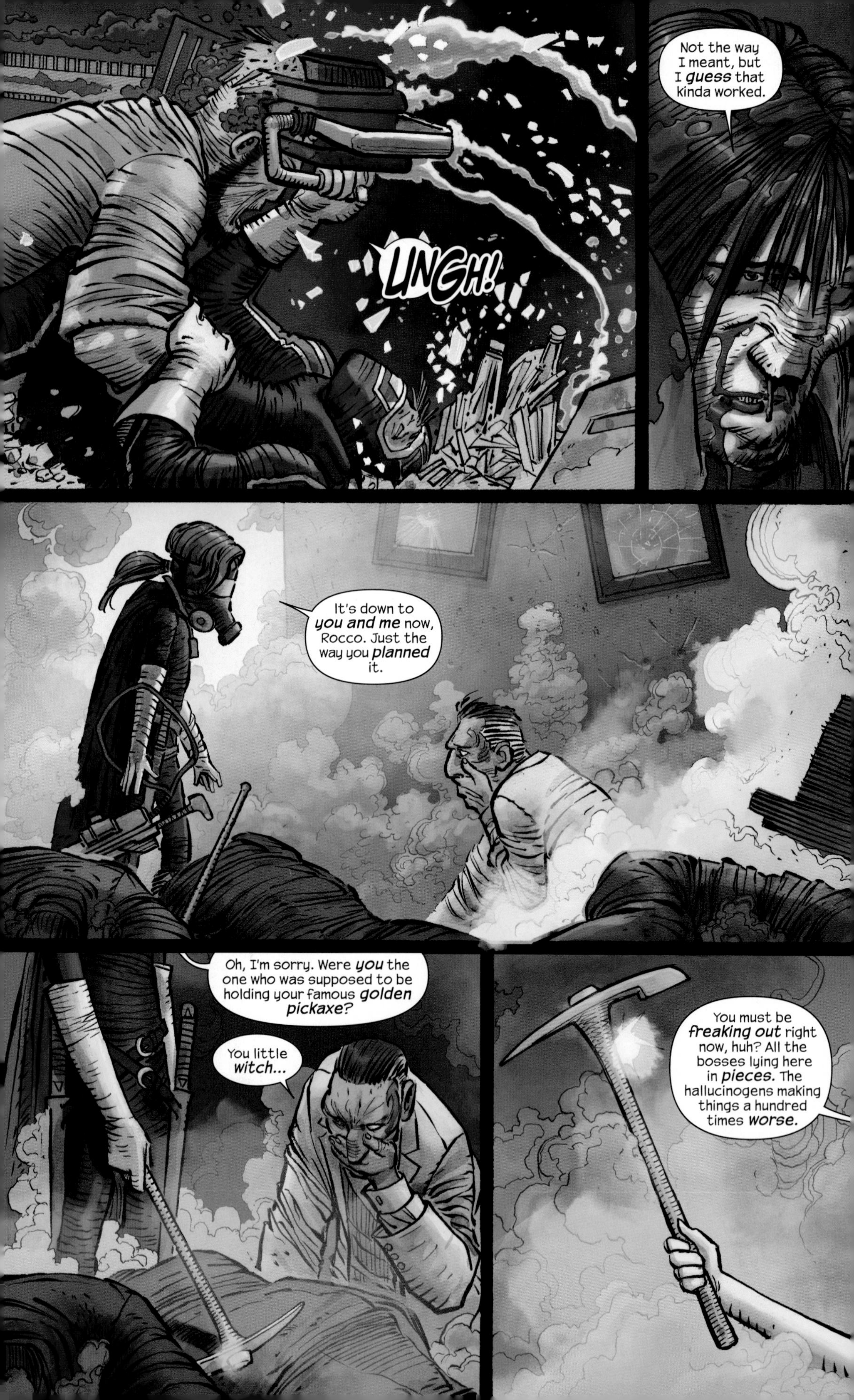
UNGH!
Not the way I meant, but I *guess* that kinda worked.
It's down to *you and me* now, Rocco. Just the way you *planned* it.
Oh, I'm sorry. Were *you* the one who was supposed to be holding your famous *golden pickaxe?*
You little *witch...*
You must be *freaking out* right now, huh? All the bosses lying here in *pieces.* The hallucinogens making things a hundred times *worse.*

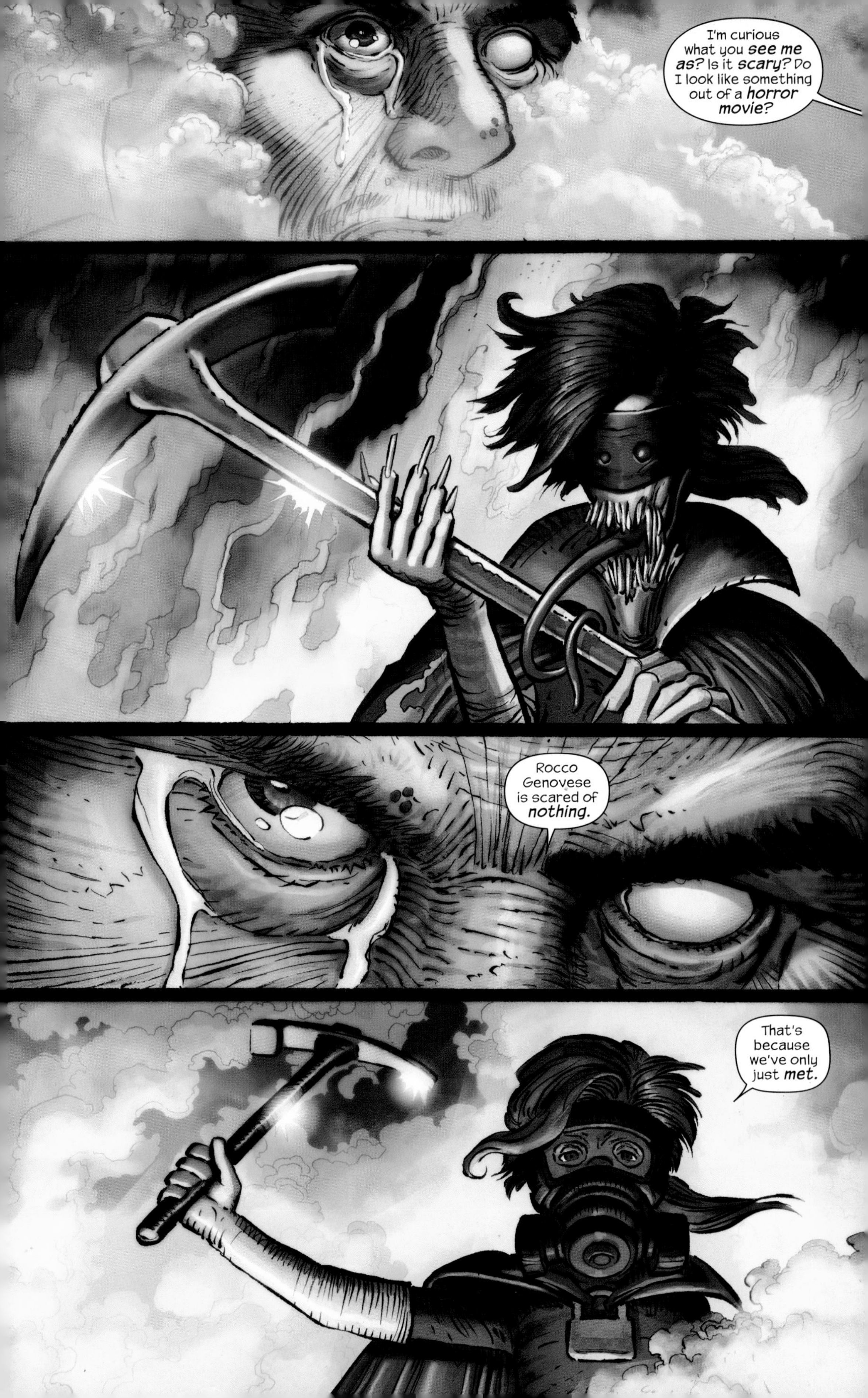
I'm curious what you **see me as?** Is it **scary?** Do I look like something out of a **horror movie?**
Rocco Genovese is scared of ***nothing.***
That's because we've only just ***met.***

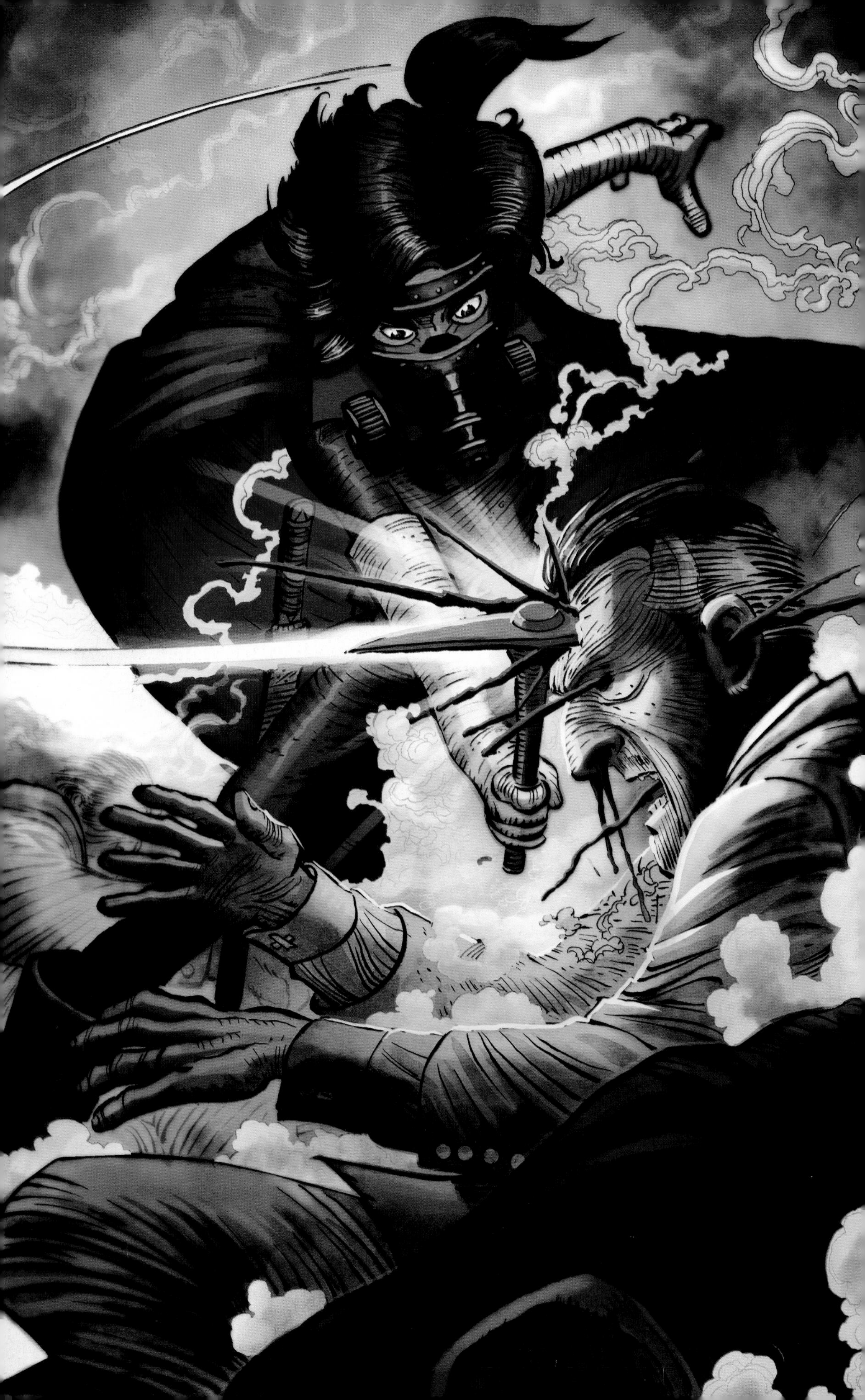

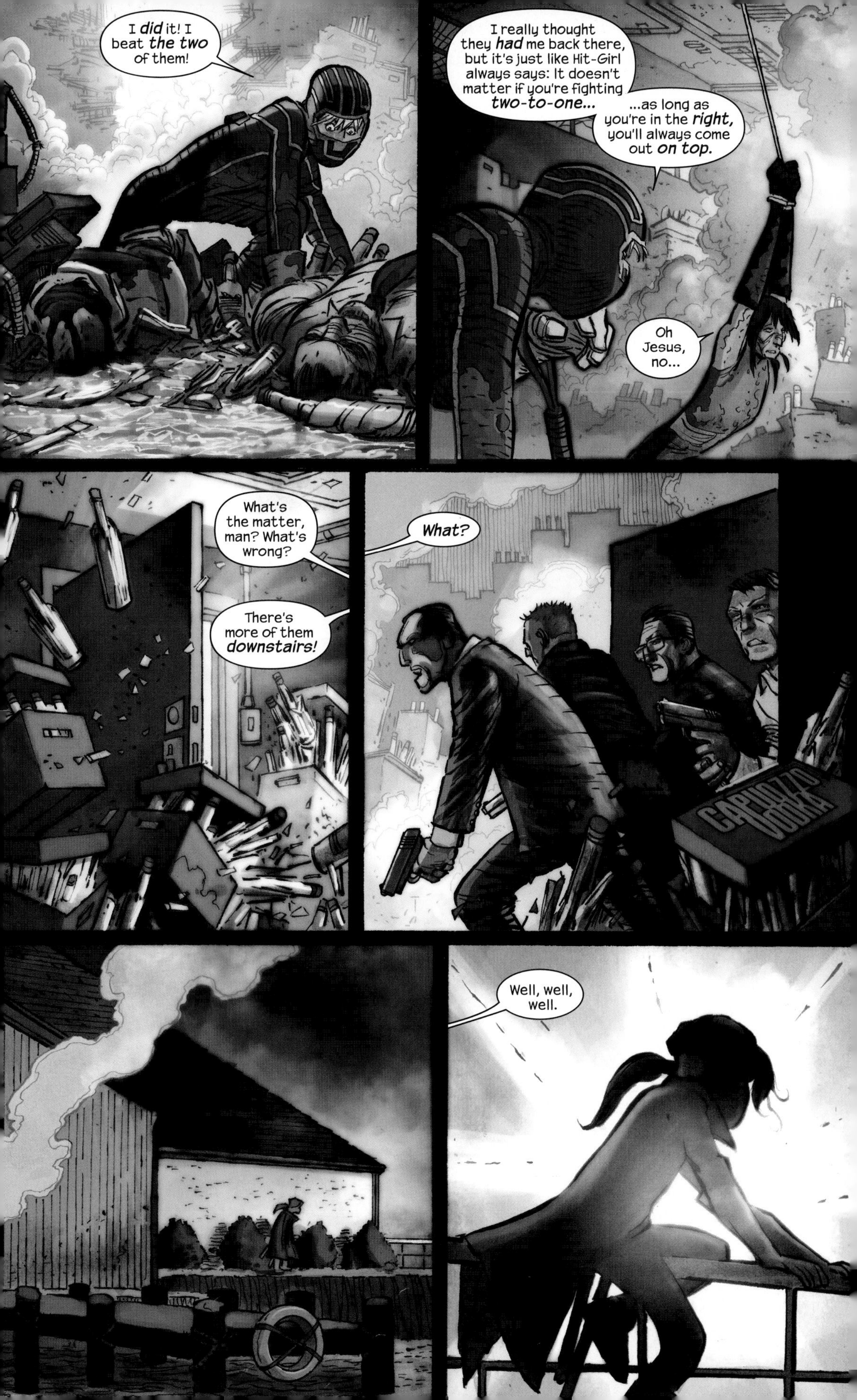
I did it! I beat the two of them!
I really thought they had me back there, but it's just like Hit-Girl always says: It doesn't matter if you're fighting two-to-one...
...as long as you're in the right, you'll always come out on top.
Oh Jesus, no...
What's the matter, man? What's wrong?
There's more of them downstairs!
What?
Well, well, well.

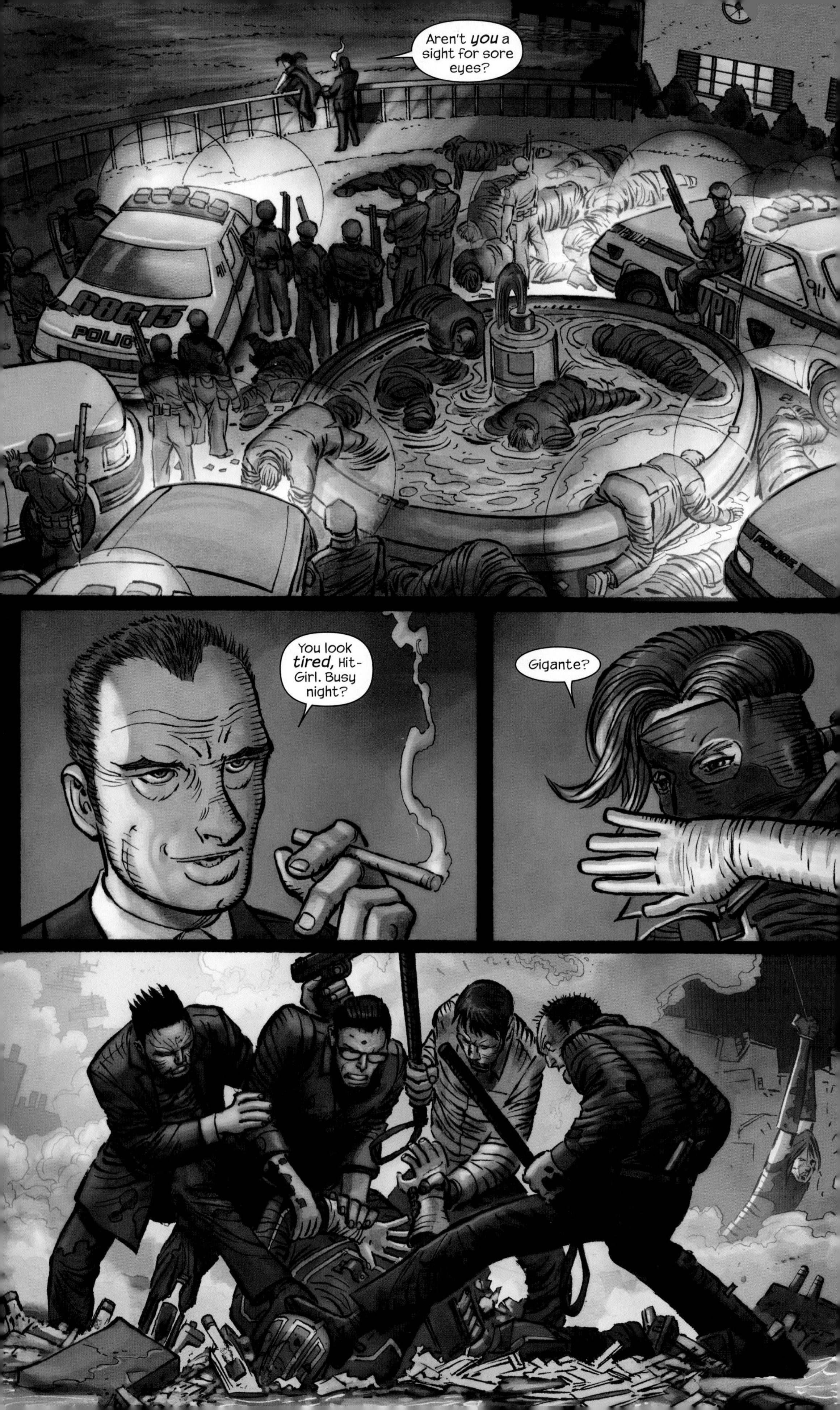
Aren't *you* a sight for sore eyes?
You look *tired,* Hit-Girl. Busy night?
Gigante?

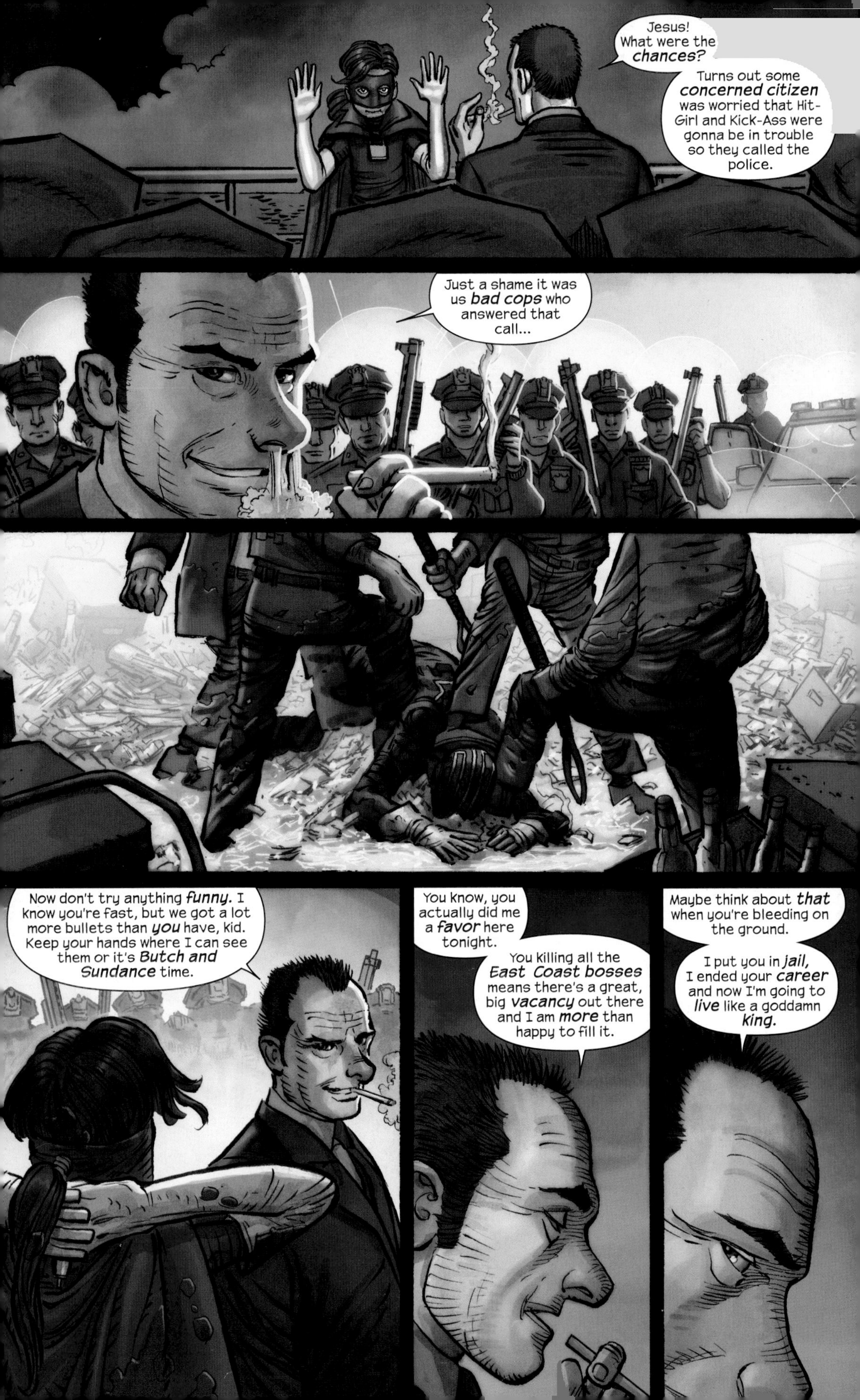
Jesus! What were the *chances?*
Turns out some *concerned citizen* was worried that Hit-Girl and Kick-Ass were gonna be in trouble so they called the police.
Just a shame it was us *bad cops* who answered that call...
Now don't try anything *funny.* I know you're fast, but we got a lot more bullets than *you* have, kid. Keep your hands where I can see them or it's *Butch and Sundance* time.
You know, you actually did me a *favor* here tonight.
You killing all the *East Coast bosses* means there's a great, big *vacancy* out there and I am *more* than happy to fill it.
Maybe think about *that* when you're bleeding on the ground.
I put you in *jail,* I ended your *career* and now I'm going to *live* like a goddamn *king.*

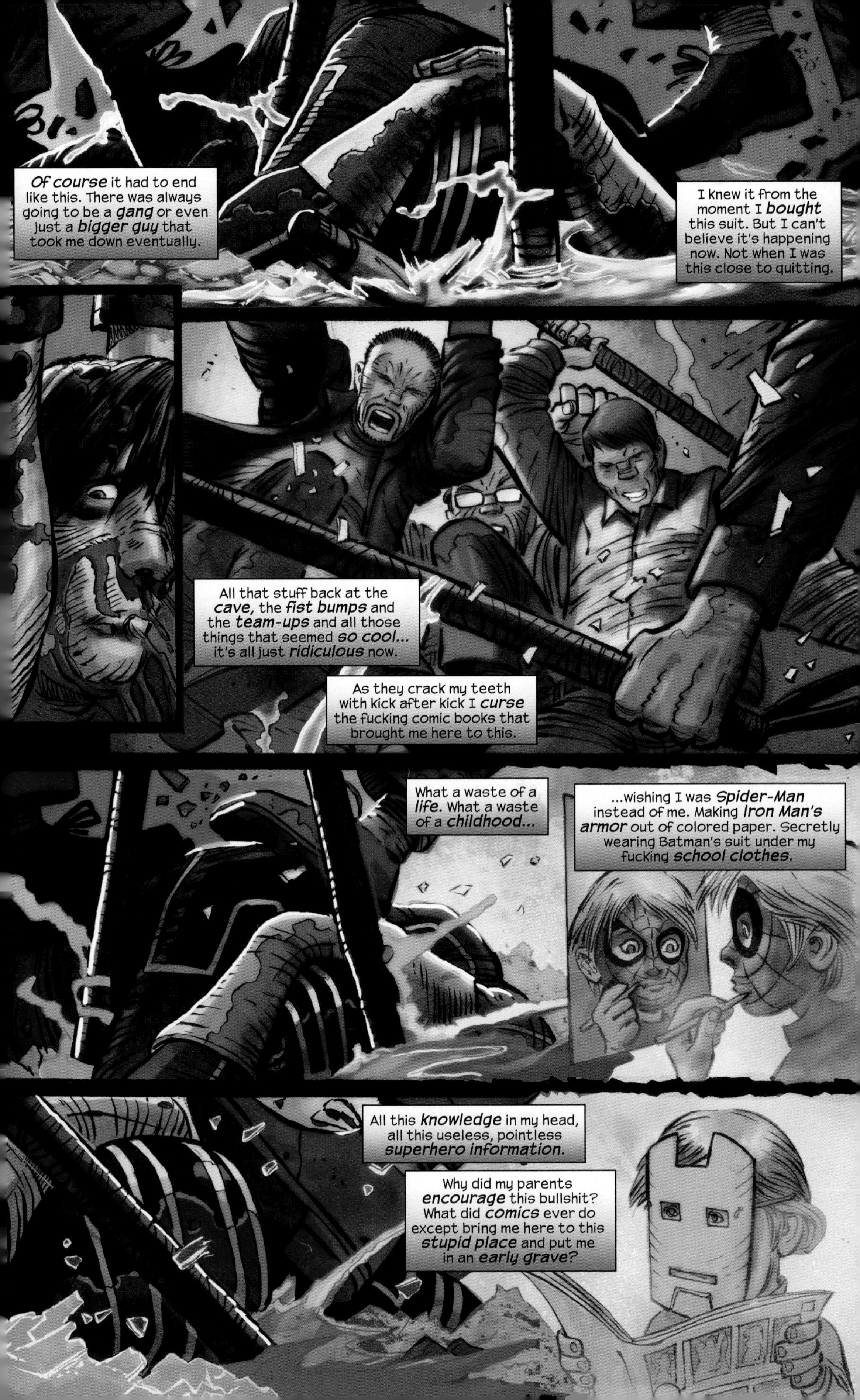
Of course it had to end like this. There was always going to be a gang or even just a bigger guy that took me down eventually.
I knew it from the moment I bought this suit. But I can't believe it's happening now. Not when I was this close to quitting.
All that stuff back at the cave, the fist bumps and the team-ups and all those things that seemed so cool... it's all just ridiculous now.
As they crack my teeth with kick after kick I curse the fucking comic books that brought me here to this.
What a waste of a life. What a waste of a childhood...
...wishing I was Spider-Man instead of me. Making Iron Man's armor out of colored paper. Secretly wearing Batman's suit under my fucking school clothes.
All this knowledge in my head, all this useless, pointless superhero information.
Why did my parents encourage this bullshit? What did comics ever do except bring me here to this stupid place and put me in an early grave?

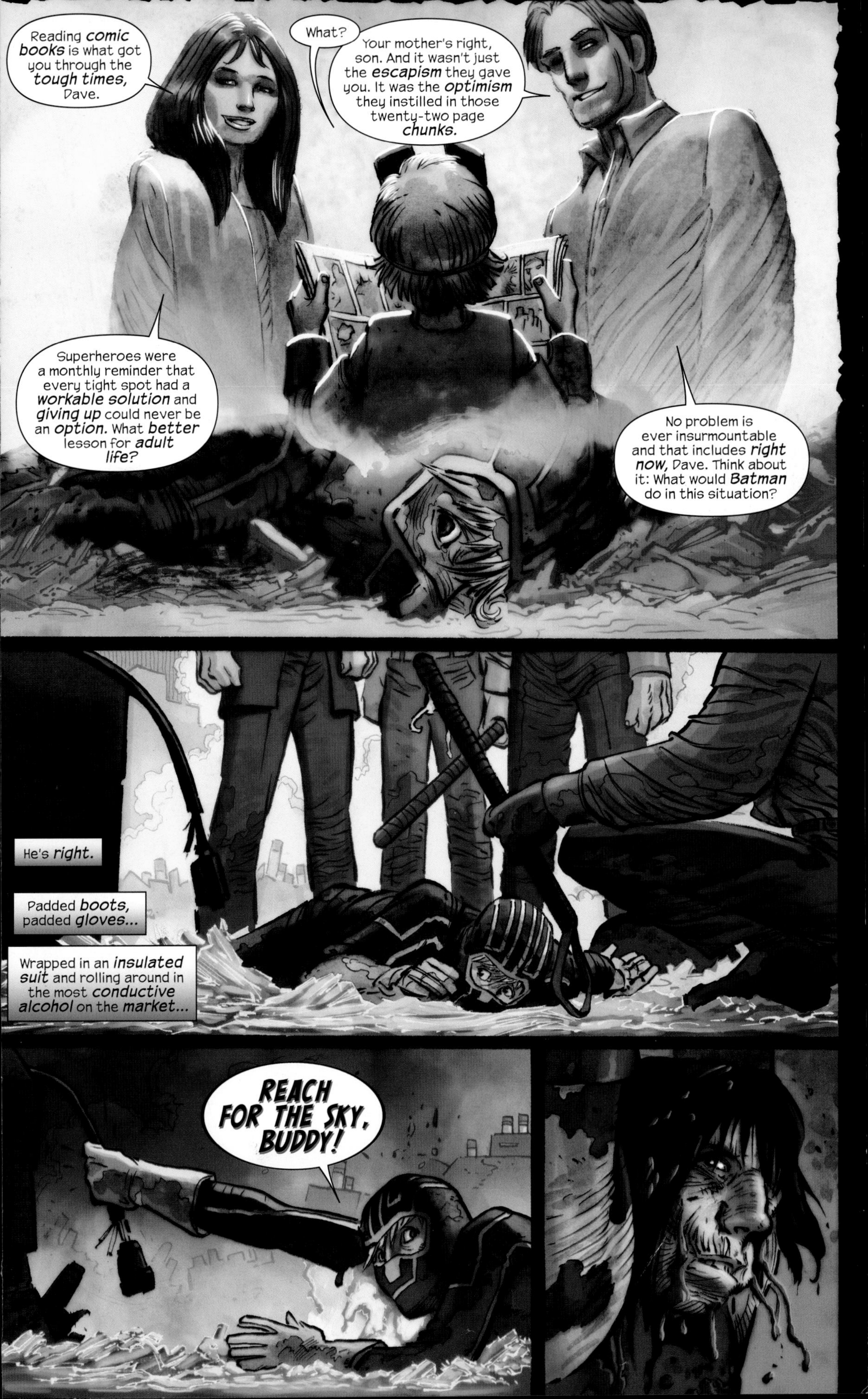

Reading comic books is what got you through the tough times, Dave.
What?
Your mother's right, son. And it wasn't just the escapism they gave you. It was the optimism they instilled in those twenty-two page chunks.
Superheroes were a monthly reminder that every tight spot had a workable solution and giving up could never be an option. What better lesson for adult life?
No problem is ever insurmountable and that includes right now, Dave. Think about it: What would Batman do in this situation?
He's right.
Padded boots, padded gloves...
Wrapped in an insulated suit and rolling around in the most conductive alcohol on the market...
REACH FOR THE SKY, BUDDY!

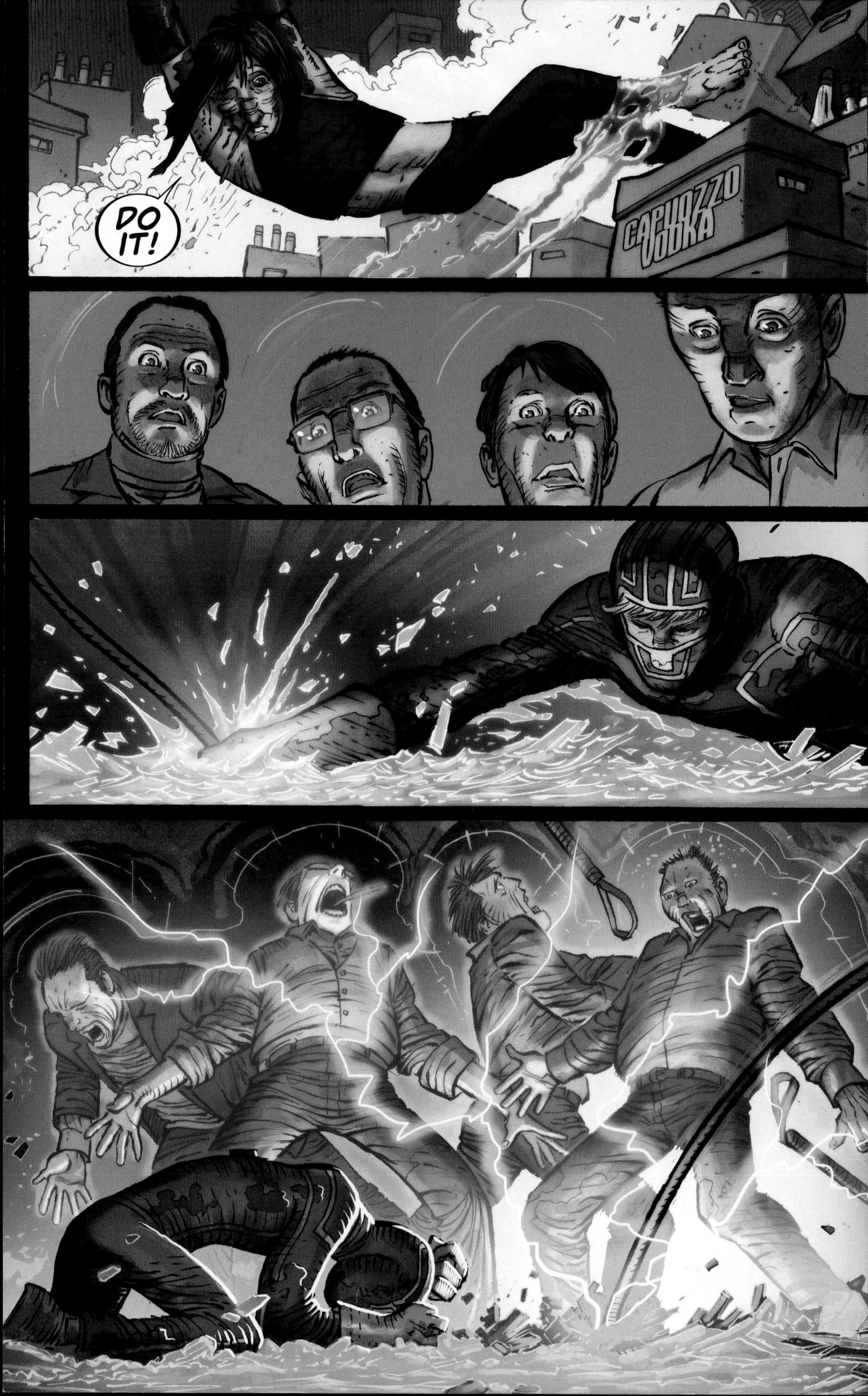
DO IT!
CAPUOZZO VODKA

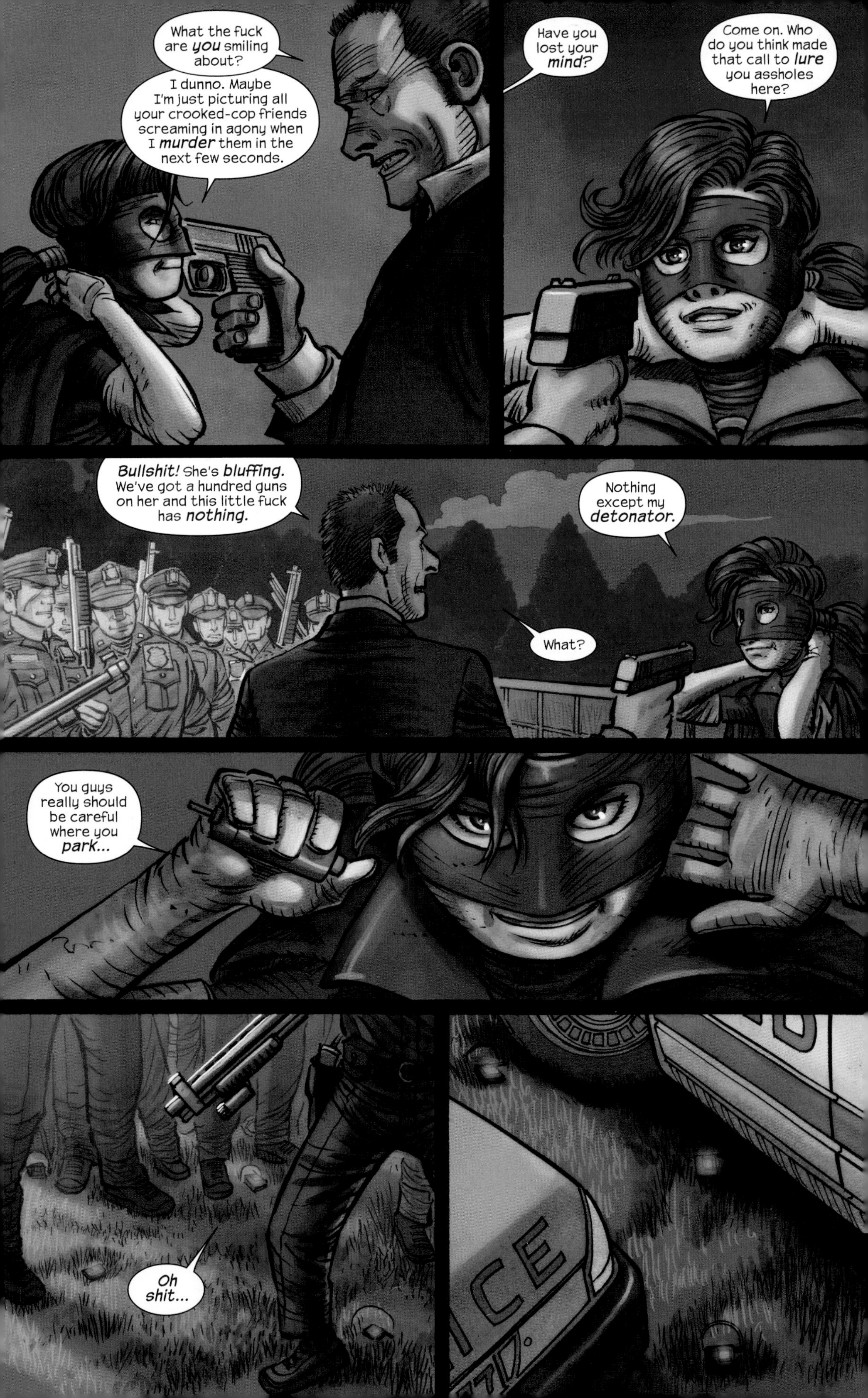
What the fuck are *you* smiling about?
I dunno. Maybe I'm just picturing all your crooked-cop friends screaming in agony when I *murder* them in the next few seconds.
Have you lost your *mind*?
Come on. Who do you think made that call to *lure* you assholes here?
Bullshit! She's *bluffing.* We've got a hundred guns on her and this little fuck has *nothing.*
Nothing except my *detonator.*
What?
You guys really should be careful where you *park...*
Oh shit...
ICE

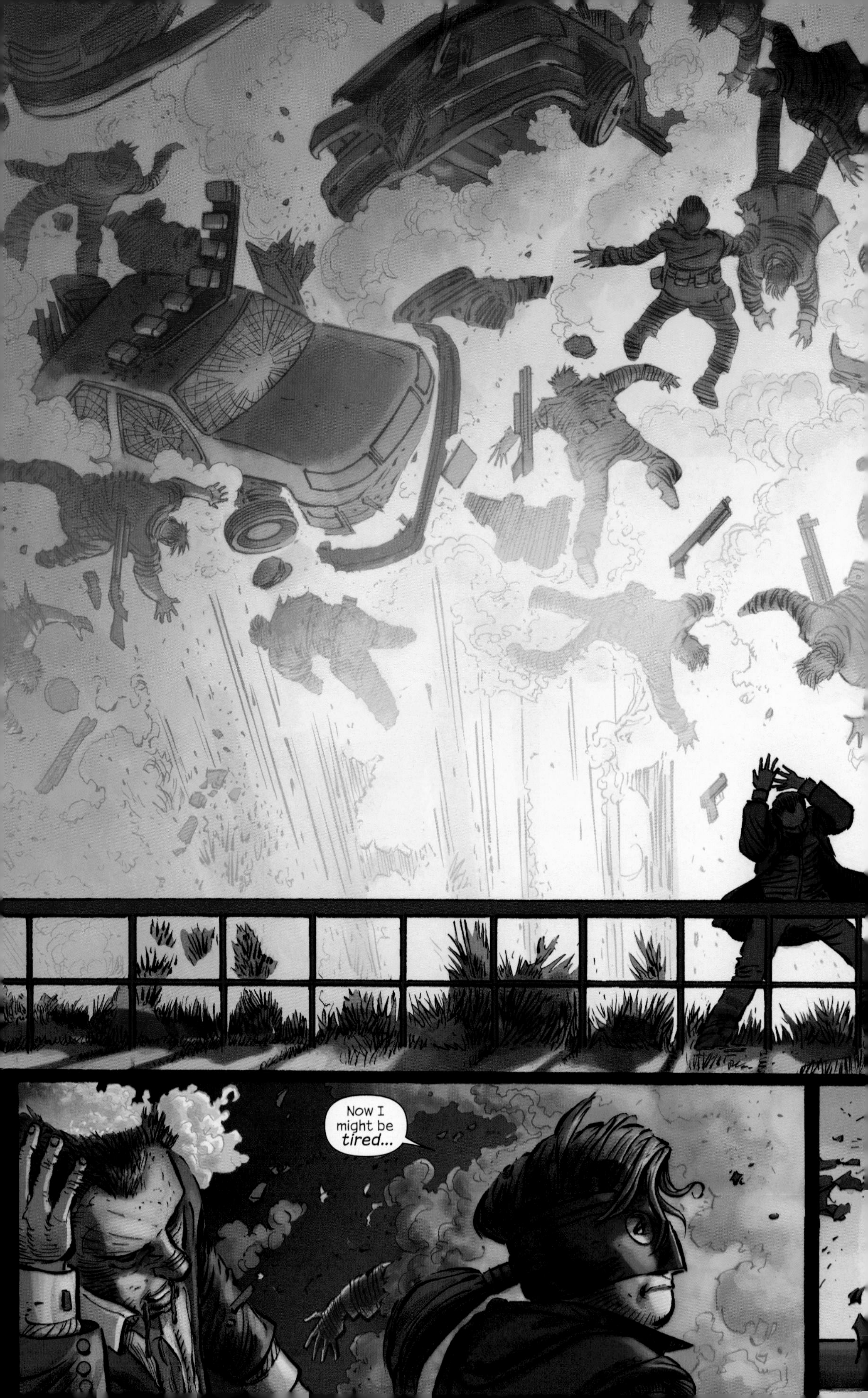
Now I might be *tired*...

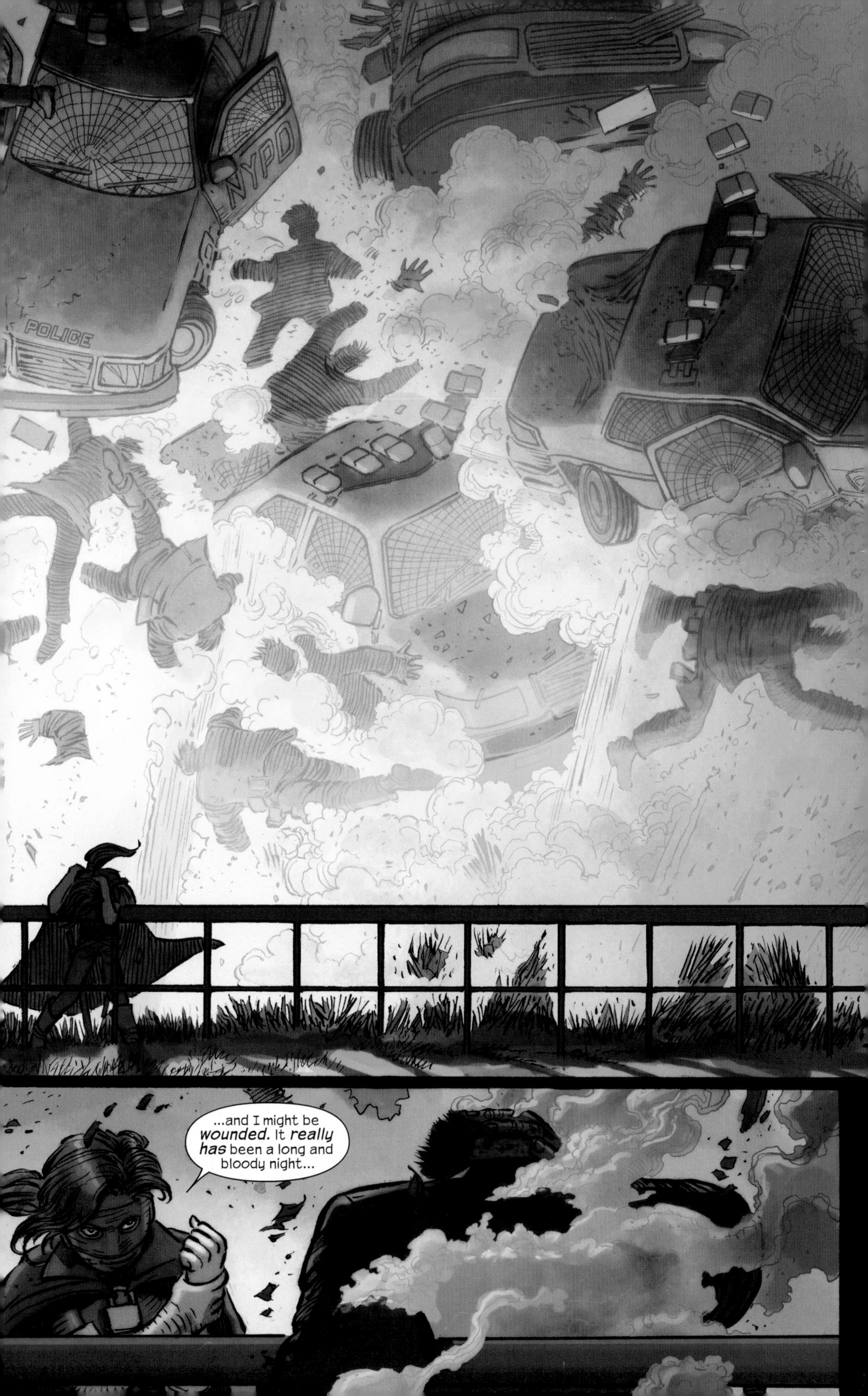
NYPD
POLICE
...and I might be *wounded.* It *really has* been a long and bloody night...

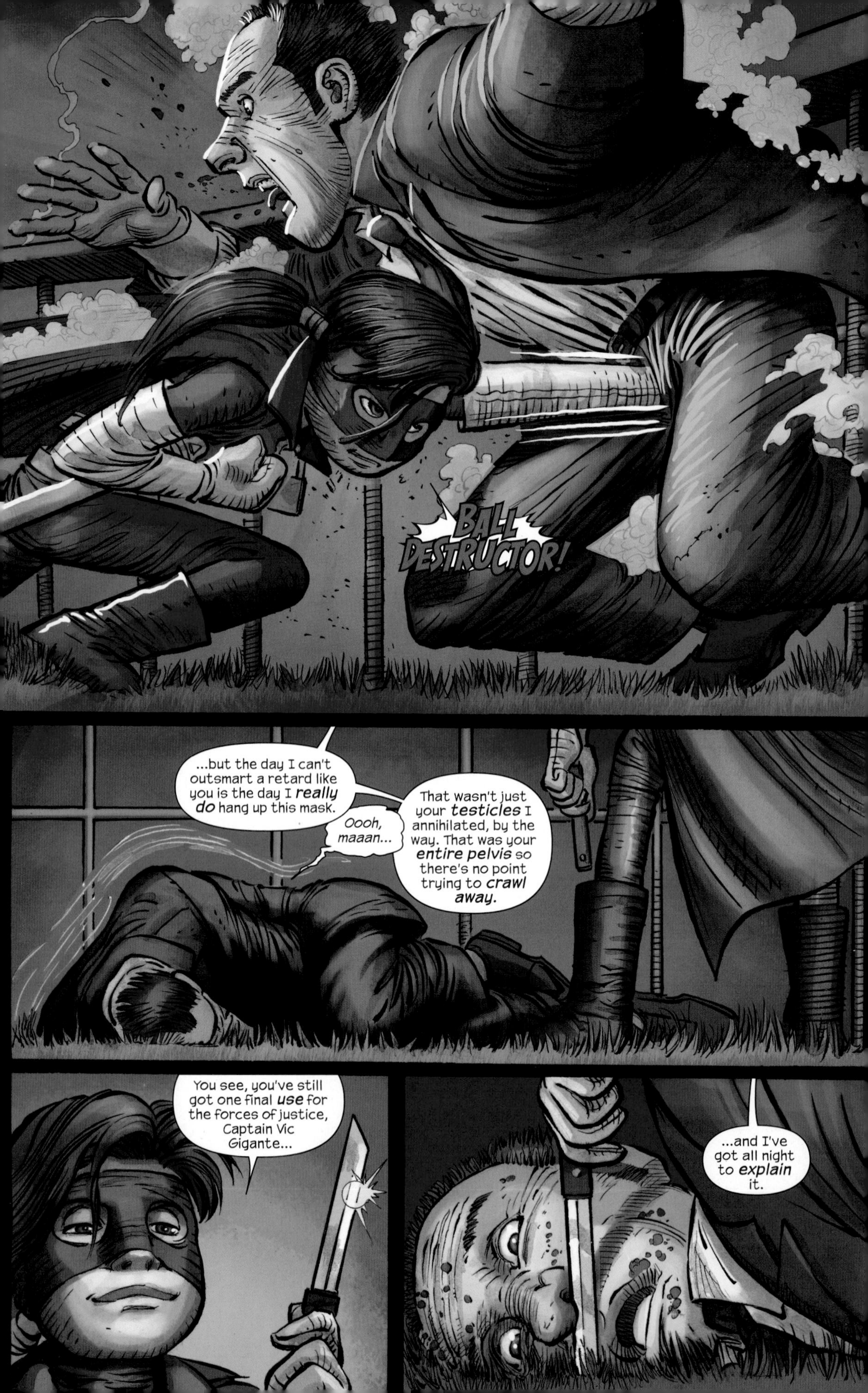
BALL DESTRUCTOR!
...but the day I can't outsmart a retard like you is the day I *really do* hang up this mask.
Oooh, maaan...
That wasn't just your *testicles* I annihilated, by the way. That was your *entire pelvis* so there's no point trying to *crawl away.*
You see, you've still got one final *use* for the forces of justice, Captain Vic Gigante...
...and I've got all night to *explain* it.

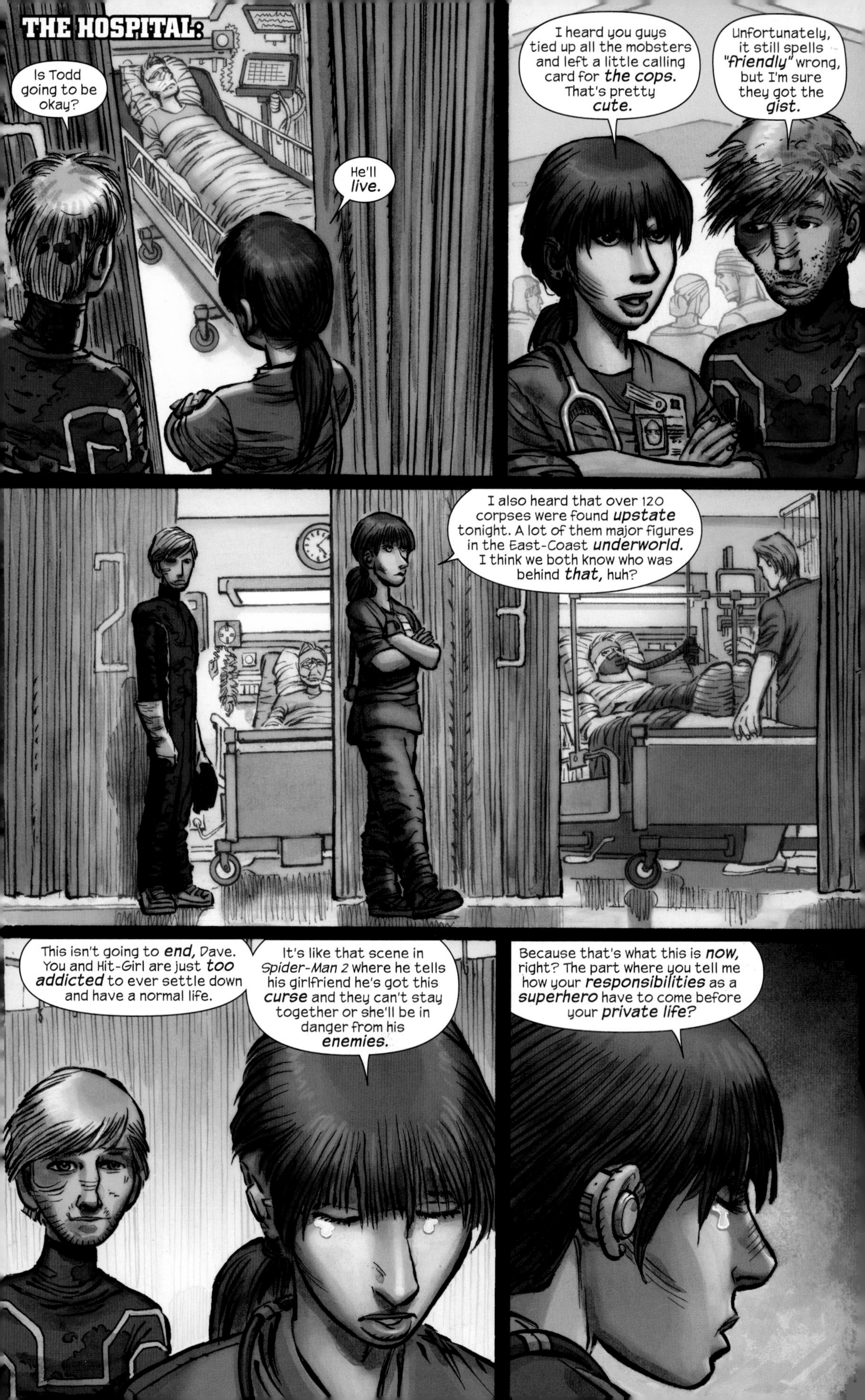
THE HOSPITAL:
Is Todd going to be okay?
He'll live.
I heard you guys tied up all the mobsters and left a little calling card for the cops. That's pretty cute.
Unfortunately, it still spells "friendly" wrong, but I'm sure they got the gist.
I also heard that over 120 corpses were found upstate tonight. A lot of them major figures in the East-Coast underworld. I think we both know who was behind that, huh?
This isn't going to end, Dave. You and Hit-Girl are just too addicted to ever settle down and have a normal life.
It's like that scene in Spider-Man 2 where he tells his girlfriend he's got this curse and they can't stay together or she'll be in danger from his enemies.
Because that's what this is now, right? The part where you tell me how your responsibilities as a superhero have to come before your private life?

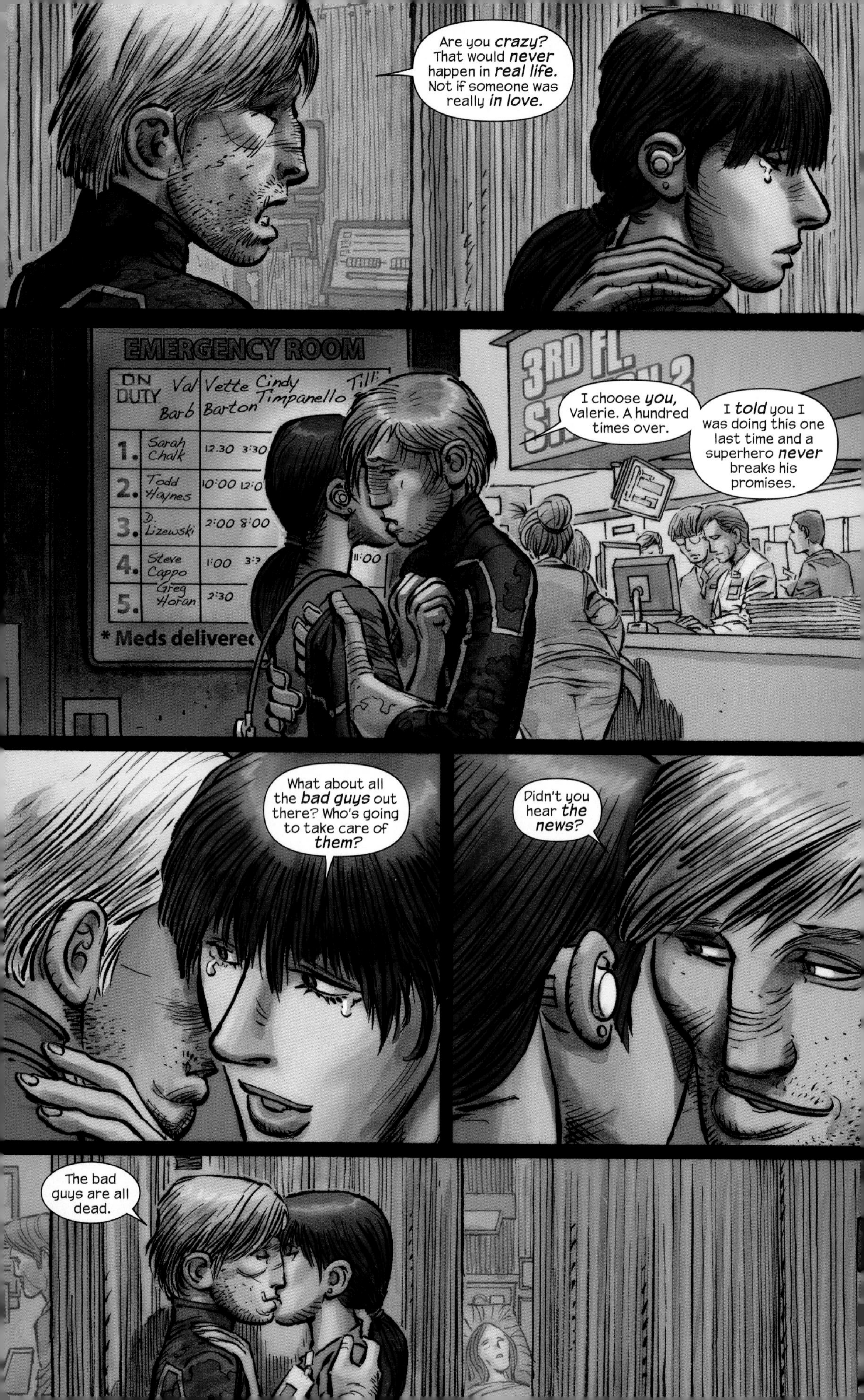
Are you *crazy?* That would *never* happen in *real life.* Not if someone was really *in love.*
EMERGENCY ROOM
ON DUTY Val Vette Cindy Timpanello Tilli Barb Barton
1. Sarah Chalk 12.30 3:30
2. Todd Haynes 10:00
3. D. Lizewski 2:00 8:00
4. Steve Cappo 1:00 11:00
5. Greg Horan 2:30
* Meds delivered
3RD FL.
I choose *you,* Valerie. A hundred times over.
I *told* you I was doing this one last time and a superhero *never* breaks his promises.
What about all the *bad guys* out there? Who's going to take care of *them?*
Didn't you hear *the news?*
The bad guys are all dead.

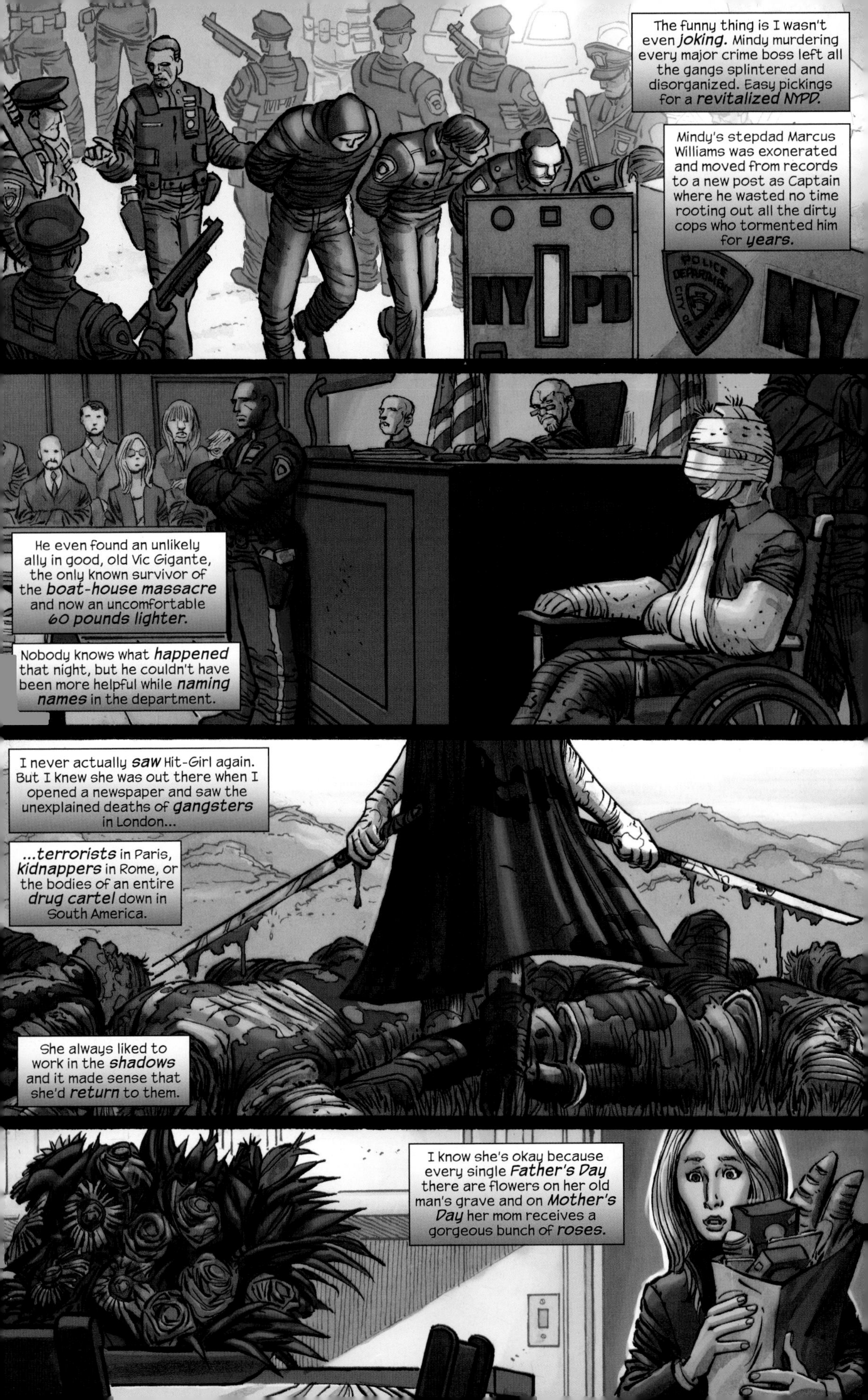
The funny thing is I wasn't even *joking.* Mindy murdering every major crime boss left all the gangs splintered and disorganized. Easy pickings for a *revitalized NYPD.*
Mindy's stepdad Marcus Williams was exonerated and moved from records to a new post as Captain where he wasted no time rooting out all the dirty cops who tormented him for *years.*
NYPD
POLICE DEPARTMENT CITY OF NEW YORK
NY
He even found an unlikely ally in good, old Vic Gigante, the only known survivor of the *boat-house massacre* and now an uncomfortable *60 pounds lighter.*
Nobody knows what *happened* that night, but he couldn't have been more helpful while *naming names* in the department.
I never actually *saw* Hit-Girl again. But I knew she was out there when I opened a newspaper and saw the unexplained deaths of *gangsters* in London...
...terrorists in Paris, *kidnappers* in Rome, or the bodies of an entire *drug cartel* down in South America.
She always liked to work in the *shadows* and it made sense that she'd *return* to them.
I know she's okay because every single *Father's Day* there are flowers on her old man's grave and on *Mother's Day* her mom receives a gorgeous bunch of *roses.*

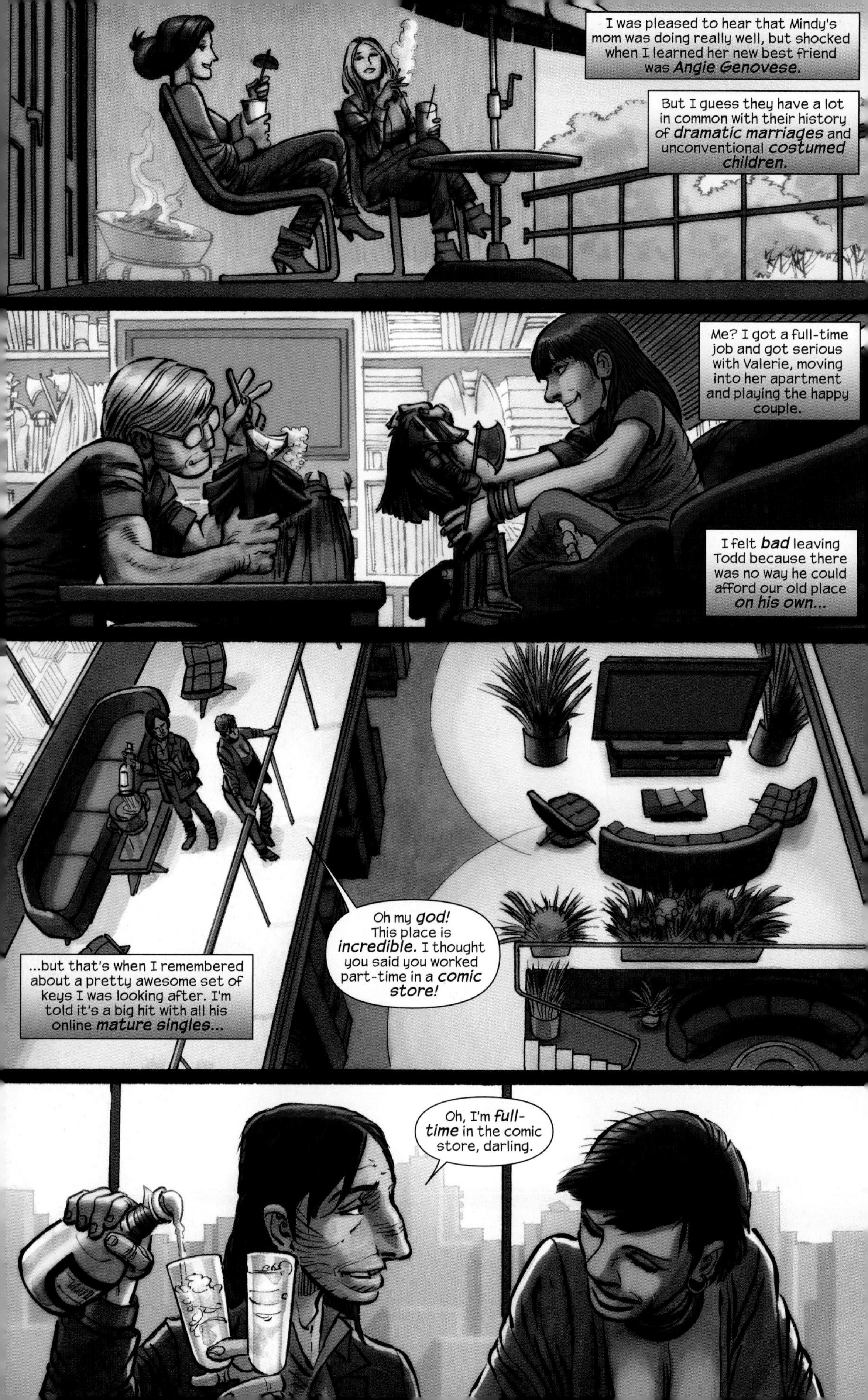
I was pleased to hear that Mindy's mom was doing really well, but shocked when I learned her new best friend was *Angie Genovese.*
But I guess they have a lot in common with their history of *dramatic marriages* and unconventional *costumed children.*
Me? I got a full-time job and got serious with Valerie, moving into her apartment and playing the happy couple.
I felt *bad* leaving Todd because there was no way he could afford our old place *on his own...*
...but that's when I remembered about a pretty awesome set of keys I was looking after. I'm told it's a big hit with all his online *mature singles...*
Oh my *god!* This place is *incredible.* I thought you said you worked part-time in a *comic store!*
Oh, I'm *full-time* in the comic store, darling.

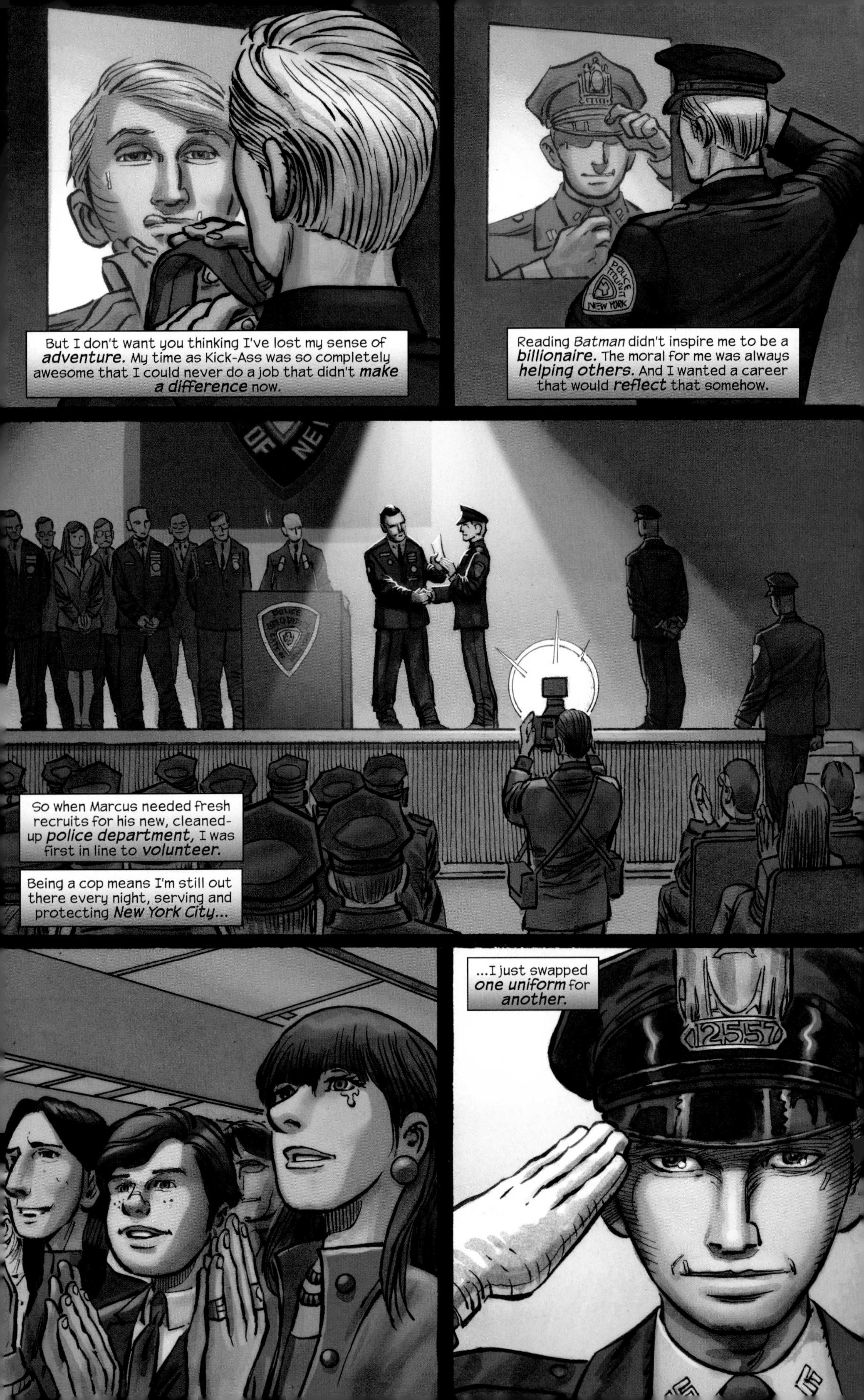
But I don't want you thinking I've lost my sense of adventure. My time as Kick-Ass was so completely awesome that I could never do a job that didn't make a difference now.
Reading Batman didn't inspire me to be a billionaire. The moral for me was always helping others. And I wanted a career that would reflect that somehow.
So when Marcus needed fresh recruits for his new, cleaned-up police department, I was first in line to volunteer.
Being a cop means I'm still out there every night, serving and protecting New York City...
...I just swapped one uniform for another.

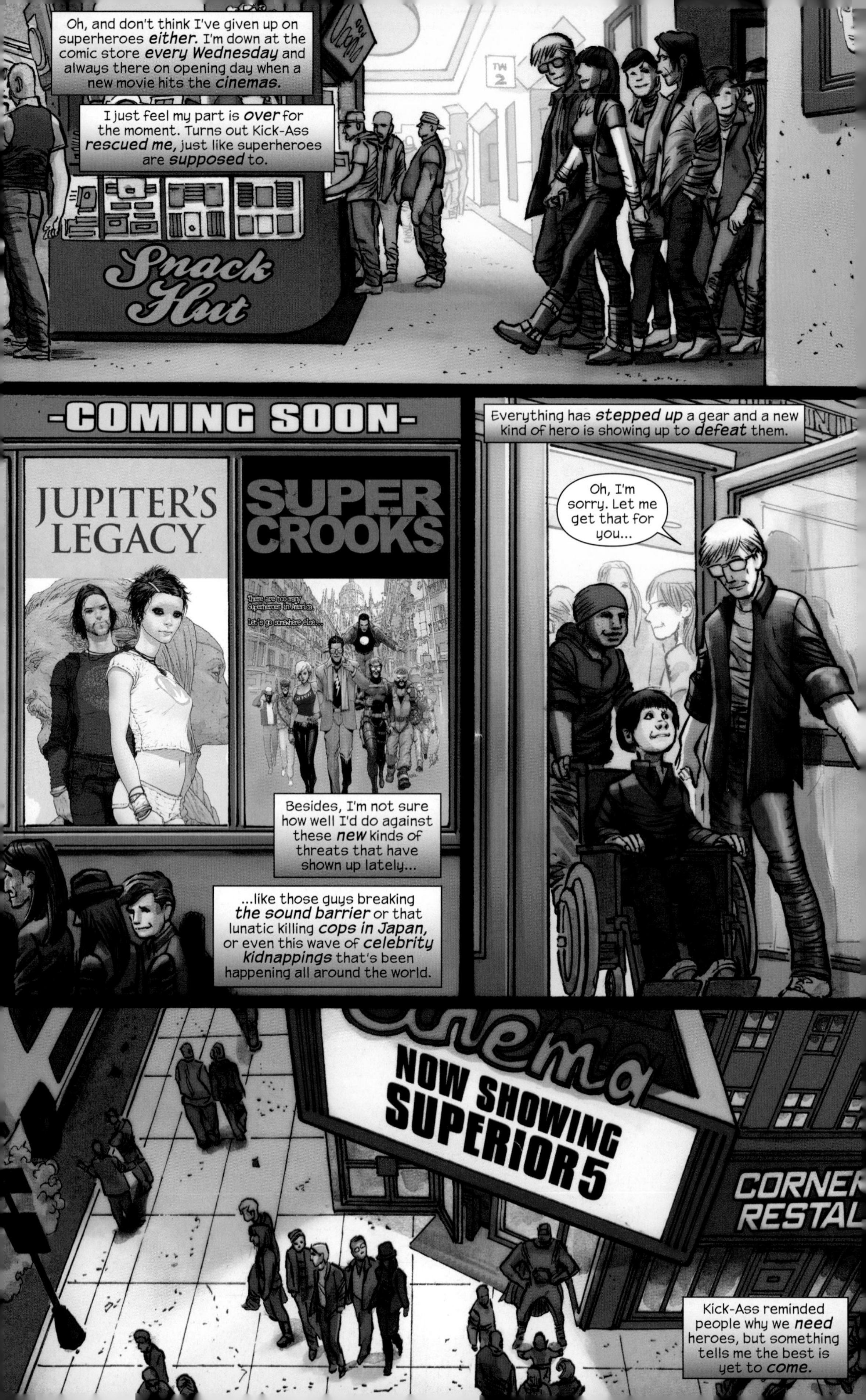
Oh, and don't think I've given up on superheroes either. I'm down at the comic store every Wednesday and always there on opening day when a new movie hits the cinemas.
I just feel my part is over for the moment. Turns out Kick-Ass rescued me, just like superheroes are supposed to.
Snack Hut
-COMING SOON-
JUPITER'S LEGACY
SUPER CROOKS
There are too many Superheroes in America.
Let's go somewhere else...
Besides, I'm not sure how well I'd do against these new kinds of threats that have shown up lately...
...like those guys breaking the sound barrier or that lunatic killing cops in Japan, or even this wave of celebrity kidnappings that's been happening all around the world.
Everything has stepped up a gear and a new kind of hero is showing up to defeat them.
Oh, I'm sorry. Let me get that for you...
NOW SHOWING SUPERIOR 5
CORNER
Kick-Ass reminded people why we need heroes, but something tells me the best is yet to come.

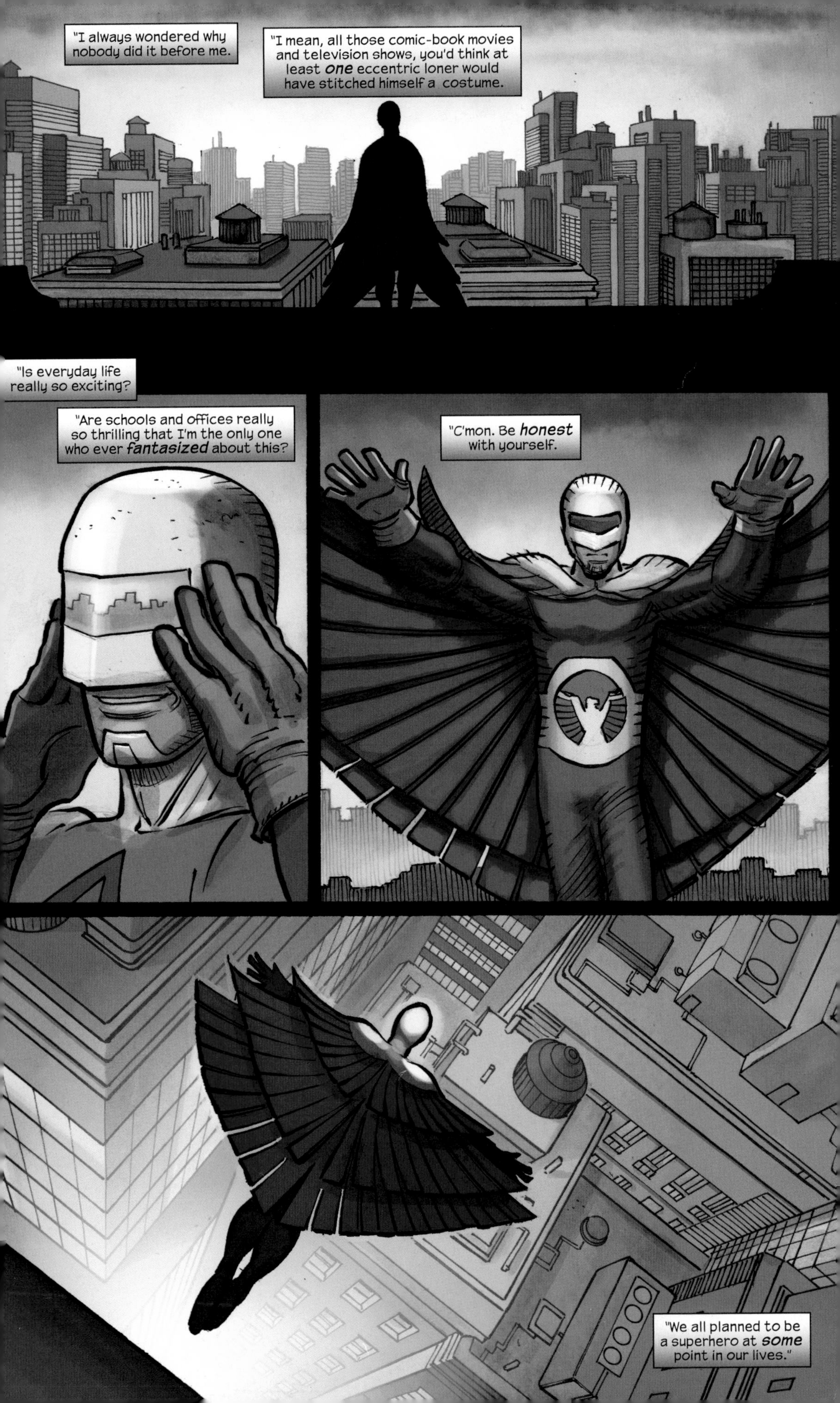
"I always wondered why nobody did it before me.
"I mean, all those comic-book movies and television shows, you'd think at least *one* eccentric loner would have stitched himself a costume.
"Is everyday life really so exciting?
"Are schools and offices really so thrilling that I'm the only one who ever *fantasized* about this?
"C'mon. Be *honest* with yourself.
"We all planned to be a superhero at *some* point in our lives."

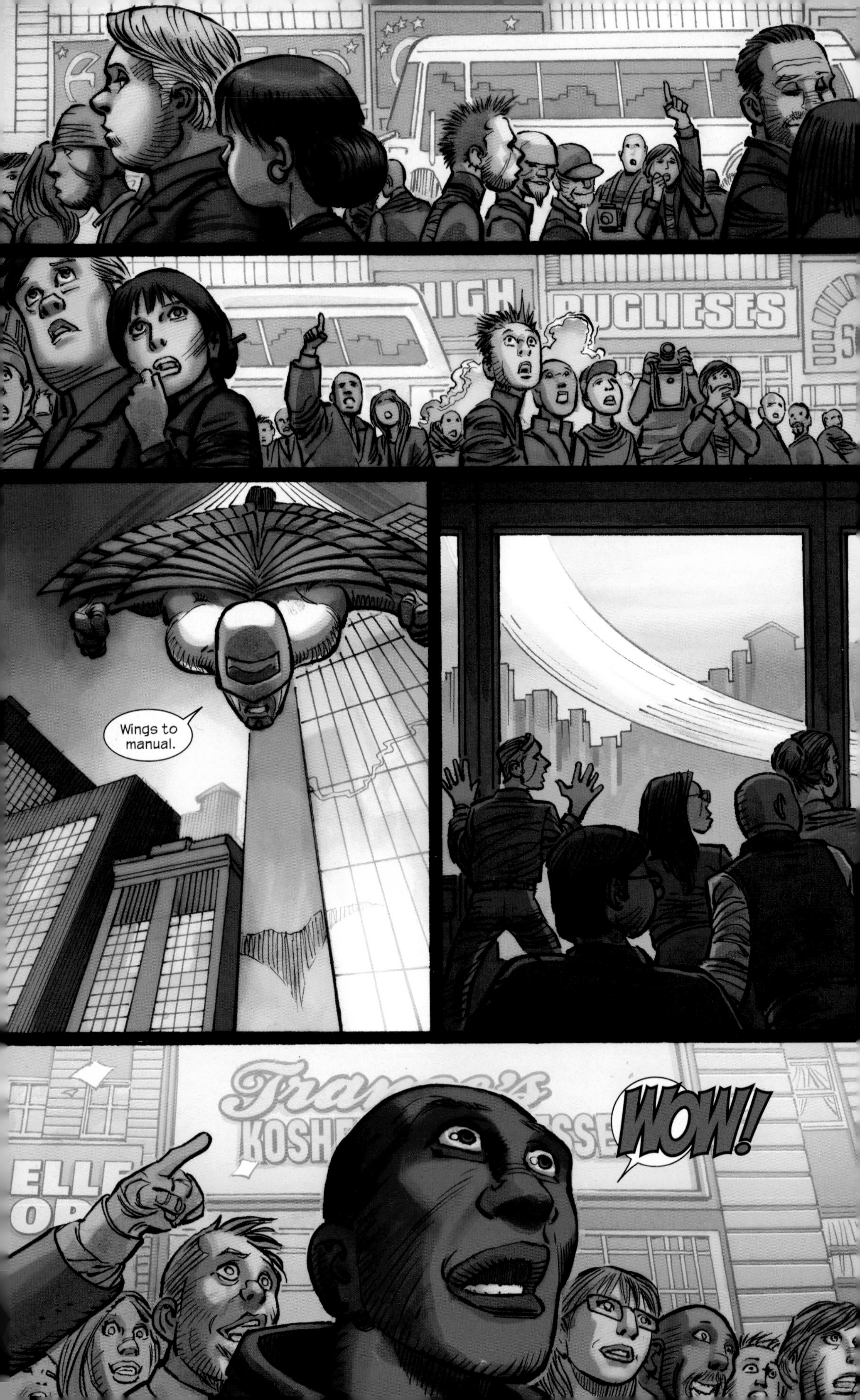
HIGH
PUGLIESES
Wings to manual.
WOW!

KICK
ASS

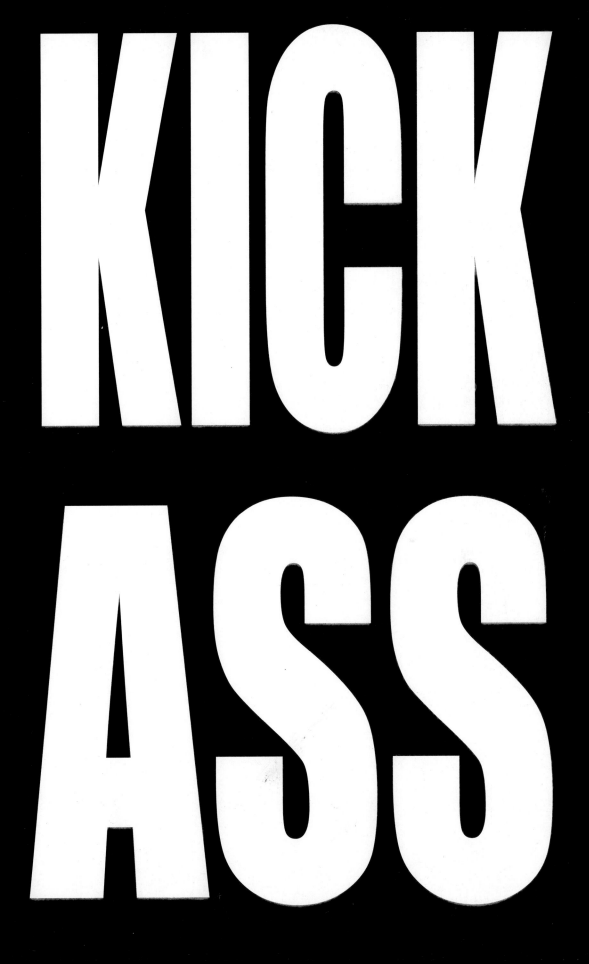

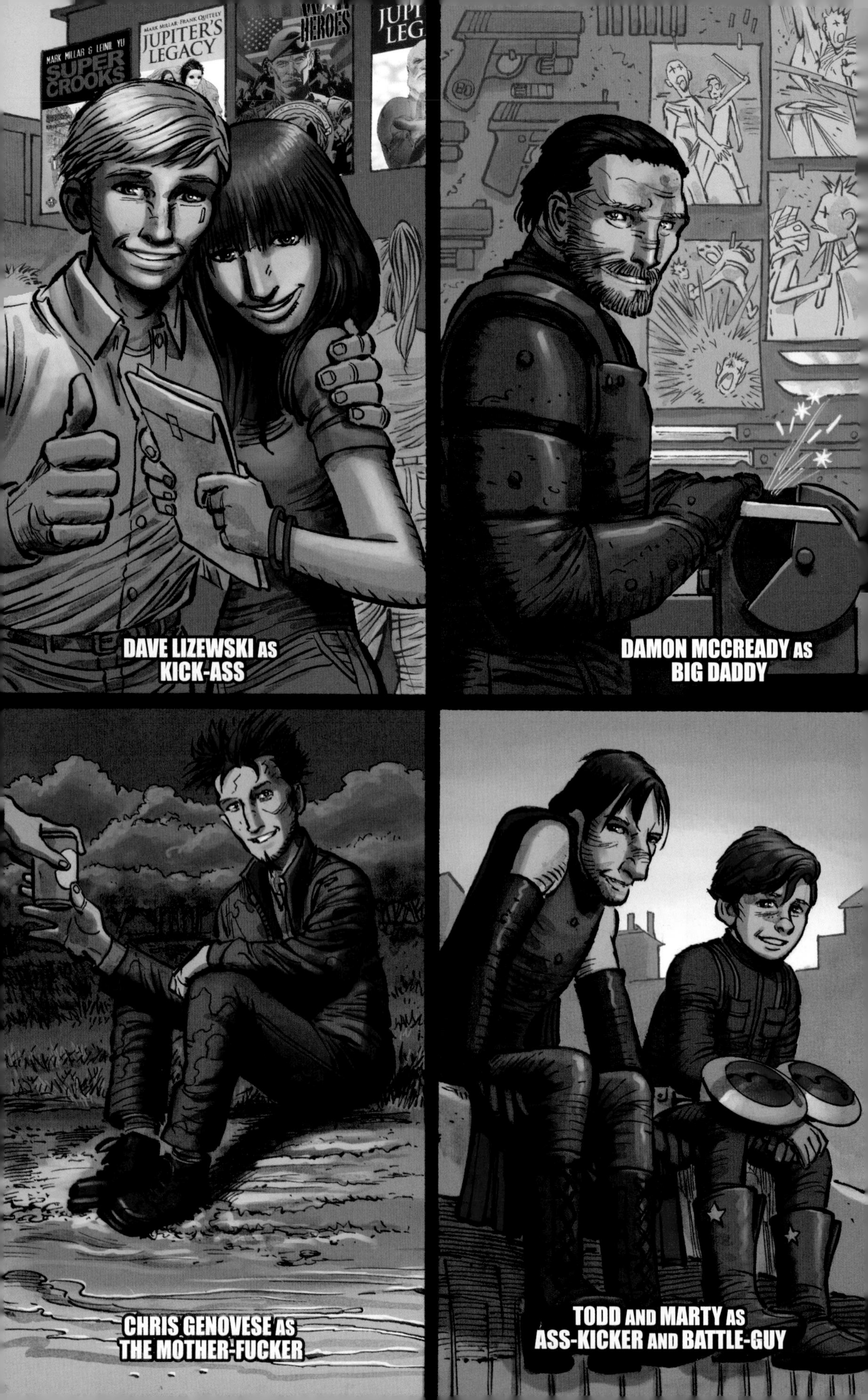
MARK MILLAR & LEINIL YU
SUPER CROOKS
MARK MILLAR·FRANK QUITELY
JUPITER'S LEGACY
DAVE LIZEWSKI AS KICK-ASS
DAMON MCCREADY AS BIG DADDY
CHRIS GENOVESE AS THE MOTHER-FUCKER
TODD AND MARTY AS ASS-KICKER AND BATTLE-GUY

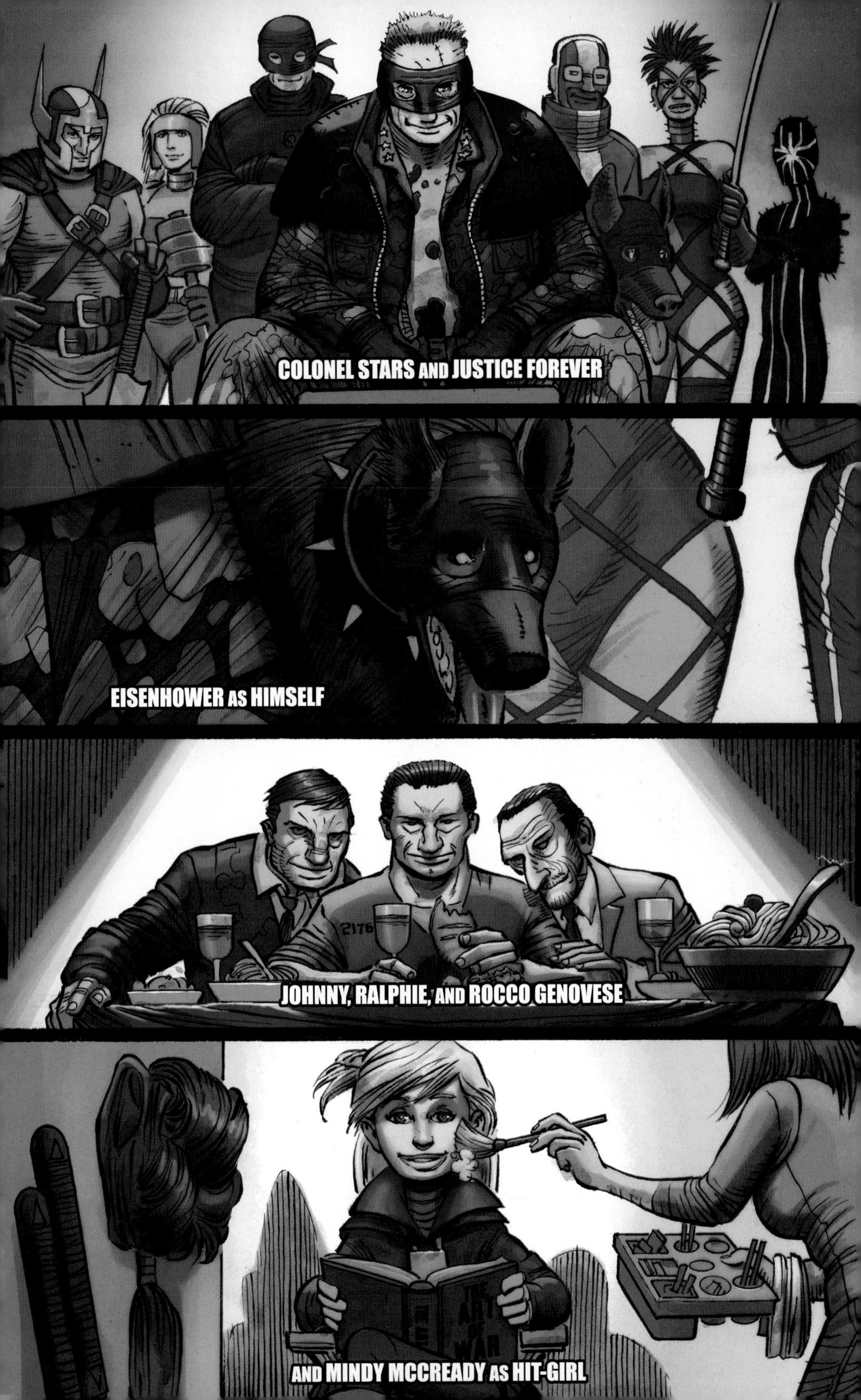
COLONEL STARS AND JUSTICE FOREVER
EISENHOWER AS HIMSELF
JOHNNY, RALPHIE, AND ROCCO GENOVESE
AND MINDY MCCREADY AS HIT-GIRL

MARK MILLAR is the *New York Times* best-selling writer of *Wanted*, the *Kick-Ass* series, *The Secret Service*, *Jupiter's Legacy*, *Nemesis*, *Superior*, *Super Crooks*, *American Jesus*, *MPH*, and *Starlight*. *Wanted*, *Kick-Ass*, *Kick-Ass 2*, and *The Secret Service* (as *Kingsman: The Secret Service*) have been adapted into feature films, and *Nemesis*, *Superior*, *Starlight*, and *War Heroes* are in development at major studios. His DC Comics work includes the seminal *Superman: Red Son*, and at Marvel Comics he created *The Ultimates*—selected by *Time* magazine as the comic book of the decade, *Wolverine: Old Man Logan*, and *Civil War*—the industry's biggest-selling series in almost two decades. Mark was a producer on the past adaptations of his works and is an Executive Producer on the feature-film and television projects currently in development. He is CEO of Millarworld Productions, an advisor on motion pictures to the Scottish government, and Creative Consultant to Fox Studios.

JOHN ROMITA JR. is a modern-day comic-art master, known for iconic runs on *Iron Man*, *Uncanny X-Men*, *Amazing Spider-Man*, *Captain America*, *Black Panther*, and *Punisher*. His work on *Wolverine* and *World War Hulk* has been hailed as some of the most explosive comic art of the last decade. Other career highlights include the relaunch of *Avengers* with Brian Michael Bendis, *Eternals* with Neil Gaiman, and *Daredevil: Man Without Fear* with Frank Miller. In addition to co-creating *Kick-Ass*, JRJR is the co-creator and illustrator of *The Gray Area*, cowritten with Glen Brunswick. He is currently developing the creator-owned series *Shmuggy and Bimbo* with Howard Chaykin and collaborating with writer Geoff Johns on DC Comics' flagship *Superman* title.

TOM PALMER has worked as an illustrator in the advertising and editorial fields, but he has spent the majority of his career in comic books. His first assignment, fresh out of art school, was on *Doctor Strange*, and he has gone on to lend his inking talents to many of Marvel's top titles, including *X-Men*, *The Avengers*, *Tomb of Dracula*, and more recently *Punisher*, *Hulk*, and *Ghost Rider*. He lives and works in New Jersey.

DEAN WHITE is one of the comic industry's best and most sought-after color artists. Well-known for his work on titles such as *The Amazing Spider-Man, Punisher, Dark Avengers, Captain America, Black Panther, Wolverine,* and countless more, Dean's envelope-pushing rendering and color palette bring a sense of urgency and power to every page he touches.

CHRIS ELIOPOULOS is a multiple award-winner for his lettering, having worked on dozens of books during the twenty years he's been in the industry – including Erik Larsen's *Savage Dragon,* for which he hand – lettered the first 100 issues. Adding to his success as a letterer, he also publishes his own strip *Misery Loves Sherman,* wrote and illustrated the popular *Franklin Richards: Son of a Genius* one-shots, and wrote Marvel's *Lockjaw and the Pet Avengers* series. Chris also illustrates the *New York Times* best-selling children's book series *Ordinary People Change The World* with author Brad Meltzer.

JENNIFER LEE is a story editor and producer working across film and comics. She's edited for both Marvel and DC Comics, and her credits include *Wolverine, Daredevil, Black Widow, 100 Bullets, Transmetropolitan,* and the award-winning illustrated prose novel *The Sandman: The Dream Hunters.* Other recent comics credits include *The Art of Millarworld* and *MPH.* Film credits include *True Adolescents, Small, Beautifully Moving Parts, Union Square, Arcadia,* and the Sundance hit *The Skeleton Twins* starring Kristen Wiig and Bill Hader. She lives in New York with her husband, comics illustrator Cliff Chiang.

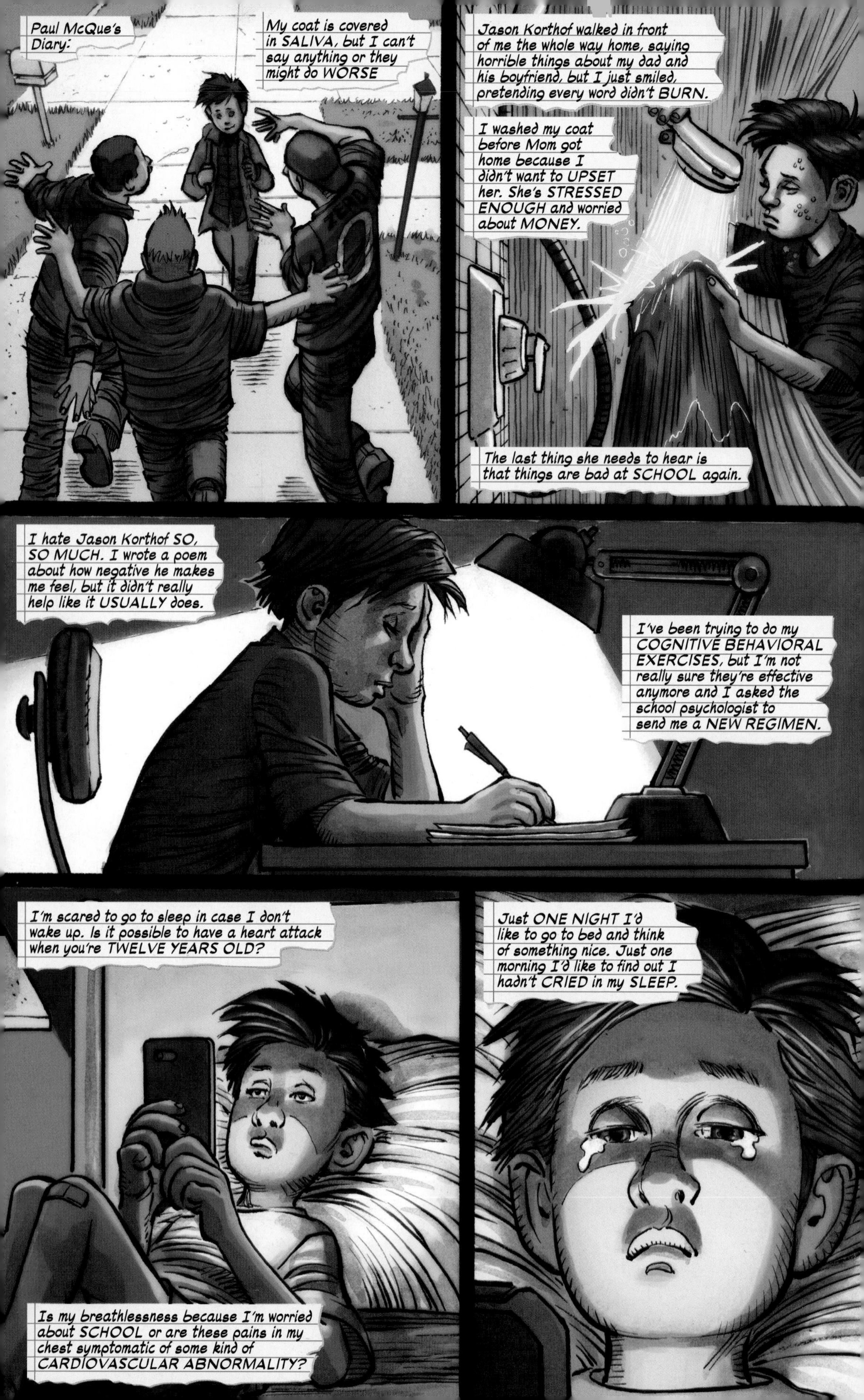
Paul McQue's Diary:
My coat is covered in SALIVA, but I can't say anything or they might do WORSE
Jason Korthof walked in front of me the whole way home, saying horrible things about my dad and his boyfriend, but I just smiled, pretending every word didn't BURN.
I washed my coat before Mom got home because I didn't want to UPSET her. She's STRESSED ENOUGH and worried about MONEY.
The last thing she needs to hear is that things are bad at SCHOOL again.
I hate Jason Korthof SO, SO MUCH. I wrote a poem about how negative he makes me feel, but it didn't really help like it USUALLY does.
I've been trying to do my COGNITIVE BEHAVIORAL EXERCISES, but I'm not really sure they're effective anymore and I asked the school psychologist to send me a NEW REGIMEN.
I'm scared to go to sleep in case I don't wake up. Is it possible to have a heart attack when you're TWELVE YEARS OLD?
Is my breathlessness because I'm worried about SCHOOL or are these pains in my chest symptomatic of some kind of CARDIOVASCULAR ABNORMALITY?
Just ONE NIGHT I'd like to go to bed and think of something nice. Just one morning I'd like to find out I hadn't CRIED in my SLEEP.

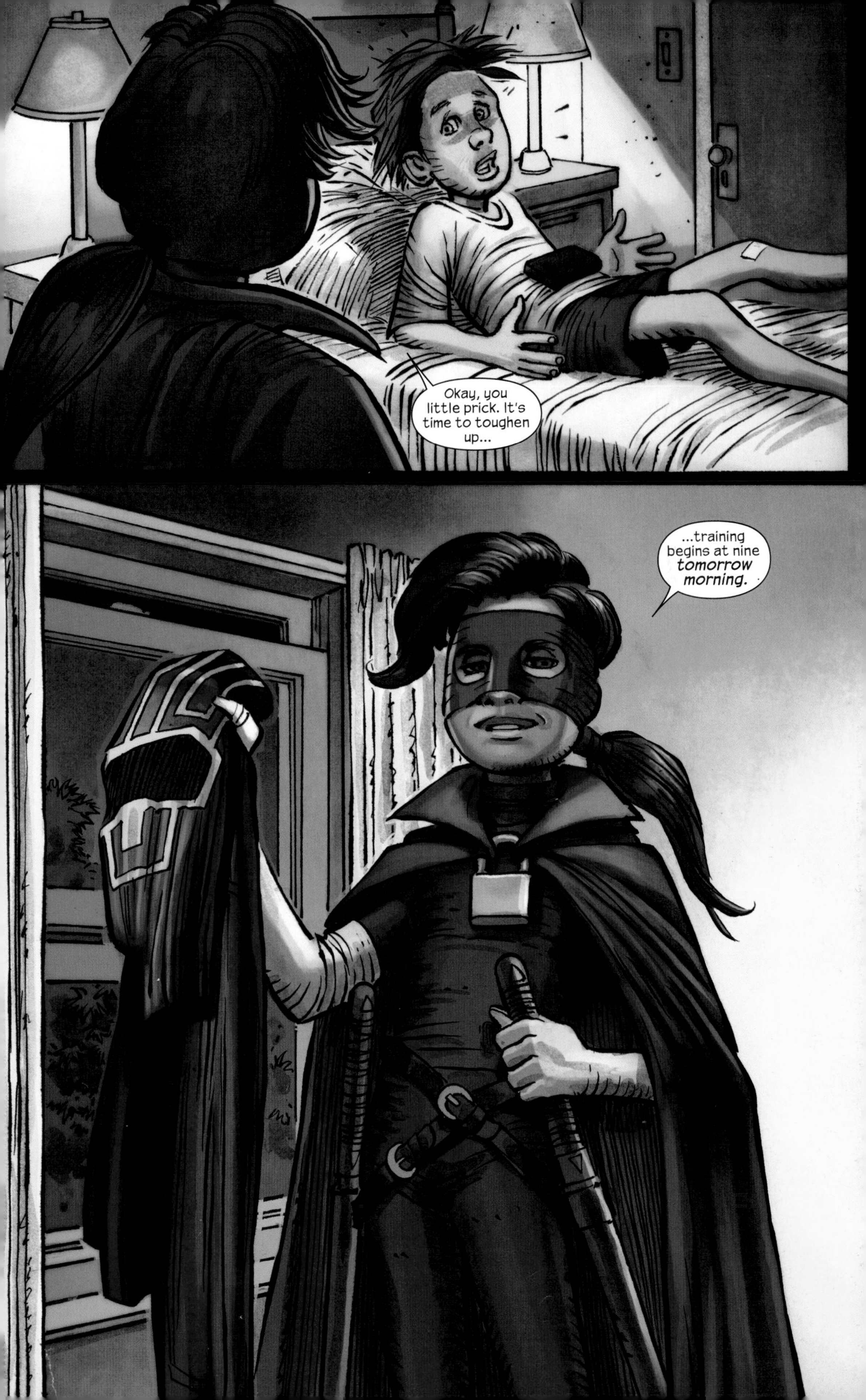
Okay, you little prick. It's time to toughen up...
...training begins at nine *tomorrow morning.*

THE

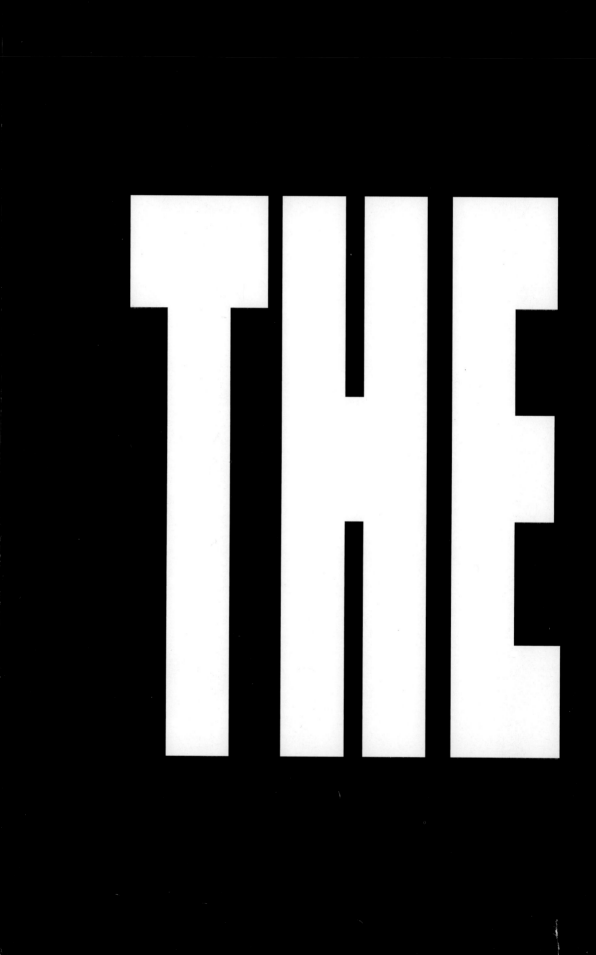

END

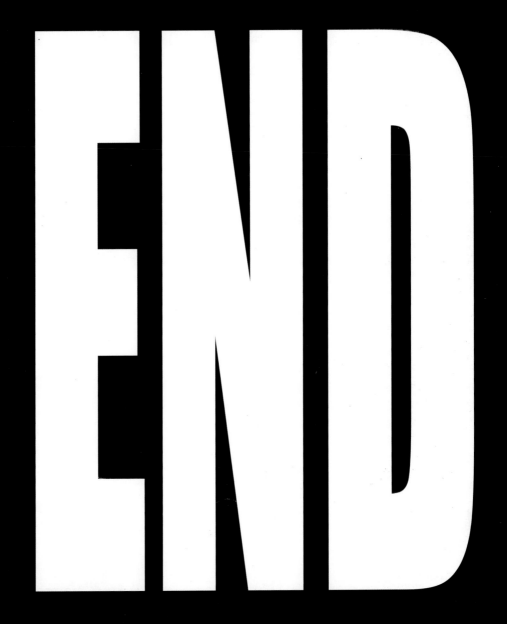

MARK MILLAR

I can't believe it's been eight years. Even worse, I can't believe it's been just twenty-eight ISSUES in eight years, but my God this wee creator-owned book went a lot further than any of us expected.

Back in 2006 I told Johnny I had a little four-issue project called BIG DADDY AND HIT-GIRL for him, but within six months it had grown into something a little bigger. Eight years on, it's been comics, collections, international editions, two Hollywood movies, two video games, bags, action figures, Halloween costumes, and Pez dispensers. Like I said, bigger than we expected, but hopefully it caught on because our enthusiasm was infectious.

We've loved telling the adventures of Dave and Mindy and I honestly can't think of a better partner to have joined me on this series than Johnny Romita. We got together on WOLVERINE and couldn't wait to get into something else again. Johnny gave me some of the best-looking pages I've ever seen in my life on this book and we've become genuine pals working so closely on this for such a long time. I thank him for that friendship and I thank him for making this book look so much cooler, classier, and exciting than it ever was in my head. Thanks also to Tom, Chris, and Dean for being completely irreplaceable and as important in this gang as myself or the Sicilian. Anyone else inking, lettering, or coloring would have just felt wrong and it's these gents who established the tone and identity that makes each page instantly identifiable.

There's a massive list of people I want to thank, from my friends who made the movies, to the surprisingly long list of editors and assistant editors, to my buddies at Marvel who gave us the chance to own and to do our own thing. But a special shout-out to Ms. Jenny Lee who came in for HIT-GIRL and stayed for KICK-ASS 3, getting the book as close as we've ever been to something resembling a schedule, a Herculean task that no one else could have done.

But most of all, thanks to you for supporting us from the moment this book launched. These last pages have been in my head since 2006. This story always had an ending. It really HAD to have an ending and we wanted to go out while we were still on a high. Thanks for gambling your $2.99 on a little book about a kid in a wet suit who fights crime with two sticks. Thanks for supporting independent creators and don't forget to pick up *Starlight, MPH, Jupiter's Legacy,* and all of Millarworld's 2015 extravaganzas.

(Did you really think I'd sign off without a plug?)

Again, thank you, and I hope you feel we did Dave and Mindy justice.

Your Pal,
Mark Millar

JOHN ROMITA JR

Every once in a good long while, an artist gets to work with a crew of talented people, who work together so well, that an amazing series like KICK-ASS is manifest. That's what happened here.

This project has been the most fun a person could have with their clothes on...professionally AND personally. (That's as far as I go with hyperbole. From this point forward, every comment is a level-headed, well-thought-out compliment, with no exaggeration...heh.)

Starting with the incredibly wild genius of Mark Millar and his fantastically, amazingly original idea to the brilliant, brilliant art of Tom Palmer, and the equally amazing art of Dean White (with color art assists from Michael Kelleher and Dan Brown), and the spectacular letter artwork of Chris Eliopoulos (with some assists from Clayton Cowles), things clicked. Vitally important to glowingly mention is the editorial strength of John Barber, Cory Levine, and Aubrey Sitterson, before they passed the very difficult job on to Jenny Lee, who dragged us all across the finish line. By the way, if one hasn't met Jenny personally, and only dealt with her professionally, you'd imagine a 6'4" 250-lb linebacker behind a computer terminal and cell phone. (I exaggerate to clarify!) Then you meet her and smile.

I would be remiss if I forgot to mention all the brilliant variant cover artists who worked with us: Steve McNiven, Tommy Lee Edwards, Bryan Hitch, Leo Fernandez, Phil Noto, Dave Johnson, Jock, Geof Darrow, Bill Sienkiewicz, Adam Hughes, Pasqual Ferry, Marc Silvestri, Cully Hamner, Adam Kubert, Duncan Fegredo, David Mack, Philip Bond, Jerome Opeña, Leinil Yu, Paolo Rivera, and Kyle Baker. Thanks to all of these artists for making MY covers look like crap! Kidding a little.

Thanks to David Gabriel, Sana Amanat, David Bogart, Dan Buckley, Joe Quesada, Axel Alonso, and the folks who made our collections: Spring Hoteling, Jen Grünwald, and Jeff Youngquist. And to the folks in production and beyond who sweat over our book every time it came in just under the wire: Idette Winecoor, Mayela Gutierrez, Alex Morales, Sue Crespi, Deb Weinstein, and Dan Carr.

I'm truly struggling to keep this as succinct as possible, because I could type for three hours about what has gone on for the last five years, and still not convey how proud I am to have worked with this group of amazing talents. Anyone who knows me knows I HATE clichés, but in this instance it truly couldn't have been done without you all.

Hugs and kisses folks,
Johnny Romita Jr

P. FRIGGIN' S. Thanks Mark, my friend, for the little bottle of Scotch whiskey, and the trophy, way back when. Thank you for calling me in the first place. This was an absolute, flippin' blast! Congrats on the beautiful family. I hope all your endeavors are as successful as you and your co-creators hope for.

Thanks, Tom (Dr. Deflector) for becoming a close friend through all this, and for saving my ass on numerous occasions.

Thanks Dean, for the same, and also for listening to my rants.

And a final thank you to Harris Miller, a great friend and advisor, and even better lawyer.

I was told by someone much smarter than me that if you make one good friend in your lifetime, you're ahead of the game. Well, this project has me WAY out in front.

A final thanks to Kathy, my drop-dead gorgeous copilot, for nudging me to try this fantastic project, when I wavered about trying something different. Thanks Vinny boy, my son, for always making me smile through the worst of the deadline crunches.

And thanks Mom and Dad, for not reading the series, and not giving me any grief for working "blue." Heh.

MILLA

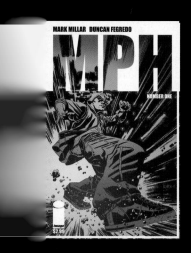

KICK-ASS

NOW A MAJOR MOTION PICTURE!

MARK MILLAR
JOHN ROMITA JR.

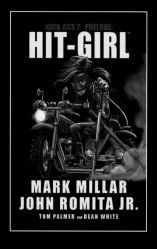

KICK-ASS 2 PRELUDE:

HIT-GIRL

MARK MILLAR
JOHN ROMITA JR.

TOM PALMER and DEAN WHITE

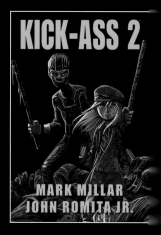

KICK-ASS 2

MARK MILLAR
JOHN ROMITA JR.

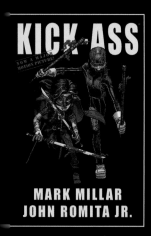

MARK MILLAR   DUNCAN FEGREDO

MPH

NUMBER ONE

Image
$2.99

WANTED

MARK MILLAR • JG JONES • PAUL MOUNTS

NOW A MAJOR MOTION PICTURE FROM
UNIVERSAL PICTURES

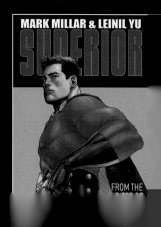

MARK MILLAR & LEINIL YU

SUPERIOR

FROM THE

WORLD
THE COLLECTION

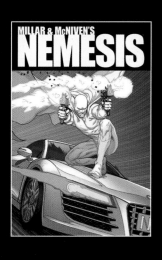

MILLAR & McNIVEN'S
NEMESIS

MARK MILLAR · GORAN PARLOV
STARLIGHT

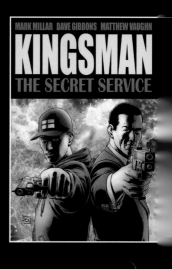

MARK MILLAR DAVE GIBBONS MATTHEW VAUGHN
KINGSMAN
THE SECRET SERVICE

MARK MILLAR · FRANK QUITELY
JUPITER'S
LEGACY

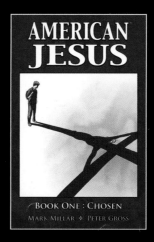

AMERICAN
JESUS

BOOK ONE : CHOSEN
MARK MILLAR ✦ PETER GROSS

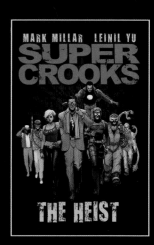

MARK MILLAR   LEINIL YU
SUPER
CROOKS

THE HEIST

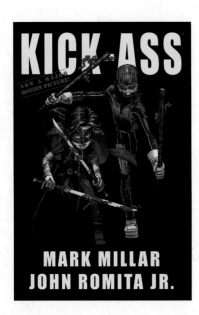

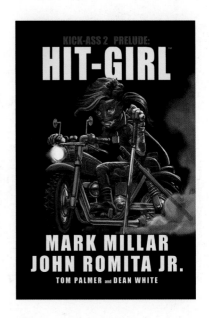

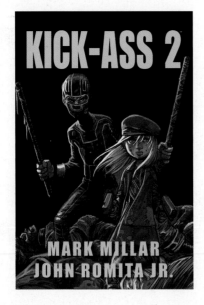

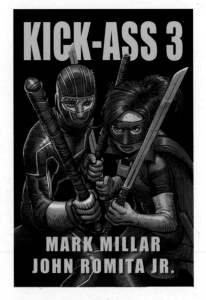